Friendship in the Book of Job

Friendship in the Book of Job

*Art, Context, and Theology
from an African Perspective*

MARK S. AIDOO

PICKWICK *Publications* · Eugene, Oregon

FRIENDSHIP IN THE BOOK OF JOB
Art, Context, and Theology from an African Perspective

Copyright © 2024 Mark S. Aidoo. All rights reserved. Except for brief quotations in critical publications or reviews, no part of this book may be reproduced in any manner without prior written permission from the publisher. Write: Permissions, Wipf and Stock Publishers, 199 W. 8th Ave., Suite 3, Eugene, OR 97401.

Pickwick Publications
An Imprint of Wipf and Stock Publishers
199 W. 8th Ave., Suite 3
Eugene, OR 97401

www.wipfandstock.com

PAPERBACK ISBN: 978-1-6667-7720-8
HARDCOVER ISBN: 978-1-6667-7721-5
EBOOK ISBN: 978-1-6667-7722-2

Cataloguing-in-Publication data:

Names: Aidoo, Mark S., author.

Title: Friendship in the book of Job : art, context, and theology from an African perspective / Mark S. Aidoo.

Description: Eugene, OR: Pickwick Publications, 2024. | Includes bibliographical references and index.

Identifiers: ISBN 978-1-6667-7720-8 (paperback). | ISBN 978-1-6667-7721-5 (hardcover). | ISBN 978-1-6667-7722-2 (ebook).

Subjects: LCSH: Bible.—Job—Criticism, interpretation, etc. | Friendship.

Classification: BS1415.52 A35 2024 (print) | BS1415.52 (ebook)

11/04/24

Dedicated to

Jannika Boafo and Jannina Boafo,
my grandchildren

Contents

	Permissions	ix
	Preface	xi
	Acknowledgments	xiii
	Abbreviations	xv
1	Introduction	1
2	Friendship as a Wisdom Tradition in the Book of Job	13
3	Friendship in Indigenous African Thought	26
4	The Bible and Friendship	55
5	History of Interpretation on Friendship	78
6	The Case of Eliphaz, Bildad, and Zophar as Friends	114
7	The Case for Job's Wife as a Friend	166
8	Extended Family Members and Acquaintances	206
9	Locating a Space for Elihu as a Friend	228
10	God as a Friend of Job	245
11	Conclusion	274
	Bibliography	285

Permissions

Unless otherwise noted, Scripture quotations are from New Revised Standard Version Bible, copyright © 1989 National Council of the Churches of Christ in the United States of America. Used by permission. All rights reserved worldwide.

Scripture quotations marked (ASV) are taken from the American Standard Version, which is in the public domain.

Scripture quotations marked (CJB) are taken from the Complete Jewish Bible by David H. Stern. Copyright © 1998. All rights reserved. Used by permission of Messianic Jewish Publishers, 6120 Day Long Lane, Clarksville, MD 21029. www.messianicjewish.net.

Scripture quotations marked (ESV) are from The Holy Bible, English Standard Version® (ESV®) © 2001 by Crossway, a publishing ministry of Good News Publishers. The Holy Bible, English Standard Version (ESV) is adapted from the Revised Standard Version of the Bible, copyright Division of Christian Education of the National Council of the Churches of Christ in the U.S.A. All rights reserved.

Scripture quotations marked JPS TANAK are taken from Tanakh: The New JPS Translation According to the Traditional Hebrew Text. Copyright © 1985, 1999 by The Jewish Publication Society with the permission of the publisher.

Scripture quotations marked (KJV) are taken from the King James Version of the Bible, which is in the public domain.

Scripture quotations marked (NASB) are taken from the (NASB®) New American Standard Bible®, Copyright © 1960, 1971, 1977, 1995, 2020 by The Lockman Foundation. Used by permission. All rights reserved. lockman.org

Scripture quotations marked (NIV) taken from The Holy Bible, New International Version® NIV® Copyright © 1973, 1978, 1984, 2011 by Biblica, Inc. Used with permission. All rights reserved worldwide.

PERMISSIONS

Scripture quotations marked (NJB) are taken from The New Jerusalem Bible, published and copyright 1985 by Darton, Longman & Todd Ltd and Les Editions du Cerf, and used by permission of the publishers.

Scripture quotations marked (NKJV) are taken from the New King James Version®. Copyright © 1982 by Thomas Nelson. Used by permission. All rights reserved.

Preface

FRIENDSHIP IS ONE OF the most beautiful things in life. It takes a friend's presence, and inspiration to see life very well and to grow mature. Friends make us feel encouraged. I have benefitted a lot from many friends. I thank God for their lives. The quest to enhance human relationship through friendship is not just an ordinary search but also a religious or theological concern. Friendship is a cardinal principle in spirituality and defines who we are as human beings. The biblical text has enabled me to fertilize a past "lived" experience to enhance contemporary mutuality and exchange.

The book of Job is notoriously difficult, in terms of text, translations, and theology. And all the characters in the story are elusive. What interpreters assume them to be easily gets out of hand. Yet, some lessons can be learnt from the vagueness and subtlety of the story. I have not found it easy at all exploring friendship in the book of Job from an African perspective since much has not been said about the African concept of friendship. My readers will admit that my findings are challenging. I cannot ignore the fact Western thinkers have given far-reaching reflections on friendship, but my African context is somehow different. So, I take a cue from the particularity of the African context to explore a biblical theology of friendship, expanding toward Old Testament ethics and psychosocial perspectives. I am an African and I draw from my experiences to interpret friendship. My dialogue with many Africans across the globe opened me to share their experiences of friendship, for which I am so grateful. I gathered some African proverbs from the dialogue I had.

This study is an insider's job, not from without or from a historical perspective. I do pretend to be part of the story itself, not more inclined toward the literary or aesthetic developments, but from a homiletic perspective. I am aware that the popular approach to the book of Job is to explore what it says about suffering. I depart from this view to concentrate on the social dynamics that influence the characters in what they say. I admit that the wisdom traditions of the Bible can teach readers about friendship, highlighting the dynamics therein. So, I try to show that there are different types of friends. Certainly, there are friends but there can be a friend among friends, and as a friend of friends. Friends can make or unmake each other.

I can say the book of Job challenges all to be good and true friends. We all need to learn lessons from the characters and develop a friendship that lasts. Job has friends but accuses them that they are no friends at all. Job accuses his wife that she is speaking like one of the foolish women and she has abandoned him. Job accuses his brothers, sisters, household members, and acquaintances that they have abandoned him. Job accuses God of treating him like an enemy and not a friend. If Job knows what it means to be a true friend, was he one to the three, his wife, brothers, sisters, household members, acquaintances, and God? How does Elihu fit into a story presumed to talk about friendship and how does he see Job? I believe all of these characters cut across real-life experiences and relationships and a fair analysis can unearth how all can live in a world that cannot do without friendship. Significantly, I use the name God throughout this book to represent all the various names of Job's deity, and affirm that they all represent Yahweh, the Creator of heaven and earth. This is intentional.

The Bible translation used, unless otherwise stated, is the New Revised Standard Version. In some cases, I provide my personal translation. All that I have done is open to be examined and challenged. Here are my views; you can add to it.

Acknowledgments

It has been a long journey for me up to this point since I have been working on friendship for more than a decade. I started writing about friendship in 2012, and it is becoming more interesting. Trinity Theological Seminary, Legon, Ghana granted me sabbatical leave from October 2022 to May 2023 to enable me to concentrate on this project. I thank God for the strength and wisdom to complete this book.

My appreciation goes to Missionsakademie an der Universität Hamburg, Germany, for granting me a short-term exposure scholarship. My time at Missionsakademie was very fulfilling. Thanks to Dr. Anton Knuth and his team, and the wonderful friends I made, who contributed to my thoughts. Prof. Dr. Corinna Korting of the Fakultät für Geisteswissenschaften, Universität Hamburg, was my advisor and I am so grateful to her for the time we spent in discussing this project. I am so grateful to God for the wonderful friends I made in Hamburg.

Another heartfelt appreciation goes to Fuller Theological Seminary, Pasadena, California. I was granted a GRI scholarship and my mentor, Professor John Goldingay, was gracious to help me out and very supportive. He carefully read through part of my work and offered useful suggestions. I have been so blessed by the quality time we spent together discussing my project. To the team at GRI and CMR, I say God bless you, especially Professor Kirsteen Kim. And to my great friends, I salute you.

As I spent time in Hamburg and Pasadena, I had the privilege of worshipping with Ghanaian Methodist churches. I am grateful to all the wonderful friends I made who encouraged me and challenged my pastoral ministry. Your support and encouragement have brought me this far. I mention my senior colleagues, Very Rev Eldad Newlove Bonney of Hamburg Circuit and Very Rev Isaac Kwabena Boamah of Atlanta Circuit, who became great friends. I mention Mr Yaw Toku Asare who was a great inspiration. I also mention the Very Rev Dr Bernard Bosompem Bamfo of the Methodist Church Antwerp, Belgium. You all gave me the opportunity to share in your ministry as a good friend and colleague. I made a special friend, Professor Johnny Ramirez-Johnson at Fuller Theological Seminary, Pasadena CA, a colleague and an acquaintance friend, who helped me to reflect on my epistemological perspective. You opened your door and your heart to me and guided me to rethink what I was writing.

In humility, I use this book to acknowledge the "friends" who are my secret admirers. Most of them are my students. I hear you are many and you always pray for me. Life without friends is empty. I pray that we can build on that friendship. It is a good relationship that enriches a healthy life. I hope to continue being a friend after learning what the discussions have to say. May all of you, whereever you are, be blessed.

Above all, I thank the Lord for how far his grace has led me. I really appreciate what the good Lord has done and is doing in your life. I say:

'ośeh gĕdolôt wĕ'ên ḥeqer niplā'ôt 'ad-'ên misppār
He does great things that cannot be searched;
  wondrous things that cannot be numbered. (Job 5:9)

MSA
2023

Abbreviations

AB	Anchor Bible
BDB	*The Brown-Driver-Briggs Hebrew and English Lexicon With an appendix containing the Biblical Aramaic*
HALOT	*The Hebrew and Aramaic Lexicon of the Old Testament*, Ludwig Koehler and Walter Baumgartner. Translated and edited under the supervision of Mervyn E. J. Richardson. 4 vols. Leiden: Brill, 1994–2001
ICC	International Critical Commentary
JSOTSup	Journal for the Study of the Old Testament Supplements
NE	*Nicomachean Ethics*
NIDOTTE	*New International Dictionary of Old Testament Theology and Exegesis.* Edited by Willem A. VanGemeren. 5 vols. Grand Rapids: Zondervan, 1997
TDNT	*Theological Dictionary of the New Testament.* Edited by Gerhard Kittel and Gerhard Friedrich. Translated by Geoffrey W. Bromiley. 10 vols. Grand Rapids: Eerdmans, 1964–1976
TDOT	*Theological Dictionary of the Old Testament.* Edited by G. Johannes Botterweck, Helmer Ringgren, and Heinz-Josef Fabry. Translated by Douglas W. Stott et al. 17 vols. Grand Rapids: Eerdmans, 1974–2021

1

Introduction

ABOUT THIS BOOK

THE TERMS "FRIEND" AND "friendship" have always been taken for granted, although there are many scholarly analyses around the concept within biblical interpretation. Friendship is used either loosely or seriously depending on the one using it. For two young people, friendship may not be the same as for two adults. A friendship between two people of different sexes may connote a wide range of expectations. Thankfully, there are categories of friends—but literature, especially in religious and theological circles, hardly focuses on the differences.

Friendship is a contextualized concept; it takes its shape in particular spaces, environments, and worldviews of the people at play. For instance, it is believed that in Africa, friendship is ignited when money is shared, but elsewhere, especially in the Western world, friendship ends when money comes into the picture. Martine Guichard rightly notes that friendship is socially constructed, culturally governed, and structurally influenced by the times and spaces in which they occur.[1] Friendship, as an important aspect of human society, has captured the attention of many since the archaic classical world, especially from the eighth and sixth centuries BCE. Various philosophical thoughts on the social, political, and civic aspects of friendship have been proposed. Such views perhaps shaped social perspectives and early Christian views about friendship

1. Guichard, "Introduction," 2.

from the Hellenistic period to Late Antiquity. The medieval period also grappled with the concept of friendship extensively, and yet still the debate continues. Despite widespread studies on friendship in the Western world, there is no unanimity of thought.

The book of Job reveals some of the various categories of friendship. It deals with both human and divine friendships. At the very least, Job had friends, and the story crystallizes the fact that the God of the Hebrew Bible always maintained a relationship with his creation, which Victor Austin calls "desired friendship."[2] I find two sentences in Harold Kushner's book highlight an aspect of what friendship means in the book of Job: "Job asked questions about God, but he did not need lessons in theology. He needed sympathy and compassion and the reassurance that he was a good person and a cherished friend."[3] Nevertheless, a gap exists in how Africans construe friendship in the light of the story in the book of Job.[4] The paucity of scholarly reflections on the concept of friendship in sub-Saharan Africa cannot be overemphasized.

This monograph explores the art of friendship in the book of Job and how it resonates in the sub-Saharan African setting. It examines the relationships between Job and his wife, Job and the three "friends," Job and God, and Job and his brothers and sisters, in the light of how friends should be. While Eliphaz, Bildad, and Zophar have been duly recognized in the story as friends even though their speeches betray them, discussions on the relationships between Job and his wife, his acquaintances, Elihu, and God seem inadequate. As will become evident, the nature of friendship is a critical feature in the biblical book of Job not only in terms of what the characters do or say to each other but how they are characterized. The details in the story about these individuals or groups of individuals teach readers and interpreters about their thoughts, histories, and dreams. Characterization in the book of Job is sometimes direct and explicit, sometimes subtle, indirect, and implicit, yet the characters' perceptions and opinions from the behavior, speech(es), and silence are real, and so the interpreter can decide who and what they are. Job is the main character of the story. He is mentioned as a historical figure in the book of Ezekiel and ranked along righteous men like Noah and Daniel (Ezek 14:14, 20). The writer of James also bears witness to Job's perseverance in

---

2. Austin, *Friendship*, 141–50.
3. Kushner, *When Bad Things Happen to Good People*, 68.
4. I italicize the title of the biblical book to distinguish it from the character, Job.

the face of suffering (Jas 5:10–11). How his characterization informs the ethic of friendship is our matter of concern.

In a recent publication, Patricia Vesely discusses friendship in the book of Job using Aristotelian ethics. She talks about virtue and addresses human flourishing, the role of tragic literature in moral formation, friendship in Hellenistic and biblical contexts, and ethics in heroic societies.[5] Vesely's thorough discussion on friendship reveals that the book of Job is not simply a theological treatise on suffering but also embodies the character traits necessary to maintain a relationship of friendship. This present book follows a similar path within the fields of philosophy, theological ethics, and biblical studies, but from an African perspective. It provides a redemptive reading of the biblical text to highlight the value of wisdom traditions of friendship for practical life, so that readers can have another perspective on the text—through an African eye. It focuses on proverbs, parables, sayings, etc., from some African communities to expose parallels from an African perspective. This study, unlike previous studies, treats Mrs. Job as a spousal friend and draws Elihu into the context of a friend. I argue that each of the characters presents a "case study" on the art of friendship, and as such a theology of friendship can be developed. The hope is to fill the gap by highlighting African voices while presenting a more nuanced view of friendship so that some biblical theological lessons can be derived from friendship. The issues that drive the discussions are: How do the speeches, actions, and inactions of the characters in the book of Job help to identify what kind of friends they are in Job's time of suffering, and how do such identities inform African readers? How can the relationships between Job and his wife, Job and the three "friends," Job and God, Job and Elihu, and Job and his brothers and sisters be described as "friendships"? What can readers learn to enrich friendship relationships?

MODUS OPERANDI

This monograph is not a commentary. Rather, it is an exploratory study of friendship drawn from the story in the book of Job. It combines various cross-disciplinary approaches. The major lens, however, through which friendship in the book of Job is understood is the African concept of friendship. It is a dialogue between my personal experiences and an

---

5. Vesely, *Friendship and Virtue Ethics in the Book of Job*.

interpretation of the book of Job. What I have experienced, and come to know in Africa, and my identity as an African is guiding my thinking and interpretation. I reiterate the point that my reference to Africa does not mean every corner and space covering Africa. Rather, I use a few language groups to represent the African experience and thought.

Much of what is known in the book of Job about friendship is derived from what the characters say and do, as well as their inactions and silence. In trying to enter into dialogue with the text and exploring the meaning and function of the speeches, the rhetorical approach to interpreting the biblical text becomes necessary and is adopted. I agree with Kennedy that rhetorical criticism can be seen as a purposeful form of communication between God and humanity, and between the biblical writers and ourselves.[6] In rhetorical analysis, the dynamics of communication within a text are explored in terms of "what the author is saying," "how the author says it," and "what is the effect on the critic concerning what the author is saying." The rhetorical critic assumes that the words, although informed by the social and cultural settings, are chosen to play a particular function. By analyzing the interrelationship of the arguments and assessing the words and their impact on a critic or an interpreter, one gets the meaning of what is conveyed. Meaning thus resides in the hearer, and not the speaker. Emphasis is on the conceptual argument rather than the means of persuasion through words. The words and language of the society in the text that are used do not lock the interpretation of that text in the distant past but reveal certain verbal realities that evoke additional meaning for the here and now.[7] To arrive at a judgment on the meaning of a speech, "it is not only necessary to consider how to make the speech (*logos*) itself demonstrative and convincing (*apodeiktikos kai pistos*), but also that the speaker should show himself to be of a certain character and should know how to put the judge into a certain frame of mind."[8]

A linear reading of the book of Job will reveal a story with a single voice and theme—suffering.[9] Interestingly, scholars who have insisted that the book of Job is about the question "Why do the righteous suffer?" have not arrived at any convincing answer. Larry Waters admits that the

---

6. Kennedy, *New Testament Interpretation through Rhetorical Criticism*, 158.
7. Russel, "Rhetorical Analysis of the Book of Galatians: Part 1," 346.
8. Garver, "Aristotle and Kinds of Rhetoric," 13.
9. Pope, *Job*, xxiii–xxx; Hartley, *Job*, 20–33; Newsom, "Book of Job" 319–25; Westermann, *Structure of the Book of Job*; Zuckerman, *Job the Silent*, 25–33; Steinmann, "Structure of the Book of Job," 85–100; Patrick, "Fourfold Structure of Job," 185–206.

suffering of the innocent does not encompass the entire purpose of the author.[10] As such, the view that this wisdom book is mainly about the suffering of the innocent cannot be sustained if it does not give the answers required to make a person wise. Truly captivating is David Penchansky's view that "the prologue, however, introduces a notion of piety that is misunderstood by the community. Legendary Job protests the traditional ideological consensus, thus creating the possibility of genuine piety that results in terrible affliction and the rejection of community."[11] Of interest here is the pointer to other possibilities that can arise due to affliction and rejection. And the questions arise: who are the community that rejected Job, and how can there be reconciliation? Hence, one cannot gloss over the reflections on relationships that lie at the heart of the book of Job.

By delineating the rhetorical unit and the various literary devices, the critic can identify the internal structures, style, and movement within the text as well as the dynamics of persuasion utilized. The process helps to identify the problem to which the author is responding with supporting arguments or proofs that justify the arguments. Analyzing the arguments also helps to demonstrate a progression that reveals the techniques used and what is at stake in the argument.[12] It is the speeches, actions, and inactions of the characters in the book of Job that can inform views on the theology of friendship. And three key functions can help us—ethos, pathos, and logos: "Ethos" explores the credibility, reputation, or trustworthiness of a speaker. It reveals the established personal credentials of the speaker. In this light, the importance of an idea can be examined through identifying the ethos that establishes the persuasive appeal of a speaker to know how trustworthy the person is. "Pathos," according to Kennedy, refers to emotional appeals that "inhere in the audience and may be defined as the emotional reactions the hearers undergo as the orator 'play upon their feelings.'"[13] The emotional appeals compel the audience or interpreter to judge what is said or read, particularly when the mood influences what is said as well as the meaning that is generated. It is important to show how the audience feels about what has been said. It shows how the audience identifies with the author's language and point of view. The "logos" is

10. Waters, "Reflections on Suffering from the Book of Job," 436.
11. Penchansky, *Betrayal of God*, 45.
12. Kennedy, *New Testament Interpretation*, 33–38; See also Wuellner, "Where Is Rhetorical Criticism Taking Us?," 455; Bitzer, "Rhetorical Situation," 247–60.
13. Kennedy, *New Testament Interpretation through Rhetorical Criticism*, 15

the logic and reason from the speech, that is, the power of proving a truth, or an apparent truth, by means of persuasive arguments.

It is necessary that a critical reader does not read against the grain of what is given and this involves developing an ability to read older and culturally distant texts "canonically," "authorially," and "narratively." As generally accepted, it is difficult to locate the author of the book of Job and know the author's intention, due to the lack of internal evidence and also the difficulties in the language of the Hebrew text. Hence, what is being done here is analyzing the canonical text rhetorically to see what it might be saying. Essentially, the analysis will be limited to micro-rhetorical forms and devices that relate to the concept of friendship.

Since the emphasis is on the single word "friendship," an exploration of the semantic range of words that are translated as "friend" in the book of Job will drive the discussions. Biblical Hebrew does not have one exact equivalent of the word "friend." The various words translated as "friend" also have a wide range of meanings. Milton Eng emphasizes that "words do not have meanings, meanings have words."[14] In fact, words carry their own lexical sense and contextual sense. Meanings from the contextual sense are usually located within the culture and context of the usage of a word. Significantly, words are merely "signs" pointing to meaning.[15]

Rhetoric carries within it many levels of deliberation, negotiation, prescription, and justification of a community of values, and it impinges upon, overlaps, and integrates the concerns of ethics.[16] Also, Kenneth Burke states that the art of rhetoric can lead to symbolic action in areas that contribute to practical wisdom.[17] Furthermore, Carolyn Miller says "the positive task of rhetoric is not to persuade others away from injustice or to promote remedies; it is to keep us constantly open to refutation, to the possibility of seeing an alternative to the inadvertent wrong we commit."[18]

Second, a psychosocial reading will help unravel the relationship styles of the characters of the story. Friendship has to do with the self and others. It is an act of belonging, making the self a part of the social world. It involves interpersonal relationships. An individual's personality

---

14. Eng, *Day of Our Years*, 23

15. Merwe, "Lexical Meaning in Biblical Hebrew," 85–95; Eng, *Days of Our Years*, 23.

16. Kimmel, "Dialectical Convergence of Rhetoric and Ethics," 2–3.

17. Burke, *Language as Symbolic Action*, 44.

18. Miller, "Review of *Rethinking the Rhetorical Tradition*," 179.

is shaped almost entirely by the relationships the person has with other people. A self-centered person hardly creates room for others and does not allow others to have an impact on their life in a meaningful way. Such a person can also create little or no room for a relationship with God. Individuals who exercise reasonable independence with a healthy sense of self create room for others and are able to relate with others meaningfully.

Psychosocial analysis focuses on social, emotional, mental, and relational capacities. It also emphasizes the strengths and abilities that promote independent functioning and fulfillment of societal roles, relying on the view that growth and recovery is a process that continuously occurs throughout each individual's life. Psychosocial analysis tends to look at situational and dispositional variables, and how the thoughts, feelings, and behavior of an individual are influenced by others. It is about the relational dimensions that shape identities. By turning away from the fallacies of objectivist science in psychology, the relationship between the self and the social world is seen as paramount for psychosocial analysis. Ruthellen Josselson says,

> Identity, then, is not only an integration of ego functions; it is not solipsistic. From many directions comes the recognition that identity is at its core psychosocial: self and other; inner and outer; being and doing; expression of self for, with, against, or despite; but certainly in response to others. It is both for those for whom one works and the work of loving.[19]

The variables mentioned above inform the exegetical and hermeneutical discussions in the book of Job. While trying to understand the relationships and behavior of the characters in the story, the basic psychosocial elements need to be highlighted. Of course, the discussions in this monograph are not intended to address the psychological attitudes and functions of the characters. Recognition is only given where necessary to the social behavior that informs the concept of friendship. It is about how the characters are described when faced with an emotionally threatening situation or tensions in relationships, and about their ways of dealing with hurting persons. The dynamism of personification is also used to help determine what it means to be a good friend or a bad friend.

Third, understanding the applicability of Hebrew biblical standards in our contemporary world is a hermeneutical task, one that unearths alternatives—a mission that African biblical scholars and ethicists are

---

19. Josselson, "Identity and Relatedness in the Life Cycle," 82.

reckoning with. African interpreters have long been engaging with the Bible in concrete situations of the struggle for survival, liberation, and life. Since the notions of friendship in the book of Job reveal the attitude and character of the people involved in the drama, an appeal to Old Testament ethics is necessary. According to Christopher Wright, "Old Testament ethics, based on history and bound for a renewed creation, is thus slung like a hammock between grace and glory."[20] It is about walking in the way of God. Here, preference is given to the paradigmatic approach to ethics. Wright asserts,

> A paradigm is a model or pattern that enables you to explain or critique many different and varying situations by means of some single concept or set of governing principles. To use a paradigm you work by analogy from a specific known reality (the paradigm) to a wider or different context in which there are problems to be solved, or answers to be found, or choices to be made. Or a paradigm may provide criteria by which you evaluate or critique some set of circumstances or proposals, positively or negatively. So a paradigm may function descriptively or prescriptively or critically.[21]

That is to say, a paradigmatic reading of the social realities of the people of God in the Hebrew Bible helps to critique the cause of how things are and explore the solutions to help people live as God intended. The Akan proverb, *Obi asɛm safoa tumi bue obi asɛm pono* ("The key to one's problem may open the doors to another person's problem"), speaks about the importance of being open-minded and willing to learn from others. The solution an individual falls on can also be relevant to another. Christopher Wright uses the term "paradigm" in two senses, first as a "wider conceptual paradigm," or "worldview," and second in a narrower sense as "a concrete model, a practical, experimental exemplar of the beliefs and values" of the wider paradigm.[22] The connection between Israel's worldview and God's universal purposes for humanity can serve as a hermeneutical principle to illuminate the relevance of the Hebrew Bible for our own ethical construction. For relating the biblical stories to our own ambition to live rightly, paradigmatic inferences bear fruit.

---

20. Wright, *Old Testament Ethics for the People of God*, 35.
21. Wright, *Old Testament Ethics for the People of God*, 63–64.
22. Wright, "Authority of Scripture in an Age of Relativism," 43–45.

Wright believes that there are some realities in the Hebrew Bible that "generate authority that governs our responsive behavior."[23] It is believed that the paradigmatic approach to Hebrew Bible interpretation will provide examples and insight for Christians today who look back to the Law to find its original function and benefit today. According to Eryl Davies, the paradigmatic approach makes "the Bible relevant to contemporary circumstances by drawing attention to the principles which underlie many of the customs and regulations of ancient Israel."[24]

Drawing on the explanations above, Old Testament ethics is fundamentally theological. The main theme in the Hebrew Bible is God initiating relationships with people. That is, ethical issues are at every point related to God—to his character, his will, his actions, and his purpose. Israelite society was to be governed by God's laws. The laws required that the relationship between an individual and God, or an individual and another individual or society, should be grounded in the fact that each and every human being is created in the image of God (Gen 1:26–27.; 5:1b; 9:6b; Ps 8), and that people ought to love their neighbor as themselves (Lev 19:17–18; cf. Mark 12:30). By putting ourselves in Israel's position and understanding how Israel perceived and experienced their relationship with God and with one another, we can learn some paradigms to guide the virtuous living. I agree with Elmer Martens that Old Testament theology should not overlook praxis but give attention to worship, ministry, and ethics, so that the messages can help in forming a community of whom God could say, "I will be their God, and they shall be my people."[25]

Essentially, the hermeneutical principles adopted here help in developing a theology of friendship. By so doing, this study will offer some insights into Old Testament theology, a discipline that is highly contested yet indisputably part of what the Bible offers. Old Testament theology, for Brueggemann, comes up when the text goes through disputation so that a new message for advocacy is created, thus flowing along testimony, dispute, and advocacy.[26] Old Testament theology is not simply confessional, although the reading community's culture has a role to play. To him, legitimation and the embrace of pain are the two principal features of Old Testament theology.[27] How society embraces pain will shape the

23. Wright, *Old Testament Ethics for the People of God*, 469.
24. Davies, *Immoral Bible*, 144.
25. Martens, "Old Testament Theology Since Walter C. Kaiser, Jr.," 690.
26. Brueggemann, *Theology of the Old Testament*, 16–20.
27. Brueggemann, *Old Testament Theology*, 1–44.

way the testimony of the text is legitimated and disputed. The same can be said for the theology of the book of Job within Wisdom literature.

For Davies, the theologies we find in the Bible are relative to the people's own time and culture, and were conditioned by their historical and socio-cultural location.[28] Hence, any discussion cannot ignore the historical particularities of the biblical prescriptions. That does not mean that what happened then has no implications for us now. John Rogerson is right in saying that Old Testament ethics should not be seen as law and precepts but as a reservoir of examples.[29] He asserts that there is a distinction between "conservative" and "liberal" approaches to the study of Old Testament ethics. While the "conservative" approach has a high regard for the moral authority and even uniqueness of biblical texts, the "liberal" approach is more concerned with the cultural context of the ancient Near East that has very little relevance for current theological–ethical discussion.[30] The conservative approach is taken in this monograph.

Generally, "virtue ethics" refers to a group of ethical theories that focus on a person's character as being central and fundamental when it comes to determining what has value and the decisions one should take. Aristotle believes that a good person is a virtuous person, and virtue is that state of character "which makes a man good and makes him perform his function well."[31] When a person lacks the basic resources to do what is good, that person cannot be said to be virtuous. From its Greek root, "virtue" literally means "function" or more aptly "excellence." Thus, a virtuous person is one who functions well from reasoned choices. What is virtuous largely depends on the situation. Within specific situations, a person should feel the right emotions or act in the right way, at the right time, toward the right people. Virtue ethics involves practical wisdom in action. The virtuous person tends to do what is best because the person desires to do so, having the proper feelings. Virtue ethics sees human character as founded in rational and moral activity, and specific virtues—such as loyalty, honesty, patience, compassionate behavior, courage, justice, and wisdom—mark such an individual. That is, virtue requires having an appropriate emotional response toward doing the right thing.

Finally, this study's interpretation is by way of African Contextual Hermeneutics. I have argued that the African contextual approach, like

---

28. Davies, *Immoral Bible*, 141.
29. Rogerson, *Theory and Practice in Old Testament Ethics*, 28, 36.
30. Rogerson, *Theory and Practice in Old Testament Ethics*, 34.
31. Aristotle, *Nicomachean Ethics* 2.6.

pragmatic or cultural analysis, is intuitive, inspirational, all-embracing, and post-critical. It tries to bring various voices to the table and allows each voice to speak without trying to harmonize them. Africans believe that a stranger cannot tell the deepest part of a stream. As a synchronic approach, it uses the context of the reader to add a voice.[32] Interpretation of the biblical text works well when it is a product of a dialogue between the reader and the text. By doing so, the meaning of a text lies within the ultimate perception not of the writer or the text but of the reader. Horsfjord asserts that dialogue is a way of exploring, describing, and discussing a reality by the use of language and speech actions, which involves committing oneself, inviting the other, acknowledging, asserting, questioning, and promising with the intention to impact the world that dialogue partners share.[33] A literary work that employs the approach of dialogue thus becomes a living word in the hands of the reader, rediscovering new life in the text since it is possible for different readers at different times to arrive at many interpretations of the same text.

ORGANIZATION OF THIS BOOK

Chapter 1 forms the preliminary pages, setting the discussions in context, and explaining the methodology and significance of the study. Chapter 2 is on the concept of wisdom in the *book of* Job. *Chapter* 3 deals with how Africans conceptualize friendship. This is undertaken by exploring some of the proverbs in African thought. To understand why is it relevant for Africans to guide their lives by ethical standards set in the Hebrew Bible, some of the African ethical norms need to be identified so as to use them to discuss their similarities and differences to biblical ethics. Chapter 4 briefly explores friendship in the Bible. Chapter 5 examines some philosophical, Christian, and psychological views about friendship throughout history that do not specifically focus on the African context. Admittedly, one cannot deal with the highly debatable concept of friendship in a few pages. However, it is necessary to set out a few ideas in an effort to isolate the conceptual field of friendship. The examination of literature demonstrates how, throughout history, many have freely made use of notions of friendship, yet significantly not in the way Africans see friendship.

32. Aidoo, *Leadership in the Book of Esther*, 5.
33. Horsfjord, "Dialogue as Speech Act and Discourse," 290.

The subsequent chapters present a close reading of the book of Job, highlighting how the conceptual field of friendship is seen in the text, and the practical moral lessons that can be gleaned from the discussion. It explores whether particular characters were friends for a season, for a reason, or for treason. Chapter 6 discusses the relationship between Job and Eliphaz, Bildad, and Zophar, exploring how they depict themselves as friends. Chapter 7 looks at the relationship between Job and his wife. The assumption is that one can marry a friend, or married couples can try to live as friends. Hence, how his wife relates to Job and how Job relates to his wife in the light of friendship is explored. Chapter 8 focuses on the relationship between Job and his extended family members and acquaintances. Friendship, it is assumed, is not only about equals—one can also make friends with children, brothers, sisters, and servants in the household. Chapter 9 is about how Elihu comes into the story and whether he qualifies to be a friend of Job. Chapter 10 is about the relationship between God and Job. It highlights the distinctiveness of divine–human friendship. Finally, chapter 11 concludes by showing the significance of wisdom and friendship for African Christians.

2

Friendship as a Wisdom Tradition in the Book of Job

THE BOOK OF JOB is traditionally classified as part of the wisdom books of the Bible. The wisdom corpus in the Bible reflects the worldview of the people of Israel and not a specific group of people, like the sages. Wisdom is a tradition of a people that reveals insights about ethical life. Although there are aspects of Wisdom literature that show intellectual reflections and speculative modes, there is also the didactic part, aimed at teaching generations how to live their lives practically in the sight of God. That is why Crenshaw says that wisdom is the reasoned search for specific ways to ensure personal well-being in everyday life, to make sense of life, and to transmit this hard-earned knowledge to successive generations.[1]

The book of Job presents critical reflections on life in sketchy detail. If the beginning of the story hints at the relationship between God and Job and notions of disappointment and rejection by the Adversary, and the end of the story shows reconciliation and relatedness between God, the three friends (henceforward, "the three"), and Job's brothers and sisters forged by friendship, then there is some form of climatic ending and some critical answers to the questions the story presents. It is in the context of kinship, affiliation, and connection, shaped by the different kinds of friendships that can make the book of Job end in the way it begins. What makes Job wise and pious, if I am not misunderstanding the text, is how he is seen by God, his family, and the three. What the story teaches

1. Crenshaw, *Old Testament Wisdom*, 4.

is how to be friends in a world that is full of rejection and suffering. Can readers come to a full understanding of suffering from *the* book of Job? Not really! Certainly, a difficult question to answer. And, if readers can come to an understanding of what friendship is all about in the book of Job should the attention only be on the poetic sections, leaving out the prose prologue and epilogue? No! If Job reconciled with God, his three friends, his wife, and his brothers and sisters in the epilogue of the book, then friendship takes center stage in the whole book of Job, and perhaps presents a resolution that has eluded most interpreters who gloss over friendship themes.

Friendship is best defined in times of suffering, as a popular saying goes: "A friend in need is a friend indeed." Needless to say, friendship in the book of Job in the context of suffering takes a large portion of the text. Therefore, attention should not be placed on suffering at the expense of the human relationships. There are friends in bad times and friends in good times. An understanding of friendship in bad times as well as good times should be a focus of the search for wisdom in this book. That does not mean that the book of Job is not a model for sufferers. In fact, Job consistently disagrees with his friends on their interpretation of suffering and insists that he is innocent—God is causing him to suffer unjustly. Job's arguments seem to portray his wife, his friends, and his acquaintances as not understanding what is going on and not reflecting on the issues well. As long as they approach suffering differently, they cannot live as true friends.

It is true that the theology of suffering in the book of Job has much to be desired because "no paradigmatic explanation is offered for why suffering takes place, but there is a lot of interest in what constitutes righteousness."[2] Therefore, focusing on suffering at the expense of the lessons in human relationships may not help the interpreter go far. Moreso, suffering in the book of Job gives rise to lots of complaints and not lamentation.[3] The inability of the three to convince Job also makes them complain, while Job complains about the attitude of the three. What happens in the story is not far removed from practical life today. People continually lose their wealth for no reason. Others cannot find appropriate ways to address the seemingly wayward thoughts of their colleagues and friends.

2. Walton and Tremper Longman, *How to Read Job*, 16.

3. Walter Brueggemann explains lament is a new situation of chaos, now devoid of the coherence that marks God's good creation that helps to identify what suffering means. See Brueggemann, *Message of the Psalms*, 20.

It is in challenging moments that one can discern good friends from bad ones. It is believed that in good times friends know you and in bad times you know them. Such a thought shows that good times will attract many people to one's side, but in bad times only those who are true friends will remain. The African perspective of suffering is rooted in socio-cultural and religious worldviews. Life was seen as a struggle, a fight, hence the adage *obra yɛ ko* ("life is war"). To the African, nothing just happens without a cause. It is therefore important to determine the spiritual root cause for everything, especially suffering.[4] Life is not compartmentalized into sacred and mundane or spiritual and physical. All aspects of life are influenced by both the physical and the spiritual. While it is easy to find physical reasons for a problem, there is a lot one has to do to understand suffering from a spiritual perspective. Suffering caused by spiritual beings like the gods or ancestors is not seen as evil, though it is not simply accepted. It is seen as punishment because the person has done what is unacceptable. However, some gods act capriciously and are very wicked, visiting the sins of one person on the community, and causing misfortunes.[5] For instance, in the traditional African worldview, there was widespread belief in witchcraft and sorcery—practices that can cause calamities in society. Africans hardly attribute suffering to God, but to the ancestors or evil spirits.[6] Nevertheless, spiritual forces can influence friendship relationships, making good friends turn to bad friends.

DECONSTRUCTING A WISDOM STORY

Traditional Wisdom literature in the Protestant/Hebrew Bible includes the book of Job. Although there are doubts about the designation, "Wisdom literature," in the Bible, the concept of wisdom found in some books cannot be denied. Wisdom's distinct category in Israel's legacy is much comparable to the law, history, prophecy, and psalmody, which shaped the life and worship of the people.

Although the Hebrew Bible does not provide a complete historical outline of how wisdom activity started or developed in ancient Israel, there is no doubt that wisdom has its roots in the history of Israel. According to James L. Crenshaw, "one can scarcely imagine a time when the

---

4. Imasogie, *Guidelines for Christian Theology in Africa*, 60.
5. Okorocha, "Religious Conversion in Africa," 173.
6. Landman, "Who/What Causes Suffering?' 3.

adjective 'wise' (*hakam*) did not function in ancient Israel." He adds that there is an allusion to "three classes of leaders in ancient Israel: priests, prophets and sages. The essential function of each professional group is thus captured in a single word. Priests promulgate instruction (*torah*), prophets proclaim the divine word (*dabar*), and sages give counsel (*'ēṣah*)."[7]

Wisdom, which is complementary with the Torah and Prophets, flourished and gave an alternative to "thus says the Lord," this time focusing on the daily happenings and experiences of life that preoccupied people, and reflecting on the difficult questions of how to get along in life. However, texts that echo wisdom call people to appreciate captivating, timeless principles that examine humanity's relationship with one another and nature, founded on a belief in God as the creator and sustainer of the universe.[8] The cultural settings within which all these occur are probably interesting to consider, for "wisdom ideas were not tied to one particular time frame. They deal with life's basic issues (What is wise and foolish, suffering, raising children, the vanity of life without God, the need to fear God), which are faced in every age."[9]

There is no doubt that wisdom refers to "points of orientation"[10] or "indispensable signposts"[11] by which people steer their course. It presents readers with virtue and the various "paths" people need to cope with life. Benjamin Wright provides four properties that underlie Wisdom literature: (1) pedagogical form and intent; (2) concern for acquiring wisdom through study and learning; (3) engagement with earlier sapiential tradition; and (4) interest in practical ethics.[12] Whether the pedagogical materials are meant to have a communalistic ethos in which the individual is submerged in the collective or not, the ethics that Wisdom literature offers maintains a balance between individuality and collectivity.[13] Wisdom describes a lifestyle (*Lebenskunst*) for people in every sphere of society including the young, parents, elders, judges, kings, prophets, courtiers, and wise scribes.[14] John Goldingay asserts that wisdom "remains a mi-

7. Crenshaw, *Old Testament Wisdom*, 27.
8. Sanders, *Torah and Canon*, 99, 100.
9. Schultz and Smith, *Exploring the Old Testament*, 127.
10. Davis, "Surprised By Wisdom," 266.
11. Von Rad, *Wisdom in Israel*, 26.
12. Wright, "Joining the Club," 298–99.
13. McKane, *Proverbs*, 415.
14. Sneed, *Social World of the Sages*, 19–20.

nority report within the Hebrew Bible itself, but post-canonical writings saw it take a more central place. Wisdom *ḥokmāh* comes to be identified with *tôrāh*; God's eternal wisdom is seen as embodied in Israel's law; general revelation is identified with special revelation."[15] The significance of wisdom to the worship life of Jews and Christians cannot be overemphasized. Yet, how the texts practically help the reader to live to become "wise" remains a matter of contention. The assumption is that wisdom is not necessarily philosophical but pragmatic and concrete.

Granting that the book of Job teaches wisdom is critical for interpreting what friends are for. And the emphasis on friendship in times of suffering is a movement away from the center, subjectively countering the dominant reading, and offering a different view of interpretation. Leong Seow's idea could have served the purpose of my reading if he had focused on the relevance of wisdom in the book of Job. He asserts that the book of Job is not about suffering but theology:

> The book is ultimately not about theodicy. It provides no satisfying solution to the question of human misfortunes . . . It does not resolve the cognitive dissonance between the notion of a just God and the reality of innocent suffering. The book is rather about theology, or more specifically, how one speaks of God in the face of chaos. It is true that the ending is anticlimactic. We do not expect, after the substantial theologies of Job, his friends, Elihu, and God, to come to this seemingly crude conclusion of a twofold restoration. Certainly after the sublime poetry and provocative theology of the divine speeches, we do not expect to come to anything so prosaic, so mundane.[16]

Much as I agree with Seow that the book of Job is essentially theological, it has its distinct voice and approach. The book of Job is wisdom, and even if the primary focus of wisdom is to teach about God, it has other things to present. Much as wisdom books presuppose canonical religion, they articulate "the religion-based, sociomoral aspects of human competences and virtue in relation to Yahweh . . . wisdom entails knowledge of and appropriate action with reference to particular circumstances, institutions, person, and other creatures."[17] As long as the book of Job begins with an affirmation of a relationship, moves into challenges and breakdowns in relationships (friendships), and closes with the

15. Goldingay, "'Salvation History' Perspective and the 'Wisdom' Perspective," 200.
16. Seow, *Job 1–21*, 108.
17. Leeuwen, "Wisdom Literature," 848–50.

restoration of relationships between Job and God, the three, his brothers and sisters, and perhaps his wife, then in that sense, there is no anticlimax.

Carol Newsom makes a pertinent observation that the book of Job constitutes a dialogic sense of consciousness and voices, in which different perspectives engage one another.[18] The dialogic idea of a text, however, may have a unified truth within a plurality of consciousness with polyphonic voices. A single voice, whether about suffering or theology, will not suffice. She observes that both historic critics and final form critics begin with the assumption that the book of Job should have a monologic idea and as such should represent a product of a single mind.[19] One may be tempted to find dissonance and tension in the prose and poetic sections of the book if working from such a perspective. This means that the book has something else to share other than suffering.

The role played by Job's three friends has had some attention in almost all studies on the book of Job. However, very little attention is placed on how they act as friends; how his wife plays the role of a friend; how his brothers, sisters, and slaves act as friends; and how God relates to Job as a friend. Most African traditional religious views hold that God originally created human beings to enjoy friendly relationships and expect all to live healthy lives, free from diseases, pain, and death.[20] Going back to the basics can help transform society.

Wisdom traditions in the Bible are not confined to a particular people for they encourage "us to be open to what there is to learn from all of human endeavor and insight."[21] Africans are mentioned in the Bible as full of authentic wisdom and knowledge.[22] Egypt and Kush are usually mentioned as having wise people (Gen 41:8, 24; Exod 7:10–12; 2 Sam 16–18; 1 Kgs 10:1–13; Ezek 29:10, Isa 18:12; 45:14, Job 28:19; Jer 13:23; Matt 2:1–12; Acts 8:26–29; cf. Exod 1:15). I agree with David Adamo that in 2 Samuel 16–18, the "African's courage to face the King and report the true situation, as well as his form of address support the view that this African was one of the royal military officers in the King's court and that he held a high position."[23] Similarly, another African, Ebed Melech,

---

18. Newsom, "Job as a Polyphonic Text," 91.

19. Newsom, "Job as a Polyphonic Text," 91; Fienberg, "Poetic Structure of the Book of Job," 286.

20. Chitando and Dube, *African Indigenous Religious*, 24.

21. Goldingay, "'Salvation History' Perspective and the 'Wisdom' Perspective," 203.

22. Adamo, *Africa and the Africans in the Old Testament*.

23. Adamo, "Africa and Africans in the Old Testament," 153.

who strategically used rags to draw the prophet Jeremiah from a cistern marks him as a wise man (Jer 38:1–12).[24] My particular interest is in how this African conveyed the news such that it did not become a problem to David. It confirms the Akan saying that *wosoma ɔba nyansafo, wonnsoma anamon tsentsen* ("it is a wise person who is sent, not the one with long legs"). The Akan say, *obiara nnyi hɔ a wɔwoo no nyansafo* ("no one was born wise").

African traditional worldview forms a part of the biblical notion of wisdom as it upholds communal values of compassion, reciprocity, harmony, and friendship in building and maintaining community. For instance, among the Akan, when one person suffers, it is imperative for all relatives, social friends, and the entire community to show their solidarity and economic obligations to support the person based on positive reciprocation. Those who are antisocial and do not support others hardly get the support of others too. Reciprocity in relationships involves an exchange of burdens and benefits.[25] Reciprocity is a way of showing gratitude, and as Ubuntu requires, it is the principle of helping others being a way of helping oneself—to show unification rather than division, respect for elders, and sharing."[26] Such a way of life emphasizes the need for the left hand to support the right hand, and the right hand to support the left hand.

Biblical wisdom may have thrived as folk wisdom in the homes and the courts but it has become part of God's plan for life, teaching society to live rightly and make the right decisions in relationships. It teaches not only how an individual can live life but also how people can be wise in their relationships with each other. Wisdom is not only speculative and reflective, but also practical, factual, and experiential. So, it is in the light of fruitful interaction and companionship that the theme of friendship is discussed, looking at Job's relationships with God, Mrs. Job, Eliphaz, Bildad, Zophar, Elihu, and Job's family members. The relationship is perceived in the prose and poetic sections. In the dialogical exchanges, the characters measure notions of friendship in times of suffering. In what category of friendship do Job himself, Job's wife, Eliphaz, Bildad, Zophar, Elihu, the brothers and sisters, the household members, and God fall?

24. Adamo, "Africa and Africans in the Old Testament," 161, 162.
25. Richardson and Cho, "Secondary Researchers' Duties," 467.
26. Mufune "African Culture and Managerial Behaviour," 21

WISDOM IN THE BOOK OF JOB AND THE BOUNDARIES OF FRIENDSHIP

Samuel Balentine observes that the book of Job is about friendship, for "it is the theology of friendship that provides the frame for the book's central concerns."[27] Again, he observes that out of the forty-two chapters, roughly 90 percent of those chapters explore the question "Who will be Job's friend?"[28] Beyond this question, one needs to explore how Job sees friendship. What image of friendship are the characters trying to create? What defines a real friend?

David Clines, looking at the ethics of injustice in the book of Job, turns to blame God and also Job for the positions they took, acting as a "fifth friend."[29] In a similar vein, Jan Fokkelman sees Elihu as a fourth friend. He designates the three as elderly friends and Elihu as younger friend.[30] Vesely's discussion in *Friendship and Virtue Ethics in the Book of Job* depends on seven moral virtues—loyalty, compassion, courage, hospitality, honesty, humility, and practical wisdom—seeking to show how they are integral to a relationship of friendship. However, emphasis is placed on the virtue of friendship between Job and the three friends and the brothers and sisters, while the friendship of God is treated as an appendix. Mrs. Job and Elihu do not feature in the discussion.[31] The position of the present monograph is not to act as one of the new friends or be the next friend, but to explore how to be a friend. The current task is to explore the ethical concepts of friendship and relate them to the African context. Identifying the friends of Job for certain means showing how to be a friend. This present monograph not only identifies the kinds of friends reflected in the book of Job but also discusses how to be friends.

A cue is taken from Norman Habel's paper, "Only the Jackal is my friend: On Friends and Redeemers in Job," which justifies a proposal that the book of Job provides a ministry of friendship that is more basic, more human, more affirming than any acceptable mode of service. The theme of friendship, to Habel, envisages partnership, cordiality, a human covenant, ultimate loyalty, and a redemptive relationship, a position helpful

---

27. Balentine, "Let Love Clasp Grief Lest Both be Drowned," 381.
28. Balentine, "Let Love Clasp Grief Lest Both be Drowned," 381.
29. Clines, "Job's Fifth Friend," 233–50.
30. Fokkelman, *Book of Job in Form*, 289, 290.
31. Vesely, *Friendship and Virtue Ethics in the Book of Job*, 8.

for this study.[32] Nevertheless, his wife and other family members are not captured within the category of "friends."

Sadly, Jennie Grillo avers that "The book of Job has not always been read as wisdom literature: the highly individualized figure of Job, vividly dramatized in the psychological realism of the speeches, had a strong exemplary role in the earliest Jewish and Christian readings and later a typological one."[33] Such an approach to the book cannot continue, in my estimation. Wisdom is for humanity to live our lives well and to relate well with one another. One of the most striking themes in the book of Job, while easily overlooked, is "friendship." Of course, this is so common a terminology that it seems to defy an investigation. In building upon the theme of friendship, analysis of some texts will be presented in light of the understanding of the multiple faces of friendship in the book of Job.

Scholars have argued that the narratives and cycles of speeches in the book of Job are disconnected units.[34] Others see more of a pattern, a continuous discourse with parts resembling each other in structure.[35] The silences, set-ups, interventions, and celebrations are impactful and support the consistency of the story. These features frame the story in its moral struggle to discover the meaning of life in the midst of tradition, experience, and faith.[36] The speeches serve as ingredients that echo tones of human identity, community, and covenant. They also show how one relates with God, others, and the self. Perhaps, that is what friends are for. The basic identifiable elements underlying the relationship Job looks for are reciprocity, other-centeredness, intimacy, and openness. As a dramatic art, speeches and responses drive the wheels of the story. As such, the attitudes and actions of the characters of the story are seen more in the speeches and responses. I argue that when friendship becomes the theme for reading the book of Job, some coherence can be found.

---

32. Habel, "Only the Jackal Is My friend," 227–36.

33. Grillo, "Wisdom Literature," 191.

34. Hartley, *Book of Job*, 38. Feinberg, "Poetic Structure of the Book of Job," 286; Parsons, "Structure and Purpose of the Book of Job," 139–42; Westermann, *Structure of the Book of Job*, esp 1–16; Lugt "Speech Cycles in the Book of Job," 554–57.

35. Anderson, *Job*, 20, 21; Weeks, *Introduction to the Study of Wisdom Literature*, 51; Timmer, "God's Speeches, Job's Responses," 288; Utzschneider, "Book of Job and an Aesthetic Theology," 93; Polak, "On Prose and Poetry in the Book of Job," 61–96; Steimann, "Structure and Message of the Book of Job," 86–88; Patrick, "Fourfold Structure of Job," 185.

36. Habel, *Book of Job*, 45.

The book of Job depicts friends in action. In fact, there is hardly any doubt about the various practical life experiences and human interactions the story demonstrates. The book of Job utilizes prose and poetry, heightened emotional feelings, and voices to draw the intuitive reader into the craft of heavenly and earthly dramas of relationship. God, on the one hand, relates with heavenly beings, including the Adversary, ending up with dialogue and planning attacks on Job. On another hand, Job relates with his wife, friends, and brothers and sisters in the prologue and epilogue sections of the book (1:1—2:13; 42:7–17), and the relationship is further reflected upon in the poetic sections (3:1—42:6). The narrative and poetic sections of the book creatively display mythological plots, disputation lament, trial speeches, ironies, wisdom poems, curses, and hymnic materials and these are arranged into scenes, cycles, and summaries. Monologues and dialogues interact with each other in a mass of complex microstructures and superstructures. It all begins with a happy and content family headed by Job and ends with a happy and content Job who lives a full life and dies gracefully.

Significantly, three basic motifs of friendship come to the fore: friends for a reason, for a season, and for treason. True friendship is motivated by personal advantages that accrue to both parties in a reciprocal relationship that lasts a lifetime and is devoid of pain. When one shares with the other and the other fails to reciprocate or disclose things about themselves, their friendship will break down. One gets to know people well by sharing "safe" thoughts with them first, not the issues that can land a person in trouble. The most important thing about friendship is how the relationship makes one feel—not how it is supposed to be or the things they have in common. The expressions and levels of involvement help to categorize the nature and category of friendship that is at play.

Friendship is also a theme in the books of Proverbs and Ecclesiastes. The sages see it prudent to explore how human relationships can support and enhance meaningful life. Good friends avoid gossiping or speaking negatively about each other (Prov 16:28). If one cannot say something good about the other, then it is better not to speak at all. Gossiping and backbiting do not promote community. The sages, in the book of Proverbs, argue that a clear identity of a good friend is love (Prov 17:9, 17). Love promotes sharing, and passion, and makes people share common interests. As soon as one goes in another direction, the friendship falls apart. An unreliable friend will ruin the other friend's life (Prov 18:24). That does not mean a friend cannot do what will adversely affect the other. Yet even if a good friend does what is hurting, it will not be taken as a big issue for the wounds of a friend can be trusted (Prov 27:6). The Akan say, *sɛ ɛdɔ ɔbaa a, ne ta koraa yɛ huam* ("when you love a woman, even her fart smells good").

The writer of Ecclesiastes says "two are better than one" (Eccl 4:9–12), thus affirming that it is not ideal to journey through life alone. Whatever the case, having another person close by is a great advantage. Nothing can replace the presence of a neighbor or friend. Whether it be a spouse, a family member, a good friend, or a colleague, our lives become enriched when carrying a burden, going through moments of joy or sadness, or fulfilling our life's goal. Africans believe that if you want to go far you need to go with someone. When we reject the presence and help of others, the progress we need in life cannot be fully achieved. Companionship erodes emptiness and loneliness.

Although many of the values taught in wisdom literature are individual in nature, it is possible to see some of them on a relational base. There are:

a. Husband–wife relationships, highlighting issues of sexual misconduct, adultery, lust, and promiscuity.
b. Parent-child relationships, highlighting admonitions to obey their parents, and parents to teach the children well.
c. Business relationships, highlighting justice, fairness, equity, and honesty.
d. Societal relationships, highlighting integrity, honesty, friendship, and care and compassion for all.

Friendship lies within the context of favor and loyalty. It may be that picking a friend or making a friend is not a difficult task. However, being a friend requires elements of favor to be accepted and to be embraced. No wonder Job sees his chaotic condition as something not to be embraced because it does not fit a coherent view of life, relationship with others, who God is, and what God does. Looking out for a "redeemer" to come to his rescue should be seen as an act of favor. John Chrysostom aptly recognizes the contributions of the story in the book of Job to grace when he says,

> There was no human misfortune, which this man did not undergo. He was the firmest and most adamant, beset by sudden tribulation by hunger, and by woe, and sickness, and bereft of children, and loss of riches, and then suffering abuse from his

wife, insult from his friends, reproach from his servants, and in everything he showed himself more solid than a stone, and a source before the Law also of Grace.[37]

God's grace has a special way of shaping lives. It is through grace that humanity comes to know more about God, who is far removed from us and beyond what we can understand. Grace plays a great role in causing hearts to change and lives to be transformed. Grace makes it possible for God not to condemn us when we sin or err. Grace can carry people far beyond where they can reach with their own strength. God's grace becomes more vivid and underlies the relationships built at the closing stages of the book of Job when God restores Job, restores the friendships Job has with the three, his wife, and his extended family.

The characters in the book of Job have some expectations of one another. As will be shown in the expositions, each one of them does meet the loyal expectation required to be a friend. They all create problems for each other and as such give the reader food for thought. Job's wife is part of the problem, as well as his servants, brothers, and sister. They are also part of the solution to identifying what true friendship means. In fact, only Eliphaz, Bildad, and Zophar are identified as friends of Job. Yet the story gives an idea that there is more to that. Much the same way, Elihu comes into the picture not as a friend of Job, but as an advocate for Job's friends. He is an ally, a concerned citizen, and can be considered a friend. The family members and servants of Job desert him when he is suffering. They have a part to play in Job's agony too. Although the family members and servants cannot strictly be called "friends," the kind of relationship that exists between Job and these people was more like friendship. Job seems to be someone who built and maintained relationships and friendships. In all, the characters in the story lack the kind of practical know-how that is a mark of a wise person. Besides all these, a contextual reading from an African perspective can further reveal aspects of friendship expectations that can enhance the understanding of the book of Job.

CONCLUDING REMARKS

Certainly, it takes the art of wisdom to learn how to relate justly with another as a friend. It is wisdom that helps one to live fully as a friend. The Wisdom traditions or corpus come to us in the context of God's Holy

---

37. See Janos, "Eclectic Commentary on the Book of Job."

Testament—The Bible. They have something to do with God's people in a covenant relationship with God, which must reflect how they live with one another. The Bible speaks of wisdom as a treasure that all should pursue, acquire, and keep. It aims at being successful in life. Wisdom helps in the mystery of life. It allows all to see clearly and to know the right way to speak and act. It offers all the opportunity to know how to make good decisions and give the right counsel when others need help. As such, wisdom protects people from falling into transitoriness, uselessness, and worthlessness. Humanity needs God's wisdom to navigate life and build solid relationships, especially in times of adversity. The significance of wisdom for today cannot be overemphasized.

3

Friendship in Indigenous African Thought

Africa is culturally diverse and the different languages, traditions, and customs of its people bear witness to this. Diversity can be a beautiful thing and Africans draw inspiration and strength from their enduring diverse cultural traditions. Indeed, Africa is not a homogenous continent. However, some forms of traditional and cultural identities seem to point in one direction, and the rich sources of knowledge for the enhancement of life look similar. Friendship is one "world" where the many diverse peoples of Africa get past their differences to share a common identity. The idea of community is another world. Also, the proverbs of African people reveal a kind of homogeneity of expectations. The allusion is that among Africans and across different groups of people there are, to a large extent, some similar beliefs and practices, or similar ways of thinking and acting and doing things, with similar expectations, most of which are positively shaped by a religio-cultural worldview. Culture embodies the beliefs and traditions that shape the way of life of a given people. Nevertheless, the ideas and values of good and evil as well as what is right or wrong may not be culture-specific. But even though the foundations may be similar, people in each specific context or place manifest the cultural beliefs differently.

In this monograph, attention is focused on sub-Saharan African proverbs. Incorporating the positive elements of the sub-Saharan African traditions and culture of friendship into a life-setting can serve as a practical response to social development and humanism. It can also help in advocating particular values while taking into cognizance cultural differences. A respect for difference somehow finds expression in language and not necessarily in the variety of social and cultural approaches to life. A Swahili saying goes, *mwacha asili ni mtumwa* ("he who discards his traditions and culture is a slave"), meaning a true child of the land must uphold the traditions and culture handed over by the ancestors. Such a view resonates with the Akan saying *nyia onnyim ne hen kyinii no yew wɔ dwabɔ ase* ("the one who does not know their chief's umbrella gets lost in a gathering"). Knowing one's tradition and culture makes the person authentic. In other words, it is not acceptable to lose one's cultural heritage, especially the positive aspects.

AFRICAN CULTURE, ETHICS, AND RELATIONSHIPS

Friendship means differently to different people. Peiqi Lu et al argue that friendships are recognized and interpreted differently across cultures and countries, and so is intimacy. While some cultures employ a looser definition of friendship and are more flexible, others are stricter in the ways they define friendship and are more stable and fixed.[1] Friendship from an African perspective cuts across all spheres of life and is about how one relates with others. African ethics is humanistic and sometimes characterized as a character-based ethics. It is concerned about the individual's character or moral development and is essentially communal. There are descriptive and prescriptive or normative aspects to the character-based notions. African ethics to a large extent is teleological, that is it derives duty or moral obligation from the end to be achieved that is good or desirable. It may not necessarily be deontological, which holds that the standards for the moral rightness of an action, on the one hand depend on a set of rules or principles, and, on the other hand are independent of the end to be achieved. Hence, issues requiring moral inquiry—such as addressing crises, bereavement management, communication, marriage, family life, and community building systems—are all shaped by communal nature and religious beliefs. These systems help not only in unveiling reality but also in the critical interpretation of thought, thereby re-creating knowledge.

Ethical principles in the African perspective focus on the individual's capacity to relate with other individuals or the community through

---

1. Lu et al, "Friendship Importance Around the World," 2.

sharing, caring, and compassion. An individual who follows the moral values, principles, and rules of society can be truly considered a good or virtuous person.² These same virtues expected of an individual make the person "friendly." Such is the spirit of Ubuntu and aptly located in Mbiti's words: "I am because we are, and since we are, therefore, I am."³ Ubuntu is a philosophy that transcends ethnic divisions, promotes working together, respects human dignity, and affirms teamwork. Laurenti Magesa stresses the importance of community: "We cannot understand persons, indeed we cannot have a personal identity without reference to others persons."⁴

According to Bhebe and Viriri, "Ubuntu philosophy is a concept that is carried through proverbs. Ubuntu means human dignity and collective sharedness. This definition means that people are people through other people."⁵ Africans believe that a person can only define oneself in the context of others. Among the Akan, the saying *wɔdze me a, nna wɔdze wo* ("if it is about me, then it is about you") expresses the commonality of action and principles of sharedness. African worldviews and knowledge systems are discerned from the proverbs, folktales, riddles, maxims, and myths, among others, that have been handed down over generations. Kwame Gyekye argues that indigenous knowledge systems are from the oral literature, beliefs, and actions of the people within a culture. According to Gyekye,

> African philosophical thought is expressed both in the oral literature and in the thoughts and actions of the people. Thus, a great deal of philosophical material is embedded in the proverbs, myths and folktales, folk songs, rituals, beliefs, customs, and traditions of the people, in their art symbols and in their socio-political institutions and practices.⁶

Proverbs are generally culture or context-specific, but it is important to establish that they are taken as universal norms.⁷ The appeal to oral tradition does not mean an unexamined thought. Basically, knowledge is based on careful observation and analysis of life, and is lived out daily. Perhaps, the daily activation of such traditions makes them more

---

2. Etieyibo, "Post-Modern Thinking and African Philosophy," 72–74.
3. Mbiti, *African Philosophy*, 108, 141.
4. Magesa, *African Religion*, 64.
5. Bhebe and Viriri, *Shona Proverbs*, ix.
6. Gyekye, *African Cultural Values*, 13.
7. Ackah, *Akan Ethics*, 16.

enduring than that kept in books. The basis of these philosophical traditions, thus, has stood the test of time.

An analysis of African philosophical thought demonstrates how societal knowledge and values lie at the bedrock of relationships. These sources of knowledge—ethno-philosophy or sage philosophy—are an essential part of indigenous critical thinking and epistemology. They are meant to guide life; they open up possibilities and affirm practical patterns of living. The cultural values, beliefs, and worldviews of African peoples as distinguished from indigenes on other continents largely construct the distinctiveness of African indigenous knowledge. Such knowledge also comes through experience of the workings of nature and its relationship with the social world. According to George Dei, "indigenous knowledge carries with it the advantage of bringing into development discourse voices from the margins. These voices may be uncritical, unscientific and crude, but they nonetheless represent the lived experiences of societies."[8] In other words, whatever comes to African people as indigenous knowledge is embraced, knowing that all knowledge is granted by the supernatural, and they can come from wherever. The experiences of people in their encounters with the African soil enhance their appreciation of indigenous knowledge.

A way to appreciate indigenous knowledge is through the use of proverbs. Such indigenous or traditional knowledge is attributed to elders and ancestors and, thus, is words of wisdom from ancient times. Language is a rich inheritance from the elders and ancestors. To make a saying authoritative, it is attributed to an unknown source—the unseen world, ancestors, or the elders. These are the foremothers and fathers of society, and it is believed that the disposition of the elderly is wisdom. Hence, if someone begins a proverb with the prelude, "the elders say . . ." or "so-and-so says . . ." or "there's a saying . . .," it is not simply a mythical quote but truth wrapped in authority. In the view of Agyekum, "proverbs are interpretations of traditional wisdom based on the experiences and sociopolitical life of our elders. The most acknowledged element of an Akan's communicative competencies is the ability to use ɛbɛ (proverbs)."[9] Hence, the use of proverbs in speech enhances the value of what is being said.

Language informs identity and gives direction in life. A Yoruba proverb goes, *owe ni esin oro, to oro ba sonu, owe ni afi nwa* ("proverbs

---

8. Dei, "Sustainable Development in the African Context," 105.
9. Agyekum, "Akan Oral Artist," 9.

are the root of words, when words get entangled, proverbs come to the rescue"). This shows that in times of difficulty, one has to use proverbs to find a way out. Knowledge is unearthed by the use of proverbs. The one who does not understand proverbs cannot reconcile with knowledge. That is to say, reality is decoded in words. Similarly, an Igbo proverb, *Ilu bu mmanu e ji eri okwu* ("Proverbs are the palm-oil with which words are eaten"), affirms the value and importance of proverbs in life. For any food to be eaten well and without difficulty, it takes a valuable ingredient. That is to say for food to be cooked, one needs a good cooking oil. A proverb happens to be such a valuable ingredient, for it is believed that a speech without a proverb is food without salt. Using African proverbs is meant to show the richness of language and its contributions to African philosophical thinking. Similarly, for one to gain an understanding of anything, there should be some lubricant that can help with the assimilation of the words. Proverbs serve as the salt of a language, without which the real taste of communication is not experienced.

Proverbs are founded on experience. Shapin says, "proverbs are oriented towards experience. They report on accumulated experience, human and natural; they make those reports efficiently available to people who mean to act in the world; they recommend courses of action in [the] light of experience; and therefore . . . represent a widely distributed form of expertise."[10] Hence, proverbs are based on human experience—not a one-time experience but on a consistent period of examinations. Sharon Bethea and Tennille Allen, dwelling on Rowe and Rowe, acknowledge that African proverbs "express guidelines for conduct and behavior, and discuss values on relationship."[11] African proverbs give direction to social situations and teach about the actions to take. A proverb is used to express a truth based on common sense and is accepted to be authoritative. It is believed that the ancestors and elders came up with proverbs based on the practical experience of humanity, to describe a basic rule of conduct or a maxim. For N. K. Dzobo, proverbs are very popular devices used to state certain general truths about life.[12] They constitute the reservoirs of indigenous cultures. Most African proverbs speak from experience and observation, which are crucial for authentic knowledge.

The structure and meaning of African proverbs as pithy wise sayings are not unique to Africa. Some proverbs in fact point to the fact that

---

10. Shapin, "Proverbial Economies," 739.

11. Bethea and Allen, "Past and Present Societal Influences," 41.

12. Dzobo, "African Symbols and Proverbs," 95.

values and norms are relative depending on their anthropological and religious beliefs. Like Western philosophy, African proverbs tend to be contradictory; every proverb has its counter-proverb. There are proverbs that answer or dispute others. The view is that there are two sides to every "coin" or proverb. A wise person, thus, knows when and how to use a particular proverb and must be made aware of the other side of it too. The apparent contradiction in proverbs demonstrates how reality is seen as a complex phenomenon. In other words, proverbs are mostly used in a comparative sense. In that sense, there is always some relationship between two statements, and the referent being compared sheds light on other aspects of life. African proverbs, thus communicate a reality that is timeless and which one cannot do without. This Akan proverb sums up the complex nature of proverbs: *wo bu ɛbɛ a, me te ɛbɛ* ("if you speak in proverbs, I also understand proverbs"). The value of proverbs is discerned in the Akan saying, *korotwa mansa tɔ nsu ma no ho na ɔfɔ na ne nsensan dze ɔwɔ hɔ daa* ("when the leopard falls into a waterbody, its skin becomes wet but its stripes are not washed away"). The relevance of these short sayings, thus, cannot be underestimated.

THE NATURE OF AFRICAN FRIENDSHIP

Friendship is a form of social organization. Every social organization is driven by social systems in which the context plays a significant role. The system defines the nature of interactions and relationships. Similarly, every social organization follows a structure. According to G. Gordon Brown and James H. Barnett, "social organization refers to the systems of obligation-relations which exist among and between the groups constituting a given society, while social structure refers to the placement and position of individuals and of groups within that system of obligation-relations."[13] As the pattern of interaction within a particular community informs acceptable behavior, culture thus plays a key role in shaping the systems and structures. In other words, certain concrete activities, roles, and functions within a culture inform social positions or participation in a particular organization.[14] Hence, friendship as a social organization can be distinct in every social system or context. In essence, the way Africans may understand friendship will not necessarily be the way others see it.

---

13. Brown and Barnett, "Social Organization and Social Structure," 31.
14. Hawley, *Human Ecology*, 31, 32.

For instance, sharing one's food with another is a way to depict friendship in African societies, but not necessarily in other contexts outside Africa. Enemies, in African thought, rather withhold food from the other person who is close by. Traditionally, greeting the people one meets is also a key virtue in Africa. Failure to greet someone who crosses paths with you is unacceptable. Among the Akan, when a person passes by without saying a word of greeting, the gesture is understood as a sign of unfriendliness or antagonism. There are acceptable forms of greetings from place to place, so one cannot greet any which way. Greeting with the left hand is a sign of disrespect. Prostration in some parts of northern Ghana and Yorubaland, for instance, is an acceptable form of greeting and a sign of courtesy or portraying respect. Bowing down is not a form of humiliation. The Yoruba say, *Ka dobale fun arara, iyen o ni ka ma ga* ("Prostrating for a dwarf does not stop one from rising up again"). In this context, waving a hand in greeting is thus seen as an act of disrespect. The absence of the appropriate greeting, where necessary, marks the beginning of hostility. All these affirm the fact that the structures inherent in the use of proverbs come with acceptable norms. And since there are some levels of homogeneity in sub-Saharan African societies, it can be assumed that there are some similarities in the way friendship is structured in sub-Saharan Africa.

The Akan[15] of Ghana use the terms *nyɛnko, yɔnkoɔ/yonko* to designate friendship. The word *nyɛnko* (spoken by Mfantse), is a compound word—*nyɛn* ("nurture") and *ko* ("fight")—perhaps echoing a call for two parties to engage in a fight. The idea of fighting may be out of place since friendship is not about competition or fighting. Nevertheless, it is also said in Akan, *ɔbra yɛ ko* ("life is war"). If life is lived as if one is at the warfront, then friendship can follow such an idea. Notice that in Swahili, the elders say, *Watu waliambiwa "kakaeni," hawakuambiwa "kashindaneni"* ("People are told 'Come and live together'; they were not told 'Come and compete with one another'"). Another word among the Twi-speaking Akan for a friend is *adamfo*, maybe from two words *adam* meaning mentally deranged, and *fo* meaning people. In such a case, friendship is when two or more people who are mentally challenged come together.

The Moosi (or Moose/Moshi) of Burkina Faso, who trace their origin to Mamprusi and Dagomba in northern Ghana, use the term

---

15. The Akan are made up of over 18 language groups from Southern Ghana to parts of La Cote D'Ivoire. I use the Mfantse, Asante Twi, and Akwapim Twi of Ghana as representatives of the Akan in this study due to the closeness of the dialects.

reementaaga to refer to comradeship that develops from neighbors, and *tadentaaga* for friendship-like relatedness within the context of associates, while *zoodo* characterizes the passionate emotional friendship, or mutual liking of one another validated by a chain of ulterior motives.[16] The Ewe of Ghana and Togo use the compound word *xɔlɔ/xɔlɔ̃* to define friendship; *xɔ* means "house" and *lɔ̃* means "agree" or "love." Hence *xɔlɔ̃* echoes agreeing with or loving someone in/of your home. The Yoruba use *ore*, *irepo*, or *aburo* to translate friendship. The word *ore* also means "intense anger" or "goodness." There is also the Yoruba word *alabaṣepọ* ("partner"), which sometimes connotes friend. Among the Ihievbe in the Edo state of Nigeria, *omomena* translates the word friendship, and it "refers to an internal openness of the self toward the other and a sense of trust brought about by the process of establishing friendship among the persons involved."[17] The Fulbe, who spread across Niger-Congo, through Sudan, Central Africa, to northern Ghana, and are commonly referred to as Fulani,[18] use terms such as *soobaajo* or *kombi* to mean "friend" or "comrade." Other Fulbe-related terms are *bandiraawo* ("relative"), *dendiraawo* ("cross-cousin," "joking partner"), *higgo* ("age-mate") and *koddo* ("guest," "stranger"). The joking relations seen as friendship among the Fulbe are parties who use teasing, exchange mutual insults, and have the right to "steal" from one another. Joking friendship is seen as a game and serves as a bridge for social interaction, but it is not taken as the exclusive form of relationship or communication.[19] The Moosi of Burkina Faso use *mzoa* to refer to an intimate friend. For the Maasai also, the term friendship is *shoreisho*, connoting a casual sense of rapport and shared company, or in the formal sense a trusted exchange partner[20]—while the Barma of Chad use the term *kapam*, indicating someone who is supposed to be of help in a lot of ways. Among the Maasai, a friend is *al-chore*, which is a mutual exchange partner, and for the Barotse of Zambia, the term *bulikani*, literally meaning the "quality of being equals," is used to denote a friend.[21] Consequently, it is not out of place to assert that in African communities, friendship relations are made up of extended family systems, distant relatives, and friends who make up a close-knit network, as well as strangers.

16. Breusers, "Friendship and Spiritual Parenting," 74–77.
17. Aihiokhai, "'Love One Another as I Have Loved You,'" 495.
18. Mogtari, "Fulani Herdsmen Traditions and Care for the Land," 179–82.
19. Breusers, "Friendship and Spiritual Parenting," 80, 81.
20. Spencer, "Comradeship and the Transformation of Alliance Theory," 49.
21. Reyna, "Afterword," 165–70.

It could be equals or non-equals, but in most cases, it is gender specific. When parties come together and see themselves as friends, they become equal. In the general sense, a friend is a person who upholds a social ethic of a supporting another. Friendship connotes striving with another, sharing, doing good, being open to another or making oneself available to others, and accepting others in a loving, friendly, and compassionate way.

Friendship and Identity

Friendship cuts across all cultures and is a necessary object of human relationships. Yet, all people have their own ideas about friendship. It is difficult to know when two people become friends because friendship develops over time.[22] It may not have a starting point but certainly has a termination point—there are times when parties cease to be friends. Friendship experiences are not particular; they are universal and central to life. However, there are different ways people look at friends and relations. There is no doubt that human beings are created to be in community and may long for friendship; a sense of belonging in meaningful relationships even outside that of the family. A lack of such interpersonal relationships has a significant negative impact on the psychological, emotional, and physical health of an individual.[23] Likewise, having too many friends can bring a negative impact on one's life. Thus, friendship, as a human institution, has its limits. Its limits are also affected by character and resources the friends bring into it.

Africans believe that in life, one cannot do without friends. The view that human beings are dangerous and not trustworthy makes people cautious in building relationships. As long as human beings are not perfect and social systems are dynamic, there is nothing like a perfect friendship. There are some parties one has to keep and others that can be allowed to go, but in all spheres of life, some types of friends are needed. There are times one needs a close friend and other times when an ordinary friend is enough. In practice, friendship is characterized by mutual understanding promoted and reinforced by a high level of interaction. It also requires a high degree of self-disclosure, trust, and intimacy.[24]

---

22. Annis, "Meaning, Value and Duties of Friendship," 353.

23. Roberts-Griffin, "What is a Good Friend," 2. See also Baumeister and Leary, "Need to Belong," 497–529.

24. Guichard, "Where Are Other's People's Friends Hiding?" 25.

Kinship and Friendship

Friendship connotes community and kinship. Among the Akan, for instance, the terms "brother" or "sister" are commonly used to emphasize the close emotional relationship between people who may not necessarily be related biological. A common thing found in another makes that person a brother or sister. Similarly, the same common substance that makes one a brother or sister also makes the person a friend. While earlier anthropological studies asserted that friendship does not exist among kin, Julian Pitt-Rivers in 1973 argued cogently that people who see themselves as mutually related because they share a common substance see themselves as friends or kin.[25] Pitt-Rivers, identifying such a structure as "consubstantiality" explained that in communal cultures, it is not possible to draw rigid distinction between friendship and kinship because friendship enters the domain of kin relations. Both friendship and kinship are based on voluntary altruism and not subject to the pressures of the political-jural domain.[26] Robert Brain also notices among the Bangwa people of Africa that kin relations are based on friendship and that one "chooses this or that uncle, this or that cousin, even this or that brother or sister to be friendly with."[27] Sjaak van der Geest also tested this assumption of consubstantiality between friendship and kinship among the Kwahu of Ghana, one of the tribes that make up the Akan, and observed that the distinction between friendship and kinship is not helpful to understand how kinship works. Kwahu people tend to freely develop friendly relations with their kin.[28] He posits that the bond between siblings and family members seems closest to the purity and endurance of friendship, although such relationships are consciously nurtured, and not simply given, handed down, or dictated by biology, tradition, or an older generation.[29] The Ga people of Ghana say, *naanyo kpakpa he fe weku* ("a friend is better than a brother"). Nevertheless, siblings make each other their friends voluntarily, free from personal interests, and this is developed independently of kinship rules and obligations.

A stranger who is welcome into a home is expected to be treated as a family member. Kwame Anthony Appiah emphasizes friends and their

---

25. Pitt-Rivers, "Kith and the Kin," 89–105.
26. Pitt-Rivers, "Kith and the Kin," 90–93.
27. Brain, *Friends and Lovers*, 16.
28. Geest, "Kinship as Friendship," 68.
29. Geest, "Kinship as Friendship," 69, 70.

responsibility toward the stranger in African societies, and says, "we have obligations to others... that stretch beyond those to whom we are related by the ties of kith and kind, or even the more formal ties of a shared citizenship."[30]

Among the Fulbe of Cameroon, "women friendship" is modeled on kinship and is valued as the purest of all friendships,[31] while in southwestern Ethiopia, the friendship developed along lines of relatedness is highly favored.[32] Guichard explains that "one advantage of having affines as friends is that their support often offers the opportunity to reduce one's own dependence upon agnates, i.e., kin with whom relationships tend to be more competitive in societies with a strong patrilineal bias."[33] Elsewhere among the Maasai of Kenya, comradeship better expresses the concept of friendship. However, marriage is a particular avenue for women and girls to build friendship networks.[34] Friendship relationships are thus less bureaucratic and full of adventure. Still focusing on friendship among pastoral Fulbe in West Africa, Michaela Pelican argues that the Mbororo understanding of kinship and friendship is rather flexible and multilayered, allowing for people to be identified at the same time as kin and friend. This is also reflected in their variable use of kinship and friendship terminology—"*dendiraawo*." She explains that the term generally refers to the person with whom you entertain a joking relationship. This may be your relative (cross-cousin) or a member of another ethnic group with whom the Mbororo are in a collective joking relationship.[35] The Mbororo conceptions of friendship are flexible enough to allow for the possibility of inequality between the partners, emphasizing shared locality and social responsibility. Moreover, friendship as including a significant economic component and may overlap with other relationships, such as kinship and patron–client relations.

Friendship is an open-ended relationship. The friends of one's friend are to be considered as friends. In the words of SimonMary Aihiokhai,

---

30. Appiah, *Cosmopolitanism*, xv.
31. Guichard, "Where Are Other's People's Friends Hiding?" 29.
32. Tadesse and Guichard, "Friendship Networks in Southwestern Ethiopia," 58.
33. Guichard, "Where Are Other's People's Friends Hiding?" 26
34. Spencer, "Comradeship and the Transformation of Alliance Theory," 43, 45.
35. Pelican, "Friendship Among Pastoral Fulbe in Northwest Cameroon," 170. It should be noted that Cameroon Grassields is made up of two sub-ethnic groups, Jaafun and Aku, who differ in their migration histories, and speak slightly different variants of Fulfulde.

One cannot be an enemy of those close to one's friends. This point is vital if one is to understand the implications of establishing bonds of friendship as a tool for enacting interreligious dialogue. To establish a bond of friendship among peoples of different religions entails an extension of that bond to those each one regards as close to oneself.[36]

The point being made is that friendship requires that one is close to the other. Friendship opens doors for people to move out of their closed context into areas of social life, and to bridge gaps with other people.

Friendship as a Mutual Support System

Among the Akan of Ghana, Emmanuel Takyi says, "friendship indicates intimacy. Among humans it is mostly casual and a mutual revealing of a symbiotic relationship with ramifications in the socio-economic and political spheres of life."[37] For the Maasai of Kenya, friendship is nurtured in hospitality, sharing, and loyalty. A friend will take a risk for the other to save the person and is expected to defend the other even to death. Breusers interprets friendship among the Fulbe of Cameroon using the maxim: "All you wish for yourself, you also wish for your friend, and whatever your friend's problem you come to his help."[38] Hence, friendship is an extension of the self.

Pelican discusses perceptions and practices of friendship among the Mbororo (pastoral Fulbe) in northwest Cameroon. She argues that the Euro-American understanding of friendship reflects a Western ideal and does not necessarily correspond with actual practices in Africa. Friendship in Africa, primarily, refers to those persons to whom one may go for assistance in situations of need. True friends are those who lend others money and grant credit. "Friends may thus be compared to a bank where one can redraw or deposit money. Mutual trust is a prerequisite in these relations and is established over continuous interaction."[39] People love to make friends and help them because they know there will come a time the friend will also be of help. Hence, the idea of reciprocity is an underlying factor.

36. Aihiokhai, "'Love one Another as I Have Loved You,'" 495.
37. Takyi, "Friendship with God in the African Context," 79.
38. Breusers, "Friendship and Spiritual Parenthood," 78.
39. Pelican, "Friendship Among Pastoral Fulbe in Northwest Cameroon," 170, 172.

Pelican further observes that the concept of friendship is perceived differently among men and women. There is a gender-sensitivity. For men, friendship encompasses elements of mutual understanding, trust, honesty, and moral and economic support. It also transcends personal, dyadic relationships to relationships of generational longevity. An individual's children are expected to continue the friendly relationships the parents established. There is also the reciprocal character of friendship, emphasizing the obligation of mutual support based on each party's strengths and capacities. Men choose their friends according to the truthfulness of the person. A good friend is somebody who sticks to his promise and who speaks honestly with you.[40] For women, friendship is founded on economic relationships, mutual sympathy, and care for each other. For them, emotional and instrumental motivations often go hand in hand, and "the continuous exchange of small gifts and the concern for each other's well-being are vital to maintaining the friendship."[41] Women choose their friends according to who is smiling at them. They stress commonalities based on everyday life. Religious and cultural differences are taken for granted and accepted as such.

Glenn Adams and Victoria C. Plaut investigated the cultural grounding of friendship from the perspective of people of North American and West African settings. They found that West Africans, unlike the North American people, feel less motivated for friendship because they devalue connection and would not prefer a big network size for friendships.[42] The reason is not the lack of opportunity to make friends; the complementary nature of social support means that if one has a large number of friends, the obligations to support each one of them can be overwhelming. "Too many friends and associated obligations can strain resources and become a source of stress."[43] However, Africans believe that having no friends stems from a refusal to take a friend, and that is considered negative behavior.[44] They also found that "people in West African settings may reserve their friendship choices to a limited number of partners that they maintain for reasons other than companionship."[45] Again, "people

---

40. Pelican, "Friendship Among Pastoral Fulbe in Northwest Cameroon," 174–76.
41. Pelican, "Friendship Among Pastoral Fulbe in Northwest Cameroon," 177.
42. Adams and Plaut, "Cultural Grounding of Personal Relationship," 335.
43. Adams and Plaut, "Cultural Grounding of Personal Relationship," 336.
44. Adams and Plaut, "Cultural Grounding of Personal Relationship," 336.
45. Adams and Plaut, "Cultural Grounding of Personal Relationship," 337.

in West African settings may be especially wary of revealing personal information, even to friends."[46]

Friendship is a communal and public affair. It cannot be a private matter. From a Nigerian linguistic point, SimonMary Aihiokhai's considers that friendship is shaped by religious perspectives, as well as that saying "you are my friend" includes a sense of public declaration of the bond that exists between two persons or groups. It also

> entails a reciprocal, intimate knowledge of one another and a sense of trust shared by those involved in the bond of friendship. While friendship is interpersonal, the fruits of friendship can be shared by those related to the persons involved in the bond. Among the Ihievbe people, there is a sense of covenantal bond that is created when two persons become friends, so *omomeiru* refers not only to the immediate persons who share the bond of friendship but also to those who are close to them. In other words, friendship is not limited to two individuals but has a communal aspect as well.[47]

Hence, friendship is founded on virtues of reciprocity, intimacy, and trust that is shared among one another. Naturally, virtue and vice exist side by side. Although it is said that "one man's meat may be another man's poison," there are basic things that are considered virtues or vices. And since each person cherishes some virtues in life, it is appropriate that friends learn to discern virtues from vices, truth from falsehood, and good from evil (for one cannot impose virtues on others). Friends cannot stay neutral on all moral matters, since human beings are necessarily moral agents.

Gender and Status

Patriarchal ideology in African societies contribute in defining social constructs of gender roles. There are specific privileges for males, females, and children. Such privileges encourage subordination, which erodes the beauty of friendship. An increase in awareness of friendship in family relations, leadership, governance, cultural practices, education, etc., has as yet failed to yield the desired results in Africa, mainly because of the resistance to change that is firmly entrenched in patriarchal ideologies.

---

46. Adams and Plaut, "Cultural Grounding of Personal Relationship," 338.
47. Aihiokhai, "'Love one Another as I Have Loved You,'" 495.

Friendship between men and women has suffered the most, while friendship between adults and young people has made inroads. For instance, a young person who is a royal can be permitted in the company of elders because of his status.

The *pater familias* ideology in that ancient world that established the man as the head of the family and priest of the household cult made Job take a central position within the familial social unit. His wife, sons, daughters, servants, and slaves were legally and economically dependent on him. More so, patriarchal power included an extensive right to punish.

Persons with different statuses or unequal people, however, can enter into friendships in some parts of African societies, although such relationships are usually tense and disappointing. M. Neelika Jayawardane reveals that in South Africa, friendship among unequal relations such as "madams" and "maids" exists. "It is not uncommon to hear families say that their domestic worker is a 'friend of the family' or even 'like family.'"[48] Writing within the context of apartheid South Africa as portrayed by artists and photographers, Jayawardane intimates that the madams strictly enforce their authority yet can sometimes engage the maids in friendly ways. This kind of friendship, though very complex, is not devoid of oppression. Yet Jayawardane says, "friendships between madams and their maids can involve, on the one hand, practices that resist structures of oppression, yet also create, maintain, and benefit from those same structures."[49] Despite the exploitation and the difference in power, there is mutuality in their relationship, and the bond they share is evident in some cases. Aspects of caring for each other allow both parties to continue to imagine the bond through the metaphors of family and friendship. "There is little chance for maids to live outside the boundaries of what constitutes their relationship with their madams, and little room for them to oppose their daily encounter with systematic degradation and injustice."[50] In short, the friendship between madams and maids comes with an agenda to exploit and impose one's will on the other; there is no mutuality, and that can be described as toxic friendship. It thrives on the principle of deception and oppression.

---

48. Jayawardane, "'Friend of the Family,'" 216.
49. Jayawardane, "'Friend of the Family,'" 239.
50. Jayawardane, "'Friend of the Family,'" 228.

UNDERSTANDING FRIENDSHIP USING AFRICAN PROVERBS

Given that African proverbs are similar everywhere, and indeed sometimes even the same, the various aspects of friendship gleaned from them present a useful perspective on its characteristics. That is to say, as one proverb or saying captured in one language is similar in another language, the following overarching themes can be said to represent African proverbs in a wider sense.

Knowing the Other Well

One should have adequate knowledge of who a friend is, otherwise such a person will be considered an ordinary friend, or casual friend, or an acquaintance. The reason is that all friends can influence one another through their behaviors, whether intimate or casual. The Akan say, *kyerɛ me wo nyɛnko na menkyerɛ wo wo suban* ("show me your friend and I will show you your character"). Friends determine the way of life of each other. It is wise, therefore, for one to take someone as a friend and share secrets only when that person is known very well. The Akan say, *wonnim nipa a, wo ne no nsi koso* ("If you don't know someone, you do not make a partnership with them"). Since, according to the Akan, *noma a hɔn ntɛkyerɛ sɛ na wotu bɔ mu* ("birds of the same feathers fly together"), it is justifiable to observe the other's behavior before embarking on a life journey with them. The assumption is that close friends try to behave in similar ways. The Akan also say, *sɛ ɛnye kɔkɔtse sian a, ɛnnhwer woara* ("if you walk with a bush pig, you will not be yourself"). That is to say, if one chooses to make friends with a pig, one should be prepared to live and play in the mud. Being a friend means one is ready to be influenced to go where the friends go and do what the friends do.

Africans caution against opening up to others without due diligence by emphasizing that if one does not choose friends with care, a big disappointment will be the outcome. It may happen that the most cherished friend causes one's downfall. It is only a friend who knows how to influence another, because they know much about the other. The Akan say, *nyɛnko dodow ntsi na kɔtɔ ennya tsir* ("it is too many friends that caused the crab not to receive a head"). The story goes that all animals were asked to go for their head, but the friends of the crab started criticizing the shapes of the heads of those who had already received one. That made the crab reluctant to go ahead for its head, and by the time the crab was ready, there were none left. The lesson is that a friend can influence another to make bad judgments, so keeping many friends can bring disastrous consequences. The view that friends can hurt each other is seen in Swahili: *rafiki yako ndiye adui yako* ("your friend is your enemy," i.e., a friend who knows much about you can harm you deeply).[51] Since friendship is opening oneself to another and allowing the other to know more about one's secrets and life, when a friendship breaks, there is the danger in how the other might use the secrets. That is why a serious friend can become a serious enemy, especially when the friend reveals a secret that is likely to bring harm to the other. The more intimate the friendship the deadlier the enmity when there is betrayal.

This does not mean that there are no friends who make a positive impact. Nor, since one cannot be sure of bad friends from the onset, should one not make friends: it is said, search for a friend with no faults and you will remain with no friends. Yet, since friends influence one another, people are expected to be careful in their choice of friends. Again, since life is a web of relationships, one cannot assume that friendship is a closed community. Every friend also has a friend elsewhere. Hence, it is necessary to know the friends of our friends. In fact, the friends of our friends are our friends. However, the Akan say, *Yɛwɔ ɔyɔnko mu yɔnko* ("There is a friend among friends"). Among a group of friends, some are more loyal than others. Knowing who is loyal is very important if one wants to continue a friendship. Similarly, within a group of friends, some will be closer than others.

Goodwill and Benevolence

Wishing someone good is an act of friendship. It takes a heart disposed to do good to help friends and to be kind to them. Friends have to share all that they can offer.[52] Goodwill grows from a myriad of virtues that result in generosity and benevolence. The Swahili elders say, *Kutoa ni moyo usambe ni utajiri* ("Charity is the matter of the heart not of the pocket"). Goodwill takes its source from love, friendliness, companionship, solidarity, and cooperation. Genuine goodwill also makes it easy for one to empathize with others. Other virtues that influence goodwill are mercy,

---

51. Scheven, *Swahili Proverbs*, 229.
52. Breusers, "Friendship and Spiritual Parenting," 78.

kindness, compassion, gratitude, and appreciation of others. Goodwill opens one to celebrate others' successes and sorrows. Friends will desire to share their good and bad times with each other because friendship is sharing. The Yoruba say, *Ore ti o ba duro tini ni ojo isoro ni ore gidi* ("A friend in need is a friend indeed"). That is to say, the one who helps you when you are in trouble is a real friend.

A heart full of goodwill does not rejoice when others are in difficulties. Friends being available in times of need gives people the motivation to cope. Such friendship enhances prosperity, and relieves adversity of its burden by halving and sharing it. The Swahili elders say, *Mchezea zuri, baya humfika* ("He who ridicules the good will be overtaken by evil"). Goodwill has to do with good behavior and good intentions. Friendships are crucial in times of great misfortune—they give hope that a friend will come to help. The practical advantages of friendship are advice, companionship, and support in difficult times. Doing good will make others feel good. The Swahili elders say, *Asiyenitua kwa hili langu, akiwa na lake n'asitumai* ("One who does not help me putting down my load, must not expect [help] when that person has a load"). And conversely, a person who loves to lend a helping hand deserves to be supported. Heavy loads require other people to help when being carried on the head or when putting them down, especially when the load is fragile or spillable, such as water pots. Hence, the principle of reciprocity is very important in life.

A friend should be a real friend. It is not acceptable to be a fake friend, pretending to be on the other's side. The Shona people say, *Chadyiwa nowako hachinzi charasika, kurasika kwacho hunge wako arizivira, risingapi* ("It is not lost when you give something to a friend, unless your friend knows not how to give"). That is to say, it is worthless to give something to someone who refuses to share it with others. Friends are expected to share whatever will build each other. The Akan say, *nsa kɔ na nsa aba* ("The hand goes and the hand comes"). This means, one needs to stretch out the hands to give and others need to stretch out their hands to give. As you do to others, you may expect another to do to you. The Akan say, *Sɛ wo fa ɔsono adamfo a, wonnte ahaesu* ("If you walk with an elephant as a friend, the dew will not bother you"). The dew on the leaves along the path will make one's clothes get wet. When one takes an elephant as a friend, the elephant will take the lead before the friend follows—the size of the elephant will clear the path of all problems for the friend to go in peace. The kind of friends one makes will determine the benefits one can accrue.

The Akan say, *Yɛyɛ kor a yegyina, yɛ paapaa mu a yɛhwe ase* ("United we stand, divided we fall"). Sticks in a bundle are not easy to break. One can break a single broom easily but when tied together, it is not easy to break. Hence, unity is strength. To build a community, people need to complement each other. Similarly, friends need to support each other and understand each other. They need to ensure each other's space and peace. A common African proverb goes, "if you want to go quickly, go alone. If you want to go far, go together."

Intimacy

Intimacy, in a general sense, is the outward expressions shown to one another. Intimacy has to do with acts of love and charity. Love, like rain, does not choose the grass upon which it wants to fall—it falls on all. Hence, everyone deserves intimacy. A friend is known in times of misfortune because that person will prove the love and intimate relationship. To know one's true intimate friends, it is said pretend to be dead and see who will cry for you.

Among the Akan, friendship is a way to express love. One way to show love is through empathic sharing and carrying each other burdens, hence the saying: *wo nyɛnko da nye wo da* ("Your friend's day is your day"). It means, whatever happens to a friend has happened to you. The day of encountering unpleasant news comes to each person, so when a friend encounters what is unpleasant, it is not simply about the friend or their day: a friend's day is seen as your day to carry that burden so that when your day comes, the friend will carry yours. The Akan say, *nya asɛm hwɛ na hɔ na ibohu w'adɔfo na w'atamfo* ("The day you encounter a problem is when you will see your lovers and enemies"). Friends show up in times of adversity while enemies desert people who are suffering. Thus, Africans believe that sorrow is like a precious treasure, shown only to friends. Distance between friends cannot be a barrier to showing one's intimacy, for it is believed that an intimate friend's house is never far away.

Although one can think of someone as a friend, it is not easy to know who if they will truly show love. The Akan says *tsir nntse dɛ burosow ma yɛapaa mu ehu dza ɔwɔ mu* ("The head is not like a pawpaw that can be cut open to see what is inside"). The time to make friends is before you need them. The Shona elders say, *Chinoshaya (Chakashaya) vanhu mushumo (murimo/ibasa), kudya hakushayi vanhu* ("He that has a piece of work to be done is friendless, but he that has a meal, has many/countless friends").[53] Those who pretend to be friends will be nowhere to be found in times of need but will show up when it is time to enjoy life.

Loyalty

Friendship is a voluntary relationship and as such requires loyalty and sincerity. Loyalty is purely expressed in relational terms. Loyal friends support each other through thick and thin and celebrate the good and bad times together. The strength of a family, like the strength of an army, is in its loyalty to each other. The Akan say, *Onipa dɔ wo a, ɔdɔ wo ne wo nkwaseasɛm* ("If a person loves you, he loves you with all your nonsense"). That is to say, tolerance is needed to prove loyalty. Patricia Mireku-Gyimah sees trust as the key aspect of friendship: "Trust is very necessary in life, but everyone must be watchful since trusting entails some risk. In all cases, traditional wisdom seems to teach the lesson often learnt too late in an individual's life that one must not trust a human being totally." She adds: "Unarguably, honesty, fairness, loyalty and dependability will remain the keys to harmony and the sustainability of friendship among people(s)."[54]

People who prove to be disloyal do not have faith in themselves and cannot stand by the words of others. Disloyal people display double-mindedness or duplicity in their words and actions, and become divided in their devotion and allegiances. In the view of Mireku-Gyimah, "betrayal of all sorts must therefore be prevented, first and foremost, by a show of genuine love and concern in dealings among people, especially friends."[55] A friend is expected to be loyal at all times. Shifting one's loyalty from one party to another amounts to disloyalty. That is why when a person has so many friends, loyalty can be divided: each friend will expect the person to stand by them in faithfulness. The Shona elders say, *Chendakose (Mutendareve) huyo yebvubvubwe inokuya mativi ose* ("A friend to everybody is a friend to nobody").[56] The larger the group of friends, the less loyal one can be to all of them. The larger the group of

---

53. Bhebe and Viriri, *Shona Proverbs*, 100.
54. Mireku-Gyimah, "Betrayal of Friendship in Akan Folktales," 42.
55. Mireku-Gyimah, "Betrayal of Friendship in Akan Folktales," 42
56. Bhebe and Viriri, *Shona Proverbs*, 59.

friends, the more influence it can bring on one's life. Having many friends may empty your pockets.

The best intentions of loyalty can go awry when there is evidence that the other cannot be trusted. Our own tongues can betray us to our friends. The Ewe people say, *Gake hafi nate ŋu adze xɔlɔ la, be nado vivi ɖe amewo ŋu* ("To make friends, you have to be friendly"). It is believed that where there is faithfulness, trust, and honesty, friendship can be developed. It begins with a genuine interest and commitment to the aspirations, goals, and dreams of the other, to offer support no matter what in small or big things. Among the Fulbe, to prove loyalty, friends give their cattle to each other to add to their stock, so they can take care of it for them, and one's ability to take good care of the animal and show accountability is a mark of friendship.

Confiding a secret to an enemy is like carrying grain in a bag with a hole—whatever is said in confidence to someone who is not trustworthy will come out into the open. Hence, loyalty can be lost either through the other's betrayal or one's own deception. Africans believe that when friends stay by each other, evil cannot thrive. When there is no enemy within, the enemy outside cannot inflict pain.

A friend will stay close when things are not good, especially when the other is willing to follow the advice given. To give advice as well as take it is a feature of true friendship. Bad friends give bad advice while good friends will speak the truth even if it hurts. In Swahili, it is said, *bora kuwa mwiba kwa upande was rafiki yako kuliko sauti yake ya mwangwi* ("It is better to be the thorn in the side of your friend than to be his echo"). That is to say, "a real friend should warn his friend in case of wrongdoing."[57]

Loyalty also helps to create lasting friendship relationships. When one is honest with others, they are more likely to trust one another and each can be honest in return. Lying may seem like an easy solution in certain circumstances, but it will only lead to problems down the road. Hence, good friends are not expected to say false things about the other. It is said that lying bites the liar at the end. Pretending to be friends is unacceptable. The Swahili elders say, *Mtu mmoja aliyejitolea ni bora kuliko wanaume kumi waliolazimishwa* ("One volunteer is better than ten forced men"). That is to say, a good friend is worth more than miserable comforters. Someone willing to help is much more admirable than

---

57. Scheven, *Swahili Proverbs*, 229.

those who do it against their will. One good friend is better than having thousands of casual friends. Good friends exhibit willingness and genuineness rather than being forced to do good to each other. When people are forced to do things against their will, it is most likely that the task undertaken will not be beneficial to those it is meant for.

Ordinary friends will flatter even when they have to correct. It takes a good and intimate friend with a good and caring heart to correct a friend. Only a real friend will risk telling the truth even if it may incur the wrath of the friend. To be a good friend, one should walk with good people who can be sincere, and welcome what they have to say.

Collaboration

In Ghana, a popular Akan saying, *nyɛnko na ɔnye wo to nsa dzidzi* ("a friend is one who eats with you in the same bowl"), gives the idea of collaboration, closeness, and togetherness. It is common for friends to go to each other's house for a meal together. There is an impression that close friends will not allow each other to use different plates for eating. A close friend, coming to meet the other when they're eating, does not expect to be invited before joining the table. Refusing to join the table, even when one is not formally invited, shows there is enmity or a problem. An open invitation is expected because whatever belongs to a close friend is there to be shared.

Similarly, friends help each other to fulfill their individual tasks. Friends are expected to lift the other when they fall. Friends are expected to share what they have with one another. Selfishness cannot be justified by the fact that human beings are necessarily egocentric beings. One should not think only of oneself, not considering the needs of others. The isiZulu saying, *Izandla ziyagezana* ("The hands wash each other"), echoes the value of reciprocity. It is expected of all, and not only among friends, to help each other and build each other up. The Igbo elders say, *Ọkọkọọ anumanu ọ kọọya na osisi ma; ọkọọ mmadu o jekuru mmaduibeya* ("If an animal feels itchy, he scratches his body on the tree, but if a man feels itchy, he goes to his fellow man"). A human being cannot do everything alone. There is a need for others to support and help. That is why in Igbo it is said, *Mmadu ka anumanu* ("No man is an island").

Africans believe that one has to hold a true friend with both hands so that they do not part ways. Friends will love to eat together, not because each one does not have enough in the house, but for friendship's sake. It is said that between true friends, even water drunk together is sweet. Friends are expected to guide and prompt each other to live by their desires. It is believed that a good friendship will not require you to act against your own values. Sometimes, people may turn a blind eye to the actions another takes, with the argument that they are minding their own business. However, since the business of your friend is your business, one cannot turn a blind eye to whatever the friend is doing. It is said that a friend is someone you share the path with. The Akan elders say, *Anoma a hɔn ntɛkyerɛ yɛ kor na wotu bɔ mu* ("Birds of the same feathers fly together"). In Swahili, it is said, *Ndege wa mbawa moja huruka pamoja* ("Birds of the same feathers fly together").

Africans believe that human beings are created to live in community and work together toward a common purpose. Life is not about each one taking their own course and pursuing individual goals. It is not about competing with one another to know who is successful. In Swahili, the elders also say, *Kazi ya kugawanywa haziishii katikati* ("Shared works don't stop halfway"). Work done together will be completed more easily and such togetherness requires less energy and less stress. Again, in Swahili, it is said, *Kidole kimoja hakivunji chawa* ("One finger does not kill a louse"). This Swahili proverb means one will need to squeeze a louse with two fingers to suffocate it. In life, doing something as a group will enhance success.

Some people have taken advantage of the goodwill of their friends and exploited them. In Swahili, it is said, *Wawili wakishirikiana mfuko wa fedha, mmoja huimba na mwingine hulia* ("When two people have a common purse, one sings and the other weeps"). That is to say, honest people will always be exploited. Hence, one needs to be careful when doing things in common with friends. Patricia Mireku-Gyimah posits that "betrayal of friendship comes in many colors as disloyalty, cheating, dishonesty, deception, and duping; and unreliability, undependability, untrustworthiness and unfairness."[58] She adds that,

> betrayal breeds societal disharmony, and so must be avoided in human relationships, especially friendship. In a society that is traditionally communalistic, bad friends and associates are a liability and constitute a drawback in development since they

---

58. Mireku-Gyimah, "Betrayal of Friendship in Akan Folktales," 41

obstruct teamwork. Ideally, friendship should lead to a good end and mutual benefits for the parties involved.[59]

It is very disheartening to find that the person holding the other end of the rope is not committed to pulling it so that the tension in the rope is sustained.

Empowerment

Friends are to be a blessing to each other. Being a friend does not mean one has to always agree with the other, but it is necessary to stand with one another. One will feel empowered knowing there is a friend nearby. To empower is to give a good part of oneself to another; it is not to capitalize on the other's failings. Empowerment is about enabling someone to perform a task or have the power to do something. Friendship is the act of making someone or oneself stronger and more confident, especially when friends stand together in times of need. Our identity depends not only on what is inside of us but also those who are around us. When people are down and have no one around them, they cannot perform to their utmost. That is why other people, especially friends, are necessary for one's life to bring change and strength. People who love each other do not rely on each other's mistakes.

Though there may be disagreements between friends, the will to stand by each other matters a lot. In Swahili, the elders say, *mtu na rafikiye ni kama kombe, haziachi* ("a man and his friends are like shells always clattering (always disagreeing)").[60] The Akan also say, *tɛkyerma na se mpo wɔko* ("even the tongue and the tooth fight"). One may expect collaboration from the tongue and teeth since they work together and stay in one place. At times, the tooth will bite the tongue, yet the tongue will need to rub the part that was bitten on the back of the teeth to gather strength. However, one needs to be careful with friends because some can bring others down. The Akan say, *afɛkubɔ te sɛ asanom, w'anhwɛ wo ho so yie a, ɛma wosopa* ("Companionship is like drinking too much palm wine; if you are not careful, it leads to disgrace"). No matter how useful wine can be, it has its destructive aspect.

---

59. Mireku-Gyimah, "Betrayal of Friendship in Akan Folktales," 42.
60. Scheven, *Swahili Proverbs*, 229.

Other-centeredness

The Akan say, *Benkum guar nyimfa and nyimfa so guar benkum* ("The left hand washes the right hand and the right hand washes the left hand"). This proverb implies dependency and cooperation. An individual cannot provide for themself all that is needed nor survive in life without others. It needs to be noted that although reciprocity is implied, what the left hand offers may not be the same as the right hand. In Swahili, the point is made that *akupaye kisogo si mwenzio* ("whoever turns his back on you is not your friend").[61] A bad friendship mentality will lead to self-centeredness and egocentric behaviors. It also leads to a sense of insecurity and insufficiency. It is also believed that bad friends will prevent one from having good friends. Some friends are so selfish that they want to enjoy whatever a friend can offer alone without allowing others to benefit. Hence, they will prevent others from coming close to a friend.

A lack of social connection can lead to a sedentary lifestyle and will have a powerful impact on one's physical health and social life. The Akan say, *nyɛnko yi nʼenyiwa a, ɔyɛ akoma sɛɛ* ("when a friend takes their eyes off you, it is heartbreaking"). Maintaining a healthy social network of friends can improve one's life. The Akan say, *awerɛkyekyer wɔfa no nyimpa ho* ("comfort is from a person"). It means loneliness can make a person's life deteriorate since there will be no one to point out what has gone wrong or needs to be fixed in their life. The Shona elders say, *Gara mumuzinda nwane shamwari ichakuruma nzeve kana yanza paunorechwa* ("Life without a friend, death without a witness").[62] A friendless life is discouraged since to be without a friend is to be poor indeed.

SOME TYPES OF FRIENDS

Interestingly, the dynamics of friendship make it easy for an individual to slide from one type to another. The type of friend one chooses also determines the level of impact made on one's life. Some are true friends, intimate/bosom friends, best friends, close friends, casual friends, social group friends, family friends, convenience/situational friends, fair-weather friends, toxic friends, or fake friends. Certainly, there cannot be perfect friends, for no human act can be perfect.

---

61. Scheven, *Swahili Proverbs*, 228.
62. Bhebe and Viriri, *Shona Proverbs*, 165.

Concerning the types listed above: True friendship is the highest and most reliable since the relationship springs from a pure loving heart. Intimate/bosom friendship seems to be the ideal; a type of relationship that involves lots of sacrifice. These friends always share their joys and pains together, especially the deep secrets of life. Best friends also, like intimate friends, build their relationships around trust and honesty, and of course common interests, but do not go as far as sharing inner or deep secrets. Best friends love to spend time together. Close friendships are more like extended family units, especially revolving around the expectations and emotional support that are commonly seen among such members. Close friendship, however, takes time to nurture and is solidly built on trust, so one cannot automatically make close friends. It is close friends who become best friends over time. Casual friendship is more than a situational friendship, but not quite a close or "best" friend. Casual friends appear in one's circle at some point but then will not be there for some time to come. They simply share common interests and enjoy spending time together once in a while. This could be with a new friend whom one is just getting to know more personally.

It has been seen from the foregoing that friendship in the African context includes confidants, constituents, or comrades. Confidants are close friends marked by their intimacy and level of shared trust. They are friends who stand by each other regardless of the situation, allowing each one to confide in the other. Such friendships can usually lead to occasional hurt, bruised feelings, or disappointments because many people cannot keep secrets. Constituents are friends around each other who share a common allegiance. Constituent friendships are like family friends and are maintained only when they are able to meet expected needs, and the relationships will dissolve when their interests change from what they were initially drawn to. Comrades, like constituents, are temporary friends who engage in the same profession. They come into one's life for a while, and will be there as long as the parties are on a particular cause. Comrades can be valuable in helping each other avoid unseen obstacles or in overcoming shared problems.[63]

Uloma Ogba, analyzing a movie, "An African City" observes five types of friends: the Lifer friend, Hustler friend, Uplifter friend, No BS'er friend, and Unlikely friend. She explains,

---

63. "Three Types of Friends."

The Lifer friend is someone who has been there with you through thick and thin and is not going anywhere, ever. You may choose different paths in life and there may come a time when you will be separated by distance and other relationships and commitments, but this is the friend that would drop everything to be by your side if you ever needed her. She will be the godmother of your children and the adopted daughter of your parents, she will be the one sitting next to you on a porch 50 years from now reminiscing about life and all the joy, sorrow, triumphs and failures it brought you both.[64]

The Hustler friend is one who always proves to have contacts and resources that a friend can tap into. The hustler knows all the backdoors through which one can navigate life easily. The Uplifter friend can always be counted on for an encouraging word when times are rough. Such a friend

> not only listens attentively but also supports all your hopes and dreams, even the crazy, impractical ones. The Uplifter's favorite word is "yes." Sometimes it seems like the world is screaming no to all your efforts and that you are constantly being met with closed doors. When you're just about ready to throw in the towel, it is refreshing to have that one voice that always says "Yes, I believe in you," "Yes, you can do it."[65]

The No BS'er friend is one who always tells the ugly or painful truth, even when it hurts. "The No BS'er friend's sole purpose in life is to burst or bruise your ego, with time you realize that they're not trying to be rude or malicious and it is all coming from a place of love. By always keeping it real, the No BS'er helps you to see a different perspective and encourages you to keep growing and changing." The Unlikely friend is a delightful medley of so many types: a social butterfly, a risk taker, and a bad influencer.[66]

It is easy to *have* friends rather than *be* friends. Having friends usually stems from a personal need. The focus is on the individual benefits one can accrue. Being a friend is a virtue based on expectations. People cannot set their own standards and expect others to see those standards as ideal for friendship. The standards are those set by the community. Being a friend, however, entails caring and meeting the expectations of the other. So personal needs have a role to play in becoming a friend. Making

---

64. Ogba, "5 Types of Friends Every Woman Needs in Her Late 20s and Early 30s."
65. Ogba, "5 Types of Friends Every Woman Needs in Her Late 20s and Early 30s."
66. Ogba, "5 Types of Friends Every Woman Needs in Her Late 20s and Early 30s."

friends is not as easy as maintaining friends. As such, those who want to have friends must first think about being a friend to others. Having a friend does not mean one is socially complete. It does not mean one can sever relationships with others to maintain a new friend. Having a close friend is not the time to avoid all other people. It is possible to have a friend but still be lonely. In that light, friendship is not a solution to overcoming loneliness.

CONCLUDING REMARKS

Africa is made up of several peoples, each with a distinct culture, but there are to a large extent some commonalities and comparable behaviors, and similar beliefs and practices. As observed, the social organizations and African proverbs preserve and inform indigenous knowledge that gives direction to life and interactions. Friendship in Africa is generally concerned with an individual's character or moral development within a social organization. Friendship leads to affective involvement with the other so both are built up. Seven of the basic expectations of friends are knowledge, goodwill, intimacy, loyalty, collaboration, empowerment, and other-centeredness. These seven are what the proverbs gathered can offer, and certainly are not the only ones.

Friendship in Africa can be voluntary or non-voluntary; some can enter into the web of friendship not by choice but by status and kinship. It has been observed that friendship in the African worldview is a personal relationship that involves degrees and types. Friendship has to do with a mutual liking of one another for one reason or another. It is seen as a mutual-exchange partnership, but men or women choose their friends based on different reasons. Friendship relations exist among extended family systems—distant relatives as well as strangers. They could be equals or non-equals, but in most cases, it is gender specific. There are true friends and pretenders; or good friends, bad friends, and those in between. There are also several types of friends. There is friendship among joking partners and acquaintances. Some are intimate/bosom friends, best friends, close friends, casual friends, social group friends, family friends, convenience/situational friends, fair-weather friends, toxic friends, and fake friends. There is also Lifer friends, Hustler friends, Uplifter friends, No BS'er friends, and Unlikely friends. One cannot be an enemy of those close to one's friends.

Refusal to take a friend is unacceptable and considered to be bad behavior. Having a large number of friends will negatively influence behavior, and the obligations of support to each one can be overwhelming. Hence, one is expected to be careful in making friends and also not to make many friends. It is also expected for one to break up with those who do not conform to social norms. In all, there are friends for a reason and for a season, be they intimate, close, casual, acquaintance, fair-weather, or fake friends. It was found that some key virtues underlying friendship are knowledge, intimacy, loyalty, collaboration, empowerment, goodwill, and other-centeredness. The degree to which a friend shows the key virtues mentioned above determines the kind or category of friend they will be.

4

The Bible and Friendship

THE TERMS "FRIEND" AND "friendship," from the biblical perspective, involve a wide range of relationships. They could be used to refer to a relationship between equals, non-equals, or patron and client.[1] The same idea can been seen from the Old English term "freond," which refers to both kin and non-kin relationships, although it tilts toward non-kinship relationships. It has more to do with a person who relates to another for a common purpose and who the other knows well in a particular capacity due to mutual commitment. Friendship involves varying degrees of companionship, intimacy, affection, and compassion, and is voluntary, cooperative, and sacrificial. Some synonyms of "friend" include companion, soulmate, comrade, associate, ally, supporter, mate, intimate associate, and close acquaintance. All these show that the word "friend" cannot be used loosely; one has to be clear about what type of friendship is meant in all cases. Some categories of friends are for the good of others and others are not; some are empowering and enduring, while others last for a brief moment.

The Bible does not give a single perspective on friendship. Some of the common terms for friendship are *rēa'* ("friend," "neighbor," "companion," "ally"), *'aḥay* ("my brother"), *yod'ay* ("my acquaintance"), *qerobāy* ("my close relatives"), and *meyuddā'ay* ("my close friends"). Another term is *sôd* (Job 29:4) that carries the nuance of "speaking with someone in a friendly way, in confidence."[2] Michael Fox defines the *rēa'* as "another per-

---

1. Witherington, *Friendship and Finances in Philippi*, 119.
2. Klassen, "Friend, Friendship," 490.

son within the pertinent sphere of affiliation."[3] Various English equivalents or parallels, however, point to the idea of friendship including: (i) brother (Exod 32:27; Isa 41:6); (ii) a confidant (Deut 13:7) (iii) kin (Exod 2:13); (iv) darling, husband, beloved, lover (Jer 3:20; Song 5:16); (v) companion, comrade (Gen 11:3, 7; 1 Sam 20:41); (vi) intimate counselor (1 Chr 27:33); (vii) one another, each other as a reciprocal expression (Gen 31:49; 43:33; Isa 3:5; Jer 23:30; Eccl 4:4; Mal 3:16); (viii) neighbor (Exod 11:2; 20:16, 17; Lev 19:18; Deut 27:24; 1 Sam 15:18); (ix) intimate friend (Pss 15:3; 38:12; Job 29:4); (x) a party in a legal dispute (Exod 22:9; 1 Sam 28:17; 2 Sam 12:11; Prov 18:17); and (xi) best man (at a wedding; in the *piel*; cf. Judg 14:20).[4] In all these instances, the emphasis is on obligation toward the other.[5] Kellermann also points out that in the Ugaritic, the form *rʿy* can be interpreted as "shepherd" while in Aramaic, *rʿn* or *rʿh* could mean "water."[6] All these meanings point to persons in close contact, a mutual acquaintance, and/or without any particular blood relationship. The biblical view of friend, thus, ranges from a relative (Exod 2:13), to someone/a relative who is like your soul (Deut 13:6), to a lover (Song 5:16), to a close companion or confidant (Gen 38:20), to a trusted one (Ps 41:9), to a helper (Eccl 4:10), to the neighbor one relations with (Gen 11:3; Lev 19:18; Jer 9:5), to an intimate royal counselor (1 Chr 27:33), to a party in a legal proceeding (Exod 22:8), or to a fellow human being.[7]

Besides the Masoretic Text (MT), the Septuagint (LXX) uses *phileō* and its cognates cognates of the Greek *phileō* occur in Gen 5:14; 27:4; Pss 38:11; 139:17; Prov 14:20; 22:24; Jer 20:6; Dan 2:17; Mic 7:5; Judg 5:30; Esth 1:3; 2:18; 9:22 as well as in Job 2:11; 6:27; 19:13,21; 32:1,3; 35:4; 42:7, 10 and is usually denoting "friend" while *hetairos* occurs in Judg 14:20; 2 Sam 13:3; 1 Kgs 2:22; Prov 22:24 and Job 30:29 and means a companion who is an imposter, that is someone posing to be a comrade but in reality only has his own interests in mind.

The Greek term *phileō* also has a range of meanings including "lover," "confidant," and "dear one."[8] The term is also founded on love and extends to the kind of concern one should have for other persons, yet *phileō*

---

3. Fox, *Proverbs 1–9*, 165–66, 212.

4. *HALOT* 2:1254; *TDOT* 13:526; Hess, "rea," in *NIDOTTE* 3:1145; Richards, *Encyclopedia of Bible Words*, 297.

5. Richards, *Encyclopedia of Bible Words*, 297.

6. *TDOT* 13:523.

7. Habel, "Only the Jackal Is My Friend," 228.

8. Spicq, *Theological Lexicon of the NT*, 3:448.

is in some ways different from what we ordinarily think of as friendship. Thus, *phileō* extends not just to friends but also to family members, business associates, and one's wider society or country. Also, contemporary accounts of friendship differ on whether family members—in particular one's children, before they become adults—can be friends. Spicq says in some usages, *phileō* is close to *agapaō*, except that *phileō* is hardly used for expressing the love that exists between God and humans.[9] Ethelbert Stauffer explains that in pre-biblical Greek, the term *phileō* is noble form of love and signifies solicitous love of gods for human beings, or friends for friends. It means love which embraces everything that bears a human countenance. However, agape could also denote regard or friendship between equals, or to esteem one person more highly than another. Hence agape may be used of the preference of God for a particular person, or active love on the other's behalf.[10]

Generally, the forms of relationships and associations between parties give clues to what friendship is all about. The relationships could be positive or otherwise, and not necessarily involve "positive feelings described by texts as 'love,'" as Saul Olyan claims.[11] Where positive emotions govern the relationship, one finds happiness, excitement, joy, hope, appreciation, authentic pride, connectedness, and inspiration that lead to a happy and healthy life.

Notice that, there may be times when one does not have any positive emotional reason to affiliate with another. The affiliation may not yield any feeling of happiness or joy. It could be affiliation for its own sake. More so, there are times when one can team up with others for a bad cause. Someone can make friends with a notorious thief to learn more about their ways. Although such an affiliation may make the person feel good, not everyone may consider it a positive feeling. In cases where the end justifies the means, one can say that if the affiliation will cause regret and pain, it is not positive.

---

9. Spicq, *Theological Lexicon of the NT*, 1:10,11.
10. Stauffer, "agape," 36, 37.
11. Olyan, *Friendship in the Hebrew Bible*, 5.

DIVINE–HUMAN FRIENDSHIP

The Bible presents a view of friendship modeled after divine–human relations. A central biblical metaphor for the divine–human relationship is friendship.

God enters into a friendship with human beings. Such friendship is akin to what is called patron–client friendship, although in the case of God, there are marked differences. God does not normally seek servants in the way human patrons do since all people are basically servants of God, and God does not receive compensation as patrons do.[12] Beyond relating with human beings as Lord, the provision to make friends with human beings is an act of grace. Patron deities in general are spiritual beings who protect and serve as guardians over people who look up to them. In Greek mythology, Apollo was the patron god of the *pólis* in Athens and was the protector of the city, but there is no record of him entering into a friendly relationship with the people. The god, Zeus, had some epithets as "Father" and "King," "Protector of Cities," "Lord of Friends," "Guardian of the Race," "protector of Suppliants," "God of Refuge," and "God of Hospitality." In the Greco-Roman world, the patron often referred to the client as *philos* or *amicus*, usually translated as "friend."[13]

The patron–client relationship is a mutual arrangement between one party who has authority, power, and resource and another who benefits from the support. Sydel Silverman defines patronage "as an informal contractual relationship between a person of unequal status and power, which imposes reciprocal obligation of a different kind on each of the parties. As a minimum, what is owed is protection and favor on the one hand and loyalty on the other."[14] To Daniel Eng, "ancient patronage involved three elements: (1) the unequal status of the parties involved, (2) the reciprocal exchange of goods and services, and (3) the establishment of a lasting relationship between the parties."[15] Eng seems to point out that it is within the vertical and instrumental bonds through which humanity secures favor and support from God. Howard Stein explains that both patron and client need each other. They can see themselves as a friend, but the client does not outgrow their status. Furthermore, the relationship

---

12. Neyrey, "God, Benefactor and Patron," 484–86.
13. Konstan, "Patron and Friend," 329; Eng, "'I Call You Friends,'" 57.
14. Silverman, "Patronage and Community," 176.
15. Eng, "'I Call You Friends,'" 56.

can evolve into different types of affective relationships.[16] Hence the relationship can be mutual but dynamic, affective but not an equal exchange, and between unequals who enjoy different levels of reciprocity. For David DeSilva, the patron–client relationship aims at a "win-win" situation,[17] not necessarily in the sense of God lacking something only to benefit from humanity, but God demanding worship. It needs to be noted that whereas the concept of patronage in general is domineering and meant to accrue some political advantage to the patron, God does not relate with humanity for such advantages. Again, God does not permit the sense of false pride, hubris, insolence, or being in an advantageous position because one is chosen by God—God's grace extends to all people.[18] There is also not the sense that if humanity fails to worship God, then no favor or support will come from God. The extension of such patronage friendship is in kinship friendship where terms like "my son," "my father," "my brother," or "my sister" can exist, a network that Julian Pitt-Rivers calls "Lop-sided friendship."[19] It also informs a sense of community. Jerome Neyrey, following Eisenstadt and Roniger, explains that divine–human patronage is quite different from human–human patronage, in the sense that "human benefactor-client relationships tend to be asymmetrical, reciprocal, voluntary, often including favoritism, focused on honor and respect, and held together by 'goodwill' or faithfulness."[20]

Adam and Eve had the special privilege of taking care of the Garden and exercising dominion over all that the Lord God had created. The concept of stewardship fits the Genesis creation story and may be seen as a patron–client relationship but not necessarily friendship. Gerhard von Rad explains that the expression for the exercise of this dominion also has a retroactive significance for all non-human creatures; it gives them a new relation to God.[21] Thus, human beings work together with God in caring for creation. Richard Bauckham also argues that Genesis 1:26–27 has always been reinterpreted through a framework very different from that which the text itself represents, leading to the legitimization of the human domination of the earth, ideas of human uniqueness and

16. Stein, "Note on Patron–Client Theory," 30–36.
17. deSilva, *Honor, Patronage, Kinship and Parity*, 97.
18. Bruce Malina posits that the concept of grace falls under the idea of patronage. See *Social World of Jesus*, 171–73.
19. Pitt-Rivers, *People of Sierra*, 140.
20. Neyrey, "God, Benefactor and Patron," 468.
21. Von Rad, *Genesis*, 59–60.

superiority over nature, and a utilitarian understanding of the world.[22] David Horrell suggests that the creation of humanity should be understood within the concept of community.[23] It is in the sense of community that human beings enjoy God's love.

Within the concept of community, the human being has to learn to be a friend of God. Enoch enjoys a friendship with God (Gen 5:22). He shows his faith first by offering to God a sacrifice that covered his sin and that pleases God (Heb 11:5, 6). God credits Enoch's faith in him as righteousness, forgives him, and purifies his heart. Enoch's friendship with God is very significant because it sets him apart from the corrupt and wicked people of his time.

Moses is a friend of God. The Lord knew Moses by name (Exod 33:17). Michael S. Sherwin asserts that the Hebrew *rēa'* most often signifies "neighbor" or even just a generic "other," and adds that the root signifies "the one guarding sheep next to you" in the sense that the relationship that is expected to exist between one shepherd and another in close proximity underlies friendship. Sherwin sees the friendly relationship between the Lord and Moses in Exodus 33:11 as affirming an intimate friendly relationship that will influence the task of shepherding the Lord's people.[24] The close friendship between God and Moses makes it possible for Moses to commune with God regularly by going to the tent: "The Lord would speak to Moses face to face, as one speaks to his friend (*rē'ēhu*)" (Exod 33:11a). The term "face to face" is a figure of speech that emphasizes close and direct communication—in a friendly interaction. So, Moses has immediate access to God, a level of intimacy that is very cordial, hence he is a friend of God. The tent of meeting is one of the places where Moses usually meets with God. Moses would leave the camp and walk to the tent of meeting to meet with God, while the people would stand and follow Moses with their eyes from a distance. When Moses enters the tent, a pillar of cloud would come down from heaven and covered the entrance, symbolizing a visible manifestation of the glorious presence of God (Exod 33:7–11).

David is described as a man after God's own heart (Acts 13:32) and such a figure of speech echoes divine-human friendship. The psalmist says, "the friendship (*sôd*) of the Lord is for those who fear him, and he

---

22. Bauckham, *God and the Crisis of Freedom*, 128–38.
23. Horrell, *Bible and the Environment*, 32.
24. Sherwin, "Friendship with God," 1326.

makes his covenant known to them" (Ps 25:14). Fearing and knowing the Lord ushers one into a special relationship with the Lord and is situated in the context of friendship (See Ps 36:10; Exod 11:7; 33:12–13; Isa 45:4; 63:16; Jer 2:8; 12:3; Hos 8:2). Those who attain wisdom become friends of God, and prophets (Wisdom 7:14, 27). Likewise, Job enjoys an intimate and friendly (*sôd*) relationship with God (Job 29:4). Spiritual values solidify the nature of friendship that was to exist between God and humanity.

Characteristics of Divine–Human Friendship

Let us turn to some of the spiritual values that characterize divine–human friendship:

Friendship as a Loving Relationship

God describes Abraham as "my friend" (Heb:*'ōhăbî;* Isa 41:8). This is because Abraham exercised special faith in God (Jas 2:23; cf. 2 Chr 20:7). Abraham is seen as a chosen one (*yĕda'ttiyw*), a term that echoes being a companion and someone the Lord knows very well (Gen 18:19).[25] The boldness of Abraham to negotiate with God to spare the righteous people in Sodom stems from the friendly relationship between them.

The prophet Malachi says God's relationship with Jacob and Israel is characterized by love (*'ăhabttî*) (Mal 1:2; cf. Rom 9:3). God loving Jacob cannot be construed as love within human emotions. Unlike the Hebrew concept of love, the Greek has various words to describe each phenomenon. Perhaps, it was out of the agape love that God reached out to Jacob; it was an amazing grace that set Israel apart and redeemed them.

Jesus sets an example of genuine friendship founded in who God is, requiring a movement into the lives of others and sharing love among themselves (John 15:9–17). Two keywords underlie friendship in the New Testament: *agapē* and *phileō*. In Christian thought, *phileō* is not the highest form of love, affection, or friendship. David Konstan does not agree with the popular interpretations of Greco-Roman friendship and holds rather that friendship provided "a space for sympathy and altruism . . . that stands as an alternative to structured forms of interaction based

---

25. The term *yĕda'ttiyw* in some cases connotes having sexual intercourse (Gen 24:6; 38:26) but can never be substantiated in a divine–human relationship.

on kinship, civic identity, or commercial activity."[26] Jesus, who is God incarnate, identifies his disciples as friends and explains that it is all about self-giving and openness. He has not hidden anything from his disciples (John 15:13–15). Such friendship, however, is dependent on obedience to the word of God. In divine–human friendship, a human being cannot choose to disobey God. Jesus chooses the disciples to be his friends not because they play a part in the "choosing"; it is purely a unilateral choice to make the disciples his friends. It is a gift with a sacramental nature. Jesus shows agape love to his disciples (John 13:1; 15:9; 21:7, 15, 20), Martha (John 11:5), and the rich lawyer who came to him (Mark 10:21), and expects his disciples to walk in *agapē* (Eph 5:2). Worship and giving should be characterized by love (2 Cor 9:7). The mark of friendship and brotherliness is to abide in the love (*agapē*) of Christ (John 15:1–9). Husbands are to show agape love to their wives (Eph 5:25, 28; Col 3:19), and not simply erotic love. A person can show *agapē* love to the community or nation (Luke 7:5). However, it needs to be noted that *agapē* simply means "charity" in ordinary use.[27] All that Jesus expects from the disciples is loyalty and obedience.

The Greek term, *agapē*, which is considered unconditional love, rather tilts more toward friendship; the selfless giving of love, seen in God, and offered to the world. From the biblical perspective, agape love is generally defined as "The attitude of God toward his Son, the human race, and to believers and the Lord Jesus Christ particularly."[28] *Agapē* is incorruptible love (Eph 6:24). It is spread abroad in the heart of humanity so that all can love God and love their neighbor. *Agapē* is love as God loves (John 3:16; Eph 2:4), because God is love (1 John 4:7–8). Agape marks the love between God and Christ (John 3:35; 10:17; 17:23–24). *Agapē* is a selfless concern for the well-being of others that is not based on what the other does or stands for. God's *agapē* love provides the basis for a philial relationship. Human beings are to exemplify agape love to God (Matt 22:37; Mark 12:30; Luke 10:27), and to one another (John 14:15–31; Rom 13:8–9; 1 Pet 2:17; 1 John 4:11, 20), including our enemies (Matt 5:43; 19:19; 22:39; Mark 12:31; Luke 6:27, 32), although it needs to be noted that the writer of James describes Abraham as a friend (*philos*) of God (Jas 2:23). God's unconditional love, despite human beings sinning against God, does not annul friendship. Even so, sin widens

26. Konstan, *Friendship in the Classical World*, 6.
27. Lidell and Scott, *Lexicon Abridged from Lidell and Scott's Lexicon*, 3.
28. Strong, *New Strong's Expanded Dictionary of Bible Words*, 907.

the gap between God and humanity and disturbs a healthy relationship, for God's holiness does not overlook unholy attitudes.

Generally, matters of love can be easily misunderstood. The ancient Greek philosophers, however, make love plain by using at least eight vocabularies or notions—*Eros* (romantic, passionate love); *Phileō* (friendly/ affectionate love/ brotherly/ sisterly love); *Storge* (familiar/ kinship-based love); *Mania* (obsessive love); *Ludus* (playful love); *Pragma* (enduring love); *Philautia* (self-love); and *Agapē* (selfless, universal love)—all of which are not exclusive in themselves. It is *philia* that best explains what human friendship is, yet the noun operates in multiple ways and can be defined differently in different situations. The noun can be related to being something loveable (*tou philētou*) or having the capacity of being loved (*philēton*) and pertain to the sphere of affection. "Friendship" points to a specific form of "love" and not any kind. It is at best seen in *philia* love, yet friendship is made perfect in agape love.

Friendship as a Demonstration of God's Holiness

God chooses the people of Israel to be close to him. The closer the people of God are to God, the more careful they should be about God's holiness. God's righteous dealings with the people of God who are close to him (*sĕbîbotām*) is a striking demonstration of God's holiness, even to the surrounding nations (Ezek 28:22–26). The Hebrew *sĕbîbotām* are those who surround God closely, and the word is set parallel to what it mean to *know* God. All actions of people close to God motivated by pride, ambition, jealousy, or impatience will attract severe punishment because such actions do not lead to a life of holiness to the Lord. Nadab and Abihu, for instance, are among those appointed to come close (*qĕrob*) to God in service as ministers of God, but they disrespect God by regarding the fire on the altar as something common (Lev 10:1–3). That is to say, God expects Nadab and Abihu to carry out their service in a way that the holiness of God will be evident so that God will honor them. The people of God, likewise, cannot worship God in a way that is improper. Acting in a way that shows disrespect to authority is unacceptable. There can be no deception or manipulation in serving God. The greater the privilege of coming close to God, the more careful one must be to fulfill one's responsibilities. Jesus says, "but one who did not know and did what deserved a beating will receive a light beating. From everyone to whom much has been given, much will be required; and from one to whom much has been entrusted, even more will be demanded" (Luke 12:48 NRSV).

Friendship as Covenant Loyalty

Covenantal loyalty surrounds the concept of friendship and this was modeled on the relationship between God and humanity. God's covenant relationship with Abraham is in the form of friendship (Gen 18–19). The covenant between God and Abraham is unilateral: God initiates it and Abraham has very little part to play to make the promise a reality.

One of the concepts that highlights a divine–human relationship is *ḥesed*, a term that fundamentally hinges on the covenant love between God and his people, which means, among other things, loyalty. About three-quarters of the 245 occurrences of the word *ḥesed* in the Hebrew Bible relate to the *ḥesed* of God.[29] In God's self-revelation to Moses in the wilderness, one of the key attributes is *ḥesed*; God abounds in *ḥesed* and keeps his *ḥesed* to succeeding generations (Exod 34:6–7). Thus, to experience God's *ḥesed* is to encounter God. Usually, the word *ḥesed* is used alongside words *raḥamim* (compassion), *ḥānān/ ḥen* (grace/mercy), *noʿam* (favor), *tôb* (goodness), *ʾāhab* (love), and *ʾāman* (faithfulness). And it would not be out of place to assume that these virtues underlie friendship. Generally, scholars have noted the difficulty in translating accurately the meaning of *ḥesed*, although words like steadfast love, loyalty, faithfulness, loving-kindness, mercy, and goodness come close to capturing the thought. Due to the difficulty of finding one English term that best encapsulates the Hebrew concept, scholars usually simply use "*ḥesed*."

A close connection between human friendship and the concept of *ḥesed* has been observed. For instance, E. A. Heath observes that "*ḥesed* is the disposition of one person toward another that surpasses ordinary kindness and friendship; it is the inclination of the heart to express 'amazing grace' to the one who is loved."[30] Nelson Glueck has argued that *ḥesed* is the "conduct in accord with a mutual relationship of rights and duties, corresponding to a mutually obligatory relationship . . . principally: reciprocity, mutual assistance, sincerity, friendliness, brotherliness, duty, loyalty and love."[31] Similarly, Hans-Jürgen Zobel seems to hint at

---

29. VanGemeren, *NIDOTTE* 2:211.
30. Heath, "Grace," 372.
31. Glueck, *Hesed in the Bible*, 55.

friendship obligations when he says that reciprocity involved the practice of *ḥesed* ensured that "the one who receives an act of *ḥesed* responds with a similar act of *ḥesed*."[32]

Gordon R. Clark's analysis of the lexical field of the word *ḥesed* in the Hebrew Bible shows that it deals with interpersonal relations, usually indicating attitudes or actions toward one another.[33] He argues that loyalty includes "mercy," "compassion," "faithfulness," "reliability," "confidence," and "love," although all these are aspects of loyalty.[34] Glueck posits that among human relationships, *ḥesed* is received or shown only by those among whom a definite relationship exists.[35] However, it can point to how a petitioner looks forward to such a relationship. Loyalty is expected between relatives by blood or marriage, guests, allies and their relatives, friends, subjects, and those who have gained merit by rendering aid and the parties thereby put under obligation.[36] In Glueck's view, it is in the context of "rights and duties" that such obligations are expected. He explains that members enjoy common rights and they have to fulfill mutual obligations because their whole existence is to be governed by reciprocity. One is obligated to the other, and such obligations expect one to act in certain ways and fulfill certain duties for mutual benefit.[37] For Baker, *ḥesed* echoes a deep, enduring, persistent commitment of one party to the other.[38]

Katherine Sakenfeld explains *ḥesed* as a "combination of commitment in a relationship, critical need of the recipient, and the freedom of the actor which characterize occasions for the exercise of loyalty."[39] For Sakenfeld, *ḥesed* among human beings operates on the level of relative positions of the two parties where the action is undertaken by a "circumstantially superior party" or a "situationally superior" party toward an inferior party.[40] That is not to say that *ḥesed* does not operate between two parties who are equal. However, she explains that two individuals may be equal on one occasion and then the situation changes, thus opening the

32. Zobel, "חֶסֶד," *TDOT* 5:47.
33. Clark, *Chesed in the Hebrew Bible*.
34. Clark, *Chesed in the Hebrew Bible*, 267–68.
35. Glueck, *Hesed in the Bible*.
36. Glueck, *Hesed in the Bible*, 37.
37. Glueck, *Hesed in the Bible*, 38–55.
38. Baker, "Aspects of Grace in the Pentateuch," 9.
39. Sakenfeld, *Faithfulness in Action*, 42.
40. Sakenfeld, *Faithfulness in Action*, 7, 12.

opportunity for a need for or the expression of *ḥesed*.[41] The need that is expected to be met is not the ordinary one that arises generally in various relationships but the extraordinary need that cannot be met by the person in need.[42] Norman Snaith posits that the Hebrew *ḥesed* is better understood as "firmness, steadfastness." Unfortunately, such understanding is often neglected. He insists that renderings such as "faithfulness, loyalty, loving-kindness, etc are often far too weak to convey the strength, the firmness, and the persistence of God's pure love."[43] That is to say, friends should stay firmly by the side of each other. Neglecting to stand by a friend amount to not showing kindness.

Reciprocity is also a key factor in *ḥesed* (loyalty). However, the divine–human notion of reciprocity is not always mutual and binding,[44] although the obligation of kindness and solidarity is mutual.[45] In the Psalms, for example, the one at prayer demands that God reciprocates kindness. Basically, however, a human being cannot blame God for not returning a favor at all costs because of an act of loyalty. The concept of *ḥesed* as kindness is what is rightly extended to the "lowly, needy, and miserable, mercy; affection; lovely appearance."[46] Sakenfeld, for instance, stresses that *ḥesed* does not entail all kinds of obligations and responsibility toward others, but in specific actions and specific situations. It is a moral responsibility in relationships for a superior to help another per the terms of the covenant, but it is not a binding obligation that is legally enforceable.[47] "It is always the provision for an essential need, never a special kindness, and an action from a superior party towards an inferior party because of the relationship with the weaker party. And it is the superior who normally renders help to the party in need, not the other way round."[48] The kindness that is shown by the superior to the inferior party is not based upon a "moral" or a "legal" obligation or responsibility but based on the freedom to either perform or not perform the act.

---

41. Sakenfeld *Faithfulness in Action*, 162.
42. Sakenfeld, *Faithfulness in Action*, 42.
43. Snaith, *Distinctive Ideas of the Old Testament*, 102.
44. Glueck, *Hesed in the Bible*, 178; Sakenfeld, "Kesed," 495–96.
45. Holloday, *Concise Hebrew and Aramaic Lexicon of the Old Testament*, 111.
46. BDB, 338.
47. Sakenfeld, *Meaning of* Hesed *in the Hebrew Bible*, 233–37.
48. Sakenfeld, *Meaning of* Hesed *in the Hebrew Bible*, 20.

HUMAN–HUMAN FRIENDSHIP

The term *rēaʿ* ("friend") is set parallel to *'ōhabāʾ* ("beloved") (Pss 38:11; 88:18) as well as *qāroba'* ("neighbor" NRSV; "nearest kin" ESV) (Exod 32:27; Pss 15:3; 38:12; Job 19:14) and *mĕyuddāʿay* ("companion"). In Jeremiah 6:21, the term *rēaʿ* ("friend") is set as synonymous with *šākēn* ("neighbor"). In Psalm 88, the companions of the psalmist have shunned him and have become like darkness because of what the Lord has done to him (v. 8, 18). The sages make a contrast between a friend and a brother, and say a friend sticks more closely than a brother (Prov 18:24). Hence, the affinity between those who stand by each other is more reliable than having a blood relation. However, the psalmist mentions that when the malicious witnesses rose against him and repaid evil for good, the psalmist continued to pray for them: "when they were sick, I wore sackcloth; I afflicted myself with fasting. I prayed with head bowed on my bosom, as though I grieved for a friend (*kĕrēaʿ*) or (*'aḥî*) brother" (Ps 35:13–14). Here, the term "friend" is set as a synonymous parallel to a brother. That is to say, friendship is more than a brotherly relationship. The emphasis is on how one relates to the other.

In any event, human–human friendship is also about people who are closely related and sometimes go beyond kinship. There are brothers and sisters who do not get along on the same path. Joseph is a great challenge to his brothers. They are jealous of him and call him "a dreamer" to ridicule him. At one point, they conspire to kill him, but on the advice of Reuben, he is spared (Gen 37:11–36). Hence, not all brothers or sisters are loving, trustworthy, and friendly. It may not matter what one offers the other, for not all friends show love to one another. If the qualities of friendship are seen in familial relationships and these have a common purpose, then they qualify as friends. Usually, the concept of friendship is not extended to a relationship between a master and a servant, or family members; essentially it is a relationship among equals. One of the reasons is that some philosophers posited that friends should be of equal status. As such, according to Sherwin, the Septuagint regularly translate *rēaʿ* as *plēsion*, the Greek equivalent of "neighbor," and not as *philia*.[49] The difficulty of the ancient Greco-Roman world to appreciate the total dynamics in the concept of "neighbor" as well as "friendship" between God and humanity, perhaps due to the relationship that was construed between

---

49. Sherwin, "Friendship with God," 1325.

the gods and humanity, made it difficult to view of divine–human relationship as a friendship.

The Christian sense of discipleship breaks down all hierarchical boundaries and makes all members of the body of Christ see themselves as brothers and sisters in the Lord (Rom 1:13; 1 Cor 1:10; Phil 4:1; 1 Tim 5:1–2; 2 Pet 1:10; cf. Matt 12:50). They are to promote brotherly and sisterly love among themselves (John 13:34; Rom 12:10). In that light, a master–servant relationship becomes blurred in the fellowship of the saints, while the household divinely sanctioned authority of the husband–wife becomes a blur in the fellowship of saints. Masters making friends with servants does not mean they are diminishing their authority but rather seeing the other as persons created in the image of God, hence a brother or sister. In fact, some philosophers such as Rorty, Badhwar, and Friedman explicitly include parent–child relationships in friendship, perhaps through the influence of the historical notion of *philia*.[50] They hold that expressing love for a friend as an end rather than a means to an end is not unconditional, but based on the friend's worth and derived from personal nature. Nonetheless, there do seem to be significant differences between, on the one hand, parental love and the relationships it generates and, on the other hand, the love of one's friends and the relationships that generates.

The New Testament generally takes *philia* as the affection of a friend or kinsman.[51] Strong defines philia as to "be a friend to," to be "fond of," or to "have affection for denoting personal attachment, as a matter of sentiment or feeling."[52] Friendship also means being a colleague (*philos*; Acts 19:31; 27:3; 3 John 14). For James, one can make friends (*philos*) with the world if the person charts a common purpose with unbelievers (Jas 4:4).

Characteristics of Human–Human Friendship

There are some characteristics of human–human friendship, which include:

---

50. Rorty, "Historicity of Psychological Attitudes," 399–412; Badhwar, "Friends as Ends in Themselves," 1–23; Friedman, "Friendship and Moral Growth," 3–13.

51. Buttrick, *Interpreter's Dictionary of the Bible*, 172.

52. Strong, *New Strong's Expanded Dictionary of Bible Words*, 1439; emphasis original.

Friendship as Enhancing Complementarity

God creates humanity not only to enjoy a relationship with God but also to be among each other. If it is not good for the man to be alone and, as such, a woman is created to be with him, then human beings are complete when they are in a relationship with one another, through a community of men and women (Gen 1:26–27). Following Barth's relational interpretation, this relationship between the man and woman is what friendship is all about.[53] Fundamentally, men and women are equal and fill the gap of loneliness in each other's lives.

Friendship is also about complementarity because the woman being the helper of the man is not about the woman becoming a servant of the man but one who stands by the other. Philip Payne says the Bible never intended the word *ʿēzer*, often translated "helper," to imply a subordinate or servant. Rather, it connotes a rescuer, savior, protector, someone of strength, or might, as in "God is our help." Hence, the woman is not subordinate to the man.[54] God's intention in creating the woman for the man is for the two to be friends in relationship and partners in stewardship.

True Friends Share Intimately and Unconditionally

Jonathan and David are intimate friends. They are not casual friends or ordinary friends. The nature of their relationship can be looked at metaphysically as desire or sincere communication, or phenomenologically as the unit-unity, collegiality/comradeship reflecting solidarity through sociality. I do not share the position that the love between David and Jonathan has sexual undertones or is erotic.[55] The friendship between David and Jonathan is described as a friendship between equals who enjoyed intimacy.[56] David calls Jonathan "my brother" (2 Sam 1:26). Jonathan promises David to speak with his father Saul, and he fulfills that promise (1 Sam 19:2–4), reporting to him everything he learns from Saul. Saul swears before Jonathan not to kill David, but he could not keep his word (1 Sam 19:6). However, when Jonathan hears that his father,

---

53. Barth, *Church Dogmatics* III/1, 184, 185.

54. Payne, "Bible Teaches the Equal Standing of Man and Woman," 3.

55. See Ackerman, *Where Heroes Love*; Olyan, "'Surpassing the Love of Women,'" 12.

56. The loving relationship between Jonathan and David has elicited divergent views and interpretations. For further reading, see Tull, "Jonathan's Gift of Friendship," 130–44. See also Ehrlich, "Book of Job as a Book of Morality," 32–34.

Saul, is hiding something from him, he goes all out to betray the trust of the father. In Francesca Murphy's view, it is David who makes Jonathan realize that some family members can be evil.[57] For Jonathan, familial loyalty cannot be compared with the value of friendship (1 Sam 20:2–3). Patricia Tull asserts that such friendship is construed along political undertones rather than personal affection and hints at unconditional loyalty as against familial loyalty.[58] David's heart is totally devoted to God and has a passion and love for God (1 Kgs 11:4), hence he shows the love of God to Jonathan. The uncommon friendship between David and Jonathan makes David extend favor to Jonathan's son, Mephibosheth, after Jonathan's death, and makes him eat with him at his table and restore all that belonged to Saul to Mephibosheth (2 Sam 9:7).

Friendship is often expressed in love shared between each other. Friends will be there to support each other when the other loses someone close or needs help. Sometimes, the only thing friends can do is to show care and comfort. David shows his love for Nahash by sending someone to express his sympathy to Nahash's family members (2 Sam 10:2). David also finds great friendship with Ittai, who pledges to support him unconditionally. Both show each other great support with little expectation of reciprocation; Ittai does not expect anything in return from David (2 Sam 15:19–21). True friendship is unconditional. However, David later changes his mind after Absalom's death and divides the inheritance of Saul between Mephibosheth and Ziba on account of Mephibosheth's refusal to travel with him (2 Sam 19:24–30). That is to say, David's friendship with Jonathan has limits.

Gary Stansell raises some arguments to explain the friendship between David and Jonathan. He establishes that while David was passive in the encounters, Jonathan chooses David as a friend, and he actively gets himself into the relationship.[59] Jonathan was hardly in the role of subservience and inferiority.[60] The friendship was not symmetrical and mutual: at first Jonathan is a prince—initially the superior person in status and legal power—while David is a servant, but later the tables change and David becomes a king, a status higher than that of Jonathan.[61] Again, the friendship is that of a ritualized friendship, similar to that found in

---

57. Murphy, *1 Samuel*, 201.
58. Tull, "Jonathan's Gift of Friendship," 134.
59. Stansell, "David and His Friends," 122.
60. Stansell, "David and His Friends," 127.
61. Stansell, "David and His Friends," 122–23.

some parts of Africa, especially between youths who experience some kind of initiatory rite together. "It is a close bond between two friends, dyadic and exclusive, established by exchanges, sacred oaths and promises, possessing the quality of loyalty that endures beyond the death of one partner."[62] Again, the David–Jonathan friendship is complex by the fact that David becomes a family member by marriage, i.e., a brother-in-law to Jonathan and son-in-law to Saul.[63] In the story, Saul and David are also like political friends, within the realm of patron–client or king–vassal relations,[64] while that between Jonathan and David is more of instrumental friendship.[65]

In Genesis 38, the story shows that Judah takes Hirah—a Canaanite who lived in Adullam—as a friend. Judah leaves Hebron and goes south to stay with his friend Hirah, meets a Canaanite woman and marries her, and has children with her. After a long while, Judah's wife dies. After grieving for her, he goes to Timnah where Hirah is shearing his sheep. It is during this visit that Judah meets Tamar, the widow of Judah's son. Believing she is a shrine prostitute, Judah had sex with her and agreed to give her a young goat or kid for her services. Because Judah had no goat with him, he left his seal, cord, and staff with the woman, promising that the next day he would send the young goat and redeem his items. The next day, Judah sends his friend Hirah with a young goat to Enaim to redeem Judah's pledges; however, he cannot find the prostitute. When Hirah inquires of the townsmen, he learns that Enaim never had a shrine prostitute. Hirah's presence in the story is an indication of how friends can share intimate secrets.

Friendship as Loyalty and Goodwill

In the Ten Commandments, friendship is equated to being a neighbor: "You shall not bear false witness against your neighbor" (*bĕrē'ăkā*; Exod 20:16). Here, the elements of loyalty and sincerity come into play. The neighbor who speaks the truth is loyal and pursues a common goal with the other. Such a loyal friend is someone who shows intimacy and love, more worthy than a blood relation, or a friend of one's friend or kinsman.

---

62. Stansell, "David and His Friends," 124.
63. Stansell, "David and His Friends," 125.
64. Stansell, "David and His Friends," 126.
65. Stansell, "David and His Friends," 129.

It also speaks of, in most cases, one who is close by and stands by the other: "Do not forsake your friend or the friend of your parent; do not go to the house of your kindred in the day of your calamity. Better is a neighbor who is nearby than kindred who are far away" (Prov 27:10).

Human–human friendship is a mutual relationship. It could be developed among equals and non-equals. Where non-equals come together as friends, there is a dynamic and complex dyadic outcome that blurs status and privileges. The face-to-face encounter between God and his friends—Abraham and Moses—makes it possible for them to speak freely and negotiate as if they are equal partners.

The idea of charting a common purpose lies at the foundation of friendship. The psalmist sees his friends as his *kĕ'erkkî* ("equal") and *'allupî* ("companion") (Ps 55:13). The word echoes one who dwells with another. For the prophet Zechariah, all who are in the same profession as the high priest is described as *rēa' e* ("friends") (Zech 3:8). Friendship carries expectations similar to those of family and neighbors.

The concept of *ḥesed* appears in many relationships: It is there between Abraham and Sarah, who were married and also relatives (Gen 20:13). When Abimelech requests *ḥesed* from Abraham, he is "asking for reciprocity."[66] Again, *ḥesed* is assumed in the relationship between Israel and Joseph, that is a father and son (Gen 47:29), and between hosts and guests (Gen 19:19; 21:23; Josh 2:12–14). The loyal relationship between families or relatives is seen in the failure of the Israelites to show *ḥesed* to the family of Gideon (Judg 8:35). For being friendly to Israel, the Kenites spare the Amalekites (1 Sam 15:6). The loving and faithful friendship between Jonathan and David makes Jonathan plead for *ḥesed* from David for his family in view of the *ḥesed* he has shown David (1 Sam 20:8, 13–17). David expresses the desire to deal kindly with (or show *ḥesed* to) a newly crowned Hanun, son of Nahash, the Ammonite king, although Hanun does not reciprocate the gesture and humiliates David's servants (2 Sam 10:1–6).

When Rehoboam is made king after the reign of Solomon, the people want him to reduce the harsh burden and heavy yoke Solomon had put on them. Rehoboam does not take the counsel of the elders who served Solomon but takes that of the young men he had grown up with, suggesting there are his friends. Their bad advice does not go well with the people and it sparks a rebellion, leading to a divided kingdom (1 Kgs 12:1–21).

---

66. Clark, *Chesed in the Hebrew Bible*, 17.

In the New Testament, Jesus is described as a friend (*philos*) of tax collectors (Luke 7:34), and refers to the crowd who had gathered to listen to him as "my friends" (*philos*; Luke 12:4) because of his intimacy with and loyalty to them. Jesus no longer relates with the disciples as master–servant or rabbi–pupil, but on a mutual-exchange level. Lazarus, Mary, and Martha are friends of Jesus (John 11:11), and their home becomes a resting place for Jesus and also a space for teaching and showing love. Hence, the gender lines become blurred in Jesus's model of friendship. Jesus calls his disciples friends (*philos*; John 15:15), with the reason that they are his followers who have the privilege of knowing the deep things of God. However, brotherly love (*philos*) springs from agape love (1 Thess 4:9).

Paul talks about the loyalty of friends and the willingness of those close to look out for one another. In this case, Timothy and Epaphroditus are the types of friends that take care of those close to them. Paul praises Timothy as caring more than anyone else. He compares Timothy with others who think only about what interests them. He also talks about his dear friend Epaphroditus, who is a fellow worker and a soldier of the Lord. Epaphroditus takes the responsibility of looking after Paul's well-being and longs for the well-being of other Christians in Philippi (Phil 2:19–26).

According to Lorriane Pangle, goodwill is rooted less in what others do for us and more in what we do for them. When we are good to others, they see our goodwill and pour themselves out in return. When there is recognition of a certain goodness, it will naturally engender goodwill. We may initially seek to do this for interesting reasons, out of hopes of honor or a return. But the more of our thought and energy and trouble we invest in others, the more those beneficiaries seem to be an extension of or a realization of our own life.[67] When a benefactor's efforts bear good fruit in us, we have no choice but to love the person deeply in return.[68]

Sharing plays a key role in friendship. When one makes friends with a wise person, all grow in wisdom: "Whoever walks with the wise becomes wise, but the companion of fools will suffer harm" (Prov 13:20 ESV). Similarly, "one who is righteous is a guide to his neighbor, but the way of the wicked leads them astray" (Prov 12:26 ESV), and "Make no friendship with a man given to anger, nor go with a wrathful man, lest you learn his ways and entangle yourself in a snare" (Prov 22:24–25 ESV). Again, "oil and perfume make the heart glad, and the sweetness of a

---

67. Pangle, *Aristotle and the Philosophy of Friendship*, 162.
68. Pangle, *Aristotle and the Philosophy of Friendship*, 162, 167, 168.

friend comes from his earnest counsel" (Prov 27:9 ESV). In other words, friends help each other, guide and correct each other so that they all grow in wisdom. The one who abhors correction and knowledge cannot be said to be a good friend. Hence, one should accept corrections. "Whoever covers an offense seeks love, but he who repeats a matter separates close friends" (Prov 17:9 ESV), and "Better is open rebuke than hidden love. Faithful are the wounds of a friend; profuse are the kisses of an enemy" (Prov 27:5–6 ESV). A true friend will give honest advice for the good of the other. "A dishonest man spreads strife, and a whisperer separates close friends" (Prov 16:28 ESV).

The writer of Hebrews sees friends as those among whom there is mutual love (*philadelphia*) and those who show hospitality (Heb 13:1–2). Similarly, Peter mentions constant love (*agapē*) and hospitality (*philoxenoi*) to be maintained among one another, for love (*agapē*) covers a multitude of sins (1 Pet 1:8–10, 2 Pet 1:5–7). A "friend" should be the identity for believers or Christians (1 Cor 10:14; Eph 6:21; 1 Thess 2:8; Phlm 1;3 John 14; cf. Zech 13:6). Paul's language of partnership among believers echoes that of friendship (Phil 1:5, 7; 2:1; 4:14, 15).

Friendship as Empowering Relationship

The Bible gives space to the idea that friends empower each other. The sages thus suggest that some relationships, including loyal friends, can lead to happiness.[69] The book of Proverbs, for instance, teaches: "As iron sharpens iron, so a friend sharpens a friend" (Prov 27:17 my translation). The one who despises the friend is also not wise (Prov 14:2) but rather a sinner (Prov 14:21). It is not easy to have a good friend, because "Many a man proclaims his own steadfast love, but a faithful man who can find?" (Prov 20:6 ESV). True friends are always reliable and dependable. "A friend loves at all times, and a brother is born for adversity" (Prov 17:17 ESV).

In the New Testament, Jesus is friends with Mary, Martha, and Lazarus. He could go and spend time in their home (Luke 10:38). When Lazarus is sick, Mary and Martha send word to Jesus that his friend is sick, but Jesus does not turn up. Four days after Lazarus has died and is buried, Jesus shows up and Martha is frank in confronting Jesus with a moral obligation to have visited and helped them when Lazarus was sick (John 11:1–45). In other words, true friends are able to speak their minds

---

69. Berry, *Introduction to Wisdom and Poetry of the Old Testament*, 155.

honestly to one another, whether right or wrong. Friends do what they can to tell each other the truth and help one another. To Paul, two are better than one, because they can support each other. If either of them falls down, the other will be available to help lift the other up (Eph 4:9–10). Nevertheless, there are others who act as friends but would not help others in times of need. Some friends are a threat to social cohesion because they deceive, slander, speak lies, commit iniquity, and oppress others. Jeremiah highlights some categories of friends as follows:

> 4 Beware of your neighbors (*mērē'ēhu*)
>   and put no trust in any of your kin (*'aḥ*);
> for all your kin (*'aḥ*) are supplanters,
>   and every neighbor (*rēa'*) goes around like a slanderer.
> 5 They all deceive their neighbors (*bĕrē'ēhu*),
>   and no one speaks the truth;
> they have taught their tongues to speak lies;
>   they commit iniquity and are too weary to repent.
> 6 Oppression upon oppression, deceit upon deceit!
>   They refuse to know me, says the Lord. (Jer 9:4–6 [Heb 9:3–5])

One should not only be cautious of such friends but also not trust them (Mic 7.5). Instead of cooperation, companionship, affection, and mutual assistance, such friends disappoint each other, particularly during a time of need. They can team up with the wicked and pay back evil for good. Such violence, deceit, and betrayal or rejoicing break up a friendship.

Sincerity also plays a key role when seeking to empower one another. The psalmist recognizes that the wicked and workers of an evil plot with their friends (*rēa'*) while evil is in their hearts (Ps 28:3). Goodwill can be seen as one of the motivating factors that makes the love between Jonathan and David stronger.

Friendship Is About Walk Together

A critical virtue among friends is the ability to agree to disagree and do things in common. God rhetorically asks Israel, "Can two walk together, unless they are agreed?" (Amos 3:3 NKJV), echoing how friends do things together. There should be a common agreement among friends, sometimes reached through compromise. Paul teaches that Christians are called together to travel on the same road with a common purpose, both outwardly and inwardly (Eph 4:4). To the psalmist, it is good when friends live together in unity (Ps 133:1).

Since Aristotle could not imagine the exact nature of divine–human friendship, he limited friendship to human–human relationships and posited that it exists in the context of commonality and equality. Aquinas disagrees with the Aristotelian concept of commonality and equality in friendship when he looks at divine–human relationships and argues that divine–human friendship is located in charity.[70] Hence, the relationship between a master and a servant, parent and child, and husband and wife may not be seen as friendship, no matter how close they are to each other. Somehow, in a restricted sense, friendship can be seen within an emotional relationship of reciprocal goodwill, erotic love, and affection between people who enjoy spending time together.

CONCLUDING REMARKS

A divine–human relationship lies at the heart of creation. God creates human beings in his own image and after his own likeness for a friendly relationship. However, there is no blurring of privileges, so human beings cannot claim to be equal to God or be like God. Divine–human friendship is a unilaterally given, marked by covenant loyalty, seen in *ḥesed*, alongside virtues like compassion, mercy, favor, goodness, love, and faithfulness. It is also founded on a striking demonstration of God's holiness. However, on the part of human beings it requires obedience to nurture the friendship. Jacqueline Lapsley rightly observes that divine–human friendship is built on habit, reciprocity, self-assertion, and emotion.[71]

Human–human friendship, on the other hand, comes in the form of complementarity, but there are fake friends, the companion who acts like an imposter. Nonetheless, human friends are equal and fill the gap of loneliness in their respective lives. Friends stand by each other. Human–human friendship is a mutual relationship. It could be developed among equals and non-equals. Where non-equals come together as friends, there is a dynamic and complex dyadic outcome that blurs status and privileges. It also calls for promoting goodwill, rooted in what one does for others without the necessity to ask for anything in return. Showing

---

70. Aquinas, *Summa Theologica* II.II Q. 23 A. 3. See also Schwatz, *Aquinas on Friendship*, 114.

71. Lapsley, "Friends with God?" 121.

hospitality is a mark of friendship. A friend cannot blame the other for not paying back a favor offered exactly, as if one party should anticipate the precise proportion of what the other gives in return. However, one good turn deserves the other. Sharing should spring from a heart of sincerity. Friends hang out with each other and do the bidding of one another. Friendship is more than a brotherly relationship and makes one feels empowered knowing that the other is nearby. A friend loves and sticks closer at all times. Nevertheless, it needs to be noted that there are different categories of friends—from intimate friends to ordinary friends, and from good friends to bad friends. A good friend can turn into a bad friend, and a bad friend can be good for a moment. C. S. Lewis is right in asserting that, "the dangers [of friendships] are perfectly real. Friendship (as the ancients saw) can be a school of virtue; but also (as they did not see) the school of vice. It is ambivalent. It makes good men better and bad men worse."[72]

---

72. Lewis, *Inspirational Writings of C. S. Lewis*, 256.

5

History of Interpretation on Friendship

STUDIES AND THEORIES ABOUT friendship since the archaic classical world, including the history of interpretation of the biblical view of friendship, have led to establishing some basic virtues that characterize the phenomenon, yet the virtues keep increasing and sometimes do not concur with each other. Different ideas always come up, some of which are slightly different from what has been established earlier. Thus, it seems there is no unanimity regarding the nature and extent of friendship relationships. This chapter looks at how Western philosophers and scholars, including theologians, have contributed to the notion of friendship. The aim is to present a historical sketch so that the similarities and differences between Western and African thought can be clear.

Given that the concept of friendship is essentially contextual yet with broad affinities, it is necessary to outline several threads of Western scholarship relating to friendship that can help delineate what the African concept of friendship looks like. Philosophically, agape is "Unselfish love of all persons,"[1] and is hardly associated with friendship. The word "*philia*" which is loosely translated as "friendship," connotes a nonpassionate affection within familial relations. Let us turn to explore how some have characterized friendship to establish a criterion for building and being friends.

---

1. Audi, *Cambridge Dictionary of Philosophy*, 14.

CLASSICAL INTERPRETATIONS

Plato

Plato (428/427–348/347 BCE) establishes that friendship (*philia*) is "a kind of affectionate regard or friendly feeling towards not just one's friends but also possibly towards family members, business partners, and one's country at large."[2] In other words, *philia* encompasses different levels of relationship that are motivated by affection. In this light, one can say it is in the form of liking, fondness, and care, of which the lack of fulfillment brings no pain. As such, friends can go and friends can come without any pain.

Philia aims at the mutual well-being and pleasure of each other. *Philia* is distinctly a personal relationship that is justified on non-sexual pleasure since that would fall under *eros*, "a kind of passionate desire for an object, typically sexual in nature."[3] Whenever the balance in pleasure tilts so that the benefit is toward oneself, the friendship relationship becomes distorted. Pleasure derived from friendship is mutual and not selfish. Whenever one goes into friendship with the aim of receiving help only, it disturbs the flow of friendship.

Plato, in his work *Lysis* explains that friendship is contrasted to desire not only because of the fact that desire cares only for bodily pleasures but also because it is a foundation of a significant part of the human intellect. If the desire is mitigated by similarity, friendship does so by identity. Friendship thus constitutes a tension between desire and love, lust and passion, poverty and wealth,[4] and affinity and affection.[5] To Plato, although friendship is distinguished from desire and love,[6] there are some similarities between the two.[7] There is the love of love but not the friendship of friendship; that is one can love himself but cannot be a friend to oneself.[8] Thus, friendship has to do with the other. A good friend can avert death,[9] but not enmity.[10]

---

2. http://plato.stanford.edu/entries/friendship.
3. http://plato.stanford.edu/entries/friendship.
4. Versenyi, "Plato's Lysis," 188.
5. Versenyi, "Plato's Lysis," 189.
6. Versenyi, "Plato's Lysis," 187, 188,
7. Derrida, *Politics of Friendship*, 154, 187.
8. Derrida, *Politics of Friendship*, 76.
9. Derrida, *Politics of Friendship*, 4–14.
10. Derrida, *Politics of Friendship*, 26, 32.

In all, Plato sees friendship as a non-passionate relationship with another for the purposes of unselfish pleasure. It thrives on liking, fondness, and care for each other. These virtues may be ideal for a close friend, but not an intimate friend. Nevertheless, it is possible to show all these but still have a friend who is selfish, not affectionate, and not ready to sacrifice for another.

Aristotle

Aristotle (384–322 BCE) argues that people who are excellent in virtue should participate in "character friendship." He holds that friendship is seen as a reflection of the other self, an idea that is founded on "do unto others what you want others to do for you" (cf. Matt 7:12). Friends try to meet the expectations of the other, and so the behavior they put up with can be a reflection of what the other stands for. A person has to relate with a friend as they would expect to relate with the self.

Aristotle distinguishes between three kinds of friendship: friendships of pleasure, utility, and virtue. These three may be classified as pleasure friendship, advantage friendship, and virtue friendship. Friendship of pleasure is based on shared enjoyment between friends and the pursuit of fleeting pleasures and emotions. It exists among friends who enjoy the company of one another. Friendship of utility is based on what friends do for one another. The final kind is the friendship of virtue or "true" friendship, or friendship of "the good." Aristotle's way of distinguishing the three may not be clear-cut, but the basic ideas of pleasure, utility, and virtue are all inherent in some categories of friendship. That is to say, there are friends who possess not only one kind but all three, hence the dividing lines are not distinct.

Friendship of virtue is enduring and immune to slander, always there to help each other avoid error, spend time with one other, support each other in making choices, and share each other's joys and sorrow. It is the type of friendship that people enjoy for each other's sake and is based on mutual respect and admiration; people push each other to be a better person. It takes longer to build a friendship of virtue than the other two kinds since it is more powerful and enduring. In the words of Aristotle,

> Perfect friendship is the friendship of men who are good, and alike in virtue; for these wish well alike to each other qua good, and they are good themselves. Now those who wish well to their

> friends for their sake are most truly friends; for they do this by reason of own nature and not accidentally; therefore their friendship lasts as long as they are good—and goodness is an enduring thing.[11]

Aristotle holds that friendships of utility and pleasure are based on the "incidental" qualities of pleasure and utility, and are therefore inferior, selfish friendships.[12] To be a self-actualized person, then, one needs to master the art of friendship of virtue. And he nurtured a thought that friendship can be permanent as long as all the good qualities one desires is found in the other:

> And such friendship is as might be expected permanent, since there meet in it all the qualities that friends should have. For all friendship is for the sake of good or of pleasure—good or pleasure either in the abstract or such as will be enjoyed by him who has the friendly feeling—and is based on certain resemblance . . . love and friendship therefore are found most and in their best form between such men.[13]

For Aristotle, there are limitations to the extent people make friends: "It is impossible to have many friends in the full meaning of the word friendship, any more than it is to be in love with many people at once."[14] What Aristotle seems to aver is that having friends of virtue is rare. Aristotle praises those who have many good friends, saying it is a noble thing. He explains that in virtue friendship, one may have all the nobility of virtuous action without sacrificing happiness. Again, such friendship goes beyond justice, for where there is true friendship, there is no need to talk about justice. From his perspective, when friendship grows to be purer, the greater the desire for the friend's good. If friendship flourishes, the friends must remain as they are: neither godlike nor even wise, but simply human. Friendship tends to consume itself in the very transcendence it desires. So, ultimately, perfect friendship can destroy itself.[15] To be perfect is not a possible human achievement, in my view, and so Aristotle is right in locating true friendship within the limitations of human abilities.

11. *NE* 8.3.
12. *NE* 8, 247–49.
13. *NE* 8.3.
14. NE 8.vi.2.
15. *NE* 8.1.1155b.7.

Aristotle holds that one can be sociable even when living a solitary life—still caring "for parents, children, wife, and in general for his friends and fellow citizens, since man is sociable in nature. But some limit must be set to this: for if we extend our requirement to ancestors and descendants and friends' friends we are in for an infinite series."[16] Ignoring ancestors and descendants in one's social life, from an African point of view, is next to impossible since that would not be sociable.

It needs to be noted that not all kinds of friendship require likemindedness, even in the case of good friends. This is because each person comes into a relationship with distinct qualities, graces, abilities, and strengths. I believe there is a requirement in Christian discipleship that enjoins the believer to bring the unbeliever close by and help the unbeliever to come to faith in Jesus Christ. That does not mean the believer and unbeliever are unequally yoked (cf. 2 Cor 6:14)—rather, for the reason of being in the same congregation of a faith group, some levels of friendship can be cultivated. Christian friendship is about building one another up in the faith. It is a way to model Jesus Christ, build a family of God, and exemplify Christlike love. Matters of pleasure and happiness do not have a place in Christian friendship. The next chapter will establish that friendship from an African perspective is not to be seen as a means to promote pleasure and happiness. Much the same way, it is as if for Aristotle that a friend should always do what is virtuous and act toward the good; however, in practicality that is not usually the case.

Aristotle locates "perfect" friendship as a relationship among equals, and in my view, that can be judged to be more restrictive. He says, "now equality and likeness are friendship and especially the likeness of those who are like in virtue"[17] Aristotle believed that God simply cannot have friends. Hence, Aristotle projects God as different from what Jesus presented, calling his disciples his friends (John 15:15). To him, individuals cannot be friends when they neither approve of the same things nor have anything in common. If their tastes are not pained by the same things or they do not agree, they cannot be friends.[18] He says,

> There are then, as we said at the outset, three kinds of friendship, and in each kind there are both friends who are on an equal footing and friends on a footing of disparity; for two equally

---

16. *NE* I, 1734.
17. *NE* 1159a35.
18. *NE* 1165b, 27–30.

good men may be friends, or one better man and one worse; and similarly with pleasant friends and with those who are friends for the sake of utility, who may be equal or may differ in the amount of the benefits which they confer. Those who are equals must make matters equal by loving each other, etc., equally; those who are unequal by making a return proportionate to the superiority of whatever kind on the one side.[19]

Here Aristotle recognizes two other characteristics of friends: first, where one of the individuals cannot bring to the table equal amounts of benefits, and second, where one is morally good and the other is not. In essence, Aristotle expands the spectrum of character friendships between unequals, explaining that—apart from husband and wife, parents and children, older men and younger—rulers and ruled, can be friends.[20] In his work, *Politics*, he asserts the superiority of men over women, saying by nature the man is superior and the woman is inferior.[21] His point is that no matter how morally good a woman is, she possesses a lower quality than that of a man. Moreover, if the one with a lower ability cannot give more, it breaks down the friendship. Aristotle argues,

And in every friendship based on superiority, the friendly affection too must become proportionate; for example, the better should be loved more than he loves; and the more beneficial; and each of the others similarly. For when the friendly affection corresponds to worth, then equality is achieved in some way, as seems indeed to be characteristic of friendship.[22]

The superiority of men over women, it needs to be admitted, is a faulty assessment and not justifiable in our postmodern world. Gender stereotyping is a barrier that stands against holistic human advancement. While there are some differences in biological and psychological makeup as well as social roles, the points that both men and women are created in the image of God (Gen 1:27) and co-heirs of the grace of God (1 Pet 3:7) cannot be ignored. In the economy of God, there is neither male nor female (Gal 3:28).

It needs to be added that Aristotle fails to see friendship within kinship relationships because of his idea of male supremacy. His emphasis

---

19. *NE* 1162a, 34–b4.
20. Konstan, "Greek Friendship," 71–94.
21. Aristotle, *Pol.* 1254b, 13–14.
22. *NE* 1158b, 24–28.

on reciprocity crowds out the whole essence of obligation to help as well as being dear to the other. Some friends play a crucial role in making their presence available in times of need and there is nothing else to contribute. The value of time, in my view, cannot be quantified.

In Aristotle's estimation, the one who is inferior has to work extra to match what the one who is superior brings to the table. That is to say, for authentic friendship to be present, each party must genuinely will the good of the other for the other's own sake and the reciprocated goodwill must be mutually known. The pursuit of a common good binds each friend to the other, and the quality of the good that is shared informs the quality of their friendship. Reciprocity is thus a requisite feature of friendship. "To a friend . . . you must wish goods for his own sake. If you wish good things in this way, but the same wish is not returned by the other, you would be said to have [only] goodwill for the other. For friendship is said to be reciprocated goodwill."[23] However, to assume that reciprocity is key to friendship would mean those who have nothing equal in measure to contribute cannot be in some circles of friends.

Aristotle agrees that like any living thing, friendship needs time to germinate and to mature. "Those who are quick to treat each other in friendly ways wish to be friends, but are not friends, unless they are also loveable, and know this. For though the wish for friendship comes quickly, friendship does not."[24] Agreeably, a friendship that takes time to grow becomes enduring. Thus, friendship does not suddenly die when friends are temporarily separated from one another. However, if communication ceases between friends for an extended period of time, their friendship bond too will fade or diminish.

In the view of Aristotle, when an individual is virtuous, that person is capable of authentically willing the good of the other person. A person can love the self, but not make friends with the self. To be virtuous means one is someone "who wishes and does goods . . . to his friend for the friend's own sake. The individual wishes to be and to live for the friend's own sake, gladly spends his time with one another, strives to make similar choices as the friend does, and shares the friend's distress and enjoyment."[25]

Good wishes are a very important factor in friendly relationships. Where like-mindedness seems to be similar, it boosts the quality of

---

23. *NE* 1155b.
24. *NE* 1156b.
25. *NE* 1166a.

friendship. That is why Aristotle believes that there is no need for rules of justice between people who are friends, since they wish for the good of each other. Such people will do what is just, and what is just is thought to be what belongs to friendship.[26]

In sum, Aristotle sees true friendship as exemplified by a virtuous life. Friends will reciprocate the good wishes extended and thus become a reflection of the other. They try to meet each other's expectations and, as such, there should be some equality among them. They must always agree on a common goal. Good friendship needs time to grow. Since it takes a human being to be a friend, there is no such thing as a perfect friend.

Epicurus

Epicurus (341–270 BCE) was a Greek philosopher who also developed ideas on the proper attitude toward friendship as an essential part of life. Epicurus, famous for propounding the theory of hedonism, says the unique goal in life is happiness based on freedom from physical pain and mental anxiety, thus placing an extremely high value on friendship (or love: *philia*). Friendship is molded by means of a community of life toward pleasure. For him, happiness is not a private affair because it is readily achieved in a society where like-minded individuals come together to help inspire one another's pursuit of happiness. Epicurus held that pleasure with happiness is the absence of pain in the body and trouble in the soul, saying "pleasure is our first and kindred good, and the starting point of every choice as long as we make feeling the rule by which to judge of every good thing."[27] Pleasure is the beginning and the end of a happy life.

In his *Vatican Sayings*, Epicurus posits that a wise man would feel the torture of a friend no less than his own, and would die for a friend rather than betray him, for otherwise his own life would be confounded.[28] J. Hilton Turner presents some Epicurus quotes on friendship:

> Of all the things wisdom prepares for the blessedness of the complete life, far the greatest is the possession of friendship.[29]

---

26. *NE* 1166a.
27. Bergsma, Poot, and Liefbroer, "Happiness in the Garden of Epicurus," 400.
28. Epicurus, *VS* 56–57.
29. Turner, "Epicurus and Friendship," 351.

> It is friendship that fills the gap and provides both the human companion and the security needed by man.[30]
>
> It is not so much our friends' help that helps us as the confidence of their help.[31]
>
> He is no friend who is continually asking for help nor he who never associates help with friendship. For the former barters gratitude for a practical return and the latter destroys the hope of good in the future.[32]
>
> Friendship too has practical needs as its motive. One must indeed lay its foundations (for we sow the ground too for the sake of crops) but it is formed and maintained through community of life among those who have reached the fullness of pleasure.[33]

For Turner, epicurean friendship revolves around fellowship. While Epicurus does not favor passionate pleasure as a basis for friendship, he does hold that friendship is not a selfish desire but that which promotes community.[34] A friend will stand by the other in times of need and that helps to maintain a sense of community.

Epicurus asserts that friendship and justice as two important features that provide us with security.[35] Although friendship has a hedonistic starting point, in its maturation a friend is no longer considered to be a means to our own happiness, but a friend has become part of our own life, a part of ourselves. Friends no longer only strive for their own pleasure; they also seek pleasure for their friends, thus becoming a mutual project. In other words, Epicurus equates friendship to the pursuit of happiness. One who finds a friend is wise, and friends provide companionship and security. Friends should be ready to help one another and not focus on one's own happiness. Friendship and justice go together.

---

30. Turner, "Epicurus and Friendship," 353.
31. Turner, "Epicurus and Friendship," 353.
32. Turner, "Epicurus and Friendship," 353.
33. Turner, "Epicurus and Friendship," 353.
34. Turner, "Epicurus and Friendship," 354.
35. Bergsma et al., "Happiness in the Garden of Epicurus," 403.

Cicero

Marcus Tullius Cicero (106–43 BCE) was born at Arpinum, Rome, and wrote a book titled *De Amicitia* (*How to Be a Friend*). The Latin word for friendship—*amicitia*—is derived from the word *amor* ("love"). Cicero believes that love is certainly the prime mover in contracting mutual affection. Commenting on Cicero's dependence on Stoic and Epicurean ideas, Martin Culy says,

> In a sense, Cicero represents a mediating position between the rival Stoic and Epicurean schools. Like the Stoics, he maintained that friendship was a natural outgrowth of human nature (cf. *Amic.* 5.19–20). He did not, however, follow the Stoic view that virtue—a necessary component of genuine friendship—was the property of sages alone. In this sense, his thinking was more akin to the Epicureans. He emphatically rejected, however, the Epicurean link between friendship and utility.[36]

In Cicero's view, "friendship" is the most valuable gift, with the exception of wisdom, that the gods have granted to humankind. He defines friendship as a complete accord on all subjects of human and divine, joined with mutual goodwill and affection.[37] He says,

> For the first thing that promotes the establishing of goodwill is love (*amor*), from which is derived the word "friendship" (*amicitial*). For it is true that many times practical advantages are obtained even by those who are cultivated under the pretense of friendship and honoured to gain a temporary benefit; but in friendship there is nothing false, nothing pretended, and whatever there is within it, is genuine and proceeds willingly. It is therefore my view that friendship has its origin in nature rather than in need, and that it derives more from an attachment of the mind together with a sense of affection than from a calculation of how much advantage the relationship will bring.[38]

In essence, fake friends or those who pretend to be friends have nothing beneficial to contribute in life and such pretense destroys the genuineness of friendship. Those who gain temporary benefits out of a relationship of friendship by pretense cannot be said to be friends.

---

36. Culy, *Echoes of Friendship in the Gospel of John*, 42.
37. Cicero, *De inventione rhetorica* 2.55.150.
38. Cicero, *De inventione rhetorica* 27–28, Cicero, "On Friendship," 157–58.

Cicero believes that there are two types of *amicitia*: public/political friendship (*popularis*), which describes the relationship between a politician or political candidate and his supporters or the broader patron–client relationships in society, and private friendship (*domestica*), which he extols as the superior nature of friendship. And to be true friends, what is required is to be good—it is not restricted only to the "wise." The "good" are those whose actions and lives leave no question as to their honor, purity, equity, and liberality; who are free from greed, lust, and violence; and who have the courage of their convictions. People of poor moral character can have friends, but they cannot be friends.

When people choose friends undiscerningly, they deprive themselves of the opportunity to experience for themselves how powerful, wonderful, and all-embracing the relationship can be.[39] Cicero cautions that people should choose their friends with care. It is more delightful to have someone to whom you can say everything with the same absolute confidence as yourself. Hence, people should take their time, hasten slowly, and discover what lies deep in a person's heart before committing or investing the self in what true friendship requires.

Cicero says that no one who is friendly can thrive in isolation because "even when a friend is absent, he is still present."[40] Friendships, however, can change over time, so they are not permanent. Old friends do not mean they are the best since there is no satiety in friendship. It is not as if the older the sweeter, as in wines that keep well. However, time can have its proper position in and influence on friendship.

For Cicero, where the demands of a friend affect one's life or reputation, the person should not make a concession. The qualities people ought to look out for in making our selection are firmness, stability, constancy. The characters of two friends must be stainless. There must be complete harmony of interests, purpose, and aims, without exception. Friendship should not precede the formation of a judgment of these virtues. Friendship and moral goodness must go together.[41] This is why true friendship is very difficult to find among those who engage in politics and the contest for office. Friends will always tell you what you need to hear, not what you want them to say. Cicero notes that there is no plague in friendship greater than flattery, fawning, and adulation.

39. Cicero, *De amicitia* 21, 79–80.

40. Shuckburgh, *Letters of Marcus Tullius Cicero*; Shuckburgh, *And Letters of Gaius Plinius Caecilius Secundus*, 9; Johnson, *Cicero, Marcus Tullius*.

41. Cicero, *De amicitia* 6, 22 and 13, 46.

In all, Cicero admits that friendship is part of human nature. It is natural. It does not come up only because there is a need. Friendship is not only motivated by happiness or pleasure. There must be goodwill and affection among friends; the two must go together. There should not be any form of pretense or hidden motives among friends. One should therefore take care in making friends.

VIEWS OF SOME CHURCH FATHERS

John Chrysostom

Saint John Chrysostom (347–407 AD), born in Antioch, was endowed with a superior genius strengthened by a brilliant education. In order to break with a world that admired and courted him, in 374 he retired for six years to a neighboring mountain, having found Christ through his friendship with Saint Basil, and was later consecrated a bishop of Constantinople on February 26, 398. Chrysostom views on friendship are strong. For a friendship to be strong and lasting in his view, it should have Christ as its basis, reason, and model. This is because Jesus showed all an example of friendship and laid down his life for his friends (John 15:13). He distinguishes between genuine friends, table companions, and mere nominal friends. Genuine friends might even die for each other, but one can see one's table companions or nominal friends and not become satiated.

Chrysostom argues that eating and drinking does not make friendships. To him, "the constant association of the two—eating, talking, laughing together—promoted a state of perpetual sexual arousal."[42] He believed that nothing can be sweeter than friendship.

> Do not stay together, thus, with friends who cause you mischief! Do not stay together with friends who love more your meals than your friendship! As all these bring to a close friendship after having eaten and enjoyed the feast; others yet, friends who value virtue, will stay together with you forever, they will abide with you in all your misery and mischief. Friends who congregate with you for eating and drinking, the pests, will avenge on you and will denigrate you.[43]

---

42. Clark, "John Chrysostom and the 'Subintroductae,'" 176.
43. Petcu, "Saint John Chrysostom, on True Friendship Between People," 450.

A faithful friend is the medicine of life and a strong defense in life. A genuine friend will share pleasure and be a treasure. When they meet together there is joy. When genuine friends are unavailable, life becomes empty, and that can lead to weeping and fond memories. Chrysostom says, "it were better for us that the sun should be extinguished, than that we should be deprived of friends; better to live in darkness, than to be without friends."[44] He also talks about spiritual friends who labor to see the friend's soul saved. Genuine friends build each other up spiritually. Such friends surpass fathers and siblings. "They are always of one heart and soul, and not one of them said that anything of the things which he possessed was his own . . . and distribution was made unto each, according as anyone had need" (Acts 4:32–35). Hence, friendship makes one not consider owned goods as something personal, rather they are also the neighbors.

Genuine friends are not so much gratified when they are recipients of good things from others as when the they are doing good. "For he wishes to oblige, rather than to be indebted to him; or rather he wishes both to be beholden to him, and to have him his debtor." And food may satiate, "but a friend never does, so long as he is a friend; nay, the desire of him rather increases, and such pleasure never admits of satiety. And a friend is sweeter than the present life."[45] Genuine friends do not abandon each other, for "friendship cannot be brought to a standstill either by the length of the roads, or the sky, or the earth, or death, or anything else, as it is stronger and more powerful than anything else; although it originates in one single soul, it can embrace many souls."[46] Likewise, with a friend even poverty is tolerable. A person without a friend will find both health and riches intolerable. Chrysostom avers,

> Though you should name infinite treasures, none of them is comparable to a genuine friend. And first let us speak of the great delight of friendship itself. A friend rejoices at seeing his friend, and his heart expands with joy. He is tied to him with a union of soul that affords unspeakable pleasure. I speak of genuine friends, men of one soul, who would even die for each other, who love each other fervently.[47]

---

44. Chrysostom, *Homily II on I Thessalonians*.
45. Chrysostom, *Homily II on I Thessalonians*.
46. Petcu, "Saint John Chrysostom, on True Friendship Between People," 451.
47. Chrysostom, *Homily II on I Thessalonians*.

In other words, Chrysostom held that genuine friendship is the purest and most reliable form of relationships. In my view, genuine friendship is the same as true friendship.

Augustine

Augustine of Hippo (354–430 AD) was an African theologian and philosopher from Hippo, Algeria. He holds that in this world two things are essential: life and friendship. Mere life is not enough. If a human being is to be a real person, there must be friendship. Augustine draws basic assumptions about the nature of friendship from the descriptions found in Plato's *Symposium* and Cicero's *Amicitia*. Augustine acknowledges the validity and usefulness of Cicero's definition in one of his letters, arguing that for true friendship to exist there must be agreement with others in goodwill and affection in things human and divine. He says,

> friendship should not be bounded by narrow limits, for it embraces all to whom we owe affection and love though it is inclined more eagerly toward some and more hesitantly toward others ... We ought to pray that, when we have these goods, we may retain them and that, when we do not have them, we may acquire them.[48]

What Augustine seems to advocate is that in life, we owe one another love, perhaps influenced by Paul (Rom 13:8–13). As such, friendship should be extended to all people, no matter what is anticipated, and it should extend as far as to our enemies. Since everyone owes the other an open affection on account of our shared nature, we should make friends.

For Augustine, friends should know each other. He believes God is knowable in some sense, for one can know that God is great, wise, just, and powerful. However, knowledge of God is not the same as knowing a human being. Knowing, or desiring to know, another person as a friend is a kind of intellectual knowledge that can be exercised with the mind.[49]

Christians should not particularly love those who love them in return. Christians should seek friendship not for what they would benefit from, as they can look forward to a future in which they will securely enjoy all the goods of human nature. In other words, Augustine sees the close link between love and friendship: love should be extended to all,

---

48. Augustine, *Epistle* 130.6.13 Augustine, *Letters*.
49. O'Daly, *Augustine's Philosophy of Mind*, 213–15.

including enemies, and so should friendship. It does not matter whether the other person reciprocates love or not in matters of friendship, in the view of Augustine. Hence, it is the responsibility of all to make friends.

Augustine also seems to believe that spousal friendship exists. When spouses are in love with one another, they grow to become friends. He says,

> Friendship perishing, there will be preserved in the mind the bonds neither of marriages, nor of kindreds and relations; because in these also there is assuredly a friendly union of sentiment. Spouse therefore will not be able to love spouse in turn, inasmuch as each believes not the other's love, because the love itself cannot be seen.[50]

Hence, no matter the responses of the husband or wife, it is the duty of spouses to be friends to one another. Augustine, in his book *On the Good of Marriage*, states,

> Every individual belongs to the human race, and by virtue of his humanity he is a social being. In addition, he possesses the great and natural blessing of a capacity for friendship. It was with these purposes that God decided to create all humanity from one man, so that all would be kept in community with each other not only by similarity of species but also by the bond of kinship. Hence the first natural link in human society is that between man and wife. Even these God did not create as separate individuals and then unite them as strangers by birth, but he fashioned the wife from the husband, and signaled the strength of their union by the flank from which she was drawn and formed; for those who walk together, and together observe the direction which they are taking, are joined side by side in unity. The next link in the chain of community is children, the sole worthy outcome not of the union between male and female, but of sexual intercourse; for even without such sexual association there could exist a true union of friendship between the two sexes, with the one governing and the other obeying.[51]

In other words, Augustine sees friendship as fundamental in all social relationships including that of the husband and wife. Males can be friends with females for good purposes. The human being was created to be a social being and as such, if a person cannot relate friendlily with others,

---

50. Augustine, "Faith in Things Unseen," § 4
51. Augustine, *De Bono Coniugali, De Sancta Virginitate*, 3.

that individual is not becoming a person in the eyes of God. Friendship, to Augustine, can develop into a kind of kinship, and even in situations where couples walk and share together in unity. The unity of purpose makes erotic love fruitful. However, "the bond of friendship between husband and wife still preceded, justified, and . . .would long outlast the relatively short interlude of active sex."[52] A relationship where two individuals are joined simply to seek pleasure or benefits for themselves through the other person either physically, biologically, emotionally, or spiritually cannot be said to be a good friendly relationship.

Augustine finds it objectionable when an individual quits being a friend just because the circumstances of the other have changed for the worse. True friends are expected to stand by each other in trouble and in joy with determined constancy. He explains that if a friend was seen as a friend when the person was rich but is not a friend when the person is poor, then it was not friendship at all, but pretense based on money. The love involved in friendship ought to be gratuitous, not simply one doing something for the other for a reward. If that were so, then it would not be true friendship or love. A friend is to be loved freely, for friendship's sake, not for the sake of something else. There is no greater consolation than the unfeigned loyalty and mutual affection of good and true friends.[53] "Such signs of friendship sprang from the hearts of friends who loved and knew their love returned, signs to be read in smiles, word, glances and a thousand gracious gestures."[54]

For Augustine, a true friend is not one who flatters, but one who dares to tell us the truth. Failure to tell the truth to one another because of its adverse consequences creates a great deal of harm. In this respect, it is often our enemies who occasionally in a burst of anger speak to other people the truth about something. Augustine says,

> Sometimes when we argued with each other it was not a bitter argument but like the kind of argument you might have with yourself. In fact sometimes the argument was the kind only friends can have when they have some disagreement—it sometimes made our usual harmony more meaningful. Each of us had something to learn from each other and something to

---

52. Brown, *Body and Society*, 403.
53. Augustine, *City of God*, 19.8
54. Augustine, *Confessions*, IV.8.13.

each in return. If someone was absent for some time they were missed and we welcomed them back warmly.[55]

Augustine believes a friend can lead another astray. A person can be a bad influence on the other. Hence, if one is not careful, one can sacrifice a good virtue to be united with another. Augustine shares his experience when he had a very dear friend about his own age who shared the same studies and interests, with whom he had a relationship sweeter to him than all the sweetness of his life thus far. However, Augustine was able to turn his friend away from true faith to superstitious and harmful fables, away from that which his mother taught him.[56] Only after his conversion did Augustine identify that his love toward his friend became misguided when he exalted the power of friendship as salvific. So, Augustine holds that friends sometimes function as spiritual advisers or as spiritual killers. In the view of Frank Valk, Augustine's thoughts on Christian friendship are that friends seek one another's well-being and happiness in this world, but the primary aim of Christian friendships is to help one's friends grow in the new life of grace.[57] Friendship which draws human beings together in a tender bond is sweet and it forges a unity. As such, friends have to teach and learn from each other what is good. The relationship should be such that when one is absent, the other will not miss anything, and when the other is around, it is a welcome joy.

In sum, Augustine sees friendship as a platform to share love and build each other in grace and faith. The human being is created not to be an island but to be friendly to all since we owe one another love. One should seek to be a friend not for what can be accrued, so it does not matter whether the other reciprocates or not. Men and women can be friends with each other, and husbands and wives can be friends as long as they stand by each other, walk together, and share in unity. Friends do not flatter each other or enter into bitter arguments, although they may sometimes disagree on certain issues. Thus, friends should not speak to each other in anger. A friend can lead the other astray so one should be careful with the friends.

---

55. Augustine, *Confessions*, IV 3.14.
56. Augustine, *Confessions*, IV.4.7.
57. Valk, "Friendship, Politics, and Augustine's Consolidation of the Self," 142.

Thomas Aquinas

Thomas Aquinas (1225-1274), an Italian Dominican friar and priest, holds that true friendship is based on unselfish love for another person for the good of that person.[58] The object of one's friendship is God through charity. "The creation of His Love within us is called the habit of charity."[59] God created people to become friends with us, so that all can share God's nature. God, thus, creates the good in people so that it can establish the common ground in relationships. Individual acts of love dispose of us for better acts of charity. To Aquinas, friendship involves a "mutual benevolent love on a common ground, and has as its normal rule, unselfishness."[60]

Only when people show intense acts of charity will they actually increase their friendship with God. "Because of this love of ourselves through God—as belonging to God and as His friend—it is possible to give all our neighbors the same supernatural love."[61] In other words, a person who loves God will have the capacity to love the neighbor. "Charity seeks only God and loves Him for Himself,"[62] and is a distinct virtue from the moral virtues in that God is its object. Aquinas, however, holds that benevolent love does not necessarily lead to friendship. Rather for friendship to exist, benevolent love must be reciprocated by both parties and recognized by both as reciprocated. Human friendship has its limits, in giving, sharing, and time spent together, and God has so ordered it that way so that the human heart can only find its fulfillment of friendship in the divine.

Thomas Aquinas does not share the viewpoint that friendship should be based on pleasure or happiness. He posits that "when friendship is based on usefulness or pleasure, a man does indeed wish his friend some good: and in this respect, the character of friendship is preserved. But since he refers this good further to his own pleasure or uses, the result is that friendship of the useful or pleasant, in so far as it is connected with love of concupiscence, loses the character of true friendship."[63] Pleasure, in this sense, is egoistic and does not help build a strong bond of friendship.

58. Aquinas, *Summa Theologiae*, IaIIae, q.23, a.1.
59. Farrell, *Companion to the Summa*, 66.
60. Farrell, *Fulness of Life*, 84.
61. Farrell, *Companion to the Summa*, 79.
62. Farrell, *Fulness of Life*, 69.
63. Aquinas, *Summa Theologica*, Ia IIae Q. 26 A. 4.

Aquinas draws on the creation story in Genesis to argue for friendship, and explains that God said it is not good for man to be alone (see Gen 2:18). As such, we are incomplete in ourselves unless we want to share our lives with others. In the view of Aquinas, friendship brings out the best in a person. Someone who cannot give totally of oneself to another does not have the capacity to share love. When friends discover the good in each other, the relationship grows.[64] He believes that when we love a friend the same love extends in some degree to the friends of our friend. We love them for the sake of our friends. When God is our friend, all of God's friends become our friends. There is nothing on this earth more prized than true friendship, and without friends even the most agreeable pursuits become tedious.

All that Aquinas seeks to project is that friendship is not based on selfish love but on the good of the other. God created us to love one another and God's love motivates us to be friends and show charity. It is not good for a person to be alone without friends. We become incomplete unless we share our lives with others. Friendship involves mutual, benevolent love that is unselfish. For individuals to become friends, there should be reciprocity of charity and recognition of such love. In the long run, friends of our friends also benefit from the love extended to friends.

OTHER CHRISTIAN LEADERS

John Wesley

John Wesley (1703–1791) was a British minister, revivalist, and one of the founders of the Methodist movement, giving some guidelines for friendship with strict limitations and cautions concerning: (1) loving all persons including the ungodly, (2) conducting temporary business with all, (3) sharing the Gospel with all, and (4) friendship with women. In a letter written June 17, 1774, John Wesley explains that "friendship is one species of love; and is, in its proper sense, a disinterested reciprocal love between two persons." Thus, friendship should not be founded on the benefits that would come out of the relationship.

Wesley thinks that Christians ought to love all people, including the ungodly. Yet he persistently points out that loving the ungodly can be dangerous to one's own spiritual well-being. Consequently, Wesley

---

64. Farrell, *Fulness of Life*, 67.

advocates love for enemies, including the enemies of God, but he also urges the Christian not to enter into friendships with the ungodly. Hence, for him, there is a difference between showing love to another and being a friend to another. For Wesley, loving one's enemies and abstaining from friendship with the ungodly are required of all Christians by plain commands in scripture. He puts the matter bluntly: the Bible "clearly requires us to keep at a distance, as far as is practicable, from all ungodly men."[65] Wesley maintains that friendship with the ungodly is a sin in itself and is "attended with most dreadful consequences."[66]

Wesley believes that it is ideal if a person who seeks friendship is of a strong natural understanding and of high learning, so that when one enters into that relationship there will be opportunities for one to learn many things, improve understanding, or gain a lot of knowledge. But still, if the friend has no fear of God, the loss will be far greater than the gain. To him, friendships that lead to a decrease in holiness should be avoided at all costs regardless of the increase in human knowledge. All the knowledge one may gain from friendship will be no relevant when holiness is affected.[67]

In a sermon entitled "On Dress," Wesley explains that one should not conform to the standards of the world by following friends who are unbelievers:

> It is one sin to contract a friendship with any that know not God . . . And this led you back into another, into that conformity to the world from which ye had clean escaped . . . But what are you to do now? . . . Now, today, before the heart is hardened by the deceitfulness of sin, cut off at one stroke that sinful friendship with the ungodly, and that sinful conformity with the world.[68]

One should cut ties with friends so that they do not deceive one into sin. Wesley also believes that people who fear God are the only ones truly capable of friendship. Thus, he says,

> Wicked persons are, it seems, incapable of friendship . . . I apprehend wicked men, under whatever dispensation, to be absolutely incapable of true friendship. By wicked men, I mean, either men openly profane, or men void of justice, mercy, and truth. There

---

65. "Sermon 81: In What Sense We Are to Leave the World," 4 (Wesley, *Works*, 3:144).
66. "Sermon 80: On Friendship with the World," 12 (Wesley, *Works*, 3:132).
67. "Sermon 80: On Friendship with the World," 20.
68. "Sermon 88: On Dress," 25 (Wesley, *Works*, 3:259).

may be a shadow of friendship between those, whether of the same, or of different sexes. But surely the substance is wanting: In all my experience, I have found no exception to this rule.[69]

Wesley goes as far as to say that if one's child does not fear God, it is better to severe relationship with the child. The same can be said of all other relations, even brothers or sisters. To him, one can be civil and friendly at a distance.

On conducting business with all people, Wesley believes that Christians may interact with the ungodly in routine business affairs. Thus, he says,

> Were we not to converse at all with men of those characters it would be impossible to transact our temporal business. So that every conscientious Christian would have nothing to do but to flee into the desert. It would not suffice to turn recluses, to shut ourselves up in monasteries or nunneries; for even then we must have some intercourse with ungodly men in order to procure the necessaries of life.[70]

Hence, there are certain things in life that are so necessary that inquiring about the faith of the one you deal with is not important. Wesley suggests that Christians ought to be careful when offering a helping hand to the ungodly. He believes the Christian can converse with the ungodly and engage in business transactions, but care should be taken. Such friendship is guided by courtesy, and Christians must take great care not to carry it too far.[71] "Otherwise you are more likely to receive hurt from them than to do them any good. For if you do not raise their hearts to heaven, they will draw yours down to earth."[72]

Wesley views friendship with women as always questionable. Maybe Wesley's bad marriage experience further reinforced his thoughts on women. In fact, Wesley not only discourages friendship between men and women, but thought the friendship between men and ungodly women was unethical. Wesley says,

> But as dangerous as it is to converse familiarly with men that know not God, it is more dangerous still for men to converse with women of that character; as they are generally more

---

69. Jackson, *Works*, 12: 295. The letter is dated June 17, 1774.
70. "Sermon 81: In What Sense We are to Leave the World," 6 (Wesley, *Works*, 3:145).
71. "Sermon 80: On Friendship with the World," 10 (Wesley, *Works*, 3:131).
72. Wesley, *Works*, 3:151.

insinuating than men, and have far greater power of persuasion; particularly if they are agreeable in their persons, or pleasing in their conversation. You must be more than man if you can converse with such and not suffer any loss.[73]

In a nutshell, as much as Wesley was troubled by the thought of friendship between men and women, or marriage between godly men and ungodly women, he was equally alarmed by the idea that Methodists would form friendships with the ungodly. For him, there is a difference between showing love to all people and being friends with all people. Friendships that make one lose one's faith are not worth engaging in. Rather, friendship should be a way to share knowledge and build each other up.

Dietrich Bonhoeffer

Dietrich Bonhoeffer (1906–1945) was a German theologian and martyr. Bonhoeffer's theology of friendship is founded on the concept of "the other" in concrete ways that affirm the worth of each other. According to Eberhard Bethge, it was only later in his life that he explicitly and intentionally wrote about friendship.[74] Bonhoeffer's views on friendship are seen in his fiction fragments, the prison letter of 1944, a poem to Bethge in 1944, and his pencil markings on the *Stifter*.[75] In the latter, Bonhoeffer describes friendship thus,

> A true and upright friend is, next to a loyal wife, the greatest good that a man can have on earth. Our parents are friends given to us by God but, loyal and sincere as they are, they are not born equal with us. Rather they stand over as recipients of our honour. Thus, our love for them does not dare to come to them with all the little foolishness and trifles with which we bother a friend who is a peer, and in so bothering him find our good fortune with him. A brother is a born friend, but the blood relationship has a sort of right to love. It appears, therefore, as an obligation and does not give the unforeseen joy that love given to us voluntarily by an outsider does. However pure, great or unselfish sibling love is, it does not completely satisfy our existence, and honourable siblings often give it to us even without

---

73. Wesley, *Works*, 3:150.
74. Bethge, *Friendship and Resistance*, 80.
75. Bethge, *Friendship and Resistance*, 81–82.

our doing anything to earn it. Friendship really completes the circle of happiness and gives us (however fine and good the friend really is) the assurance of our own value. An unworthy person has only accomplices, not friends.[76]

What Bonhoeffer seeks to say is that friendship is very important in life. Friendship has some liberality and freedom attached to it, a kind of expectation that is outside what is expected in families. For him, family members cannot be our friends as such, although they are obliged to show some loyalty to us. Friendship exists in a relationship where there is deepening trust in which freedom and love promote a sense of value and become fulfilled in the circles of happiness. Friendship also admits a little foolishness and triviality.

Bonhoeffer in his 1927 doctoral thesis, *Sanctorum Communio: Eine dogmatische Untersuchung zur Soziologie der Kirche* describes friendship as an ecclesiological issue—a life that the Christian should live. For Bonhoeffer, the I-Thou relationship between a human being and God is analogous to the relationship between the neighbor, the friend, and the stranger. He adds, "the individual becomes a person ever and again through the other; in the 'moment'. The other person presents us with the same challenge to our knowing as does God. My real relationship to another person is oriented to my relationship with God."[77] Individualism destroys the essence of the Church.[78] For him, the other ought to be always regarded in one's thinking and functioning without trying to compel that person to be like an abstract idea in one's mind.[79] It is in the act of giving oneself to the other that our true humanity is affirmed. In Bethge's words,

> Bonhoeffer sees that friendship cannot be defined according to interests, goals and purposes, which could be institutionally codified and then also protected, whether by professionals or groups. Rather, it can be defined only by what binding content exists between two people. This content can be very different individually. The different kinds of content give friendships their individual character and intensity. For that reason, they must remain free.[80]

---

76. Bethge, *Friendship and Resistance*, 90.
77. Bonhoeffer, "Sanctorum Communio," 55–56.
78. DBW 11, 145.
79. DBW 1, 29–31.
80. Bethge, *Friendship and Resistance*, 92.

Friendship is therefore understood not as something that is exclusive or individualistic, but rather necessitates relationship, care, community, and freedom.

Bonhoeffer sees friendship on two levels: friends in the plural, and friends in the singular. Friends in the plural can be understood as a circle made up of many brothers and sisters—as well as their friends—that can meet their needs for stimulation, entertainment, and competition. He specifically mentions friends for a common purpose, such as for hiking and traveling, professional colleagues, fellow lovers of music, like-minded allies, and co-experimenters with liturgy and monasticism.[81] In a sense, some within the family and beyond who offer support systems are part of the group of friends in the plural. That does not mean Bonhoeffer saw family members as being strictly part of the circle of friends. To Bethge, "absolute reliability is not an unconditional element of family relationships. But it is one of friendship, and in this they formed a unity, in which family strengthened the friendship element and friendship strengthened the family element."[82]

Friends in the singular were particular individuals, whether family members, younger people, or in fraternities, each maintaining their independence in unique ways. Such friends could even enter into heated debates and still remain best friends.[83] Bonhoeffer asserts that "the human heart is created in such a way that it seeks and finds refuge in the singular rather than in the plural . . .There are individual relationships without loyalty and loyalty without individual relationships. Both are to be found in the plural."[84] In other words, building individual friends can be more rewarding than striving for group friendships. Bethge explains that the kind of friendship Bonhoeffer espouses is not defined by theological or christological notions or an understanding of *agapē*. "The conception flows out of an act of accepting a gift and not from the arduousness of dogmatic logical deductions or from the exegesis of the biblical *philia*."[85] In that sense, matters of erotic love cannot find space in Bonhoeffer's view of friendship. Bonhoeffer did not believe that couples could remain friends because there are recognized rights expected from each other.

---

81. Bethge, *Friendship and Resistance*, 83.
82. Bethge, *Friendship and Resistance*, 84.
83. Bethge, *Friendship and Resistance*, 86.
84. Bethge, *Friendship and Resistance*, 88.
85. Bethge, *Friendship and Resistance*, 88.

Bonhoeffer shows a deep appreciation for honest and sincere friendship because he holds that it contributes to the full flourishing of human life. Friendship is a personal encounter with the "other" in communality or community. Bonhoeffer thus sees communality as a crucial part of what it means to be a friend. He feels that the church is designed to display a visible concern for communality and therefore should promote friendship. He is of the view that Christians ought not to live in seclusion but as people living among other people and should not take the privilege of living in the midst of other Christians for granted.[86] To be in community is from the grace of God. Friendship within the Christian community should constitute freedom.

Bonhoeffer emphasizes the principle of freedom in a poem from Tegel prison—a birthday gift for Bethge in August 1944, titled "The Friend." An excerpt goes:[87]

> Not from the heavy soil
> where blood and ancestry and oath
> are powerful and sacred,
> where the earth itself
> guards and protects and avenges
> the consecrated ancient orders
> against madness and wickedness—
> not from the heavy soil of earth,
> but from free affection
> and the spirit's free desires,
> needing no oath or legal bond,
> friend is given to friend.

In essence, when people enter into a relationship based on an oath or legal bond, that cannot constitute friendship. To liv e with the "other" in friendship requires a level of trust, affection, and vulnerability that is rooted in freedom, and not toward ill feelings and wickedness.

Bonhoeffer emphasizes the ethic of intercession in friendship. The intercessor is more than a brother to the friend. It takes a friendly heart to spend time praying for another:

> A Christian fellowship lives and exists by the intercession of its members for one another, or it collapses. I can no longer condemn or hate a brother for whom I pray, no matter how much trouble he causes me. His face, that hitherto may have been

---

86. Bonhoeffer, *Life Together*, 27.
87. Bethge, *Friendship and Resistance*, 99.

> strange and intolerable to me, is transformed in intercession into the countenance of a brother for whom Christ died, the face of a forgiven sinner. Intercessory prayer is the purifying bath into which the individual and the fellowship must enter every day . . . Intercession means no more than to bring our brother into the presence of God, to see him under the cross of Jesus . . . Then everything in him that repels us falls away; we see him in all his destitution and need . . . To make intercession means to grant our brother the same right that we have received, namely, to stand before Christ and share in his mercy.[88]

For Bonhoeffer, friendship is about doing good to another and standing in for the other. Doing good is contrary to being vicious, lawless, and scandalous. Rather, it involves a wide range of actions from "purely external observance of good order to the most intimate self-examination and character-formation and to personal self-sacrifice for the most sublime human values."[89] Intercession has to do with speaking on behalf of another, whether an individual, a group, a situation, or a community. Through intercession, we make sacrifices of ourselves and our time so that the other can be built up in an act of love.

In all, what Bonhoeffer seeks to advocate is that friendship is best seen in the qualities of a loyal wife. Ideally, there are expectations on family members to act in certain ways and those acts cannot be adequately seen arising from friendship. There is trust and freedom in friendship and the relationship allows some trivialities. Friends make one another better. When we give ourselves to others, we become what God created us to be. So, friendship contributes immensely to the flourishing of human life. It is expected of people not to live in seclusion but in community, and friends live to intercede for each other.

A CONTEMPORARY NOTION OF FRIENDSHIP

Basically, the assumption that when the word "friend" or "friendship" is used, it connotes true friendship is not true. The sample drawn in the foregoing shows that everyone means something different when talking about friendship. The reader should therefore decipher what type of friendship is assumed. I have also established that intimate friendship is a personal and voluntary relationship but one cannot live without it. To begin, it

88. Bonhoeffer, *Life Together*, 86.
89. Bonhoeffer, *Ethics*, 62.

behooves friends to know each other well. The degree of knowledge will determine whether the relationship is on the level of an intimate/bosom friend, best friend, close friend, family friend, friend of convenience/situational friend, ordinary/casual friend, fair-weather friend, toxic friend, or fake friend. The differences matter. Inadequate knowledge of a friend will not help one be careful in relating with the other.

The terms "friend" and "friendship" involve or describe a wide range of relationships. It is held that friendship is a personal and voluntary relationship that involves degrees of intimacy. It is grounded in concern for each other. Each degree determines what kind or category of friend the other is. Hence, there are the companion, soulmate, comrade, associate, ally, supporter, mate, intimate associate, and close acquaintance. It can extend to relationships between a master and a servant or family members.

"Friendship" is different from "love" and has its limits, so there is nothing like perfect friendship. Friendship is indispensable in life. If a human being is to be a real person, then there must be friendship. Friendship is a kind of non-passionate, affectionate love. It aims at the well-being of the other. Unhealthy friendships and relationships are like cancer. They can eat a person up, destroy, and even kills a person.

The ancient philosophers saw friendship as for individuals with equal status or between nations. The recognition that friendship is an exchange of virtuous actions and that friendly affection must become proportionate disqualifies those who cannot give in equal measure. What is equally difficult to accept is that if one person becomes incurably vicious, friendship breaks down. However, it is possible that even though one friend is deficient in a particular virtue, the other can improve the friend through help and guidance. The principle of reciprocity that lies at the heart of friendship makes the expectations in the relationship a kind of duty; without this a person fails to qualify as a friend. Charity is one of the key requirements in friendship.

Virtue friendship causes justice to reign. Friendship is human companionship and aims at making life complete. If one does not feel the suffering of a friend nor will sacrifice for a friend rather than betray them, that person is not a friend at all. Although friendship has a hedonistic starting point, as it matures, it does not become a means to our own happiness, but the happiness of all. There should be the unfeigned loyalty and mutual affection of good and true friends.

A bitter argument between friends should not break the relationship, since friends can have some disagreement among themselves. They agree to disagree so that harmony is more meaningful. Disagreements between friends are not seen in angry outbursts but in the love of helping the other to realize what the other sees. Since a friend can lead the other astray.

True friendship can be cultivated where there is a spirit and a heart that is ready to accept the other no matter what, reconcile, and forge relationships to create a beloved community. Even where the other is not ready for a communal relationship, the essence of embrace and love can spark a light of transformation and help friendship to grow. Friendship is not a selfish desire but that which promotes community. It springs from a genuine concern for the other and proceeds willingly. Friendship is crucial in times of great misfortunes. If there are some friends available in times of need, one can cope. True friends are expected to stand by each other in trouble and in joy with determined constancy. Friendship, meant to meet the needs of others, can be likened to hospitality. It can begin with unmotivated kindness.

Friendship is not permanent. As such, there can be times when the friendship relationship can be discontinued. Where some challenges erupt to affect the relationship, the ability to manage the challenges and hold on to one another makes a person a good friend. To be friends requires opening up to penetrating interaction, exposing the strengths and weaknesses of each other. Spousal friendship is possible and is a key aspect of marriage. A man and a woman can be friends even where there is no sexual association.

Friendship is an act of grace extended through sharing. It comes freely to those who do not deserve it. God created humanity to show acts of charity and to be gracious to one another. Individual acts of charity dispose us to become better friends since charity erodes selfishness. In Christian friendship, if one party has no fear of God, the loss the other accrues will be far greater than the gain. Friendship can be renewed through spiritual bonding.

Friendship comes with a price. It calls for laying one's life down for the other, not counting how the other will be willing to lay down their life. Being nonjudgmental does not mean relating with people who do what is unacceptable in the relationship. As long as friends share fellowship and build each other up, those who come with bad attitudes may end up badly influencing those with good attitudes. The desire to boost one's status makes people hide behind the curtains of technology to make friends they never wanted to associate with in the first place. One can have a friend online yet would not like to share what is essential to life with that person.

THE SEVEN VIRTUES OF TRUE FRIENDSHIP

If a person cannot show love, it does not mean that person cannot be a friend or have a friend. If a person is not thinking as one expects, there might be another quality the person possesses that the other can benefit from. Friendship fills the gap and provides both human companionship and the security needed by humanity.[90] That is to say, a person is not an island but needs others. To be fully human, there must be a relationship with others. Friendship, thus, involves a mutual relationship between parties in such a way that neither can lay claim to a neutral standpoint. In this sense, one cannot call the other a friend when the other person is not ready to be a friend. P. Wright seems more comprehensive when he says that friendship is a "voluntary or unrestrained interaction in which the participants respond to one another personally, that is, as unique individuals rather than as packages of discrete attributes or mere role occupants."[91]

A person's identity as a human being is enhanced through friendship. Thus, it is necessary to relate with those who help to build virtuous personalities and not bad reputations. If friendship is founded on virtue, then one must make friends with those who promote similar virtues. It is said, "birds of the same feathers flock together." According to Roberts-Griffin, "people tend to like other people that are similar to themselves."[92] As such, friends should be selective in those they walk with or the behaviors and lifestyles the other brings into the relationship. To be selective, one has to adopt the attitude of being judgmental. One cannot say "It's not up to me to judge anybody" and so move along with people who practice what is unacceptable to the relationship. Being "nonjudgmental" means you do not find anything wrong with what others do because it is their life. As long as friends share fellowship and build each other up, those who come into the friendship relationship with bad actions may end up influencing those with good actions.

Let us turn to the seven virtues that characterize true friendship.

First, true friends know themselves and each other very well. Looking at a friend as if a reflection of the self, however, will not work for

---

90. Turner, "Epicurus and Friendship," 353.
91. Wright, "Self-Referent Motivation and the Intrinsic Quality of Friendship," 115–30.
92. Roberts-Griffin, "What Is a Good Friend," 3.

ordinary or casual friends. Casual friendship assumes that all friends are friends, and relationships are on a superficial level. In such cases, it is difficult to know much about a friend. Significantly, when it comes to intimate friends, close friends, and bosom friends, the expectation is that each one knows the other very well. Such friendship involves a considerable amount of bonding and care, while casual friends and ordinary friends exist for mere social interaction. There are also fair-weather friends, i.e., people who continue as friends when things are going on smoothly and shy away when life is rough. Since they are not reliable, it is disheartening to rely on them. In essence, one must know who such fair-weather friends are. People may call others their friends as long as they stay close by within a particular community. Others claim the neighbor who is known is a friend as long as there is no problem between the two. Friends could be those whom one plays with or who stick around all the time. It could also be those who care or are willing to help. Knowing who a friend is can serve as a guide to the level of involvement and sharing in friendship relationships.

Second, there should be an element of intimacy between true friends. The relationship between love and friendship has always been very difficult to discern. William Rawlins differentiates between five distinct love styles. These are friendship, platonic love, friendship love, physical love, and romantic love. He argues that friendship is "a voluntary, mutual, personal and affectionate relationship devoid of expressed sexuality." Platonic love is an even deeper sense of intimacy and emotional commitment without sexual activity. Friendship love, which is the interplay between friendships and sexual relationships, is often characterized by the use of terms such as "boyfriend" and "girlfriend" as distinguishing characteristics to denote paired romantic attachments. Physical love tends to involve high levels of sexual intimacy with levels of relationship commitment, while romantic love revolves around sexual intimacy.[93] In all love depends on how chooses to define it. And intimacy has to do with a feeling of closeness and connection. The other should feel that the closeness of a friend is an expression of love.

Friendship has to do with social interactions such as communicating—verbally and/or non-verbally—at least once with another person. However, "friendship" suggests a deeper, more meaningful connection that may include intimacy and shared love. This means that what

---

93. Rawlins, "Cross-Sex Friendship and the Communicative Management of Sex-Role Expectations," 343–52.

friendship offers is deeper than all social relationships. According to Dennis Annis, friends seek each other out, and enjoy each other's company. They share beliefs and values and are open to sharing experiences.[94] Friendship is necessary for our existence in a community, but it is very important to live a human life fully. Friendship affirms our worth and self-esteem, adding something important to our lives.[95] Friendship requires that people perform some special duties for their family members and community, the failure of which leads to being seen as not caring. Paying attention to another person at the expense of one's spouse or children is considered to be unacceptable because there must be some preferential treatment among some types of friends. When a friend does not live up to expectations, we see a breach of understanding.[96]

Friendship does not use sexual fulfillment as its measure of happiness. It seems people tend to portray that happiness and fulfillment are achieved through romantic relationships. But it is true that some have ended up in regret after a long bout of romantic sharing. Friendship rather exerts a powerful impact on relationships and well-being for its own sake. It is said that good friends add special meaning to life. They are there to help in sharing good times and to overcome difficult ones. They can elevate one's spirit and boost one's mood. In the view of Dana Robert, friendship is like a mustard seed that is planted. It starts small and grows over time, even though there are times when weeds of personal failures and social injustice can compete with it and grow alongside it.[97] Ideally, a friend is a trustworthy person who shares a deep level of understanding and love.

Third, loyalty is expected from true friends. When two people become friends, the hierarchical strings break down. Both are expected to come to the level of the other. Rawlins posits that friendship is pervaded by what he calls "the spirit of equality,"[98] in which friends emphasize attributes that make them appear more or less equal to each other, but fail to recognize and address the differences between complementary and symmetrical relationships. He explains that whereas friendship is a private and voluntary interpersonal relationship, society or the public enforce a certain framework that guides the making of friendship in a socially acceptable manner. The dialectic of the ideal and the real, according to

---

94. Annis, "Meaning, Value, and Duties of Friendship," 349.
95. Annis, "Meaning, Value, and Duties of Friendship," 351.
96. Annis, "Meaning, Value, and Duties of Friendship," 353, 354.
97. Robert, *Faithful Friendship*, 83.
98. Rawlins, *Friendship Matters*, 9.

Rawlins, connects with how friends deal with the tension between the cultural ideals associated with friendship, and the real nature of their relationship. In this sense, it is possible for the real demands of a friend to cause another to break cultural laws and expectations in an attempt to help the friend.[99]

From the Western perspective, C. S. Lewis differentiates between friendship and companionship. He says companionship is cooperation and mutual respect rather than a form of love, and he likens that to people who come together at golf clubs, mess halls, and bars. For him, companionship is an important type of relationship, while friendship is a love that involves more than one person who is absorbed in a common interest.[100] Companionship is when two or more people discover that "they have in common some insight or interest or even taste which the others do not share" and "instantly they stand together in an immense solitude."[101] However, he is aware that the foundation of all levels of friendship is companionship. It seems Lewis is concerned about the levels of friendship and assumes that only close, intimate, bosom friends are true friends. However, platonic, casual, or ordinary friendship is implied, in the view of Lewis, when he says that we become someone's friend without knowing or caring about that person's past, previous history, profession, or family.[102]

Some friends are dependable while others are not. Neera K. Badhwar mentions instrumental friendship and end friendship. She argues that instrumental friendship is based on features that are tangential to the friend and is on what one can achieve, and that here a friend ceases to be useful if they cannot help the other achieve their goals. On the other hand, an end friendship is a relationship in which one loves and cares for the friend as the person is, and as an essential part of one's end.[103] Instrumental friendship cannot be said to promote loyalty, but end friendship promotes trustworthiness.

True friends must be sincere with each other. Any relationship that puts pressure on the other in such a way that the freedom and will of that person is bound to a need is not an ideal form of friendship. An individual, for the sake of friendship, cannot be a slave to necessity or the

---

99. Rawlins, *Friendship Matters*, 13–35.
100. Lewis, *Four Loves*, 61.
101. Lewis, *Four Loves*, 65.
102. Lewis, *Four Loves*, 70.
103. Badhwar, "Friends as Ends in Themselves," 1–23.

whims and expectations of another.[104] Real friendship does not promote making promises that call for absolute commitment, the failure of which brings pain.

With the premise that friendship is a human institution, I do not agree with Agnes Heller that there is something like perfect friendship: "Perfect friendship is morally good, and it is also beautiful; it contains and embodies the promise of happiness. It is where virtue and grace, possession and desire, coalesce. Friendship, not erotic love, is the beautiful human relationship."[105] As a human institution, it would be farfetched to expect a friend to be perfect, but one's sincerity should not be questioned.

Fourth, it behooves friends to support each other, since collaboration enhances true friendship. Collaboration stands for a cooperative alliance between two or more people toward a common goal. It is when people come together and contribute what will be of benefit to each other in a shared objective. It is about teamwork and bringing people together. It requires mutual support, as well as a willingness to stand by each other, and share ideas and knowledge. Good friends come up with ideas when one is exhausted. When good friends collaborate with each other on a task, it is seen as a learning experience that each party can make the most of.

Fifth, in true friendship, there should be empowerment from affective involvement with the other. Friendship has the tendency to motivate all parties and build up individuals, enhancing one's own self-image when the friend does well—although it can be demotivating when the friend fails in life. In the view of Campbell et al., "friendship allows and enables both persons to be self-enhancing without fear of negative consequences for an already secure relationship. Friends may tolerate, even promote, each other's self-enhancement strivings with a resulting mutually beneficial psychological outcome (e.g., increased individual self-esteem)."[106]

Sixth, there should be an amount of goodwill expected of true friends. Friendship cannot exist as a covenantal agreement demanding specific rights and privileges. Hence, the expectations from friends are less demanding. Friendship usually starts as a temporary relationship and grows into a stronger relationship of trust. Not all friendships grow into responsible and mature relationships. As such, friendship does not

---

104. Hilton, "Epicurus and Friendship," 353.
105. Heller, "Beauty of Friendship," 10.
106. Campbell et al., "Among Friends?" 232.

always lead to the time to "settle down" for a committed, mature relationship, such as marriage.

Friendship is seen as a reflection of the other self, an idea that is founded on "do unto others what you want others to do for you." A sign of goodwill in a friendship is when a person wishes good things for the other. Goodwill, then, can be a starting point of friendship although not all who have goodwill love each other, since a person may wish good things to those for whom they have goodwill but not do anything to help them nor be inconvenienced by them.

Bennett Helmm defines friendship as a "distinctively personal relationship that is grounded in a concern on the part of each friend for the welfare of the other, for the other's sake, and that involves some degree of intimacy."[107] Daniel Hruschka says friendship is "a social relationship in which partners provide support according to their abilities in times of need, and in which this behavior is motivated in part by positive affect between partners."[108] For John Reisman, it is "someone who likes and wishes to do well for someone else and who believes that these feelings and good intentions are reciprocated by the other party."[109] It is known, however, that some friends do what would hurt the other and may not mean good for the other. Others would not support a friend lower than their abilities.

Friendship, meant to meet the needs of others, can be likened to hospitality. In the view of Patricia Tull, "friendship often begins with the unmotivated kindness of one person toward another, a generous, uncalculated action offered simply from the joy of companionship."[110] Walter Donlan also sees hospitality as "guest-friendship" when he discusses the distinction between temporary and permanent hospitality. For him, temporary hospitality toward a stranger is "simple hospitality" since custom, reinforced by divine sanction, demands that any stranger who appeared at the door be given protection and sustenance. Permanent hospitality, on the other hand, is the formal bond of guest friendship and is like altruistic hospitality that does establish a continuing relationship.[111]

Finally, true friends are expected to walk together, stand together, and help each other toward a common purpose. Rawlins argues that

107. Helmm, "Friendship."
108. Hruschka, *Friendship*.
109. Reisman, *Anatomy of Friendship*, 94–95.
110. Tull, "Jonathan's Friendship," 142.
111. Donlan, *Aristocratic Ideal and Selected Papers*, 272.

friendship is an "institutionalized non-institution."[112] Friendship is by definition private and is something that is worked out between two people and cannot be forced upon anyone. However, there are strong societal and cultural expectations as to what a friendship is and means, and Rawlin's theory argues there is a dialectic between what society says a friendship should be (the public) and how two friends actually view their friendship (the private).

Hruschka claims that friendship reflects a capacity to cultivate corporate ties beyond parental and biological ties.[113] In fact, he thinks indigenous cultures maintain kinship beyond family relations and blood ties, but it is also known that friendship existed in those cultures. Friendship is more of a social and emotional response. It yields itself to attract like-minded people, align with them and cooperate with them. Such cooperation can fall within mutual benevolence, intimacy, love, and positive goals. "It involves mutual liking, prosocial behavior, companionship, and a relative lack of conflict."[114] However, it needs to be noted that an understanding of friendship based on mutuality and equality cannot work in all kinds of friendships. Some friends fail to walk closely with others. When a friend does not participate in a common cause that is before them in a friendship relationship, it does not mean that person ceases to be a friend. As Benedict Ssettuuma explains, "human relationships that are authentic and mutual, reciprocal and intimate, result into genuine friendships."[115]

The expectations one has for friends must be placed within a broader set of moral concerns. There are real friends and fake friends. Real friends are believed to empower each other and share in the satisfaction, security, and stock of each other. As such, real friends bring what they have to the table to share with one another for the common good. Bad friends do otherwise for their selfish interests. Fake friends are people who pose as friends for what they can benefit from, only to betray, hurt, or disappoint the other.

---

112. Rawlins, *Friendship Matters*, 9.
113. Hruschka, *Friendship: Development*, 77.
114. Hruschka, *Friendship*, 156.
115. Ssettuuma, "Friendship," 57.

CONCLUDING REMARKS

The seven key virtues that have been espoused in relation to true friendship are knowing each other well, intimacy, loyalty, collaboration, empowerment, goodwill, and common purpose. These seven virtues may not be all that it takes, but I find these to be the basic, running through the exploration made above. Note that one cannot be perfect in all these virtues. Again, friendships, at every stage in life, come with a complex set of dialectical contradictions that challenge the nature of a relationship. The ability to withstand challenges and hold on to the other makes a person a good friend. Every notion of friendship must consider some dialectics: how human imperfections come to play in relationships, how each appreciates certain virtues, and how the ideal and the real are understood. It is easy to talk about friendship as an enduring cultural ideal, but real-life experiences can make it an elusive reality. Also, there is tension between seeing a friendship as an end in itself or as a means to another end. Hence, the guiding principles can be the reason for having a friend, when to be a friend, and to what end. In other words, it needs to be established whether the relationship is for a reason, a season, or treason.

6

The Case of Eliphaz, Bildad, and Zophar as Friends

In the book of Job, the three—Eliphaz the Temanite, Bildad the Shuhite, and Zophar the Naamathite—are specifically described as friends of Job. Generally, critics see the three as bad friends because of what they say to Job and how they say it. The three do not believe in Job and vigorously urge him to accept their point of view. Such categorization as "bad friends" cannot paint a holistic picture of what the story seeks to teach. Although in the epilogue God's verdict was that the three did not speak well about God, rather than about Job (42:7), it does not make them bad friends. A critical look at the three from an African perspective of friendship, in my view, can reveal that they may not be totally bad friends although Job did not approve of what they did. The issue is, when did the strongly held opinions of friends make them bad friends? Why should friends holding a different perspective, even from ignorance, fall into the category of bad friends? In what way does an argument between friends make one party bad? Should friends always share the same point of view? I contend that the inadequate knowledge or one-sided perspective of the three some good qualities of friendship.

CATEGORIZATION OF THE THREE FRIENDS

The root $r'h$ and its cognates occur 172 times in the Hebrew Bible. In the book of Job, the noun $rēa'$ ("friend") and its cognates occur 14 times. It is commonly interpreted as "friend" (2:11; 6:27; 12:4; 16:20; 17:5; 19:21; 32:3; 42:7, 10), "companion" (30:29; 35:4), and "neighbor" (16:21; 31:9, 19). John Hartley assumes that the friendship between Job and the three is based on a covenant (6:14–15, 21–23, 27),[1] a view that is not stated explicitly in the text.

The storywriter describes the three as *šělošēt rēʿêʾiyyōb* (2:11), popularly translated as "Job's three friends." The phrase *šělošēt rēʿêʾiyyōb* may be read in various ways: "Three friends of Job," or "Three of Job's Friends," bearing in mind that *šělošēt* is an adjective construct and *rēʿê* is a noun construct. I agree with Robert Alden, that it is better to read "three of Job's friends" than the usual "Job's three friends" to show that Job had many friends and these three, in particular, made it here in the story.[2] The three are from different places,[3] but all within the Mesopotamian region. Hence, the story is not Jewish. The references to geography and history relate to northern Arabia. Like Abraham who comes from Ur in the land of the Chaldeans (Gen 11:20), Job and his three friends know and worship Yahweh, the Creator God of the whole earth.

The three are believed to be professional wise men from the east, with Habel linking them with Edom or its associated regions.[4] Edom is noted for its wisdom (Jer 49:7; Obad 1:8). Job is from the land of Uz (1:1), a place closely linked with Edom (Gen 36:28; Lam 4:21). R. H. Pfeiffer mentions the presence of Edomite wisdom traditions,[5] while Victor Sasson notes that there was Yahweh worship in Edom, arguing from an inscription written on a bowl found in Hovat ʿUza in Northern Neveg that looks like a parallel version of Job 27:10–17.[6] If the three are friends of Job by virtue of their profession as wise men, then Job might also be a wise man. Colleagues in the same profession are said to be ordinary friends. However, the three show how close they were to Job when they heard about what had happened to him, even though they were separated by distance, indicating that they were not merely colleagues.

1. Hartley, Job, 85.
2. Alden, *Job*, 68.
3. Scholars are not sure about the exact location of the places of origin of the three friends. The name Teman occurs in the genealogies of Edom (Gen 36:4, 15). Elsewhere in Jeremiah 49:7, Teman is described as a place noted for wisdom. The geographical sites for Shuah and Naamath do not occur in the Hebrew Bible. The character Shuah is the son of Abraham and Keturah (Gen 25:2).
4. Habel, *Book of Job*, 19.
5. Pfeiffer, "Edomite Wisdom," 13–25.
6. Sasson, "Edomite Joban Text," 601–15.

As friends, they were in close proximity in thought, and concerned about the well-being of each other. They were not minding their own business or disconnected from each other's lives. Certainly, true friends must think about each other, stay in touch, and meet. They show intimacy, compassion, and goodwill, knowing that showing real presence makes friendship grow.

The three make high demands on Job and even make it difficult for him to meet their demands. Making demands from friends fits into the African worldview, but may not be so in other contexts. Jürgen Moltmann, for instance, analyzing friendship from a Western perspective, argues that friendship is a personal relationship that makes no claims. He adds that there are no compulsions in the relationship, for a "friend" is not an official category, a title of sovereignty, nor a function that is exercised only for a certain period of time.[7] Moltmann's view is inconsistent with African thought because it is rather friends who have to demand compliance from each other. Much as friendship is personal, voluntary, and non-permanent; it is a commitment that lays ethical and moral claims. A friend has the right to insist that the other lives in a particular way and follows a particular path so that the friendship can stand. To introduce someone as a friend from the African perspective is to make an official claim and expect people to accept such identification as someone who influences behavior. It is said in Akan, *kyerɛ me wo nyenko na menkyerɛ wo wo suban* ("show me your friend and I will show you your character"). Friendship is not simply by name; it is in action and character. Habel rightly notes that in the Hebrew Bible, "a 'friend' (*reaʽ*) is characterized by deep loyalty and close bonds of faithfulness (*hesed*)."[8] That is to say, friendship is based on how an individual knows the other, the level of intimacy and loyalty, and motivated by how they collaborate, help each other, and follow a common path.

It seems likely that these three of the friends of Job are also friends to one another; they know each other. Perhaps it reinforces the idea that the friends of our friends are our friends. They are from different countries yet are in contact with each other—*wayyābo'ûʾîš mimməqomô* "and they came each man from his place" (2:11). Each of them comes from a different place, but the close contact solidifies their friendship. The phrase *yaḥddāw lābōʾ* "they came together" (2:11) connotes an arranged

---

7. Moltmann, *Living God and the Fullness of Life*, 118.
8. Habel, *Book of Job*, 97.

THE CASE OF ELIPHAZ, BILDAD, AND ZOPHAR AS FRIENDS 117

meeting at an appointed place. The verb *lābo'* is a *qal* infinitive construct, giving an impression of constant commitment or agreement in a form of an oath. It is not indicated how they hear about Job's affliction, but as long as good friends are concerned about each other, they usually try to stay in contact. That is why they hear about what is happening to Job. Friends find time to collaborate with each other. Upon hearing the calamity that has befallen Job, they contact each other and agree to meet and visit Job. The Akan say, *Yɔnko-yɔnko na ɛma asɛm trɛ* ("Friend–friend spreads the news wider"). In other words, when a friend hears what has happened to another, it behooves the friend to tell a friend, and the other friend will tell a friend, making the news spread faster among each other. That is what friends are for.

The three travel together to meet Job. They do not stay in their homes and send messages to Job that they were praying for him. They decide to do what friends do by visiting their friend periodically. The three sacrifice their own personal time for their friend, leaving their jobs and families behind to spend time with Job. The three decide to go and console and comfort their friend (2:11). Such a thought shows how close friends can reach out to one another and plan together for the sake of their friend. Even if the thought may have come from an individual, eventually the three decide that the best course of action is to show up together as one group. Among the Akan, to say "please, remember me to him" means one cannot meet the expectations of being a good friend. Such a pronouncement is not the same as *yɛnkɔ* [backwards c character] "let's go" (semantically similar to *yɔnko/yɔnkoɔ* "friend"). That is to say, it is unacceptable to give excuses for not visiting a friend in times of need.

SYMBOLIC EXCHANGES AMONG THE FRIENDS

Eliphaz, Zophar, and Bildad show some intimacy through their actions and words when they meet their friend, Job. When they see Job from a distance, they do not recognize him, perhaps due to the effect of the illness. When they finally identify him, they "raised their voices and wept aloud" (2:12). The three are deeply sorry for Job and express sad emotions. The Hebrew *lanûd-lô*, translated as "sympathy" or "console," literally means "to shake the head" (cf. Isa 51:19; Jer 16:5; 18:16; 48:17). Maybe, the three shake their heads in disbelief and disappointment. They doubt the reality and are in disagreement with the predicament. Perhaps, the denial of reality reflects how they have known him in the past and echoes how the three are beginning to disagree with Job while expressing their disappointment. Sympathy, as contrasted with empathy, makes a person look at another with pity and puts the struggling person in a place of judgment more than understanding. Sympathy is a way of showing care but also keeps one at an appropriate distance. Empathy, on the other hand, is accepting and listening without judgment, and seeing oneself in another person's struggle. It is connectedness and understanding that encourages those struggling to feel motivated because they are not alone.

The three also show solidarity with Job. Ancient traditions reveal how people tear their clothes and put dust and ashes on their heads in times of sorrow and grief (2 Sam 3:31; 1 Kgs 21:27; Neh 9:1; Jer 49:3; Ezek 27:31; Lam 2:10; Jon 3:5–9). When the adversary first strikes Job and destroys all of his property, Job tears his robe and puts dust on his head (1:20). The three do likewise (2:12). The three, however, do something unusual. Instead of simply placing dust upon their head (Josh 7:6, Ezek 27:30, Lam 2:10), they toss it upward. Eliphaz, Zophar, and Bildad stay with Job on the ground and spend time with him. Good friends usually manage to identify with each other, laugh, or cry together. The three sit with Job for at least seven days and nights (2:13), thus showing their willingness to be with Job as long as he needs them. Instead of delivering words of comfort, they fall short of words, expressing solidarity through silence for seven days. Frank Delitzsch argues that "their long silence shows that they had not fully realized the purpose of their visit. Their feeling is overpowered by reflection, their sympathy by dismay."[9] Alternatively, David Atkinson sounds more convincing when he sees the silence of the three as that of compassion since a silent presence is more eloquent than words.[10] Actually, these are friends who do what they can to identify with Job, who was silent. Their condoling presence, however, cannot abate Job's dimming greatness.[11] Francis Andersen also sees the silence as an act of compassion for Job who sat down in ashes.[12]

Silence, however, has multiple meanings. It can set in when one is in shock. The massive traumatic sight and shock renders the three friends speechless. Silence can be a way for people to organize their thoughts and give meaning to experiences. Silence is a therapeutic communication

9. Delitzsch, *Job*, 75.
10. Atkinson, *Message of Job*, 30.
11. Janzen, *Job*, 60.
12. Andersen, *Job*, 142.

technique, but it also tends to influence evil thoughts. Bruce Knight believes there are many forms, experiences, and occasions for silence, welcomed or unwelcomed. Silence can be moments of intentional solitude when we experience the awe of spiritual awakening and intimacy.[13] Also, there is that moment of silence that comes before the storm of shock, anger, bargaining, depression, and acceptance when first we realize that something valuable to us has died. Silence becomes a reaction when one feels overwhelmed, sinking in the shame of a relationship-destructive behavior, and fights back a watershed of tears. The silencing power of shame and the silence that comes from the dawning realization of pain, loss, and death can be devastating. "Whether the silence is unwanted, unwelcome, desired, treasured, avoided, or embraced, it is a reality of the human condition, a teacher of the soul, if we allow ourselves to embrace it with a curious mind and willing heart."[14]

Furthermore, silence is one of the therapeutic ways of affirming one's presence. It can also influence calmness, and lead to healing. There is complete articulation and communication in silence. Silence might not always be used as a way of showing consent, for it can convey an act of dissent. Maria Sifiano argues that silence can function as a tool in the exercise of power and adds that "in general, remaining silent in order to avoid acts which clearly jeopardize the addressee's face indicates consideration and is thus polite."[15] Still, Guilaine Kinouani, from a psychological perspective, describes silence as an instrument of violence, to smother unpalatable voices, or to stop one from expressing unbearable content, and keep the same out of conscious awareness.[16]

Keeping silent for seven days and nights, however, may be highly irregular and may serve as a rhetorical plot to reveal the character of the three friends. When the three friends begin to speak in the dialogue section of the story, they cannot speak words of comfort, thus affirming what the author wants to portray. Still, silence is key to the unspoken world of the patient. In the face of trauma, the cessation of speech can be contrasted with the disintegration of language into sounds such as screams and sighs.[17] The three may have wanted to protest but were taken aback. Their silence is louder than words and gives a good impression

13. Knight, "Voices."
14. Knight, "Voices."
15. Sifiano, "Do We Need to Be Silent to Be Extremely Polite?" 103.
16. Kinouani, "Silencing, Power and Racial Trauma in Groups," 145–61.
17. Ritter, "Silence as the Voice of Trauma," 176–94.

of them. It cannot be that when they start speaking that they show their true value.

It happens that people's first inclination in an emotional situation is to say something to make the situation better. They get agitated and fill the dead air with the sound of their voice or even weep with those who are weeping. Nevertheless, it is known that in moments of pain, anger, and suffering, people often speak at the wrong time and choose the wrong words. The three recognize from the moment they arrive on the scene that Job is not ready to process words. So, they simply sat there with him and express their empathy through silence.

Before Eliphaz, Zophar, and Bildad arrive on the scene, Job consoles himself by taking a potshed to scratch himself and sitting among ashes (2:8). He is not yet ready to give up. The rhetorical question to his wife, "shall we receive the good at the hand of God and not receive the bad?" (2:10), is ironically an act of confidence and resilience. He is ready to embrace his situation and not throw his hands in the air in desperation. Such an expression fits how the three come to see Job and then introduce the impact it has on them. How Job managed to motivate himself into accepting all that has befallen him is certainly a lesson that can be explored. The three come to Job, however, weeping in loud voices (2:12). Significantly, Job had already torn his robes (1:20), and the three identify with him by tearing theirs also. The ritual performance of raising the voice to weep and throwing dust in the air shows the difference between the three and Job, and marks the three as not true friends. While Job is in the mood for self-comforting, the three are not able to comfort themselves. Gary Anderson explains that comfort "does not connote a simple act of emotional identification. Comfort can imply either a symbolic action of *assuming the state of mourning* alongside the mourner, or it can have the nuance of *bringing about the cessation of mourning*."[18] The day of the Lord can bring comfort to all who mourn so that they receive the oil of gladness instead of a mourning garment (Isa 61:2, 10). Isaac ceases mourning when his Rebekah comforts him (Gen 24:67), and Ephraim after being comforted by his brothers has sexual relations with his wife and has a son (1 Chr 7:22–23). Xuan Pham also explains that comforting can be done in two ways: "by identifying with the mourner through participating in the mourning rites; and, secondly, by speaking to the

---

18. Anderson, *Time to Mourn and a Time to Dance*, 84; emphasis original.

THE CASE OF ELIPHAZ, BILDAD, AND ZOPHAR AS FRIENDS 121

mourner, giving him or her advice on how to get over his or her pain."[19] Job shaving his head is a mourning rite (1:20; cf. Jer 7:29, Mic 1:16), but falling in worship is not necessarily a mourning rite. The histapel verb *wayyištṭāḥûʿ* (meaning "and he prostrated himself in worship") does not connote mourning, although one can worship in sadness. However, Job sitting on the ash heap is a clear sign of mourning, yet he does not use a sackcloth. While Job is not ready to give up and cease mourning, the three had already given up. The three in some aspect fail from the onset to be a source of empowerment.

There are varied opinions given about the ritual of weeping and throwing dust into the air. Delitzsch supports a spiritualization of the actions of the three and claims they were crying to heaven.[20] As such, it was a form of protest. Habel is very sympathetic when he opines that the three wanted to empathize with Job and identify with his boils, hence their weeping.[21] Yet to weep loudly would naturally make the sufferer also weep. Robert Gordis, however, goes too far when he claims these actions are more magical gestures toward themselves about the evil that has come on Job than acts of sympathy.[22] Also, Gerald Janzen sees the friends' attitude toward Job as similar to that "portrayed in Ezekiel 3:15 and Ezra 9:3, where one is portrayed (without the dust) as being *appalled* over the fate announced over others (Ezekiel) or the judgment implicitly invoked on others by their actions (Ezra)."[23] In essence, they are stunned, disgusted, and already revolted, perhaps using some cultural practices.

If the actions of the three in a way seem to portray people who are dejected, depleted, and disappointed, then they were not on the side of Job who was quiet and had accepted that fate. Though there is some plausibility in the view that the friends were protesting, one should not lose sight of the fact that the sufferer is the object of consolation. Friends try to be with each other by following a common purpose and not reacting differently from one another. Some people react to issues that occur in the lives of their friends to accrue some advantage for themselves. They cry so that others will see that they are sad, and not support the sufferer. Alden is right in noting, "nowhere in the book did Job weep for himself;

---

19. Pham, *Mourning in the Ancient Near East and the Hebrew Bible*, 28.
20. Delitzsch, *Book of Job*, 74.
21. Habel, *Book of Job*, 76.
22. Gordis, *Book of Job*, 24.
23. Janzen, *Job*, 58–59; emphasis original

perhaps he was beyond that point of grief."[24] So, when the three act contrary to what Job stands for, they are doing so for themselves. It is not what sympathizers do that matters, for they were not there to perform for the mourner or to appease themselves. They had come to console the bereaved, the helpless, and the sick but eventually arrive without peace in their hearts. Job seems more at peace within than the three.

By performing their obligations to Job, mourning with him like a close companion, and providing counsel, Eliphaz, Zophar, and Bildad show they had good intentions, but missed the mark. Their identity as friends should not be taken for granted.[25] Hartley also mentions: "Friends often solemnized their relationship with a covenant, promising to care for each other under kinds of circumstances."[26] That is to say, the three stand true to their commitment to visit and comfort Job in the prologue. Their mere presence can be an act of comfort. It is friends who stick by one another during hard times who can be counted on. Trials and adversity can usually separate true friends from those who are just fair-weather friends. It is said, "a friend loves at all times, and a brother is born for a time of adversity" (Prov 17:17 NIV). Loyalty is a mark of true, close, and intimate friendship. There is something special about having an intimate friend whom one can confide in, explore troubles and joys with, and share life with. Someone who cannot show love, cannot be trusted. Someone who cannot stand with a sufferer in times of need is not a good friend. Such people may be seen as ordinary or casual friends.

The Three's Dialogue as Verbal Strategies

Eliphaz, Zophar, and Bildad show themselves as people whose emotional, intellectual, and religious capacities provide a platform to nurture a level of friendship with Job. Good friends share and listen to each other to build each other up with their words, while bad friends tear each other apart with their words. The value of true friendship is seen in terms of the non-verbal and verbal support each gives the other (Eccl 4:9–14). I emphasize that intimacy, loyalty, collaboration, empowerment, goodwill,

---

24. Alden, *Job*, 70.

25. The nature of the book of Job makes the real identity of the characters of the story complicated. Job and the three are depicted as wealthy aristocrats. Newsom ("Book of Job," 327) says such a depiction does not necessarily assume they were of that class. However, the friendship between the characters has never been an issue.

26. Hartley, *Book of Job*, 85.

and promoting similar values matter a lot in friendship. Though no two people share the same thought, good friends learn to agree to disagree.

First Cycle of Dialogue (4:1—14:22)

The motivation to enter into dialogue with Job expresses a view of friendship. It shows what friends are for, and certainly the nature of good people. C. White remarks that friends are not useful because "they stand by us in danger or provide us with various external benefits but because they are the means whereby we may be led to wisdom and truth."[27] In other words, the arguments of the three are expected to be lessons for Job to build himself up in wisdom and truth. Staying close to a friend is not enough unless the individual's presence can build up knowledge, wisdom, and power in the friend. Unfortunately, that is what the three failed to do. James Reynierse considers Job's friends as embarking on a systematic desensitization with a gradient of increasing intensity from the beginning of the dialogue to the end, to condition fear stimuli into Job.[28] Fear is a tool that breaks friendship relationships and destroys communality. Fear destroys intimacy, a key dynamic in bad friendships.

The Bible emphasizes "fear not" more, especially the unhealthy emotion of fear that is obnoxious and crippling, although there is the healthy experience of fear that helps people to confront the truth about their circumstances. Bill Arnold explains that fear has a broad lexical field that includes the nuance of respectful awe or reverence (Deut 1:21; 5:5), and obedience that will make people not act presumptuously again (13:11; 17:13; 19:20; cf. 21:21). "At one end of the spectrum stands a 'pathological anxiety' in the face of the threat, resulting in crippling inactivity. At the other end of the spectrum stands a positive course of action, which when used to characterize one's relationship with YHWH/God is a response of obedience or exclusive worship."[29] Arnold concludes his study on Deuteronomy 5–11 by saying that "Ancient Israel has here learned that 'love' and 'fear' are not, in fact, mutually exclusive, but complement each other, so that love prevents terror and fear prevents irreverent familiarity."[30] In fact, Job admits that what he feared has come upon him (3:25). To dispel

---

27. White, *Friendship in the Fourth Century*, 24.
28. Reynierse, "Behaviour Therapy and Job's Recovery," 189.
29. Arnold, "Love–Fear Antinomy in Deuteronomy 5–11," 563, 564.
30. Arnold, "Love–Fear Antinomy in Deuteronomy 5–11," 567.

such fear, a friend will have to make the one who is battling fear confront the fear. Even if the three's persistent calls to Job to accept his sins and recant are tools to instill fear in Job, the object is to help Job recover. Such a fear is not a destructive or crippling fear but that which translates into humility, submission, and openness. It is also not paralyzing inducement or discouragement but rather fear that leads to recovery and encouragement. The three were afraid of the unknown and were trying to prevent it in Job's life.

The tendency to see friendship only when soothing words are spoken can be a setback. Friendship is not only expressed in comforting words but also in healthy and positive confrontations. Lamentation is a legitimate part of spirituality. Those who go through challenges are expected to pour out laments to God, and the psalmist goes as far as to blame God for the cause of his woes (Pss 13:1–3; 22:1; 30:7–12; 102:23–24). A lament is an act of finding a voice to call to God for help in facing the vulnerabilities of life. It is an act of raising a complaint, confronting the fears that seem to overtake one in prayer, and offering the burdens to God in an open way based on who God is to the one in prayer. It gives an opportunity to break the silence and thoughts of giving up on God, to appeal and speak up with raw faith, naming and interpreting reality. Walter Brueggemann explains that a lament is "a profound yearning for a transformation that will end the unbearable reality of present arrangements."[31] To John Goldingay, laments are "expressions of pain and protest."[32]

Deryck Sheriffs argues that confrontation is part of intimacy and inherently evident in the journey of spirituality.[33] The three confront Job to recognize his own past and reconcile with himself. Janzen shares a similar thought when he notes, "on Eliphaz's behalf, it may be noted that in certain contexts the reminder of one's frailty, ignorance, and sinfulness may come as a distinct means of comfort in the form of acceptance of the way things are."[34] Within the context of confrontation, they share ideas with each other, with everyone standing their ground. The confrontation by the three, in a sense, was aimed at giving Job some hope, but Job saw it otherwise. According to Carol Newsom,

---

31. Brueggemann, "Lament as Wake Up Call," 221–36.
32. Goldingay, *Psalms*, 1:62.
33. Sheriffs, *Friendship of the Lord*, 210.
34. Janzen, *Job*, 118.

the friends offer Job not simply a story about the hope of the pious but rather a story incorporated into a religious practice is of the utmost importance. The practice, like the story, is oriented toward transformation, and so subordinates issues of explanation. Regardless of the reasons for the misfortune, there is always something one can do about the situation, and doing gives the sufferer a degree of agency. Thus the question "Why?" simply has less urgency. Moreover, the practice embodies a mimetic power that could not be achieved in narrative alone because it involves active imitation of the underlying order to which it refers. It bridges the now and the not yet of hope.[35]

What Carol Newsom wants to establish is that the story is meant to teach about how to transform the lives of people who are broken, suffering, and hopeless. What is done in such situations matters a lot and not the reasons why. A similar view is expressed by Bonhoeffer when he says that the Christian "must learn to regard people less in the light of what they do or omit to do, and more in the light of what they suffer."[36] Love is better seen in action than in words, but the tone of words can depict the actions intended.

Eliphaz indeed accuses Job of being impatient and inconsistent (4:2-6) while he concedes that Job has been a good friend and a source of strength to others (4:3-4):

A	Behold, you have	instructed	many
B	and you have	strengthened	the weak hands.
A1	Your words have	upheld	him who was stumbling,
B1	and you have	made firm	the feeble knees.

The repetition of the power of Job's words in subsequent lines in synonymous parallelism amplifies the extent of his support. The "many" in Line A are the weak. They are also those who are stumbling or have feeble knees. The weak hands mentioned here may not be literal (needed for work) but rhetorical (for defending oneself). Such people are further described as having feeble knees, connoting that they are not in a position to plead for themselves. The knees are symbols of pleading, prayer, and supplication. The prophet Isaiah picks up on such an analogy of strengthening weak knees, stating God will come with vengeance upon

---

35. Newsom, "Job and His Friends," 245-46.
36. Bonhoeffer, *Letters and Papers from Prison*, 10.

the enemies who are causing those problems (Isa 35:3–4). The prophet Isaiah's message is meant to produce hope in God's afflicted people in the midst of disappointment. Perhaps they could not pray to God because they could not see their way forward. Isaiah promised the people that they would experience new life and hoped that they would see the glory of God revealed. Such a message of hope is not about physical deliverance from Assyria and their return from exile to the Promised Land, but points to the future when God's glory will be revealed. A similar idea is echoed in Hebrews 12:12: "Therefore lift your drooping hands and strengthen your weak knees." The Greek *pareimenas cheiras* specifically connotes hands that hang down in the midst of fear or discouragement. The writer of Hebrews, perhaps quoting from Job and Isaiah, makes the point that even in a time of chastening, the believers should take strength and courage in the Lord with the hope that that Lord answers prayer, and knowing that they will be partakers of the goodness of God. In all, a heart of friendship positively drives the virtue of compassion, and care for the weak and stumbling.

Eliphaz's description of Job's generosity connotes virtues of solidarity and goodwill aimed at improving quality of life. Job's responses seem to help explore moods and behaviors, provide fresh perspectives on how one should be friendly to all, and offer a better understanding of shared emotions to address issues of depression, anxiety, psychosocial adjustment, antisocial behaviors, abuse, and conflict. Such people possess skills like self-awareness, active listening, and communication skills, as well as a specific mindfulness that is ready to support those who are weak. Job was thus an advocate for the weak. So, Job spent his time changing and transforming lives.

Norman Habel's thematic study on friendship in the book of Job focuses on Eliphaz, Bildad, and Zophar as patriarchal examples of true friendship, a view I disagree with.[37] Noting the variety of ways and the various levels friendship used in the Hebrew Bible, Habel finds in the three a true example of friends whose bonding and obligation make them travel from distant places to comfort and sympathize with Job. Habel writes:

> They appear to have been Job's peers, wearing robes as marks of their nobility, robes which they rend in sympathy with Job (cf. 1:20). They weep in empathetic response to his tragic condition;

---

37. Habel, "Only the Jackal Is My Friend," 228.

they join him in abject self-negation by throwing dust on their heads and flinging it heavenward (cf. Josh. 7:6; 1 Sam. 4:12). They identify with Job as a man reduced to the dust (cf. Ps. 35:13–14). They are ideal friends who commiserate with Job as he suffers in perfect submission. While Job is stunned into patient silence, they have the strength to say nothing, nothing at all. Job's plight is too appalling for words. Such is the legend and the foil for the poet's study of friendship.[38]

The act of joining hands, as Habel notes, is a mark of friendship. These three friends choose to act the same way as Job, matching to feel how he is feeling, so as to understand what he is going through. As Benedict Ssettuuma avers, "human relationships that are authentic and mutual, reciprocal and intimate, result into genuine friendships."[39] These are good marks that the three depicted.

The pointer to instruction and strengthening in Job's social service fits the sage paradigm, where wisdom is the hallmark that provides such guidance in life. The wise person invites people to a way of life that is in harmony with both the created order and God's redemptive work through instruction and encouragement. The sage is not simply an instructor and advocate but also a supporter, and transformer, focusing on what people need to understand in order to live well and cope with the central problems of life, and helping them overcome their predicaments so that they can be happy. The wise person is capable of making a good judgment, bringing his knowledge to bear on the other's actions (cf. Prov 8:12; 1 Kgs 2:9; 3:9).

Eliphaz does not understand why Job would urge people to hold on in the midst of affliction, suffering, disappointment, and persecution, but not do the same. If Job has been encouraging those who are weak and chastened, why is he failing to apply the same principle to console himself? Eliphaz is not sure what happened along the line for a good person like Job to lose the power to empower himself. Perhaps Eliphaz means that Job has himself to blame as if to doubt that Job didn't do something untoward to his clients. Similarly, Eliphaz quizzes,

> Think now, who that was innocent ever perished?
> Or where were the upright cut off?
> As I have seen, those who plough iniquity
> and sow trouble reap the same. (4:7–8)

38. Habel, "Only the Jackal Is My Friend," 228.
39. Ssettuuma, "Friendship," 57.

Eliphaz believes that those who instruct, transform, and empower others will benefit from their own actions. Eliphaz's idea of righteous judgment and retribution is that it is not possible for the righteous to suffer (cf. Prov 16:17; 19:3; 22:5). The innocent, for Eliphaz, will never perish or suffer destruction. Sowing evil will reap evil. Based on such a principle of retribution, Eliphaz claims that Job has not been a good person from the way he is talking (4:12–13). Although Job has helped the poor, he is not a good friend because his motive was not right. Just like in the cases of Elijah (1 Kings 18, 19), Daniel (Dan 7), and Ezekiel (Ezek 1:28), Eliphaz believes a person can have a direct encounter with a supernatural being but can only see its form. The encounter will make the person understand something little since a mere mortal cannot stand right and pure before God. Eliphaz declares that his arguments were not based on speculations. As the Igbo say, *otu onye tu izu, o gbue ochu* ("knowledge is never complete, for two heads are better than one"). Hence, Job must take him seriously and disabuse his mind that he knows God, and take responsibility for his sins.

Eliphaz appears sarcastic when he asks, "Can mortals be righteous before God? Can human beings be purer before their maker?" (4:17). Although Eliphaz knows that human beings cannot be righteous more than God or before God, what he says is a rhetorical way to distinguish Job from God and affirm that Job is nobody.[40] Note also how Eliphaz uses his divine-inspired vision to support his argument:

> 12 "Now a word came stealing to me;
>   my ear received the whisper of it.
> 13 Amid thoughts from visions of the night,
>   when deep sleep falls on mortals,
> 14 dread came upon me and trembling,
>   which made all my bones shake.
> 15 A spirit glided past my face;
>   the hair of my flesh bristled.
> 16 It stood still,
>   but I could not discern its appearance.
> A form was before my eyes;
>   there was silence; then I heard a voice (4:12–16)

Eliphaz shows that he submitted himself when he had a vision from God and could not grasp all that came. What Job did was a secret but it has been revealed. The Igbo elders say, *Ihe di woro ogori azuala na ohia*

---

40. Whitekettle, "When More Leads to Less," 447.

("What was secret is revealed in the marketplace"). No matter how an issue is kept secret, it will become plain out in the open. According to James Harding, Eliphaz "seems to believe he is justified in launching an outrageous, slanderous tirade against Job's manifold iniquities, which foregrounds Eliphaz's total ignorance of Job's actual moral status in the starkest way. This is the point to which Eliphaz's trust in the words of the supernatural visitor ultimately leads."[41] So, he wants to impress upon Job to take a similar posture of humility when words of wisdom are spoken to him. Good friends usually impress upon others to follow a known path and not something they were unsure about. The three believe that when Job listens to them and follows what they have been saying, it will go well for him, but it was based on half-knowledge. As long as Job remains their friend, they have a duty to help him, knowing that Job would react the same way when they encounter similar incidents. Eliphaz seems disappointed at Job's stance for not listening to them and also points out the attitude of Job when he says, "Surely vexation (kāʻaś) kills the fool, and jealousy slays the simple" (5:2 NRSV; ESV). Hence, Job is making himself a fool who is impatient.

Friends are not supposed to be jealous or act foolishly. To Eliphaz, what he sees about Job is not temperance, which a friend should have. The noun kāʻaś also means jealousy, suspicion, or mistrustfulness. In other words, Job was worried beyond measure and jumping to irrational conclusions. That is how he saw Job, not counting on any earlier knowledge of him. It is not the sores or pain that is killing Job. Rather, the worries are eating up Job and will eventually kill him.

Bildad also sees Job as an evildoer who must admit his guilt. Bildad, following the same line of argument as Eliphaz, argues: "See, God will not reject a blameless person nor take the hand of evildoers" (8:20). Bildad affirms that God is just because he never rejects an innocent man (8:3, 20–22). Bildad seems to be assuring Job that things will change for the better and that God will fill his mouth with laughter and joy if he accepts that he has not been a good person. He was actually forcing Job to accept that he is in the wrong. If Job is pure and upright, he will prosper (8:6). And if Job consults with the ancestors and bygone generations to ascertain his innocence, he will know what went wrong and God will restore him. For Bildad, someone who does evil cannot be a good friend.

---

41. Harding, "Spirit of Deception in Job 4:15?," 157.

In the mind of Bildad, repentance is the key to restoration, if Job wants to be a good person. Bildad directs Job to "make supplication to the Almighty" (8:5) in repentance. By so doing, Job's fortunes will turn around and be "very great" (8:7), and he will as well be filled with "laughter" and "shouts of joy" (8:21). Bildad shares the same view as Epicurus, who avers that the goal of life is happiness and joy. Bildad thinks that as long as he wishes Job to pursue pleasure, he is a friend.

Similarly, Zophar, within the first cycle of dialogue, tries to explain to Job "the deep things of God" (11:6–9 cf. Isa 55:8) that have made him come to the realization that Job is a sinner. The deep things of life, or secrets of heaven, belong to God. God is the one who reveals secrets (12:22 cf. Dan 2:22, 47). It is only the wise and those who fear God who can have access to them (Deut 29:29; Ps 25:14; Amos 3:7). In the New Testament, Matthew and Paul explain that the secrets of heaven are revealed to the saints (Matt 13:11; Eph 3:3–8; Col 1:26). Zophar wants to see Job turn sober and plead for forgiveness of sins because he has some insights about Job's situation from God (11:13–20). To Zophar, "God has even forgotten some of your sins" (11:6b). Perhaps what Zophar seeks to say is that Job's sins are so numerous that God could not count all of them, or God has intentionally refused to add some of Job's sins to the compilation so that he can be forgiven. Zophar feels that Job was deceiving himself by claiming he had not sinned. God recognizes deceivers and sees evil when it happens (11:11). If Job were good, he would prosper; but since he suffers, he must be evil (11:13–20).

Zophar claims that Job used his hands to do iniquity. He likens Job to the wicked who have no hope after breathing the last (11:20). Perhaps he extorted money, collected bribes, or attacked the unfortunate, unlike what Eliphaz said about Job. What Job has done amounts to injustice, and it has come to reside in his tents. His iniquity (*'āwen*) hand is used synonymously parallel to injustice (*'awāh*) in the tents (11:14). The Hebrew *'awāh* also means "iniquity," hence a word used with double meaning for emphasis. If Job lifts his face, he will "forget his troubles," that is, being released from "the obligations and penalties that attend his former deeds."[42]

All three friends of Job in the first cycle of speeches find fault with Job. They show how they have come to see Job, even if in the past he was their friend. They want Job to be like them, although it is said among the Akan that *wonnim nipa a, wo ne no nsi koso* (If you don't know someone,

---

42. Hartley, *Job*, 202.

you do not make a partnership with them). It seems the three do not know Job well. Or they have decided to be Job's antagonist. Africans believe that when one searches for a friend with no faults, the person will remain with no friends. In other words, everybody has flaws in life so one will never get someone without flaws. Those who believe themselves to be self-righteous would expect that their friend will be just as they are. Others become so disappointed when they dwell so much on the flaws of their friends. Hence, one needs to avoid focusing on the flaws that friends have and focus on their bright sides. The three focus so much on the flaws they see in Job. It is therefore right to say that they were not acting as friends at all.

Second Cycle of Dialogue (15:1—21:34)

In the second cycle of dialogue, Eliphaz begins by affirming that Job's words are convincing but meaningless (15:3–6). Rather, the sages have taught him a lesson and he would like to share it with Job. It is all about humility and the punishment of the wicked but Job does not listen. Eliphaz quizzes Job if he knew better than his forefather (15:9), and he seems to say that he is a person with grey hair and that he has walked with the aged. As such, they are capable of declaring wisdom. And Job should never come to think that he knows better than his aged friends.

Friendship should aim at identifying the worth of the other. Bildad saw that Job was looking down on them and that is not what friends should do. Bildad tells him to take a cue from the patriarchs. Truth, wisdom, and experience reside in the people of old. Zophar also gives a straightforward answer to Job that he has done something causing all to desert him, because "it is of old, since man was placed on earth" (20:4). Bildad thinks Job is comparing them to cattle and thus stupid:

> Then Bildad the Shuhite answered:
> ² "How long will you hunt for words?
>   Consider, and then we shall speak.
> ³ Why are we counted as cattle (*kabbĕhēmāh*)?
>   Why are we stupid in your sight?" (18:1–3)

The noun *kabbĕhēmāh* translated "as cattle" also denotes "like a beast." Such comparison is sometimes taken as a measure or symbol of wealth, power, and virility (Deut 33:17; Pss 22:12; 68:30; 92:10; Isa 66:3), or brute force. Synonymous with cattle is a cow (Heb: *pārāh*; Gen 32:16;

Job 21:10) beast/animal/behemoth (Heb: *behēmôt*; Ps 49:12, 20; Job 18:3; 40:15), and oxen (*miqneh*; 1:3). Cattle are the main animal workforce in ancient agricultural societies and are also reared to provide meat, milk, and other by-products.

Bildad also has the impression that Job is a sinner. Since Job is suffering like the wicked, he is guilty (15:17–35). Eliphaz feels Job does not deserve the comfort that ought to be offered to a sufferer. He also claims Job is treading the same path taken by the wicked people of old (cf. 22:15–18). In fact, Eliphaz claims Job is a sinner (15:5–6). As friends, Bildad and Eliphaz did not want Job to remain in his sins. Eliphaz finds wisdom in the ancients who contended that God will not cast away the blameless if Job's assertion is anything to go by. Yair Hoffman remarks that "the status of prosecutor assumed by Eliphaz is made possible by the kind of accusations which he hurls against Job—accusations belonging to the realm of visible social transgressions, of the type for which human beings are wont to sue their fellows and against which, should the transgressors claim innocence, they need to defend themselves."[43] That is to say, Eliphaz saw Job as a wicked man in society and that alone disqualifies him from attracting the grace of God.

Bildad angrily wonders how long will Job keep comparing them to animals (18:2). He asked why Job regards his friends as stupid (18:3). Bildad rebukes Job for being arrogant, and affirms that the life of the wicked is shortened, weakened, diseased, and will be wiped out. Job will suffer the fate of those who do not know God (18:1–21). Bildad admonishes Job to be sensible and stop the nonsense talk (18:2). He thinks Job has been tearing himself to pieces with his anger (18:4).

Zophar reminds Job that the wicked may be blessed for a short time, but God will make them lose their riches (20:1–29). Perhaps, Zophar has an impatient heart, and he said he could not stand the rebuke of Job (20:1–2). Perhaps, Job has become a wicked person because he is among those who "have crushed and abandoned the poor, they have seized a house that they did not build" (20:19). Zophar's conviction is based on the fact that wicked people cannot enjoy their riches because God will make their stomachs "vomit them up again" (20:15). He states that wicked people may get some produce out of their toil but it will be short lived: "They will give back the fruit of their toil, and will not swallow it down; from the profit of their trading, they will get no fruit of their enjoyment"

---

43. Hoffman, *Blemished Perfection*, 154.

(20:18). Zophar the Naamathite posits that Job has actually received less suffering than he deserves so he should be grateful. For him, Job does not have the capacity to search out the deep things of God.

Although the three are trying their best to be friends, they are judgmental instead of suggesting their opinion. Their approach is unacceptable. Africans believe that to remove a fly from a friend's forehead, never use a hatchet. That is to say, one needs not to use harsh means to correct another. The hatchet will inflict wounds while using it to help a friend, and that is what true friends normally avoid.

Third Cycle of Dialogue (22:1—27:23)

Eliphaz is convinced that he is not conjecturing or totally wrong in his observations about Job since, in his estimation, he knows him too well. Proclaiming God's disinterest in Job's piety and his ego in the third cycle of dialogue, Eliphaz impresses upon Job to repent because God is transcendent (22:12–14), since God is so lofty in heaven and does not care what is happening on earth (22:17–20). Eliphaz hardens his heart against his supposed friend. He cannot trust Job that he is innocent. Faced with the self-imposed choice of blaming Job, he continues to ask, "Is there no end to your iniquities?" (22:5). He consistently accuses Job of iniquity, not only in the past but as a continuous practice. And then he mentions some of the iniquities he has on the charge sheet against Job: "You gave no water to the weary, and you have withheld bread from the hungry" (22:7; NIV). "You sent widows away empty-handed, and the arms of the orphans was crushed" (22:9). It appears Eliphaz knows something that no one else knows, for not even God knows that Job has iniquity in his hands!

A friend can only empower the other if there is submission and acceptance. Eliphaz concentrates on forcing Job to submit to him even if he will not accept his fault. To Eliphaz, if a person of worth and a person of wisdom cannot enjoy peace, then God has to grant it. "Is not God high in the heavens?" (22:12); "Agree (*haskken-nā'*) with God and be at peace" (22:21). The use of the verb, *haskken-nā'* from the root *skn* also means "be used" or "submit." The word has been translated variously: "agree" (NRSV; ESV), "acquaint" (KJV; ASV), "give yourself" (ERV), and "submit" (NIV). In the view of Hartley, *haskken-nā'* means "repent."[44] However, according to Clines, it does not mean repentance but is the

---

44. Hartley, *Job*, 332.

language used among equals or friends who have fallen out with each other, a view I share.[45] In the view of Eliphaz, if Job submits to what he (Eliphaz) is saying, Shaddai will be his gold and silver. It will then happen that Job will delight himself in Shaddai, and will lift up his face to God. Job will pray to Shaddai and he will hear (22:25–27). Eliphaz holds the traditional thought that God has abandoned Job because of his sins. God's presence is likened to gold and silver in the life of a person and if Job accepts his faults, God will come back to him again.

Bildad also affirms in the third cycle of dialogue that Job has to stop blaming God and accept that he is a sinner. God has sovereign power and rules over the world (25:2–3). God cannot be compared to human beings, and there is no sense for Job to claim he is just and clean (25:4–6). God does not see how a human being can claim innocence (25:4). As Atkinson observes, Bildad fails to meet Job where he really is. His orthodox views of God's omnipotence rather meant Job is a puppet in the hands of God.[46] Newsom concurs:

> The advice they offer remains consistent: seek God (chaps. 5, 8, 11, 22). The turmoil that is experienced—whether it arises from inexplicable calamity (chap. 5), from a disharmony with the right clouded by false consciousness (chap. 11), or as punishment consequent on deep moral disorder (chap. 22)—can be addressed by means of the reordering practices of seeking God.[47]

Applying their theological assumptions about God and justice to Job's circumstances as a way of comforting does not result in the three encouraging Job to endure in hope.

Africans believe that a good friend should know everything about the other and still want to be with the friend. The three, in their minds' eye, intend to stay by Job and be his friend but their actions are distancing themselves from Job. They do not want to accept the piety of Job. They know that honest advice does not destroy true friendship. Ignorance, however, breeds distrust. The truth hurts, if really what they are saying is the truth. Also, it is believed that a wound inflicted by a friend does not heal. Anytime the friend comes close, and remembers what the other has done, it should bring joy and relief rather than cause grief and regret.

---

45. Clines, *Job 21–37*, 562.
46. Atkinson, *Message of Job*, 56.
47. Newsom, *Book of Job*, 106.

AN ETHIC OF FRIENDSHIP: HOW JOB SEES THE THREE

Job's thoughts and articulations are examined, shaped, and revitalized by the opposing views of the three. Job particularly saw the negative criticisms and could not stand those views. Yair Hoffman also observes, "another character trait that typifies Job is his great sensitivity, despite the harsh words which he directs towards God . . . Job's sensitivity is likewise expressed in the appeals to the friends."[48] Be as it may, the three contribute something to Job's capacity for reflection. Job knew that the three were his friends. Now, what type of friends have they become if even they were formerly his bosom friends?

In the three dialogue cycles, Job identifies the three as his friends (*yr'*; 6:14, 27; 12:4; 16:20; 19:21) and brothers (*'ḥ*; 6:15; 19:3). Indeed, Job has some blood brothers and sisters (42:11), but it is these three that assume such kinship categories due to some prior relationship. Unfortunately, the ones who were supposed to be brothers have become like intermittent streams. They flow only when there is abundant water (6:15-20). They have become fair-weather friends. The brotherhood or solidarity that is seen between Job and the three should have been more like a covenant. In the words of Hartley,

> The relationship between Job and his three friends gives every evidence of being based on a covenant (6:14-15, 21-23, 27). Such a relationship was characterized by loyal love (*hesed*; e.g., Jonathan and David, 1 Sam. 20:14-15). Motivated by love and their commitment, these men came *to console* and *to comfort* Job . . . With the noblest intentions, these three earnestly desired to help Job bear his sorrows.[49]

Unfortunately, the kind of reciprocity demanded in such a human–human covenant did not Appear particularly. It is not just about showing sympathy or being with a sufferer. It is about seeking an attachment due to some social bond. Newsom notes that the act of visiting a bereaved person is a traditional expression of solidarity.[50] Visiting a friend is good but there should be more to it. Unfortunately, the friends could not perform the role of consoling and comforting.

Job accuses the three friends of showing empty consolation. Job compares the words from Eliphaz to tasteless food that is difficult to eat

---

48. Yair Hoffman, *Blemished Perfection*, 132.
49. Hartley, *Job*, 85.
50. Newson, "Book of Job," 357.

(6:6–7). Naturally, it is very difficult to eat tasteless food unless one adds some sweetener or salt. That is to say, Job does not have any appetite for the words of his friend. Their words are in bad taste and thus Job refuses to have anything to do with them. Their failure to show kindness becomes a matter of concern. Job responds to Eliphaz this way:

> [14] Those who withhold kindness (*ḥāsed*) from a friend (*mērē'ēhu*)
> forsake the fear of the Almighty (6:14)

The Masoretic Text for 6:14 is uncertain and therefore has been translated variously:

> JPS TANAK:
> A friend owes loyalty to one who fails,
> though he forsakes the fear of the Almighty.
>
> NASB:
> For the despairing man there should be kindness from his friend;
> So that he does not abandon the fear of the Almighty.
>
> ASV:
> To him that is ready to faint kindness should be showed from his friend;
> Even to him that forsaketh the fear of the Almighty.
>
> CJB:
> A friend should be kind to an unhappy man,
> even to one who abandons Shaddai.
>
> NKJV:
> To him who is afflicted, kindness should be shown by his friend,
> even though he forsakes the fear of the Almighty.
>
> ESV:
> He who withholds kindness from a friend
> forsakes the fear of the Almighty.
>
> NIV:
> Anyone who withholds kindness from a friend
> forsakes the fear of the Almighty.

The major issue in the text is who loses the fear of God. Is it the one who withholds kindness or the one to whom kindness is not shown? The JPS TANAK makes it clear that even if a friend would forsake to fear the

Almighty, that person should not forsake to show loyalty to one who is in need.

Notice that the ESV and NIV do not include "to the despairing one." The Hebrew does not have the negation but it is so in the NASB. Gordis thinks it is the one who seeks kindness who has forsaken the fear of God and also suggests a reading: "If anyone seeks mercy from his friend, he forsakes the reverence due God."[51] Seow prefers to interpret the adjective *lammās* as "abandoned" and adds that the waw in *wĕyit'at* should be treated as a circumstantial clause, "even though," thus it is the one who is seeking the favor who has abandoned God.[52] Tremper Longman III follows the NRSV, NIV, and ESV to explain that since the friends are not protecting him but rather intensifying the problems, they are not truly following God because that is not the proper attitude when one fears God.[53] In my estimation, both renderings are valid. If someone withholds kindness from a friend, that is unacceptable before God, since God expects that people show kindness to one another. Also, if a person trusts a friend to show kindness in times of need, then the person is trusting another human being (cf. Isa 26:3–4; Jer 17:7; Prov 3:5–6; Pss 20:7; 56:3; 62:8; 118:8). However, the context of Job's words shows more of a critique to their actions. They do not fear God and that has led them to withhold kindness. Whatever one does to a friend, he is doing it to God.

One comprehensive term that lies at the heart of Job 6:14, which comes so close to friendship, is *ḥesed*.[54] In Chapter 4 of this book, it has been shown that the Hebrew term *ḥesed*, which occurs 237 times in the Hebrew Bible and 3 times in *the* book of Job (6:14; 10:12; 37:13), is obviously a difficult word to translate and carries a wide range of meanings. In the Bible, it is often translated as "loving-kindness," "steadfast love," "loyalty," and "faithfulness." In its basic forms, it is used as the object of a sentence to connote an act or something shown. The Hebrew Bible presents both the unconditional aspect and the conditional aspect of *ḥesed*. The unconditional aspect is a gift that does not require any response from the benefactor. Fundamentally, the concept of *ḥesed* is not tied to legal notions, yet it goes as far as to "joint obligation," "goodness," "graciousness," "godly action," "achievements," "proofs of mercy," and the like. The

---

51. Gordis, *Book of Job*, 73–74.
52. Seow, *Job 1–21*, 477.
53. Longman, "Job," 144.
54. See chapter 3.

term *ḥesed* points to conduct in accordance with social norms. It is identical to life and justice. It is also a demonstration of trust.

If Job is looking for loyalty, then the three are not loyal; if kindness, then the three are not showing kindness. The three, by showing solidarity with Job and trying to restore him, are loyal to their friendship requirements, although that was not the way Job expected. Loyalty is a key virtue and a paradigmatic expression found in friendship. Loyalty is contextual, so the extent to which loyalty must be maintained sometimes depends on the situation. Nevertheless, the idea of perseverance in a relationship to which one has become intrinsically committed is what is expected. A person who desires to be in a friendship with another is expected to show some amount of loyalty. One expects loyalty from the spouse, family members, and group members. Organizations demand loyalty, and to be a member of a country, one has to pledge loyalty.

The link between loyalty to a friend and fear of God underlies Job's argument, although there was nothing in the argument of the three to indicate that they did not fear God. It takes a person who fears God to obey the word of God. Fearing God also means respect, reverence, and worship. Those who fear the Lord walk in his ways (Deut 10:12–13). God expects that his people show kindness to all, especially the poor and needy (Deut 15:11; Ps 37:21; Prov 19:17; Matt 19:21; Gal 2:10; Jas 1:27). Anyone who fails to do so does not fear God (Prov 14:21, 31). In another vein, the Akan says: *sɛ obi yɛ wo papa a, due* ("if someone does good to you, it gives you a burden"). That is to say, it is obligatory to reciprocate kindness as long as we accept kindness. When we do kindness to another, we do it to God (Prov 19:17; Matt 25:40, 45; 1 John 3:17; 4:20–21). Without the fear of God, one cannot turn from evil (Ps 11:10; Prov 1:7; 9:10; 10:27; 14:27; 16:6). Hence, Job equates loyalty from a friend to fear of the Lord (6:14). He also seems to posit that one may forsake fearing the Lord, but one should not forsake a friend. He sees that his friends lack loyalty, which is most unacceptable. They have become fair-weather friends. Gordis understands the text in 6:14—*lammās mērēʿēhû ḥāsed wĕyirʾit šaddaʿ yaʿăzwob* ("If anyone seeks mercy from his friends, he forsakes the reverence due God")—as a conditional sentence rather than a statement of fact.[55] It seems such a translation is about relying on human beings rather than God. Nonetheless, it is God who expects his people to show

---

55. Gordis, *Book of Job*, 74.

kindness, so such a meaning may be farfetched. If Job affirms that "such you have become to me" (6:21a), the three are not good friends.

Job continues to explain that instead of showing kindness, reliability, and love, the three were becoming disloyal and untrustworthy. Job says,

> ¹⁵ My companions (ʾaḥa) are treacherous like a torrent-bed,
>   like freshets that pass away,
> ¹⁶ that run dark with ice,
>   turbid with melting snow.
> ¹⁷ In time of heat they disappear;
>   when it is hot, they vanish from their place.
> ¹⁸ The caravans turn aside from their course;
>   they go up into the waste, and perish.
> ¹⁹ The caravans of Tema look,
>   the travelers of Sheba hope.
> ²⁰ They are disappointed because they were confident;
>   they come there and are confounded.
> ²¹ Such you have now become to me;
>   you see my calamity, and are afraid. (6:15–21)

The NRSV translates the noun ʾaḥaʿ "my companions," perhaps trying to be more inclusive. Realistically, "my brothers" seems more acceptable. A companion may not have the kind of obligation a brother has. Delitschz also sets ʾaḥaʿ as friends who are beloved as brothers.[56] Unfortunately, Alden claims that ʾaḥ aʿ here does "not carry with it any sense of commitment."[57] Being a companion without showing any commitment is strange. However, from the preceding verse, Job was looking for a commitment from the three. They, by withholding their loyalty, which is a commitment due to a friend, have forsaken the Lord's teaching and, as such, are not acting as friends.

A brother is one who stays close to the side of the kin and that is what the three are exhibiting. However, Job sees them as unreliable and treacherous as a torrent bed (6:15). When rain falls, it creates a pathway to run along instead of seeping into the ground. The pathway becomes a gully as the violent rushing waters scoop deep into the bed of the earth and carry off what it has taken. The torrent bed only becomes a useful channel when rain or water passes through it. When it is dry, the bed becomes dangerous for human use and passage, and it destroys the topography. Such has been the attitude of the three friends. They were

---

56. Delitschz, *Job*, 115.
57. Alden, *Job*, 102.

not useful when the rains came, and the channel they created had become waste and unproductive for further action and interaction among friends. The channel, during snowy times, becomes filled with ice as if they are passable. When the ice melts, one cannot use the torrent bed. Job observes that such incidents happen to travelers on a caravan who wish to use the route in which the torrent bed is filled with ice, but will soon discover that the ice has melted and they cannot use the road again. He says the caravans "are disappointed because they were confident, they come there and are confounded" (6:20).

Job sees the three as people who act treacherously when needed and go up into the waste (6:15). They are a bunch of confused people, stunned by their own fears. Job expresses his disappointment about the three using the metaphor of a stream that flows in a particular season and dries in another. He counted on them to show some kindness, but their fear of sharing in Job's calamity has made them turn their backs on him. The confidence he had in them has become a disappointment and he thus feel ashamed. The use of *bošuʿ* ("your shame"; 6:20) strengthened by the verb *wayyeḥppārûʿ* ("and confounded/abashed you"; 6:20) expresses a feeling of shame caused by deception.[58] Here, *boš* connotes shame as disgrace or disappointment, which is a negative disorienting effect that causes diminishment in the image one sees in the eyes of others. "Shame as disgrace, usually a negative experience, describes a feeling of worthlessness, embarrassment, discouragement and failure while shame as discretion is believed to be a proper shame that plays a role in sustaining personal and social relationships."[59] Newsom also remarks that the failure of Job's friends leaves Job publicly shamed.[60] Job accuses the three of being dry streams that disappoint people at a time when they need water most (see Isa 8:3; Nah 1:8; Dan 11:10).[61] After reproaching them as acting like a deceitful stream of fresh water that has gone bad, he also challenges them to show him where he has sinned. In that sense, the three were insincere in their judgment. David Konstan makes an observation that explains the friends' actions succinctly. He says, "the opposite of friendship is not so much betrayal or the exploitation of an

---

58. Aidoo, *Shame in the Individual Lament Psalms*, 85; Avrahami, "בוש in the Psalms," 295–313. See also Pss 35:26; 40:15.

59. Aidoo, *Shame in the Individual Lament Psalms*, 70.

60. Newsom, "Book of Job," 389.

61. Zophar later uses the metaphor of waters that pass away quickly in 11:16.

THE CASE OF ELIPHAZ, BILDAD, AND ZOPHAR AS FRIENDS 141

intimate friendship, as the earlier tradition has represented it, but rather a failure of sincerity that presents a false image to the admirer."[62]

Although Eliphaz, Bildad, and Zophar set out to comfort and sympathize with Job, much of what they do and say turns them into accusers. They become Job's inquisitors.[63] Try as they might to maintain their original mission to Job, their actions speak differently. Job avers,

> ^{22} Have I said, "Make me a gift"?
> Or, "From your wealth offer a bribe for me"?
> ^{23} Or, "Save me from an opponent's hand"?
> Or, "Ransom me from the hand of oppressors"?
> ^{24} Teach me, and I will be silent;
> make me understand how I have gone wrong.
> ^{25} How forceful are honest words!
> But your reproof, what does it reprove?
> ^{26} Do you think that you can reprove words,
> as if the speech of the desperate were wind?
> ^{27} You would even cast lots over the orphan,
> and bargain over your friends (*reʿăkem*)
> ^{28} But now, be pleased to look at me;
> for I will not lie to your face.
> ^{29} Turn, I pray, let no wrong be done.
> Turn now, my vindication is at stake.
> ^{30} Is there any wrong on my tongue?
> Cannot my taste discern calamity? (6:22–30)

From the above, Job makes it clear that words hurt, especially when coming from a friend. To reprove a friend in a harsh manner is like casting lots over an orphan, or like trying to see who is the highest bidder in an act of sale. A good friend cannot dispense with a friend for money, as if money can buy friendship. Job has not asked for any favor from his friends. He has not asked for a gift, wealth, or a helping hand to fight his oppressor. As friends, they are obligated to speak kindly to him. All he needs from them is honest words of judgment that could reprove him even if the words were hurting; to show if "there is any wrong on my tongue" (6:30). Yet the force of their words makes it sound more like they are fighting against him than reproving. He sarcastically describes their words as "honest words" (Heb: *'imrê-yōšer*; v 25); perhaps they are saying what really comes from their hearts but without any evidence. These

---

62. Konstan, "Friendship, Frankness, and Flattery," 17.
63. Balentine, "Let Love Clasp Grief Lest Both be Drowned," 386.

friends are opposing him and, as such, in their bid to hurt him they are not honest (*yōšer*). If they are right, why is Job not ready to accept them? On the other hand, Job might be admitting that what their friends are saying is the true product of their hearts, but rather his problem with them is that they are forceful (*nimrĕṭû*), a niphal perfect of the root *mrṭ* also meaning "to be sick, violent." The honest words are therefore sick or violent. Their words lack the power to empower but rather destroy. Yet to ask rhetorically whether friends can reproof with words (v. 26) means their words are not to be taken seriously.

Job sees the three as bargaining over who will win the argument against him. He will be happy if the friends accept their mistake because he is not lying to them. The words of the three friends are not merely reflecting on their established theological stance but forcing Job to conform to their worldview and also to admit a sin Job knows he has not committed. Job finds the arguments of the three unacceptable. They are firmly holding on to what they know, the traditions they have been following and teaching for a long time. They absolutize their long-cherished traditions and cling to them so much that there is no room for further reflection or change of position. They are like a wheel spinning in the air: though there is some movement, it does not go anywhere.[64]

In the three cycles of dialogue between Job and his three friends, there was no agreement between them. Their dialogue was more of disputation with arguments and counter-arguments, or accusations and counter-accusations. Proverbs 6:1–5 teaches that if there is an agreement between friends and it comes to a point where one of them is trapped in what has been said, a friend should give the other no respite until that friend settles the matter. Forcing one's thoughts on another's can cause lots of harm.

In the third cycle, the three also engage Job in a way that makes it difficult for him to respond. Job has said all that he feels necessary, but the three do not listen to him. According to Janzen, "the friends serve as the dramatic and dialectical means by which Job's own settled views come to articulation alongside the new tones which his sufferings have given to his voice."[65] Similarly, William Young reflects on how Thomas Aquinas argues that the three provided Job with the opportunity to exercise intellectual virtue.[66] According to Julius Moster, "the image of the

---

64. Gutiérrez, *On Job*, 29.
65. Janzen, *Job*, 59.
66. Young, "Patience of Job," 597.

three friends that emerges from a careful survey of the Dialogue is not one of sympathetic comforters, but rather one of rigid fanatics who are your friends as long as you accept their religious beliefs but who turn on you viciously if you do not."[67] Hence the three are at an international dialogue conference to give meaning to Job's suffering when friends are not supposed to do so. Elsewhere, rēaʿ is used, for instance, to emphasize goodwill, that is to say, generosity and faithfulness among friends (Prov 3:28–29). A friend also needs to provide security (Prov 6:1, 3, 29). The friend is contrasted with a stranger (Prov 6:1).

Job sarcastically rebukes his friends because their counsel lacks wisdom. They do not take time to engage in a deep reflection before speaking and thus, make their thoughts useless. Job sees his three friends as people who cannot see beyond what they know. They do not understand the mystery of suffering and will not be sober to learn from Job. They love to jump to hasty conclusions. The reader knows that Job is suffering through no fault of his own, but the friends who have no such preknowledge are making invalid conclusions. Their error stems from the fact that they are making generalizations and not considering Job's situation as a special case. Job feels the three do not help at all in this situation; they only make it worse him. And their claim to be wise and understand words of wisdom is challenged by Job:

> Then Job answered:
> "No doubt you are the people,
>   and wisdom will die with you.
> But I have understanding as well as you;
>   I am not inferior to you.
> Who does not know such things as these?" (12:1–3)

Job sees his friends as trying to show that they are better than him, especially in terms of knowledge and understanding. They are people who look down on others, to make them inferior. Such an attitude does not show that they are wise. Ignorance cannot be an excuse. If Job is without wisdom, how are they helping him out? Job's question has been put variously by translators:

> How have you counseled one who has no wisdom!
>   and given much good advice! (26:3)

---

67. Moster, "Punishment of Job's friends," 217.

> What advice you have offered to one without wisdom
> And what great insight you have displayed! (NIV)

> Without having the wisdom, you offer advice
> And freely give your counsel (JPS TANAK)

Whereas in the NRSV and NIV it is the recipient of the advice who is without wisdom, it can be observed that the JPS TANAK assumes that it is the one who was giving the advice who has no wisdom.

Job also describes his three friends as a company (*'attem-'ām*; 12:2). The idea of "company" means the three were no longer his bosom or close friends. They are like colleagues in the same profession. These three friends, unfortunately, seem closer to each other than to Job. As Seow observes, the three friends are in cohort with one another and think of themselves more highly than Job.[68] Their words are causing more harm than healing, so Job says,

> As for you, you whitewash with lies;
>   all of you are worthless physicians.
> If you would only keep silent,
>   that would be your wisdom! (13:4–5)

A physician is expected to make a proper diagnosis and offer the right kind of treatment. To Job, the wrong choice of words makes them worthless. Using wrong words may cause or lead to harm to another. It takes a person who knows how to keep silent to display wisdom. Such words bring adverse reactions and negative outcomes. Elaine Phillips says, "while the inherently moral nature of the universe does necessitate a basic sense of retributive justice, the friends inhabited a 'flat deistic universe' and they failed to perceive and/or acknowledge the vast complexity of the powers and principalities in the heavenly court."[69]

The thrust of the arguments of the three is that their protestation will grant Job the perspective to stand right before God. The real sense of perplexity, however, is captured in these words; Eliphaz makes himself like "a gentle, confident mystic, Bildad as a firm traditionalist, Zophar as a rash dogmatist."[70] The three want Job to see things the way they do while Job expects their loyalty and a demonstration of their friendship in

---

68. Seow, *Job 1–21*, 82.
69. Phillips, "Speaking Truthfully," 35.
70. LaSor et al., *Old Testament Survey*, 476.

community.⁷¹ In their rebuttals, the three cannot see eye to eye with Job. They reject what Job is saying (8:1–2; 11:1–4; 15:1–16; 18:1–4; 20:1–4).

Job, however, maintains that he has held on to his integrity (2:3; 6:28–30; 19:6; 27:5–6). He rebuts the accusation of sin. He says even if it were so, how they are putting it is disproportionate to the suffering he is going through. Job tries to defend himself against known sins (10:2–7), although he admits sinning when he was a youth (13:26). Accepting his guilt does not make him a sinner. At least, he knows he had offered sacrifices to appease his sins already. Furthermore, Job feels the friends make him feel worse when they speak untruths about him (13:4–5). Job seeks a true friend who will cast his mind on who he is and what he stands for because these other friends have had their eyes closed all along. For Job, the devotion of his friends is being put to the test. They are showing that they do not believe him when he speaks. In fact, Eliphaz posits that he knows why Job is suffering. He sees Job as a stubborn old man. What Eliphaz says is that Job should acknowledge his "sins of oppression, exploitation and terrorizing others."⁷² Job, however, does admit that as a human he has his sins to contend with (14:16–17). He is conscious of his own limitations, weaknesses, and mortality. Yet, the three are not listening to him. They are not satisfied that Job rather desires to confront God and demand a fair trial. They are prejudging without any substantive evidence. To accuse Job of being prideful and boastful is in fact unwarranted—the friends are only conjecturing.⁷³ They did not have any concrete proof of a wrongdoing Job has done.

Job touches on the theme of fake friends also in 16:2–6 and 16:18–22 in his response to Eliphaz. The first addresses what the friends are doing and closes with how it has affected him. Job makes a point about the words that come from the three:

> Then Job answered:
> ² "I have heard many such things;
>   miserable comforters are you all.
> ³ Have windy words no limit?
>   Or what provokes you that you keep on talking?
> ⁴ I also could talk as you do,
>   if you were in my place;

---

71. Balentine, "Let Love Clasp Grief Lest Both be Drowned," 392.
72. Hoffman, *Blemished Perfection*, 139.
73. Schifferbecker, *Out of the Whirlwind*, 60.

>   I could join words together against you,
>   and shake my head at you.
> ⁵ I could encourage you with my mouth,
>   and the solace of my lips would assuage your pain.
> ⁶ If I speak, my pain is not assuaged,
>   and if I forbear, how much of it leaves me?" (16:1–6)

This stanza is made up of two movements: 16:2–3 and 4–6. In the first movement, Job says he has "heard" (v. 2) "windy words" (v. 3a); they "keep on talking" (v. 3b). He describes the three as miserable comforters. The Akan say, *nnyɛ hɔn a wosu wɔ weyi ase nyina na wɔyɛ w' anyɛnkofo* ("not all who cry during your funeral are your friends"). As such, some people pretend to be friends—fake friends. Such a type of friendship is how Job saw the three. Fake friends do not have your best interest at heart and are not invested in your well-being. They make friends feel insecure, used, or judged.

In the second movement (16:4–6), there is a shift from what the friends are doing to what Job could do in retaliation. Friendship can be seen within the notion of the golden rule: "Do to others what you want others to do to you" (Matt 7:12; Luke 6:31). Job makes it clear that he could do the same thing to his friends, talk as they do, and join words together against them (16:4; cf. Isa 8:10). The prudent know how to hold their mouth (Prov 10:19; 11:9). Job shakes his head at them as a sign of disappointment and disbelief (16:4; cf. Pss 22:7; 64:8; Jer 18:16; Matt 27:39). All of the above are the outworking of how words can be hurtful. Job then adds the positive sense: "I could encourage you with my mouth, and the solace of my lips would assuage your pain" (16:5; cf. Prov 15:4; Eph 4:29). To him, whether he speaks or keeps his mouth shut, the pain he is going through will not be assuaged (16:6; cf. Prov 10:21, 31; 12:18).

In 16:18–22, Job expects the earth "to be a friend" who will accept him after human beings and God have rejected him. He calls the earth to be a witness and an advocate that stands in and gives an undertaking for a client, an echo of how the blood of Abel cried from the ground (Gen 4:10–11). Although Job has an advocate in heaven, he looks to the earth to plead his cause just as a friend would do. Job gives a "bitingly sarcastic address to the three companions" for not being empathic.[74]

The translations of 16:20 suggest various ways whereby a friend is seen:

---

74. Alter, *Wisdom Books*, 136.

MT: *mĕlîṣay rē'ay 'el-ĕloâh dālpâ 'ênî*

JPS TANAK:
Mine inward thoughts are my intercessors,
   Mine eye pour out tears to God;

NIV: My intercessor is my friend as my eyes pour out tears to God

NRSV:
My friends scorn me;
   my eye pours out tears to God

ASV:
My friends scoff at me:
   But mine eye poureth out tears unto God

Alter:
My advocates, my companions!
   Before God my eyes sheds tears

The hiphil participle construct *mĕlîṣay* from the root *lyṣ*, has been translated as "intercessor" (JPS TANAK; NIV), "scorn" (NRSV), or "scoff" (ASV). The word can also mean "mediator" (33:23; Isa 43:27), "envoy" (2 Chr 32:31), or "interpreter" (Gen 42:23). In other words, the three should have been interceding and mediating for him but they are not doing so. Their attitude is to scoff at the other (cf. Ps 119:51). It can be surmised that Job wants to see the three as comforters who intercede on his behalf but they have turned out to make fun of him. True friends intercede for one another. Instead of acting as mediators for him, they laugh at him and ridicule him. He complains about the miserable comfort the friends are giving him (16:1–5; 19:3; 21:34). Job seems to be saying that the three know what is right, but for fear of being implicated, they are withholding themselves. Janzen makes the point clearer by saying that, "not only have the friends refused to risk themselves in surety for him; they are informing against him in hopes of gain at his expense."[75]

The posture of the three makes one assume that they will never put up a smile while speaking with Job. A Swahili proverb goes, *Cheko la rafiki lina bei ghali* ("The smile of a friend costs dearly"). This means friendships should be built on trust. When a friend is going through a rough time, that is when other friends have to come in to cheer the person up

75. Janzen, *Job*, 125–26.

and make the person smile. In other words, true friends become a source of empowerment to each other through their genuine smiles. Additionally, when one accomplishes something and the friend is happy about it, it gives satisfaction, but a bad friend will bring much sorrow. The writer of Sirach also distinguishes between true and false friendship:

> [5] Pleasant speech multiplies friends,
>   and a gracious tongue multiplies courtesies.
> [6] Let those who are at peace with you be many,
>   but let your advisers be one in a thousand.
> [7] When you gain friends, gain them through testing,
>   and do not trust them hastily.
> [8] For there are friends who are such when it suits them,
>   but they will not stand by you in time of trouble.
> [9] And there are friends who turn to enmity
>   and tell of the quarrel to your disgrace.
> [10] And there are friends who are companions at the table,
>   but they will not stand by you in time of trouble.
> [11] When you are prosperous, they become your second self
>   and boldly command your slaves,
> [12] but if you are brought low, they turn against you
>   and hide themselves from you.
> [13] Keep away from your enemies,
>   and be on guard with your friends.
> [14] Faithful friends are a sturdy shelter;
>   whoever finds one has found a treasure.
> [15] Faithful friends are beyond price;
>   no amount can balance their worth.
> [16] Faithful friends are life-saving medicine,
>   and those who fear the Lord will find them.
> [17] Those who fear the Lord direct their friendship aright,
>   for as they are, so are their neighbors also. (Sir 6:5–17)

A close friend can be around for a while but a true and intimate friend is a great treasure for an entire lifetime. It is great to have many friends, but one has to "test" the relationship to know who is close and who is intimate. One need be careful not only with enemies but with all types of friends. The nature of true friendship, according to Sirach, is a proper use of speech and harmony that brings empowerment. Building a close spiritual friendship. True friends focus on virtues that the Lord desires. They invest their whole life in seeking wisdom and directing each other to fear God. Thus, there is a need to distance oneself from fake friends, since they try to destroy others.

THE CASE OF ELIPHAZ, BILDAD, AND ZOPHAR AS FRIENDS 149

Job continues to address his friends in a negative light by using the wrong words. For him, that amounts to mockery and exploitation:

> 1 My spirit is broken, my days are extinct,
>   the grave is ready for me.
> 2 Surely there are mockers (*hătulîm*) around me,
>   and my eye dwells on their provocation.
> 3 Lay down a pledge for me with yourself;
>   who is there that will give surety for me?
> 4 Since you have closed their minds to understanding,
>   therefore you will not let them triumph.
> 5 Those who denounce friends (*rē'îm*) for reward—
>   the eyes of their children will fail. (17:1–5)

In this pericope, Job describes the three as mockers around him (17:2). The Hebrew *hătulîm* ("mockers") appears only here in the Hebrew Bible, and may form a semantic parallel with "scoffers." They are making fun of him as a form of deception to discredit him (cf. 30:1). They have become people who turn against friends because of the reward they can receive (17:5). Job expects them to stay with him for friendship's sake, but they turn out to be defenders and ridiculers, and have closed their minds to understand what friendship is all about (17:2–3). As such, they will not triumph (Heb: *teromēm* root *rûm*), i.e., be exalted, grow up, or prosper. The eyes of their children will also fail (17:4b, 5b), meaning that failure to be a good friend will bring repercussions on one's children. To Job, the consequence of treating a friend badly is an eye-defect for one's children.

The three do not have sympathetic hearts. They do not have any pity for the sufferer but attack him. Job laments:

> 2 How long will you torment me,
>   and break me in pieces with words?
> 3 These ten times you have cast reproach upon me;
>   are you not ashamed to wrong me?
> 4 And even if it is true that I have erred,
>   my error remains with me.
> 5 If indeed you magnify yourselves against me,
>   and make my humiliation an argument against me. (19:2–5)

A true friend is expected to empower the other. A Yoruba proverb goes, *bia ole gbe mi, bi o tib a mi* ("if you cannot improve my lot, do not worsen it"). The Akan elders also say, *sɛ rennyi m'ayɛw a, mma nnsɛɛ me dzin* ("if you will not praise me, do not destroy my name"). It is the words of the three that are most hurtful (cf. Prov 18:21). The psalmist also laments about betrayal and disappointment from friends (Pss 38:11; 88:18). The tongue is a powerful tool, and unpleasant words can hurt, destroy, and pull people down (Jas 3:5–8). It is more harmful than the deadliest ammunition. Hence, one should not utter corrupt words (Matt 12:36–37; Eph 4:29; 1 Pet 3:10). Words can determine one's attitude. The words of the three are clothing him with "shame/disgrace." The massive weight of the three's accusations is "ten times" (v. 3), more humiliating than any pain. Alden does not see any significance in the number ten, saying that it is an unspecified number.[76] The hyperbole of the number ten, juxtaposed with the Adversary's attack, shows that the three have caused more pain than the Adversary. In fact, it is Job who is not accepting the fact that he has been crushed, and moreover the effect of what the three are doing is also great. Effectively, the intensity of Job's voice is intended to inject vigor into his "crushed" situation. Job has received more than enough of the blame and shame. All along, Job has asserted his innocence. At 19:4, Job hypothetically says, assuming he had erred, his actions did not affect anyone. Why Job refuses to accept that one person's sin can affect another is interesting. Is he claiming some sins do not have an effect on others? For him, his sins stayed with him. The Akan say,*ssɛ oguan kor dɔ ntwom a, dze saa nguan pem* ("if one sheep is affected by scabs, it infects a thousand others"). In fact, there is some selfishness in Job's assertion. Perhaps Job is claiming that it is not the business of the friends to judge him even if he has erred.

Job feels that as his family is far away from him, acquaintances are nowhere to be found, relatives and close friends have failed him, guests have forgotten him, servants do not recognize his authority, young children despise him, and intimate friends abhor him, then the three should act differently—"have mercy on me, have mercy on me, you who are my friends" (19:13–21). The three should be more than family members, acquaintances, close friends, and intimate friends. It is interesting that Job sees a virtue beyond intimate friendship. That is to say, true friends do not stay away from the other, fail to respond to the needs of the other, despise the other, or abhor the other. The effect of the words of the three is compared to the pursuit of God. Like a ruthless beast trying to catch its prey, the three want their hands to "touch" Job just like the hand of God has touched him. Job's assertion that "I have escaped by the skin of my teeth" (19:20, my translation) depicts a narrow escape from his

---

76. Alden, *Job*, 199.

THE CASE OF ELIPHAZ, BILDAD, AND ZOPHAR AS FRIENDS 151

pursuers. The tone of the speech indicates that Job exercised some calm in his next appeal:

> ²¹ Have mercy on me, have mercy on me,
>   You who are my friends (rēʻa)
>   for the hand of God has touched me!
> ²² Why do you, like God, pursue me,
>   Are you not satisfied with my flesh? (19:21–22)

Here, Job does not shift from his aggressive position as he uses the vocative—"you who my friends" (v. 21a). Thus, it is a statement of disbelief. The tone here, according to Clines, seems solemn in appealing for mercy,[77] but it is captured in the *qal* imperative. It is deeper than an appeal. Their attack upon Job is somewhat equated with what God has done. They are pursuing and striking Job just like God. For Job, being a true friend means being able to show compassion and mercy. A friend should not be on the side of the assailant, pursuing, and striking the one supposed to be a friend. To Job, what the friends are doing is an attack on his flesh. They do not know what is enough. They are tearing off his flesh to the last bit. Instead of supporting him to have faith in the Lord, they are making it difficult for him. To Job, even if he has given up faith in God, that does not mean his friends should go against him. Rather, what true friends do is stay close because they owe each other kindness and loyalty. Seow explains that "friendship in a time of need may help those who are discouraged not lose faith and abandon God. One must stay with one's desperate friend so that the friend might not give up on God. Yet it is hard to imagine Job implicitly threatening that if the friends should abandon him, then he might give up on God and that they will be responsible for his loss of faith."[78]

After failing to convince the three, Job prefers being silent to further confrontation. Silence, in the entire story of Job has a profound impact on the story's interpretation. Looking at their speeches, the three are not prepared to give up until they see that Job stops speaking. Their choice to deliberate on Job's opening soliloquy (3.3–26) and also on his subsequent responses may have been an investment the three make to comfort Job. Yet, how far such a choice is successful in consoling the sufferer may be another matter.

77. Clines, *Job 1–20*, 453.
78. Seow, *Job 1–21*, 461.

The sensitivity of the three to the environment and the sufferer most likely ignited their psychological feelings so much that they ended up in fear and anger. What they saw must have tuned their verbal processing to jump to conclusions at will. It is their wickedness that has brought all those calamities upon him. They do not see any good in him (23:5). Job also says the three do not have insight into whatever is going on, and their words are futile (26:3). As a result, when he is brought before the courts of justice, he will be cleared and acquitted (19:25-27; 23:3-7; 35:2).[79] He pronounces an oath of innocence (27:2-6; 31:1-34, 37-40). In the story of Job, we see the crushing effects of destructive criticism and the judgment of the three. As Roy Zuck asserts, the three friends are "truncating His sovereignty, suggesting that He could use suffering for only one purpose, namely, discipline for sin."[80] They attack Job for telling them the truth about himself.

Harkening to the cries of the sufferer and seeking to find justice for a friend lies at the heart of Job's speeches. Social justice is a prominent theme in wisdom discourse.[81] Friends are not supposed to harm the childless woman (24:21). So now that he has no children, they should stand by him. Job rhetorically asked how his friends, especially Bildad, have helped him when he had no power (26:2). Unfortunately, the three could not sustain the trust that existed between themselves and Job. They knew him but thought it was possible he had changed. In the words of James Crenshaw,

> earlier appeals to Job's nobility of character give way to one primary concern, and that is to vindicate themselves. In the process a decisive shift occurs; whereas the friends were at the outset genuinely interested in helping Job return to his former estate, in the end their consuming passion was to justify themselves. This recognizable change explains why Job came to identify the three friends as agents of the enemy, in this instance, God.[82]

---

79. Commentators hold that the book of Job can be seen as a "lawsuit." Chapters 4-14 are assumed to be a preliminary attempt to settle the dispute out of court. Chapter 15-31 serves as a formal court proceeding where there is cross-examination between Job and the friends, while the case is resumed with Elihu serving as a witness in 38, and finally, God the judge pronounces his judgment. See Crenshaw, "Wisdom," 253, 254; Parsons, "Literary Features of the Book of Job," 213, 214.

80. Zuck, "Theology of Wisdom Literature and Song of Songs," 220.

81. Torrance, "Friendship as a Mode for Theological Engagement," 126.

82. Crenshaw, *Whirlwind of Torment*, 70.

THE CASE OF ELIPHAZ, BILDAD, AND ZOPHAR AS FRIENDS 153

For Job, the appropriate use of words and gestures plays an important role in promoting good relationships. Job is someone who provides good counsel, and people listen attentively when he speaks (29:21–23). In the words of Elaine Phillips, "the friends not only spoke falsely about Job, but their words failed to acknowledge the dynamic cosmic dimension of what was happening."[83] Speaking well is emphasized here, but not in the sense that there is nothing wrong in whatever he says or that his words overshadow others. The aged, nobles, chiefs, and rulers accord him all the respect when he speaks (29:8–9). He says: "my words dropped upon them like dew" (29:22b). Moreover, he puts up a charming face that influences confidence. The power of his smile is enough. A smile is infectious and has priceless value. It is one of the most effective methods of non-communication which overcomes barriers, evokes trust and controls emotions.

The comforters have become accusers in their claim to impart wisdom to Job but, in the end, God reveals how the three did not speak well. They thought they were honoring God with their theological views, not knowing they were speaking what was not right about God (42:7). Some interpreters find it strange for God to rebuke Job for speaking in ignorance and then commend him for having spoken the truth. I agree with Marvin Pope that the word in the Hebrew text does not mean "sincerity," but rather "correct."[84] Of course, anytime people do not speak about what is true about God, they fall into the trap the three friends fell in, and it takes the prayers and sacrifices of friends to restore them. While claiming to be friends who sustain trust, identify with each other, and stand by one another in times of joy and pain, they choose to attack Job with their harsh criticism. Job's intercession is meant to reestablish a renewed relationship with his friends. They become good friends once again; there is no hostility between them. Job will certainly intercede for them, not with a sad heart or as an enemy. He does so as a true friend, meaning he has to renew the relationship before praying for them. Hence, "reconciliation between Job and his three friends must have taken place before."[85] Habel avers, "the ministry of friendship is not judged by our capacity to explain God's ways or defend God's teachings, but by our ability to stand with an alienated human against the insidious forces of our world and to believe,

---

83. Phillips, "Speaking Truthfully," 35.
84. Pope, *Job*, 350.
85. Iwanski, *Dynamics of Job's Intercession*, 355.

at all costs, in that person."⁸⁶ If this assertion is anything to go by, then the three are not true friends as readers are made to believe.

Job does not abandon his three friends or condemn them. Even though he does not see them as true friends, he desires to continue relating with them. Only when Job prays for his friends is he himself restored. In the words of Moster,

> This portrayal of the three friends as critical and heartless is supplemented by Job's rantings against them. They are disloyal, fickle, cowards, liars, quacks, unjust, deceitful, full of empty platitudes, mischievous, mockers, unwise, aggrievers, humiliators, abusers, overbearing, deserters, maligners, offerers of empty consolation, and talkers of nonsense.⁸⁷

That is to say, the three friends do not know how to live with the concept of Ubuntu where one's well-being is dependent on the other. If Job fails to forgive the three friends, his restoration may be hampered: "After Job prayed for his friends, the Lord made him prosperous again" (42:10). Job praying for his three friends initiates a process of reconciliation and renewed friendship. They are no longer miserable comforters or treacherous, but new friends who can be relied on.

IMPLICATIONS

It seems the book of Job is a critique of what friendship should be. The relationship between Job and the three provides a range of opportunities for the emotional expression and self-disclosure expected in friendship relationships. As Evan Howard posits, "self-disclosure involves every aspect of human experience."⁸⁸ The three display their anger and who they truly are, and Job cannot control his temper any longer after going through all that suffering either. Earlier, Job had tried to accept the outcome of the disaster, but after his wife intervened, his true sense of anger erupted. The capacity to evaluate one's actions and speech is inherently human. Anyone can jump to conclusions after hearing what the other is saying. The Akan say, *nyɛnko bi sen onua* ("there are friends who are more loyal than siblings"). How does God expect humanity to give up our lives for our friends? What can Christians do to show that depth of love for their friends? How can the

---

86. Habel, "Only the Jackal Is My Friend," 227.
87. Moster, "Punishment of Job's Friends," 217.
88. Howard, *Brazos Introduction to Christian Spirituality*, 24.

stories between Job and the three help to produce an ethic that embodies the qualities of justice, love, and friendship?

First, true friends should know each other very well. The problem with the three is that they do not know Job well. They accuse him of sinning when they do not have credible information. They jump to conclusions based on misleading theology. Job feels that he has to correct his friends who are misrepresenting him. The Akan believes that *sɛ annkasa wo tsir wo a, woyi wo eyi bɔn* ("if you do not speak out, the barber will give you a bad haircut"). In other words, one has to explain issues to others so that one is not misrepresented. The Igbo elders also say, *Agwo emeghi nke o jiri buru agwo, umuaka achiri ya hie nku* ("If a snake fails to show its venom, little kids will use it in tying firewood"). In other words, there are times when one has to defend one's position.

Friends who know each other well learn to trust another. It may be that the three did not know Job well just as the Lord did. The Lord knew Job as a righteous man, but not so in the eyes of the three. The words "righteous" and "equity" are rich with both ethical meaning and sheer simplicity. Christians often attach overtly religious overtones when perceiving what it means to be "righteous." The basic meaning of the word in Hebrew is "to do the right thing." The three apparently do not know Job well enough to know that he can do the right thing. If they had spent the time really getting to know him, they would have believed and trusted that he was a righteous man. Africans also believe that "there is no better mirror than a best friend." Cocking and Kennett can be understood in a sense when they say, "the self my friend sees is, at least in part, a product of the friendship."[89] That is to mean, if it were not for the friendship between Job and the three, they would not have accused him the way they did.

Good and intimate friends know things about each other, especially their values, struggles, goals, and interests. They strive to elevate each other's mood and boost their outlook, thus ensuring the happiness of each other. They also support one another to achieve each other's goals, in good times or bad times. A good friend will show a genuine interest in what's going on in the friend's life. It is not the best for friends to "own" each other. Job had confidence in himself that he was not at fault. He could not get himself to think that he might have wronged anyone or sinned. This can be a dangerous position for a contemporary Christian to take for all have sinned (Rom 3:23; 1 John 1:8–9). Self-righteousness makes people

---

89. Cocking and Kennett, "Friendship and the Self," 505.

search through their hearts and motives and conclude that they have not sinned, thus showing the limits of their knowledge. That does not mean that a Christian cannot be said to be holy and blameless before God. But it is possible for some people to see themselves as righteous and not listen to their friends. Such friends cannot end up being true friends.

Good friends will find a positive way to express themselves when they do not agree. Good friends are honest about themselves to one another, but bad ones hide themselves. The characters of friends must be stainless. They should be completely open without any hidden agendas, interests, and aims. The sages say, "Whoever conceals his transgressions will not prosper, but he who confesses and forsakes them will obtain mercy" (Prov 28:13). This means friends confess sin to each other (Prov 17:9). Friends are accountable to one another. It is not acceptable to confess only the outward life and leave what is dear to the heart. Friends do not simply share what is enough to soothe their consciences but heavily edit and sanitize their stories. Nevertheless, some friends turn out to act with a police mentality when inquiring about the secrets of their friends. A bad friend tries to control, criticize, and abuse the friend's generosity.

Second, true friends should aim at helping each other as a sign of goodwill. Job is depicted as a person who shows care and compassion—not just a feeling but an action. Caring people think of others with love and actively seek their well-being in times of need. Good friends stand together when the other is weak and fearful, usually showing respect for them through solidarity. Friendship is love expressed in acceptance, forgiveness, and commitment, regardless of what the other has done in the past. It is consistently about looking forward to the future with unfailing love. Job has to pray for his friends when God finally brings judgment against them, for they did not speak rightly about God (42:8). Jesus enjoins believers to extend love to one another and abide in love, and even love your enemies and pray for those who persecute you (Matt 5:43–45). To forgive a friend will pave the way for the heavenly Father to also forgive us when we make mistakes. When we forgive others, it makes it possible for us to be forgiven (Matt 6:14–15). People who do this display goodwill and can be trusted.

The three promote misleading theologies, understood as theologies that are one-sided, undermine fundamental biblical doctrines, and lack a sound theological ethos. Misleading theologies lead to a violation of the God-given dignity of others and do not restore the poor and needy to a place of honor. Trying to defend God without taking into cognizance the full account of the facts is not the best. The position the three take mirrors how some fail to consider all the revelations of God in making their arguments. Taking a portion of scripture and developing a theology out of it is like taking one thread in a cloth and assuming it is a cloth, or cutting a small piece out of a cloth and assuming it is a full cloth. God's relationship with humanity is always mysterious and beyond our understanding, but the whole Bible is enough to help us arrive at some appreciable view of life. Holding on to the idea that God is only on the side of the righteous and prosperous person cannot be the whole truth of the Bible. God's ways are very wonderful and greater than what our feeble minds can grasp (Ps 139:6).

Third, the problem with the three is that they lack intimacy. True friends are expected to show empathy and stand by each other. They should be ready to trust the other friend's opinion and appreciate what is going on. The Akan say, *nyia a ɔhyɛ ne mpaaboa na onyim mbrɛ osi mia no fa* ("the one wearing the shoes knows how it is squeezing the legs"). Since a person cannot imagine the exact nature of hurt in another person, taking the other by their word is enough, and that is what friends have to do. Job's point about arguing with God in the debate with his friends has something to do with caring for one another and teaching one another how to live as friends. He does not want the friendship between him and the three to be severed. Many a time, friends will walk away when they find no comfort in one another. The Akan say, *Wo amma wo nyɛnko anntwa anko a, wo ronntwa nnuru* ("If you don't let your friend cross and reach his destination, you will also not cross and reach yours").

A true friend is someone who helps out when the other friend is possibly suffering harm, just out of love and friendship. That is to say, it is the foundation upon which friendship relationships are built. Some friends are always available, especially in days of trouble, but it is not enough to be available yet not show love. Such is the teaching of Proverbs 18:24: "There is a friend who sticks closer than a brother." In other words, what a friend can do for another, brothers or sisters cannot do the same or may not go as far. However, the three do not help Job at all in his situation; they only make it worse for Job.

The story encourages all to see themselves as friends who will not violently accuse others when we do not know the facts or we presume the facts. Bearing false witness is a grave sin (Exod 20:16; 23:1; Prov 24:28; 25:18), and such people will not go unpunished (Prov 19:19; 21:28). The Akan say, *Wohu sɛ wo yonko abodwesɛ rehye a na wasa nsuo asi wo deɛ ho* ("If you see your neighbor's beard on fire, fetch water and place by yours"). That is to say, one is supposed to learn from the experiences and circumstances of others. Likewise, the Akan cautions that one should not ignore what has happened to another. The Akan say, *Otua wo nyɛnko ho a, otua dua mu* ("If it is in the body of your neighbor, it is in a tree") to mean what has happened to one person can happen to another person. If Job deserves harsh treatment, then they also deserve it because Job cannot be classified as different or someone with no feelings. What Job is going through could also happen to the friends. However, the significance of the proverb is that one should never fail to empathize with one another. However, it is more common for people to not genuinely care about another because they do not feel what the other feels. In the epilogue, the three friends will come to learn what it means to have not spoken what is right about God. If how they treated Job was to be how Job would treat them, they would find it unacceptable. When they are pronounced to be in the wrong, they may have a better appreciation for it and demand the empathy that they were unable to offer Job. To develop true friendship, one should be prepared to support the other out of love because one good turn deserves the other. The most important thing about friendship is how the relationship makes one feel—not how it is supposed to be or the things they have in common.

Fourth, loyal friends are the ones to be trusted. Bad friends see friendship as a way to expose others, not knowing that they are exposing themselves. The three seek to expose Job to knowledge about God, but eventually, they expose themselves in terms of their paucity of knowledge. They are not prepared to learn from the thoughts and concerns of others and assume that putting themselves out there is scary and dangerous. Lack of openness also makes bad friends assume that there will be no guarantee that a friendship relationship can last. Developing and maintaining friendships does take time and effort, so those who do not have time for others are not good friends. It is possible to see bad friends as those who are too busy and may not have time for friends. They cannot allow some space and time, and cannot prioritize friendships. They see friendship as pleasure and assume that they cannot mix business with pleasure. Being there for one another can help fight depression. Sharing problems with friends can help to cope with most of the challenges that come from a life crisis.

Close friends can turn against one another (Ps 41:9), but not loyal friends. The psalmist decries that it is not one's enemies who taunt their friends and accuse wrongly, "but it is you, my equal, my companion, my familiar friend, with whom I kept pleasant company; we walked in the house of God with the throng" (Ps 55:12–14). He goes on to say,

> My companion laid hands on a friend
>   and violated a covenant with me
> with speech smoother than butter
>   but with a heart set on war;
> with words that were softer than oil
>   but in fact were drawn swords. (Ps 55:20–21)

The three urge Job to listen to them no matter what. Job knows they are not right, so he is not ready to listen to them and accept their judgement. The Igbo elders say, *Mmadu a dighi mma ilo aso mmri maka iza onye oma* ("One should not swallow phlegm in the name of decorum"). This proverb teaches that no one should not accept fault when innocent, just because it is the friend who is speaking. A person is not expected to do what is wrong in order to be praised or called good.

Fifth, true friends learn to collaborate with one another. They try to agree to disagree. In life, it is possible to do the right thing in the wrong way. The three purpose in their hearts to help Job come to a realization of life—they feel they are doing good to their friend, Job—but their approach is not acceptable to Job. A good friend will feel comfortable pointing out the truth about themselves and the friend because they share a bond of trust and loyalty. They do not imagine that their approach to doing good would turn out to be a stab in the back. An African proverb goes that whoever turns his back on you is not your friend. It is also said, "better to have an enemy who slaps you in the face than a friend who stabs you in the back."

The three become entrapped by the view that Job is not being fair to them. Again, they find fault with Job's claim to his own righteousness. Although they are ignorant of God's affirmations that Job is righteous and blameless (1:8; 2:3), they are not prepared to listen to Job, for a person should not boast about oneself. What fuels their passion to contend with Job and argue strongly is the understanding that all misfortune is caused by sin and that Job's claim to innocence makes God come out to be unjust (8:3). Such a bid to defend God as not being unjust separates them from Job and becomes a point of departure which breaks their friendship. Perhaps the three feel being confrontational will make Job see them as friends. As it is said in Swahili, *bora kuwa mwiba kwa upande was rafiki yako kuliko sauti yake ya mwangwi* ("it is better to be the thorn in the side of your friend than to be his echo"). Confronting a friend does not mean one should be disloyal or treasonable.

The three friends assert that Job is not showing humility in that he claims to know better than the aged. An Akan proverb says, *adze a abofra bɛtsen no kɔn ahwɛ no, panyin tsena ase hu* ("what a child will stretch his neck to see, an elder will sit and see it"). In other words, the elders have a highly discerning eye that transcends beyond the ordinary. The three assume that Job has lost touch with tradition—he is refusing to accept what the elders have proposed and established.

Friendship is about oneness and togetherness; colleagues follow a common agenda. Jesus's prayer in John 15–17 emphasizes that "oneness" among believers is to be a sign to the world, pointing out the love of God for us in Jesus Christ. Human relationships have constantly been bedeviled with disagreements and squabbling. However, the mystery of the incarnation is that God came to dwell among us (John 1:1–14) revealing the extent of the desired loving relationship that God expects from everyone. Cocking and Kennett say, "it is not the sharing of private information nor even of very personal information, as such, that contributes to the bonds of trust and intimacy between companion friends. At best it is the sharing of what friends care about that is relevant here."[90]

Friends cannot easily or faithfully walk together when they hold divergent opinions. At least, they should agree to disagree with one another so that they can follow a common purpose. Friends ought to focus on others, not themselves, showing interest in the friend's feelings, experiences, stories, and opinions. They are not pretending when they listen, care, and simply foster a connection, and they do not look for their own benefit in the other person. Wilson writes,

> when the pursuit of survival exhausts our energies, we have little left to sustain our faith. This is when we most need believing friends who resist the temptation to criticize our struggling faith, and instead come alongside us to give testimony of the continuing faithfulness of God that we have difficulty seeing through our pain. This is what Job's friends fail to do.[91]

Many a time, the best thing friends need is an encouraging word that will make the sufferer reflect on life critically. Sometimes, all that

---

90. Cocking and Kennett, "Friendship and the Self," 518.
91. Wilson, *Job*, 61.

friends need is someone to lean on, cry with, or offer a comforting hug. Showing a positive presence makes the friend stand in times of adversity. Friendship should not be for a season. It is possible to listen to friends and not hear what the friend has actually said. When friends listen, it is easier for them to understand what the other's needs are because they know them. If a friend desires to speak or offer advice, it should be an encouraging word.

Sixth, friends are supposed to empower each other, especially in times of difficulty. The three friends could not "comfort" Job as they had purposed to do. Their presence made Job broken and disappointed rather than empowering him. Friends are more important to psychological well-being than even our love and family relationships. Friends bring more happiness into our lives than virtually anything else. Establishing and maintaining a friendship takes time and effort because friendship has to be nurtured from simple acquaintance to intimate friendship. Friends should always have a reason to be there for each other. Africans believe that since life is cyclical, something may happen to one person at one moment and in the next moment happen to another. It is not a realistic way of viewing life to think that it is only the other who will encounter problems.

A fake friend will not care how the other feels when giving counsel or advice. Since the motive is not friendly, the approach is to put the other down even after you are talking. They are not prepared to listen to friends or know how the person feels. The fake friend will try to help friends understand "the why" or try to offer solutions to their problems but will lead the friend astray so that the friend fails in life. All the solutions the three proffer are about themselves and not about the one they desire to help. It is believed that a close friend can become a close enemy. Dana Roberts is right in saying,

> The path of friendship is shaped by its context—both the socio-politico-economic realities of the day and the particular characteristics of the friends themselves . . . Even if friends are fellow followers of Christ, their definitions of friendship are influenced by differences in culture, differences in generation and even generational differences within the same culture.[92]

In some cases, Christian pastors and healers accuse people who are going through suffering and challenges of the need to confess hidden sins

---

92. Robert, *Faithful Friendship*, 168.

before their petitions are brought before God. The sufferers are accused of a sin they may not be aware of. At worst, they are reminded of universal sin (Rom 3:10, 23; Pss 14:3; 53:3). Much as a person cannot lay claim to righteousness, it does not mean God has not acquitted some to be righteous. The sad reality is that wrongly accusing someone who is suffering of sin is a grave sin in itself. The book of Job teaches all who accuse others falsely to learn from the three.

An Akan proverb says, *nyɛnko na ɔka nyɛnko enyim sɛ ɔfom a* ("a real friend should warn his friend in case of wrongdoing"). Yet, friends need to speak the truth in love so that each one can grow up in every way into Christlikeness (Eph 4:15). Friendship is courteous in every respect. The three take their "friend" Job for granted. They think Job is heading for trouble, so they find ways to talk about it. However, their approach is not caring and empathic.

Job's words to his friends are not only intended to build their knowledge or help people to gain insights and skills. To Job, the three should aim at upholding those who are stumbling and strengthening feeble knees. Closely connected with Job's notion of friendship is an exhortation, admonition, confrontation, and an encouragement, urging, begging, and appealing to the three to empower all who come to them. Encouragement is a virtue all friends must owe each other. Encouragement means cheering up. Encouragement from a friend can boost one's confidence, sense of self-worth, and chances of success. Those who come to Job should go back differently, having an assurance of support, and knowing that their problems are solved. His influence transforms the hopeless to have hope. He is a mature person, helping others who are weak to stand on their feet.

Finally, true friendship is about putting others' need above one's own need. Selfishness darkens how people treat others and speak to them. The three cannot create any space to empathize with Job or listen to him. Their own thoughts cloud their imaginations and whatever they say was how they feel. Failure to be other-centered breeds mistrust, negativity, and quarrel. True friendship also involves actively seeking what is best for someone else. It is about putting the other first without grumbling and using what we have in serving others (1 Pet 4:9–11). Sometimes, being other-centered will come at a great personal cost, yet it should be seen as the love that is shared. Friendly love should be shared with the notion of not receiving anything in return. Other-centeredness is an extension of hospitality. Friends can accommodate each other's thoughts, words, and behavior and also give encouraging words or wise counsel to each other. It is about helping out with the various needs of others that arise in day-to-day life. It is a privilege to have a friend who does not think about themself but others.

CONCLUDING REMARKS

The foregoing has revealed the relationship between the three and Job. It has shown how the three were friends for a season and a reason. A friend should also not be seditious. Seven lessons gleaned from the foregoing are (1) knowing the other well, (2) goodwill and benevolence, (3) intimacy, (4) loyalty, (5) collaboration, (6) empowerment, and (7) other-centeredness. Contrary to popular thought, the three are more likely to be categorized as good friends in African thought. At least, they show some positive virtues expected of friends like collaboration, loyalty, goodwill, and common purpose. The three are from different places, but they stay committed to each other as friends. They show that friendship is based on how an individual knows the other, and the level of intimacy and loyalty, and is motivated by how they collaborate, help each other, and follow a common path. True friends think about each other and stay in touch.

Friendship is a commitment that lays ethical and moral claims. It calls for knowing each other well, which the friends fall short of. Staying close to a friend is not enough unless the individual's presence can build up knowledge, wisdom, and power in the friend. In contemporary times, many are caught up in the social media web of "friendship" which is measured by people one cannot know too well. It is about the number of people who show "likes" over quality relationships; people one cannot know much about or meet in person. Again, the three feel it is their duty to correct Job when he goes out of line, but they do not show intimacy and empathy in their approach. They thus make high demands on Job, and even make it difficult for him to meet their demands. Hence, they do the right thing in the wrong way. Moreso, the three try to identify with Job in his predicament but rather expressed their uncontrolled disappointment, disbelief, and grief by raising their voices and weeping aloud. Hence, their attitude is not empowering. The three are deeply sorry for Job and express sad emotions. Even when Job is not ready to give up, the three had already given up, thus failing from the onset to be a source of empowerment. They also use silence at a point in time as a therapeutic way of affirming their presence.

Friendship is also expressed in healthy and positive confrontations but not imposing one's opinion on the other. The three think Job is not motivating himself in the midst of affliction, suffering, disappointment, and persecution. To them, for Job to lose his temper and begin cursing everything was not the best. Friends show their worth when others are in the wrong because when one searches for a friend with no faults, the person will remain with no friends. Yet, friends do not dwell so much on the flaws of the other. A friend can only empower the other if there is submission, hence the three resort to forcing Job to submit.

Doing the right thing in the wrong way robs the action of its rightness. Yet making a mistake or using the wrong approach does not make a person bad. Job feels that the three are not living up to expectations and, as such, are bad friends. Nevertheless, a lack of experience and knowledge does not make one necessarily bad. As long as the three assume that Job has sinned, they will never stray from the view that God has punished Job. They are using the wrong approach to judge him, so the three are not loyal. And anyone who withholds loyalty from a friend is not a good friend.

One has to know a friend well and learn to listen to and trust the other. True friends are expected to show intimacy and empathy and promote the psychological well-being of each other. Where friends hold divergent opinions, they should agree to disagree with one another so that they can follow a common purpose. Job does not value the solidarity and sympathy the three are showing, because they are not trying to restore him but rather accuse him wrongly. They do not believe him as a brother because a brother stays on the side of the kin in difficult circumstances. Friends have to do to others what they want others to do to them. The appropriate use of words and gestures plays an important role in promoting good relationships. Job feels that even if he had given up faith in God, fierce confrontation should not be the approach of a friend. The words of the three are most hurtful. Words can be like arrows attacking a person's flesh and piercing the soul. For Job, once the three are hurting him, they do not fear God. Job expresses his disappointment about how the three are acting, speaking of a stream that dries in a hot season, at a time when people need water so badly. The three are miserable comforters, using windy words and unfounded arguments. A friend does not make it difficult for others to share their opinion. A friend should be able to show compassion and mercy and not pursue the other into exasperation. A friend should not be on the side of the assailant and strike the one supposed to be a friend.

The three lack wisdom, for they do not provide well-balanced counsel. They do not take time to listen to all sides of the story before speaking. The three become accusers instead of encouragers, and thus make a fool of themselves by speaking what is not true about God. Often, critics do not pay attention to their interpretations. As long as their claims are logical, they promote them. They may not consider whether their arguments are "right" or "wrong" since in our postmodern age, rightness and wrongness are relative. Some Christians judge others as sinners without any proof. At times, they erroneously interpret a scriptural passage to support their claim, thereby drawing conclusions out of false premises. The assumption that to err is human and there is none that is righteous is true, yet wisdom teaches that sometimes God looks at issues differently. The proper use of speech is necessary for building friendships. A good speech that leads to an increase in wisdom brings harmony that brings empowerment. Friends should help each other in seeking wisdom and direct each other to fear God. Christians need a similarly balanced understanding of friendship in a world where relationships thrive virtually, a world that is part of God's world.

7

The Case for Job's Wife as a Friend

THE RELATIONSHIP BETWEEN JOB and Mrs. Job is worth exploring while considering spousal friendship. Seeking out the presuppositions underlying the text, finding emotive influences in the choice of words and actions between Job and his wife, and locating the discussion in the context of what is called spousal friendship can show whether they can be seen as friends. I have posited that the book of Job does not give a satisfactory answer to the problem of evil but reveals some answers to the question of human nature and relationships. Therefore, an exploration of spousal friendship can give critics some perspectives on the story. The story about Job and Mrs. Job presents some possibilities about how their marriage worked, which can be deduced due to the apparent amplification of verbal attacks. Generally, it can be argued that their relationship was full of suspicion and disappointment because they did not nurture friendship in their relationship. Some questions are worth pondering: Is it possible to show from the story how to be good friends in marriage? What could have been the issues between Job and Mrs. Job that led to the use of words and actions against one another? How trustworthy are they in the eyes of each other? How does the story play upon the hearer's feelings? What mood influences what is said and the meaning that is generated? How does the relationship between Job and his wife demonstrate friendship or otherwise?

MARRIAGE AND FRIENDSHIP IN THE AFRICAN CONTEXT

Marriage is a contract between couples—an agreement to help and support each other in a relationship—but it can become a platform for oppressing and exploiting one another. The reasons why some enter into marriage cannot be easily seen, but how the couple lives together matters, and may make their motives clear. The Akan say, *awar tse dɛ nkatse, wɔpaa mu ansaana yeehu dza ɔwɔ mu* ("marriage is like groundnut; one has to crack it to see what is inside"). In a world where marriages are hanging on a thin line of loyalty and get broken easily, and where "for better or worse" means so little or rather "for better for best," living together in marriage is more of a burden than a blessing. Hence, disappointments usually set in. Fredrich Nietzsche is right in saying, "it is not a lack of love, but a lack of friendship that makes unhappy marriages." Hence, the similarities between the expectations of marriage and friendship cannot be overemphasized. Spousal friendship thrives in authentic love and serves as a bedrock for a loving expression. Spousal or marital friendship is the love, affection, time, energy, attention, gifts, and sacrifices shared between husband and wife. The grace to hold on to one's spouse in spite of all the challenges in life, however, depends on how the couple builds friendship.

Marriage in most parts of Africa is founded on the *pater familias* ideology; the man is the head of the family, household, or social unit. His wife, sons, daughters, servants, and slaves are legally and economically dependent on him. In such a system, the man or husband relying on patriarchal power has the right to punish or correct any member of the family, including the wife. In traditional African societies, the wife is expected to be a good housekeeper, a mother, and nurturer of children in the household, and to show respect to her husband. She is expected to submit and care for her husband no matter what. She should seek the best interest of her husband, and humility must be her watchword. She is not to see herself as an equal companion and must sacrifice her personal desires and ambitions for her husband's. The wife, in some sense, is one of the "properties" of her husband. If there can be peace at home, then it should come from her. African women are always blamed as the cause of dissatisfaction in marriage. The Akan say, *yer tse dɛ kuntu; sɛ edze kata wo do a, nna woho keka wo, na sɛ iyi gu hɔ a nna awaw dze wo* ("the wife is like a blanket; when you use it to cover yourself you will feel itches, and when you put it away you feel cold"). However, abuse of one's spouse is a serious offense and can lead to divorce. No wonder most mothers take their children as their intimate friends.

Interpretations of love in the African worldview are also contextual and based on intimacy, goodwill, and the ability to support one another. Among the Akan, for instance, most of the proverbs on love echo how unreliable lovers can be. For instance, *suro nea ɔdɔ wo* ("fear the one who loves you"). Similarly, in Swahili it is said, *Mahaba ni tamu, mahaba ni sumu* ("Love is sweet, love is poison"). Again, in Swahili it is said, *Akipenda chongo huita kengeza* ("A person who loves calls one-eyed a squint"). In other words, couples should be cautious when it comes to love, for it can be misleading. Nwando Achebe argues that African expressions of love appear different from what is seen in the Global North, but that does not mean that Africans are incapable of communicating and experiencing amorous or romantic love for one another.[1]

In the absence of love, couples focus on the challenges of life and not the requirements and dedication that friendship relationships require. The reality, however, is that friendship plays a key role in building relationships prior to marriage and it can continue throughout marriage. Loyal or true friends stand by each other no matter what happens. Loyal friends celebrate both the good and bad times together, as in the Akan saying, *Onipa dɔ wo a, ɔdɔ wo ne wo nkwaseasɛm* ("If a person loves you, he loves you with all your nonsense"). Friendship in marriage makes the couple work toward a common goal. The unvoiced commitment in friendship provides the basis of the laws governing the relationship. If dating and courtship become a time to see how each other is a good friend, then the real discoveries and virtues that grow in a relationship should not die off when the two become married. Hence, couples are to move from being ordinary friends and companions to being true or intimate friends.

Traditional marriage in most African communities is arranged by families, yet some aspects are based on the friendship between the groom and bride. In some communities, like in Botswana, courtship stages (*go kokota / go itshupa*) and bride-seeking (*patlo*) are permitted. For instance, among the Fulbe, marriage is endogamous, but the women are allowed to make their choice of the man they wish to marry. People of the same lineage and caste are expected to marry to preserve their bloodline and identity, yet those intending to marry are allowed to make friends in order to choose well.

---

1. Achebe, "Love, Courtship, and Marriage in Africa," 119–42.

Women are sometimes socialized to focus on the benefits they can accrue from marriage. During customary marriages, the wife is told that when she gets anything in the marriage, she should bring it to the extended family, but when she incurs a debt, she should leave it to the husband. It shows that some societies honor women when good is happening to them, and try to take advantage of it, but when times are adverse, the woman cannot be part of it and the man should absorb the adversity that comes up. As such the Akan say, *mmaa pɛ adze kyir ka* ("women like to enjoy possessions, but they hate debt"). That is to say, some women love where they can be enriched, not where they have to carry a burden. However, in Botswana, there is a system of community of property where the couple become co-owners of all property that each one acquires or brings into the marriage.

Africans generally feel that a woman has destructive powers and cannot reflect on issues very well. Hence, men should control the thoughts and speech of women, a situation which is very unfortunate. For instance, the Akan say, *Oyere te sɛ kuntu: wode kata wo so a wo ho keka wo; woyi gu ho nso a, awo de wo* ("A woman can be compared to a blanket; if you cover yourself with it, you may feel irritation on your skin, and if you remove it you become cold"). Another Akan proverb, *ɔbaa tse dɛ hurui, mogya mmpa ne tsir mu da* ("a woman is like the tsetsefly; blood will always be in its head"), shows that no matter how good a woman is, she will always do what is evil).

It is not out of place to add that in African communities, friendship relations are made up of extended family systems, distant relatives, and friends who make up a close-knit network, as well as strangers. Friendships can be between equals or non-equals, but in most cases, it is gender specific. When parties come together and see themselves as friends, they become equal. In the general sense, a friend is one who upholds a social ethic of collaboration toward a common goal. Friendship connotes striving with another, sharing, doing good, being open to another, or making oneself available to others, and accepting others in a loving, friendly, and compassionate way.

Goodwill and support for one another are also key virtues in marriage and friendship. The Shona people say, *Chadyiwa nowako hachinzi charasika, kurasika kwacho hunge wako arizivira, risingapi* ("It is not lost when you give something to a friend, unless your friend knows not how to give"). That is to say, it is worthless to give something to someone who refuses to share with others. Among the Fulbe, to prove loyalty, friends give their cattle to each other to add to their stock and take care of it for them—and one's ability to take good care of the animal and show accountability is a mark of friendship.

Friends are expected to share whatever will build up each other. Friends share things in common. When a family is experiencing difficulty, the proper response of a faithful member of a family is friendship. Such expression of presence involves giving one's self to the other and sharing resources to help one another. The Akan say, *Hwɛ me so mma minni bi nti na atwe mmienu nam* ("Watch over me while I eat makes two antelopes walk together"). It is also said *Huu m'ani so ma me nti na atwe mmienu nam* ("it is because one has to blow the dust from the other's eyes that two antelopes walk together"). The African idea of sacrificial giving is different from what Nietzsche says (quoted by Derrida): "Here and there on earth we may encounter a kind of continuation of love in which this possessive craving of two people for each other gives way to a new desire and lust for possession, a *shared* higher thirst for an ideal above them. But who knows such love? Who has experienced it? Its right name is *friendship*."[2] In other words, it is not desire or lust that defines love but a relationship of empathic sharing and carrying each other burdens, hence the saying, *wo nyɛnko da nye wo da* ("your friend's day is your day"). It means whatever happens to a friend has happened to you. Each person has a day when unpleasant news comes, and when a friend encounters what is unpleasant, it is not only the friend's day. Yet the Akan say, *nya asem hwɛ na hɔ na ibohu w'adɔfo na w'atamfo* ("the day you encounter a problem is when you will see your lovers and enemies"). True friends show up in times of adversity and stand by each other while enemies desert people who are suffering.

A friend will stay close when things are not good, especially when the other is willing to follow the advice given. To give advice as well as take it is a feature of true friendship. Bad friends give bad advice while good friends will speak the truth even if it hurts. In Swahili it is said, *bora kuwa mwiba kwa upande was rafiki yako kuliko sauti yake ya mwangwi* ("it is better to be the thorn in the side of your friend than to be his echo"). That is to say, "a real friend should warn his friend in case of wrongdoing."[3]

---

2. Derrida, *Politics of Friendship*, 71, quoting Nietzsche; emphasis original.

3. Scheven, *Swahili Proverbs*, 229.

The Ewe people say, *Gake hafi nate ŋu adze xɔlɔ la, be nado vivi ɖe amewo ŋu* ("To make friends, you have to be friendly"). It is believed that where there is faithfulness, trust, and honesty, friendship can be developed. Such a relationship begins with a genuine interest and commitment to the aspirations, goals, and dreams of the other, to offer support no matter what in both small and big things.

Friends are expected to lift the other when they fall. Selfishness cannot be justified by the fact that human beings are necessarily egocentric beings. One should not think only of oneself, not considering the needs of others. The isiZulu saying *Izandla ziyagezana* ("Hands wash each other") echoes the value of reciprocity. It is expected of all, and not only among friends, to help each other, and build each other up. The Igbo elders say, *Ọkọkọọ anumanu ọ kọọya na osisi ma; ọkọọ mmadu o jekuru mmaduibeya* ("If an animal feels itchy, he scratches his body on the tree, but if a man feels itchy, he goes to his fellow man"). A human being cannot do everything alone. There is a need for others to support and help. That is why in Igbo, it is said, *Mmadu ka anumanu* ("No man is an island").

Although there may be disagreements between friends, the will to stand by each other matters a lot. In Swahili, the elders say, *mtu na rafikiye ni kama kombe, haziachi* ("a man and his friends are like shells always clattering/disagreeing").[4] The Akan also say, *tɛkyerma na se mpo wɔko* ("even the tongue and the tooth fight") to connote how two individuals should tolerate one another. The collaboration between the tongue and teeth is unquestionable. At times, the tooth will bite the tongue, yet the tongue will need to rub its surface at the back of the teeth to know the extent of the damage. However, one needs to be careful with friends because some can bring others down. The Akan say, *Afɛkubɔ te sɛ asanom, wànhwɛ wo ho so yie a, ɛma wosopa* ("Friendship is like drinking too much palm wine; if you are not careful, it leads to disgrace"). No matter how useful wine can be, there is its destructive aspect.

WHO IS JOB TO HIS WIFE?

This section focuses on the relationship between Mr. and Mrs. Job.

---

4. Scheven, *Swahili Proverbs*, 229.

Credibility and Credentials: General Discussions

The prologue begins with the family of Job, mentioning that Job has seven sons and three daughters (1:2). Nothing is said about his wife. The omission of Mrs. Job in this description may imply that she is not someone of importance in the story, perhaps revealing the patriarchal nature of the storyteller and the community. The intuitive reader is thus given the opportunity to have some preknowledge about the relationship between Job and the household.[5] The story does Mrs. Job a great disservice by not acknowledging here that she gave birth to seven sons and three daughters to Job (1:2). And nothing is said in the epilogue; Job's wife was not mentioned at all. Job rather gave birth to sons and daughters (42:13). The daughters were very beautiful but nothing was heard about his wife (42:15).

In the ancient Near East, marriages were usually arranged, based on either political or economic reasons rather than love. Marriage was seen as an effective way for men to control the desires of women because it was believed that women lacked self-control. "Control of her desires had to be imposed from outside and achieved through guardianship and marriage, as well as through strict codes of behavior and veiling in public."[6]

After the description of Job and his family, the story moves to the heavenly realm where dialogue between God and the Adversary (*hāśāṭān*) or simply, Satan,[7] ensues. The scene portrays a form of a council, where heavenly beings of a common interest meet to discuss issues. In this meeting, God moderates the affairs of all the sons of God, one of which is the Adversary. The story moves to what is happening on earth and speaks about Job as a man who desires that his children follow his example by maintaining their closeness and intimacy with God. The children of Job are old enough to organize parties for themselves. Job's sons would invite their sisters to have a feast. After the festive days, Job would bring his seven sons and three daughters close to where he is, sanctify them, and offer burnt sacrifices on their behalf, with the assumption that they might have sinned and cursed (Heb: *ūbērăkū* // root *brk*) God in their hearts (1:5).[8] This is a routine for Job. The silence about Job not

---

5. "Preknowledge" is used courtesy of Gerald Wilson. See Wilson, "Preknowledge, Anticipation and the Poetics of Job," 243–56.

6. Glazebrook and Olson, "Greek and Roman Marriage," 71.

7. The Hebrew has a definite article, thus not a proper noun.

8. The Hebrew simply says Job will send for them and consecrate them. Whether Job sends someone or sends for them is not mentioned.

offering sacrifices for his wife is instructive. She is incapable of sinning or cursing God in her heart. Nonetheless, it reveals the kind of relationship between the two, and it may not be out of place to conjecture that some distance existed between Job and his wife. Perhaps the storyteller wants the intuitive reader to imagine a seeming lack of oneness between Job and his wife.

At the first heavenly council meeting, the Lord projects Job as the Lord's servant who is blameless (Heb: *tām*) and upright, fears God, and turns away from evil (1:8). The adjective *tām* has a wide range of meanings including "blameless" (2 Sam 22:24; Ps 18:25), "without blemish" (Ezek 43:22–23), "sincerity" (Josh 24:14), "whole"/"full" (Lev 25:30; Josh 10:13), and "perfect" (Deut 32:4; Ps 18:30; Job 37:16). In Proverbs 11:3, the sages contrast *tummat* ("integrity") with *selep* ("crooked") (11:3, 20), and *mašggeh* ("someone who misleads others"; Prov 28:10). Again, the righteousness of one with integrity (*tāmmîm*) keeps the person on a straight way (Prov 11:5). In all, the Lord knows Job well, but the Adversary does not know Job that way. It is not clear whether Mrs. Job knows her husband the way the Lord knows him. The Adversary does not accept what the Lord says about Job and tries to prove that there is some other reason that Job is blameless and upright; Job does not fear God for nothing (1:9). It is the children and possessions that Job has acquired that make him fear God! The Adversary then asks permission to "touch all that he [Job] has, and he will curse you [God] to your face" (1:11). The Lord instructs the Adversary: "only do not to stretch his hand against him" (1:12), implying that only Job should be spared. His wife is not included and should not be spared.

To prove whether Job is who the Lord says he is—and would not curse (Heb: *yĕbārăkā* i.e., *piel* imperfect 3ms // root *brk*) the Lord—permission is given to the Adversary to destroy everything Job has. The Lord gives the Adversary power over everything Job has (1:12). The Adversary, however, does not touch or strike Mrs. Job when God gives that permission. Perhaps Job does not have her at that time. Job rather blesses (Heb: *mĕborākĕ* i.e., pual participle ms // root *brk*) God after losing all that he has and does not sin or charge God with wrongdoing (1:21–22). Actually, the Lord does not give the Adversary permission to kill Job; he has to spare his life. Eventually, the Adversary spares the life of both Job and his wife without giving any reason why his wife is spared.

At another heavenly council meeting, the Lord draws the Adversary's attention to Job, repeating that "there is none like him on the earth, a blameless and upright man, who fears God and turns away from evil" (2:3). The Lord also explains that Job has maintained his integrity even after the Adversary incited the Lord to permit the destruction of all that Job had for no reason. Nevertheless, the Adversary gives a new reason why this might be so: in the first instance, the Lord had not allowed the Adversary to touch Job's bones and flesh (*ʾel-ʿaṣmôʿ wĕʾel bĕśārô*; 2:5). If such permission is given and the task carried out, Job will curse (*yĕbārakĕkkā*) God to God's face (2:5). With permission given by the Lord, the Adversary "struck Job with a bad boil from the sole of his foot to the crown of his head. And he took a piece of pottery to scrape himself while he sat in the ashes" (2:7–8).

The two Hebrew words—bones and flesh—are as when Jacob comes to stay with Laban, and Laban welcomes him with the words: "Surely you are my bone and my flesh" (*ʿaṣmî ûbĕśārî*; Gen 29:14), and as in Ezekiel 37 and the bones and flesh that God brings back together in the valley. In Genesis 29, "bone and flesh" is used as a motif for kinship, which is why Ezekiel takes it as a symbol of creation. David Shepherd also cogently views the Adversary's attack on the bone and flesh of Job as an attack on Job's wife since according to the Genesis tradition of marriage, the woman was the man's flesh and bone. Marriage, by implication, has made the two become one flesh:

> Then the man said,
> 'This at last is bone of my bones (*ʿeṣem mēʿăṣāmay*)
>   and flesh of my flesh (*wĕbāśāro mibbeśārî*);
> she shall be called Woman,
>   because she was taken out of man." (Gen 2:23 ESV)

Shepherd tactfully notes that "the Satan's insistence on the destruction of Job's bone and flesh is a reminder that Job's wife is in fact a crucial part of him, insofar as she is the part of him which is necessary for his securing of the future of his house."[9] Much as this argument can be justified, it still stands that Mrs. Job is not attacked directly. Strangely, Seow explains that bones and flesh would commonly refer to Job's children, and since they have already been destroyed, the reference should be taken literally.[10]

If it is the wife of Job who, by the attack on the "bones and flesh," is indirectly meant to be the real target, then the Adversary succeeds, at

---

9. Shepherd, "Strike His Bone and His Flesh," 81–97
10. Seow, *Job 1–21*, 293.

least from a psychological and rhetorical angle. After all, it is common to see that those who stay with a sick relative or bosom friend also deteriorate and usually pass away, leaving the sick person. Unsurprisingly, the wife of Job, out of great emotional pain, confronts her husband: "Do you still hold fast your integrity? Curse (*bārēk*) God and die" (2:9). On the one hand, it seems Mrs. Job does not trust Job's spirituality. He is maintaining his integrity at a time Mrs. Job thinks differently. Maybe she assumes that Job was like anyone else and would do what some normally do by changing their position. She is wrong and disappointed in the behavior of her husband.

Note that there is a relationship between personal integrity and collective action. The word "integrity," from *integer*, the Latin word for "whole" or "complete," points to a human state of "wholeness" or "completeness." It is an all-encompassing virtue that includes honesty, honor, respect, restraint, and authenticity, as well as responsibility. Job can be complete in his relationship with the Lord, but he is incomplete if he does not likewise maintain a relationship with other people. The writer of the Epistle of John says a person who professes love to God but does not love the neighbor is a liar (1 John 4:20). Individual integrity is a moral attribute that does not stand against the common good. Job has a set of positive attitudes that enhances his honest and ethical relationship with God, but does not show values that impact the overall atmosphere, credibility, and functioning of his entire family. Maybe, Mrs. Job questions Job's integrity because she sees it as incomplete; it does not have any impact on her. I have established elsewhere that for Mrs. Job to find her voice in the midst of perceived betrayal and sidelining means she rises above her personal sufferings and seeks the common good.[11]

On the other hand, it is also possible to assume that Mrs. Job does not have any doubt about her husband's integrity. She knows he has persisted with or maintained his integrity for a long time. Her problem is why should one maintain a position that will continue to bring suffering? Should a person not change their mind so that torture will come to an end? To her, Job is ready to accept suffering but not ready to prepare her to embrace suffering. He had not shown his wife how to cope in adversity. Job's motivation to accept suffering is because he believes it comes from God, just as good things do (2:10).

---

11. Aidoo, "Standing on the Side of Mrs Job," 137.

The unnamed wife of Job is the first to enter into dialogue with her husband in the second chapter.[12] The storyteller identifies her as the wife of Job (2:9) and Job later refers to her twice as "my wife" (19:17; 31:10). Her voice is heard only in her outcry to her husband. Scholars have observed, with mixed reactions, how Job's wife confronts her husband.[13] It seems, of all the women in the Bible, Job's wife is one of the most despised and abused. Perhaps, her nameless identity is better for her and preserves who she is than the many "names" commentators have given to her.

In fact, there is a similarity between God's description of Job to the Adversary and Mrs. Job's words to Job:

"And he still maintains his integrity" (2:3e)

"Are you still maintaining your integrity?" (2:9a)

The first statement is from God while the second is from Job's wife. In a sense, Job has to prove to his wife that he is who he claims to be, as God sees him. Possibly, Mrs. Job feels her husband is not blameless, or is insincere. Job's quietness is deceptive, and as such, his integrity is questionable. In other words, Mrs. Job is quizzing the husband's spirituality if he is still claiming that he was blameless. He should prove his integrity by either cursing God or remaining quiet. And her question does not mean she is faithless.

The Rhetoric of bārak

Generally, it is accepted that *bārak* is euphemistic for "curse" (see 1 Kgs 21:10, 13, Ps 10:3) in some rare cases.[14] The verb *bārak* occurs over 325 times in the Hebrew Bible, most frequently translated "to bless." The Hebrew verbal root *brk* and its derivatives are also used to mean "give thanks" (Gen 24:48, Deut 8:10, Judg 5:2, 9, Neh 8:6, 9:5), "to kneel down" (e.g., 2 Chr 6:13; Ps 95:6), "be strong" (Deut 29:18; Ps 147:13), or "to greet" (1 Sam 13:10; 2 Kgs 4:29; 10:15). There are five occurrences in the

---

12. Elsewhere, the name of Job's wife is provided. In the Aramaic Targum, she is Dinah, perhaps pointing to Dinah in Gen 34. In the *Testament of Job*, she is called Sitis.

13. Schweitzer, "'Curse God and Die," 38; Wolde, "Development of Job," 201–21; Sasson, "Literary and Theological Function of Job's Wife," 86–90; Magdalene, "Job's Wife as a Hero," 209–58; Seow, "Job's Wife—With Due Respect," 1–39.

14. Clines, *Dictionary of Classical Hebrew*, 268; HALOT 1:160; BDB 1907:139; Scharbert, "*rr*," TDOT, 1:415.

book of Job with the normal meaning "bless" (1:10, 21, 29:13, 31:20, and 42:12), and there are four others that are conventionally translated with the opposite meaning of "curse" (1:5, 11, 2:5, 9). That is to say, while the literal meaning of "blessing" fits logically into the context of Job 1:10, when the same verb is used in the contexts of Job 1:5, 11; 2:5, 9, interpreters find that the translation "to bless" is not tenable.

John Walton argues that the word *bārak* is used to mean the tendency to think that one's success was achieved by one's own effort and so fail to give credit to God.[15] Gerald Wilson also rightly considers Mrs. Job's use of *bārak* as a circumlocution, that is in a deliberate attempt to be vague or evasive.[16] Job, who is afraid always that his children may have sinned "and cursed God in their hearts" (1:5) and sacrifices a burnt offering on their behalf, does not curse God but blesses God. Mrs. Job, of whom Job was not worried about cursing God in her heart, rather advises the husband to curse God and die. Job assumes that his wife is foolish and is leading him astray. Meir Weiss states, "her intention was good; her action was not. Job—at least this time—does not understand his wife, and takes her words not as she intends, but literally."[17] Like Job, E. van Wolde misses the point by saying that *bārak* usually has only one meaning, and in the context of Job 1–2 a contradictory meaning is created, making it have two meanings. Mrs. Job claims that Job can curse God, which might make God leave him and result in his death.[18]

From one angle, the tone in Mrs. Job's voice echoes pain and distress. A person in pain can do the unthinkable. When Elijah runs away from Bathsheba, who wants to take his life, he pleads with God to take his life because he has had enough (1 Kgs 19:4). Similarly, Jonah has to plead with God to take his life for he feels it is better for him to die than to live (Jonah 4:3). Job indeed affirms that God controls the breath of all living things (12:10). Pain, in most cases, cannot simply be understood as a cause-and-effect thing. Psychic distress or pain is as real as physical pain; the two are phenomenologically akin to each other and, therefore, should be categorized under the same rubric. Some scholars hold that pain should not always be considered strictly as a physical phenomenon, only that from injury to the body. When people experience overwhelming fear, anxiety, and isolation, their feelings are not what the professionals

15. Walton, *Job*, 60,61.
16. Wilson, *Job*, 27.
17. Weiss, *Job's Beginning*, 70.
18. Wolde, "Development of Job," 204.

prefer to call suffering or anguish but pain.[19] Such people experience distress that correlates with increased blood flow to the brain like in the anterior cingular and insular cortices, the same way that usually occurs when in physical pain. The greater the social distress generated, the more the affective pain becomes destructive. David Biro establishes:

> While psychological pain may be unpleasant, the fact remains that it is "in our heads," not our bodies ... those who suffer without any physical corroboration to show for it inevitably begin to appear suspect. They are either crazy (mentally ill), deceitful (because there is no real pain), or weak (everything is painful to such people). They don't need pain doctors or pain medication, but psychiatrists and priests.[20]

Emotional pain can also set in when there is deep sorrow, depression, unfulfilled desires, panic, rage, or feelings of worthlessness, and it has been associated with a higher risk of suicidal ideation.[21] It is possible to see Mrs. Job with a suicidal lens (she may not be contemplating suicide but wishes so for her husband), and accept her pain, even if it has made her slip into a situation where she makes unacceptable outbursts or expresses negative emotions.

Whether Mrs. Job is challenging God's assertion that "he still holds on to his integrity" (2:3), casting doubt on what God says about Job, or urging her husband to follow the Adversary's lead to "curse" God, she is not depicted as a silent looker, an uncaring wife, a heartless woman, or a sycophant. She sees lamentation as a tool to use. She shows that Job is selfish by not lamenting. As seen in the books of Psalms and Lamentations, the concept of lament deals with disrupted well-being and social relations. It also challenges notions about the character of God. A lament is a raw, honest, emotional outburst and may show that the one at prayer considers themself cut off from God. The laments teach people to protest in the face of challenges.[22] As long as the church has not come to fully grasp the place of lamentation, Mrs. Job's words are damning.

---

19. Papini et al., "Behavioral Neuroscience of Psychological Pain," 53–69; Biro, "Is There Such a Thing as Psychological Pain?" 658–67.

20. Biro, "Is There Such a Thing as Psychological Pain?" 664.

21. Conejero et al., "Psychological Pain, Depression, and Suicide."

22. Westermann, *Praise and Lament in the Psalms*, 267. See also Goldingay, *Book of Lamentation*.

The assumption of Mrs. Job that God kills those who curse him seems to be a popular view. There is certainty in the argument of the Adversary that curses do not necessarily end life; they show that one does not fear God. Destroying all that Job has would lead Job to curse God and thus make him lose his blamelessness. Perhaps, Job's periodic sacrifices to God on the pretext that his children might have cursed God in their hearts while making merry raised the pitch in the words of Mrs. Job: "curse God and die." If indeed the children had cursed God, as Job assumed, they did not immediately die. Curses, then, do not imply a punishment a death. The power of death is not dependent on curses or not. Even Job's prayers and sacrifices for his children did not insulate them from death when the Adversary destroyed all that Job had.

To some commentators, Mrs. Job's words were a theological method of committing euthanasia.[23] Mrs. Job's advice seems to them to border on euthanasia—that is, an act of deliberately ending a person's life to relieve suffering—to keep her husband free from pain in his last days. If such an idea is anything to go by, she was deliberately encouraging her husband to kill himself. Generally, taking one's life is both a rejection of God's sovereignty over life and an attack upon the sanctity of life. In contemporary times, euthanasia has come to mean many other things. For instance, the Webster's Dictionary provides two definitions: (1) "An easy death or means of inducing one" and (2) "The act of practice of painlessly putting death to a person who is suffering from incurable conditions or disease."[24] Mrs. Job may have desired an easy death for Job. It is generally believed that God alone is the author and finisher of life and that no life is not worth living. Society or individuals do not have the right to declare certain sick people as unfit to live. One cannot usurp God's sovereign's right over life and death. In any case, arguments for euthanasia usually appeal to cases of incurable suffering, where the level of pain is presumably intolerable and beyond the range of medical relief.

Euthanasia can be classified into two main types: voluntary euthanasia, where a person makes a conscious decision to die and asks for help to do so, and non-voluntary euthanasia, where a person is unable to give their consent due to their current health condition. Some factors that are included in the decision-making may be classified as physical or psychological. Physical conditions include paralysis, unbearable pain,

---

23. Terrien, *Job*, 42; Andersen, *Job*, 93.
24. Orr et al., *Life and Death Decisions*, 152.

incontinence, and inability to breath, while psychological factors include depression, feeling a burden, fearing loss of control or dignity, or a dislike of being dependent.[25] With such an understanding of psychological factors, it can be argued that Mrs. Job did intend mercy killing.

Among the Akan of Ghana, a harsh tone in the voice when one says *Nyame nhyira wo* ("God bless you") is understood as a curse. To indicate that the pronouncement means a blessing, the tone of the language should be friendly and motivated by a good gesture. A similar statement is *Nyame ntua wo kaw* ("God recompenses you"); this is a curse in disguise. Kofi Agyekum notices how in certain contexts specific curses or punishments are omitted in imprecatory grievances by the imprecator, with the intention that the gods will decide for themselves the punishment fit for the wrongdoer.[26] He shows the close link between grievous imprecation (Akan: *duabɔ*) and ordinary curses, and he avers that *duabɔ* has three main parts: "the protactic proposition, which is the invocation, the apodictic proposition, stating the reason(s) of the imprecation, and the commissive proposition, stating the punishment. It is possible to omit either the protactic, apodictic content, the commissive proposition or the imprecate in certain contexts."[27] So, whether one addresses a deity, giving reasons for the prayer, or prescribes a desire, does not matter. A fitting punishment will come since the deities will investigate and ascertain the intended cause and effect.

In some African cultures, however, cursing a deity or a person of authority is illegitimate. When a person of authority like a chief, parent, or elder curses a subordinate, it is legitimate, but when a person curses another who is of a higher authority, it is illegitimate. Agyekum explains that in Akan culture, there is no justification for a spiteful grievance imprecation because it is egoistic and occurs in situations that go contrary to the laid down customs of the people.[28] Since relationships are reciprocal and meant to promote the worth of each other, one is not expected to repay evil with evil. Hence, in many African communities, engaging in anything that disrupts life is not only a crime but also an abomination.[29] It is the unrighteous person whose mouth is filled with curses (Ps 10:7). Paul says that believers should not utter filthy or foolish words (Eph 4:29;

25. BBC, "Ethics Guide. Euthanasia," 2014.
26. Agyekum, "Pragmatics of *Duabɔ*," 362, 363.
27. Agyekum, "Pragmatics of *Duabɔ*," 379.
28. Agyekum, Pragmatics of *Duabɔ*," 371.
29. Aidoo, "'If This Is of God," 18.

5:4). Again, they should bless those who bless them and not curse them (Rom 12:14). Such an idea is similar to the view of the writer of the book of Proverbs that one should put away all crooked speech (Prov 4:24). Note that, "an undeserved curse will go nowhere" (Prov 26:2); it will not land or cause any harm to its intended victim.

Roger Scholtz sets out to see how the words of Job's wife intersect with Job's, and how her influence contributes to Job's transformation. To Scholtz, it would be strange to say that she was not one of the instruments that God used to make Job prosperous, and also in the restoration of Job's economic fortunes in the epilogue.[30] Again, for Job to make an impact within the wider social sphere by helping the poor, widow, and needy during the prime of his life largely depended on the support within his own household.[31] She had a hand in raising the children Job had. Her speech for Job to curse God and die serves as a motivation for God to comfort God in the dialogue section of the story, and makes her "the forerunner of God in the divine speeches, where the vision of this alternative worldview is fleshed out in all its vibrant, stirring, risky glory."[32]

If Job fears God and holds fast to his integrity, as God states, it will not be possible for Job to appeal to the gods of the ancient world to curse God. He would certainly not appeal to God to curse God. Job thinks the children may have cursed God and thus there would be a need for sacrifices and sanctification. For Job, curses are unacceptable in a person's spiritual life. Mrs. Job asks Job to curse God and that becomes another issue Job will not tolerate. The power behind curses or blessings is from God and not from a human being or other deities. In Deuteronomy, God offers his people pathways of blessings and curses, and urges all to choose the path that leads to blessing. Claus Westermann explains that God's blessing has to do with God's continual work to provide for people's daily well-being, but the use of blessings, as well as curses, underwent evolutionary development. Similarly, Jeff Anderson admits that, "in the Old Testament, the sole subject of the curse is Yahweh, and only in the Old Testament can a curse be changed into a blessing."[33] For Anderson, both blessings and curses are incredibly potent in proper social contexts. He goes too far in saying, "these performatives can at once both maintain and challenge social structures, serving as social propagandists and

30. Scholtz, "I Had Heard of You," 826.
31. Scholtz, "Re-Visioning Job's Wife," 827.
32. Scholtz, "Re-Visioning Job's Wife," 837.
33. Anderson, *Blessing and the Curse*, 46.

iconoclasts alike."[34] Michael D. Swartz also argues that in the Hebrew Bible, blessings and curses are closely related semantically and formally in the sense that the same style used to pronounce blessings is used to pronounce curses.[35] I also do not agree with Anderson that blessings and curses do not have any magical element and are not self-fulfilling. Also, there is no instance where a person's words become effective on their own accord, or a person has the power to bless and curse by physical attribution. The words are picked up by the supernatural and acted upon. Divine sovereignty and authority are at play in these magical words of blessings and curses. The pronouncements are essentially wishes. In the view of Anne Marie Kitz, curses are associated with several properties, including (i) divine judgment; (ii) the arousal of divine wrath; (iii) separation from the deities; (iv) separation from society; (v) and finally, if left unforgiven, separation from life.[36] Consequently, such can be the intended meaning of "curse God and die."

Job does not curse (*bārak*) God but curses everything under the sun (3:1–26), and commentators do not see that as unacceptable, or see him as a bad person. Job thinks his children may have "sinned and cursed (*ubērakū*) God in their hearts" (1:5), and that to Job is unacceptable. The conditional nature of the thought points out that the children may not have cursed God, but Job wants to be forearmed. So, it would out of place to posit that when Mrs. Job urges her husband to curse God and die, she is playing the devil's advocate. The Adversary's use of the *piel* form of the root *brk* to God about Job is clear: "you have blessed (*bētaktā*) the work of his hands. But stretch out your hand now, and touch all that he has, and he will curse you (*yĕbārakĕkkā*) to your face" (1:10–11; cf. 2:5). And Job did not want to pay back with curses after he had been blessed by God.

It would be strange to believe that Mrs. Job is acting as the Adversary's advocate. Such an idea, in a sense, is to suggest that she is her own enemy. She supports the destruction of her own property that was part of what Job had, destroys her own ten children she bore for nine months, only to live impoverished, poor, and miserable. Any human being with the right senses will not destroy children and property so as to live in loneliness and poverty, unless bewitched and possessed by an evil spirit that does not cherish good things. In other words, Mrs. Job cannot be a

---

34. Anderson, *Blessing and the Curse*, 50.

35. Swartz, "Aesthetics of Blessing and Cursing," 187. See also Uusimäki, "Blessings and Curses in the Biblical World," 161.

36. Kitz, "Curse and Cursing in the Ancient Near East," 618.

witch or an evil person because she does not destroy her own family. Unless there are enough grounds to prove that Mrs. Job is not affected in any way when her own children perish and her husband loses his property, making them fall from grace to grass, she should be seen as a victim. The point is that, despite the interpretations forced on the text and woven around her image, Mrs. Job's role in the tale, as it appears in the MT, is clear and unequivocal.

It is ironic that when Job curses all of creation in chapter 3, it is not a problem, but when his children curse God in their hearts, it is unacceptable (1:5). Certainly, Job does not want to curse God (1:21), and so Mrs. Job cannot urge her husband to curse God and die (2:9). Of course, the negative meanings of cursing by the Adversary and Mrs. Job cannot be accidental and could be a "leading word" to convey to the reader that Job's wife should be seen on the same level as the Adversary. After all, the Adversary, like Mrs. Job, does not know Job well just as the Lord knows him. The Adversary does not agree with the Lord as to the reason Job fears God. However, Mrs. Job is not acting on the Adversary's bidding. Such tendencies to equate women and satanic acts have not been helpful. No wonder women have consistently raised their voices to patriarchal interpretations that color them as "satan," "evil," "destroyer," and "witch."

Mrs. Job's Logic: What Is Going On?

Mrs. Job's words to her husband are an outburst of her own frustration. She intends for Job to find his voice against God. Incidentally, that is what Job finds and does throughout his dialogue with his three friends. Perhaps, Job responds negatively when his wife prompts him because of "fear" of the Almighty. In chapter 9, Job affirms his innocence and recounts an unjustifiable attack from God. He cannot fight back because "who has resisted him and come out unscratched?" (9:4b). God does what he pleases and does not restrain his anger. Therefore, Job cannot dispute him (9:13–15). He knows that if he dares, God will crush him (9:16–18). No wonder he looks for an opportunity for someone to mediate between himself and God and remove God's rod that is punishing him so that he "would speak up without fear of him" (9:35a).

It may be out of place to opine that Mrs. Job is insensitive and wants Job to die so that she can be free because she is influenced to speak by the strong emotional and marital bond between them.³⁷ Perhaps, such an outcry comes from a partner who has endured enough pain and affliction. She definitely shares in the distress of Job but does not see Job that way. Going through the emotional, psychological, and physical loss of children, wealth, and honor, as well as enduring the pain from a suffering husband, seems to have gravely affected her. She cannot imagine herself deserting her husband in such a situation, but the painful sores and the eruptions of skin she sees on her husband are a source of her own affliction. At least, staying with her husband up to that time deserves some commendation. In the view of Anne Stewart,

> Job's wife takes on a life of her own in the history of interpretation. Her character gathers different names, various characterizations, and longer speeches. Despite the diversity among them, each tradition continues to grapple with the serious issues the biblical woman raises as she witnesses both the integrity and the anguish of the one who suffers. The lively interpretive tradition surrounding Job's wife thus ultimately points us back to the ambiguity of her words in the biblical text.³⁸

In other words, her paucity of words, her passive actions, and her identity as a woman have influenced many to look at her with suspicious eyes. The Akan elders say, |sɛ wo tamfo resaw w'asaw a, ɔkyea ne pa ("if your enemy is emulating your dance, they will twist the waist"). By twisting the waist, the dancing steps will be awkward. That is to say, if someone does not love you, the person will not speak well about whatever you are doing. After all, it is not only Job who is not friendly.

Hartley picks up the position Job's wife assumes and says that she "portrays another dimension of Job's trial, namely, the alienation that his affliction caused between him and his wife."³⁹ Certainly, a bad wife will be happy that the husband is suffering and would inflict more pain. As pointed out, the alienation between the couple did not start after the affliction; rather, it worsens as both suffer loss. The Akan say, sɛ ɛkoto de awarfo roko a, mma mbisa de ebɛnasɛm na ɔrokɔ do, na mbom ebɛnadze na ɔkɔɔ do ("if you meet a couple fighting, do not ask what is going on, but rather what went on previously"). An earlier problem might have influenced wife to attack husband.

---

37. Hartley, *Job*, 84.
38. Stewart, "Job's Wife and her Interpreters," 219–20.
39. Hartley, *Job*, 83.

WHO IS MRS. JOB TO JOB?

Let us now explore how Job saw his wife and the possible meanings of the words he used for his wife.

The Credibility of Mrs. Job

Robert Alden may be right in suggesting sympathetically that critics and readers should not be too hard on Job's wife.[40] After all, she is showing us how she sees her husband. Job's answer implies that his wife is not supporting him in his time of tribulation. For Job, the suffering was *his* suffering. He is not looking for answers or strength to resist God who has brought that calamity upon him. Being sentimental and judgmental at that point in time is not an option Job's looking for. That may be what foolish wives do, which is how Job, uncomfortably, sees his wife. He prefers to protest silently at that time than to raise his voice against affliction. He fails to recognize that friendly advice is like medicine to the soul, and good advice from a friend is like perfume that brings joy to the heart (Prov 27:9). Such heartfelt advice heals brokenness with time. In fact, "Mrs. Job suggests that an alternative course of action must be taken to lodge the objection to God's brutal deeds. Job's wife offers Job this alternative; she gives him the option of dying proudly in resistance to the violence of God's law."[41] Offering alternatives is what friends should give.

If Mrs. Job makes Job realize that he can stand up to God and challenge God's friendship, and if Job's challenge really ended up his vindication, then his wife is a good advisor. She has something to offer readers of the story. Moreover, Rachel Magdalene asserts that Mrs. Job is a hero, a great and wise mother whose contribution shapes the present view of wisdom. Magdalene, for instance, argues that Mrs. Job makes all the difference in Job's life by effecting the change from passivity to assertiveness in his relationship with God.[42] Magdalene strongly objects to unsympathetic critics who claim that Job's wife is a fool, that there is nothing good in her, or that she wants Job dead. She says such comments are insensitive

---

40. Alden, *Job*, 66.
41. Magdalene, "Job's Wife as a Hero," 238.
42. Magdalene, "Job's Wife as a Hero," 209–58.

to women's reality at the time.⁴³ To her, Job's wife believes in the husband's integrity and innocence by raising her question to Job.⁴⁴

Some women can trick their husbands into taking wrong decisions. An Igbo proverb seems to suggest how the husband can outwit his wife if she plays any trick on her: *Nwaanyi muta ite ofe mmri mmiri, da ya amuta ipi utara aka were suru ofe* ("If a woman decides to make the soup watery, the husband will learn to dent the gari before dipping it into the soup"). That is to say, the soup for the gari meal is supposed to be thick. If the wife makes it watery, the man will mold the gari so that it can take much soup.

In "Job's Wife—With Due Respect," Leong Seow painstakingly explores—using the Septuagint's version of Job, ancient and medieval Church Fathers, Jewish exegetes, mystery plays, movies, documentaries, and paintings—negative and positive images of Mrs. Job. In the long run, Seow praises Mrs. Job for her intuition and knowledge by arguing that the unnamed wife is portrayed as knowing how God sees Job as a man of integrity.⁴⁵ God says to the Adversary that Job "maintains his integrity" (2:3) and Job's wife uses the same diction when in her desperation she asks her husband, "Are you still maintaining your integrity?" (2:9). Seow also concludes that Job's wife "is neither a hero nor villain. Her function in the book is, rather, a literary and theological one: to present before mortals a dialectic. How a human being like Job responds to that dialectic is another question altogether, however. It is a question pursued throughout the book, a question with which the reader must grapple."⁴⁶ Seow may be right because the image of wisdom is that it does not aim to stand out as a hero. So, Mrs. Job is an epitome of wisdom, not necessarily of showing heroic actions.

Mrs. Job has her own unique identity in the story. I agree with John Walton who says that Job's wife's speech accomplishes four purposes:⁴⁷

1. It avoids a quick win for the Adversary.

2. It provides an opportunity for Job to express his faithfulness yet again.

3. It serves as a prelude and transition to the friends.

---

43. Magdalene, "Job's Wife as Hero," 213
44. Magdalene, "Job's Wife as Hero," 233
45. Seow, "Job's Wife—With Due Respect," 27.
46. Seow, "Job's Wife—With Due Respect," 28.
47. Walton, *Job*, 106.

4. It proposes a solution opposite the direction the friends would go. They want to tell him how to live (with renewed benefits) while she tells him life is not worth living.

Hence, Mrs. Job cannot be judged just like the three friends. She represents a counselor who does not give false hope. She shows Job how to live and how to die, unlike the three who focus only on how to live.

Being married to Job at a time when *pater familias* reigned may have obscured the identity of Mrs. Job in the home. She may well have been the one who had borne sons and daughters to Job, nursed them, and raised them into a family that could come together to dine (1:13). She may not have enjoyed a cordial relationship with her husband if Job had drawn the line in the home that he was the one with absolute authority. When the personal comfort of mothers in their children is taken away, it is more devastating than the loss of wealth and property. She is left only with a husband who will not involve her in prayers and sacrifices and who will not recognize that the loss of children and family property is not *his* loss but *their* loss. She sees in Job a man who cannot move beyond himself to think about his wife's situation and emotional trauma.

I have pointed out that the silence about Job not offering sacrifices for his wife echoes a seeming lack of knowledge, coordination, distance, intimacy, and goodwill between Job and his wife. To Job, his wife is one of the foolish women who destroys her own home down and questions God's action. She is only in it for good things and not bad things. A foolish woman lacks understanding and sound judgment. She is weak in intellect and imprudent in her choice of words. The book of Proverbs says "The foolish woman is loud; she is ignorant and knows nothing" (Prov 9:13 NRSV). The babbling of a fool brings ruin near (Prov 10:14), and throws off restraint, and is careless (14:16). It is "the wise woman builds her house, but the foolish tears it down with her own hands" (14:1 NRSV). To Job, his wife is not wise. She is rash and intolerant. It is from this premise that Ilana Pardes comments that "Job's wife prefigures or perhaps even generates the impatience of the dialogues. She opens the possibility of suspending belief, of speaking against God."[48] At face value, Job's wife seems to be a nagging but assertive woman. Emily Gravett says that her speech depicts her as some sort of frustrated woman and that she "may end up sounding like an impatient nag here—a wife who finds her

---

48. Pardes, "Wife of Job: Bible."

husband's integrity and faith ridiculous and wishes for him to do something about her troubles."[49]

Mrs. Job's assertiveness, however, does indeed affect Job. Later in the story, Job curses the day he was born and struggles to maintain his integrity before his friends with a strong voice, and it is his wife's voice that moves Job into speaking, making the story possible.[50] In fact, Job makes a profound statement that echoes what his wife wants him to do (Job 6:8–9):

A	O that	I		might	have my request,
C	and that	God		would	grant my desire;
B	that		it would please God	to	crush me,
B1	that		he would let loose his hand	and	cut me off.

Gordis translates line B1 instructively as "let it please God to crush me."[51] Mrs. Job has asked him to make a request, and Job wishes he would have the opportunity to make the request. Now it is not what his wife wants but, as Job says, "my request" (6:8a). The end-goal of the request will make God crush him, and the power of God's hand will come against him and cut him off (6:9). The *wayitol* verb *wîbaṣṣe'nî* translated as "and cut me off" also means "to die." Hence, what Mrs. Job wants Job to do is the same thing Job is affirming, that God would cut him off. In essence, Mrs. Job empowered Job to confront God.

Nevertheless, Job's wife can be seen to be a selfish woman, looking out for her own interest and honor. If Job dies, she will be free to find another man who will protect her positive shame.[52] As long as Job lives, her positive shame and discretion-shame or disgrace-shame[53] stand in tension against each other. Positive shame, Bruce Malina explains, concerns sensitivity about one's own reputation and sensitivity to the opinion of others.[54] In the Mediterranean world, it is the woman who symbolizes the corporate aspect of honor and shame, and the man has a responsibility

---

49. Gravett, "Biblical Responses," 106–7.
50. Magdalene, "Job's Wife as a Hero," 257.
51. Gordis, *Book of Job*, 72.
52. Mbuvi, "Ancient Mediterranean Values of Honor and Shame," 761.
53. For a discussion on discretion-shame and disgrace-shame, see Aidoo, *Shame in the Individual Lament Psalms*, 68–69.
54. Malina, *New Testament World*, 49.

to protect both the corporate honor and the woman.[55] Women are said to achieve honor through the positive value of shame which is "characterized by deference and submission to male authority, by docile and timorous behavior, by hiding nakedness, by sexual exclusiveness, and by modesty in attire and deportment."[56] Job, in that miserable state, is unable to protect the positive shame of his wife.

JOB'S EMOTIONAL APPEAL: BALANCING THE MOOD

The first time Job speaks to his wife is when he challenges her suggestion—"curse God and die" (2:9). Job finds what his wife says touchy, so he gives a stereotypical or "fitting" reply as the man of the house. Job's reply had a loaded diction:

> You speak as any foolish woman (*hannĕbālôt*) would speak.
> Shall we receive the good at the hand of God, and not receive the bad? (2:10)

The tone in Job's voice is rather harsh, abusive, and insulting. He likens his wife to "the senseless women" or "the disgraceful women" (*hannĕbālôt*) who bear no sense of shame. Such women, in most African cultures, cannot reason in accordance with social norms, and are unfit to be acknowledged in society. In fact, to say she is "like any foolish woman" does not mean she is merely behaving as such, but rather she *is* foolish, senseless, and disgraceful. Pardes admits that, "Job's initial response to his wife's provocative suggestion is harsh."[57] Is Job trying to pay his wife back for something else or simply for what his wife has said? If it is a fool who says in their heart that there is no God (Ps 14:1), does Mrs. Job make such a claim and does she engage in such thing that the psalmist talked about? Does she believe in God or is she morally disgraceful? Does Job help his wife in any way to "believe" in his God? Perhaps Crenshaw is right in saying that Job's faith and reasoning are foreign to his wife's comprehension.[58]

Job fears God and is a man of integrity. He is blameless and shuns evil (1:8; 2:3). A person of integrity will not easily give up on his values,

---

55. Malina, *New Testament World*, 53.
56. Klein, "Honor and Shame in Esther," 151.
57. Pardes, "Wife of Job: Bible."
58. Crenshaw, "Concept of God," 11.

cast off restraint, and become dishonest, abusive, and intolerant. If God sees Job as blameless, does that justify what he says to his wife, and can such a description be "blameless"? Maybe before his wife confronted him Job was blameless, but can we continue to say so after showing his other side? It is normal to assume that Job does not agree with his wife in all things. It is one thing to point out a disagreement, no matter how forceful it can be, and another to be abusive. In all, for Job to see Mrs. Job as speaking like a foolish woman tells us who Mrs. Job is to Job.

There is no doubt that Job is casting invectives at his wife by comparing her to other foolish women. Verbal abuse can be likened to other forms of physical and emotional abuse. The infliction of ill-treatment—such as punches, slaps, kicks, truncheon blows, severe beatings, use of pepper spray, electric shocks, suspension or hyperextension by means of handcuffs, burns to various parts of the body, asphyxiation with a plastic bag or a gas mask, lock-up, stress building, and mock executions for the purpose of obtaining a confession or other information during or in the context of police interviews—serves as a way to break a person's willpower, and such use of violence remains a very serious problem in the world. Sometimes, it happens that people subjected to such ill-treatment and unlawful actions change their minds and plead guilty even when they know that they are innocent, so that the abuse can stop. Perhaps in the case of Job, a way to whip his wife into line is to attack her verbally.

In her work, "'Battered love': Exposing abuse in the Book of Job," Marlene Underwood fails to recognize all the abuse Mrs. Job suffered. She sets out to explore abuses of both men and women but fell short of naming the violence against Mrs. Job. She does, however, mention the abuse perpetrated on women's and children's bodies as she espoused androcentrism and biblical patriarchy seen in the story of Job, but concentrates only on how God abused Job.[59] Her summary of Lenore Walker's work on the cycle of domestic violence, its effects on battered women and families, and the role public policy can play in assisting survivors is insightful. Walker demarcates the abuse cycle into three distinct phases: (1) tension building, (2) the acute battering incident, and (3) loving-contrition. In my view, Mrs. Job went through lots of tension before disaster struck the family. Her husband batters her when she approaches him, but at the end of the story she gives Job beautiful sons and daughters. Marlene Underwood summarizes Walker's views as follows:

---

59. Underwood, "Battered Love," 165–84.

Phase one involves the gradual escalation of tension displayed by discrete acts causing increased friction, such as name-calling, other mean intentional behaviors, and/or physical abuse . . . The victim (usually a woman) attempts to placate the batterer, doing what she thinks might please, calm down, or, at least, what will not further aggravate the abuser (usually a man). Exhausted from the constant stress, the victim usually withdraws from the abuser . . . Phase two is characterized by the uncontrollable discharge of the tensions that have built up during phase one. The violator typically lets loose a barrage of verbal and physical aggression that can leave the victim severely shaken and injured. The victim does her best to protect herself, often covering parts of her face and body to block some of the blows. This phase ends when the battering stops . . . during phase three, the batterer may apologize profusely, try to assist the victim, show kindness and remorse, and shower the victim with gifts and/or promises. at this point, the batterer may believe that he will never allow himself to be violent again. Because the victim wants to believe the batter, she may continue to hope in his ability to change.[60]

Mrs. Job can be considered to have gone through the first phase of intimate partner violence because of Job's words. She does not go through any physical abuse, but something might have gone on to warrant Mrs. Job withdrawing from her abuser. She was exhausted from indescribable, unbroken stress. The friction between Job and his wife is discrete, but it takes a heavy toll on Mrs. Job. Job's words are spoken to appear to correct Mrs. Job, yet it is probable that Job is soothing himself. Mrs. Job, after being exhausted from the loss of property and children, and now with the one sentence that was more than a barrage of verbal abuse, withdraws into silence and away from the husband (see 19:17). Job knows that words could torment a person (19:1).

Seow seems to miss something when he argues that Job's words to his wife do not mean she spoke foolishly, as women are wont to do, but that he was cautioning her against reckless reaction and disregard for theological, ethical, and social norms. To him, the term "foolish/senseless" refers to one who speaks, acts, or is simply outside the acceptable theological, ethical, and social norms.[61] Yet certainly Mrs. Job crosses the line and is speaking or acting without regard to ethical behavior. So, if such a person is not a fool ("theologically speaking" or "socially

---

60. Underwood, "Battered Love," 172.
61. Seow, *Job 1–21*, 296, 297.

speaking"), the less said about this view, the better. She speaks and Job understands what she is saying. She acts and is being judged.

Significantly, Job's question using the plural "we receive" (2:10) draws his wife into the picture. She is also a target of the Lord's action. To Job, his wife has to be prepared to receive whatever comes their way. Hence, everything that had happened affects both of them. It is easy to praise God for the good but very difficult when the unexpected is encountered. Paul talks about the value of contentment either in good times or bad times (Phil 4:6–12). The people of God need to stand their ground in times of trouble (Rom 12:12). And in the book of Proverbs, poverty or riches are extreme points in life and make people either deny or profane the name of God (Prov 30:8–9).

The second time Mrs. Job is mentioned in the story is when Job complains about everyone not behaving like true friends, after Bildad speaks in the second round of the first cycle of dialogue. Job speaks about his wife in these words:

> My breath (*rûḥî*) is repulsive to my wife;
> I am loathsome to children of my womb. (19:17 my trans.)

The import of such a statement is that bad breath has greatly affected the relationship between him and his wife. It seems Job's tenor about his repugnant *rûaḥ*, "breath," causing his wife to desert him, is a rhetorical way to echo the kind of spirit he was exhibiting.[62] The noun *rûaḥ* also means spirit as a seat of emotion (Mal 2:15), disposition (Isa 4:4; Prov 15:4), anger (Prov 16:32), a blast of nostrils (Exod 15:8), and mind (1 Chr 28:12). Gordis takes it as "my passion, desire" and fits the idea that his wife does not agree with his line of action.[63] Katherine Southwood sees *rûḥî* as hyperbole and translates it as "my wind" and arrives at a translation "my wind is repulsive to my wife," thus evoking the meaning of flatulence. Though recognizing the socially degrading nature of Job's situation, Southwood argues that "wind" may also be appropriate since the characters in the dialogues regularly refer to each other's speeches as "windy" words.[64] Windy words may be repulsive but how she arrives at flatulence is not clear. Job looks to have depicted a disposition of

---

62. Elsewhere in Genesis, the human being God created from the dust of the ground becomes a living because of the *nišmat ḥayyîm* "breath of life" (Gen 2:7).

63. Gordis, *Book of Job*, 202.

64. Southwood, *Job and the Dramatised Comedy of Moralising*, 152.

intemperance, impatience, and sorrow, and as such it is not easy to stay close to him. His anger might have taken a better part of him.

From a literal point of view, bad breath is interfering with their love life to the point that Mrs. Job fears interacting with him. She opts to keep herself away. Job seems to be making a concession about him being the cause of the problem by talking about his breath. He is indicating that the painful sores from the soles of his feet to the crown of his head have not only caused his outer skin to be nauseating but also whatever comes from within him to smell bad. Beyond that, Job literally complained about God causing alienation between him and his family members, acquaintances, relatives, closest friends, guests, female servants, male servants, his wife, and intimate friends (19:13–19).

To be clear, it is known that oral infection and poor dental care are the leading causes of bad breath. Bacteria on the tongue act on food trapped between the teeth, under the gums, or in the mouth, resulting in bad breath. Sulfurous gases in the mouth such as sulfide and methylmercaptan lead to bad breath. There are other strong-scented foods that interfere with breathing and cause bad breath. The odor of smoking creates the infamous "smoker's breath." Some medications can also dry out your mouth, contributing to bad breath. When the person breathes, the air gives an offensive smell, causing bystanders to suffocate. Generally, people try to go far away to take a good breath. In his sorry state, Job may be incapable of giving proper attention to his skin and his mouth. Whatever the cause of his bad breath, it makes his wife stay at a distance. Perhaps she cannot bear the shame of living with a man who lives in ashes, full of skin disease and pain.

In the dialogue section, the three friends complain about the words of Job. Eliphaz, for example, explains that an unwise man will not guard the answers he gives. The words that are uttered are unprofitable, for they come from windy knowledge (*da'at-rûaḥ*) or the east wind (*qādîm*) that fills the belly (15:2). He goes further to say that with such words, one will not depart from darkness, but the breath of his mouth (*rûaḥ pîw*) will make the person depart into darkness (15:30).

The next reference to Job's wife in the story is seen in his rebuttal to prove his innocence and loyalty. Job sounds a loud trumpet about his good deeds, boasting about his credentials and ethical relationship with members of his household and that in his community. He does not imagine doing anything untoward to anyone. However, he is ready to pay if he has sinned against them. To pay for his sexual sins, if any, his wife has to be the object of the price:

> If my heart has been enticed by a woman,
>   and I have lain in wait at my neighbor's door;
> then let my wife grind for another,
>   and let other men kneel over her. (31:9–10)

Gordis explains that Job was using the legal-moral principle of retribution in connection with the sin of adultery. The neighbor's door has sexual connotations (Songs 4:12). The wife grinding for another also carries a sexual connotation. She would be sexually used.[65] Using one's wife to pay for sexual sins committed is violence by an intimate partner. Such violence, whether domestic violence or intimate partner violence, causes physical, psychological, verbal, or sexual harm to persons in that relationship. The main perpetrators of abuse are the males, although it is important to note that some males have also been victims of domestic abuse.

Job knows that sleeping with someone's wife is a heinous crime. To him, getting very close to the private part of someone's wife is equally a serious crime. It is like "fire consuming down to Abaddon and it would burn to the root all my harvest" (31:12). The use of "fire" echoes the devastating nature of sexual transgression. Its destructive power is beyond measure (Prov 6:26–35; Song 8:6). The sages wonder why the young person is intoxicated by the love of another woman who is not his wife (Prov 5:20). However, would his wife paying for such a crime under the principle of retribution or *lex talionis* not itself constitute a crime? Would giving over his wife to another to have sexual intercourse with her as a form of punishment not constitute a grievous crime?

God does not approve of violence (Prov 12:18; 18:21; Eph 4:26; Col 3:18) and expects his people to be protected from violent people (Prov 27:12; Prov 11:9). Definitely, sexual violence is an affront to God (Deut 22:23–27). Victor Matthews explains that in Genesis 19—when the men of Benjamin demand that Lot bring out the male visitors who have been offered hospitality for them to have sex with the visitors—Lot rather offers them his daughters, pleading with them to have sex with his daughters, even though they were virgins. That action speaks of Lot's view about women and girls as if they deserve to be raped. Lot gives out

---

65. Gordis, *Book of Job*, 346.

his daughters without any consideration for their rights as persons, but as property that can be used to compensate for improper actions.[66]

Similarly, in Judges 19, the cycle of intimate partner violence is witnessed in the story of the Levite and his concubine, who is a guest to an Ephraimite living in Gibeah. Mieke Bal sees the story of the Levite and her concubine in Judges 19 as the most horrible story in the Bible of the rejection, gang-rape, murder and dismemberment of a young woman.[67] The story depicts the first actors of violence as the men of Gibeah, but it is the brutality of the Levite against his wife that makes it so outrageous. In the evening, the gang come to the door demanding to have sex with the Levite who had entered the house. The Ephraimite host defends the rights of this guest, and offers an alternative—his own virgin daughter as well as the Levite's concubine—to be taken away and raped, since it was an "outrageous thing" to abuse a male visitor (Judg 19:23–24). Cheryl Exum points out that male rape by another male would have been a "de-gendering" of the man.[68] In the course of the exchanges, the Levite throws his concubine at the men and boys, who ravage her. After being gang raped throughout the night, the Levite's concubine had nowhere to go, not back to her husband who had sold her out. She drags herself to the threshold of the house, and there the Levite finds her the next morning. He cannot rouse her from her unconscious state, so he places her on the donkey and makes the trip home (Judg 19:27–28). As Alice Keefe intimates, "there is an element of dark absurdity in both the horror of the woman's fate at the hands of the Levite and the horror of a war among the tribes which is to no purpose except mass death and more rape."[69]

There is moral disorder throughout the story of the Levite and the concubine. There is a band of evildoers outside, threatening the old man and the Levite inside. A man who takes his wife or concubine as a good friend would not sacrifice her in such an atrocious way. A father who sees his daughters as friends will not throw them out to be sexually abused. Such compromises and complicities with wickedness make women dehumanized, speechless, and lifeless. Women cannot be sacrificed as a substitution for the safety of men.

---

66. Matthews, "Hospitality and Hostility in Genesis 19 and Judges 19," 5.
67. Bal, "Body of Writing: Judges 19," 209.
68. Exum, *Fragmented Women*, 183.
69. Keefe, "Rapes of Women/Wars of Men," 92.

DEMONSTRATION OF FRIENDSHIP

Friendship is the oil that lubricates the engine of marriage, vitalizes its beauty and vigor, and makes couples thrive in times of crisis. And Mrs. Job is not depicted as a silent looker, but a caring friend. Her position in the story reflects what friends go through. In her bruised state after losing all that she had, she cannot find empathy from her husband. The sharp difference between Job and his wife is seen in his words to his wife: "You speak as any foolish woman would speak" (2:10). Has she shown him any such traits as sharing the thoughts of foolish women? Mrs. Job has crossed the line and is speaking or acting without regard to ethical behavior. Job cannot accept his wife's point of view. Her silence after Job "insults" her was not only a form of protestation, but also what wisdom teaches. It is an appeal to find space to ponder over how Job sees her. Her silence also functions as a communicative strategy not only to indict God but also to stand behind her husband in seeking a resolution. Job's wife intends for Job to find his voice against God. Incidentally, that is what Job finds and does throughout his dialogue with his three friends.

It is necessary to state that couples who are friends show more enduring intimacy, loyalty, trust, and connection. Here, I tentatively add Fredrich Nietzsche's famous quote: "It is not a lack of love, but a lack of friendship that makes unhappy marriages." Spousal friendship thrives in authentic love and serves as a bedrock for loving expression. Spousal or marital friendship is the love, affection, time, energy, attention, gifts, and sacrifices shared between husband and wife. It is within the context of marriage that the most basic of the experiences of love can be expressed, whether *philia, agape, eros, storge, ludus,* or *pragma.*

Friendship is therefore a strong factor in relationships, making the couple become partners even in the context of marriage that is seen as a contract or alliance. If friendship plays a key role in marriage, then the idea of spousal friendship cannot be underestimated. Pope Pius seems to promote spousal friendship when he says,

> This outward expression of love in the home demands not only mutual help but must go further; must have as its primary purpose that man and wife help each other day by day in forming and perfecting themselves in the interior life, so that through their partnership in life they may advance ever more and more in virtue, and above all that they may grow in true love toward

God and their neighbor, on which indeed "dependeth the whole Law and the Prophets."[70]

In other words, for marriage to thrive and endure, it should be strengthened through friendship. A friendship that easily breaks down is not built on a good foundation. Friendship is a medium through which the home of a couple is most beautifully established. Seeing the value of the spouse and seeking the good of the spouse gives hope for an enduring relationship and sustains it once it is established. Dana Robert, dwelling on Jeremy Taylor who holds that Christian marriage is the queen of friendship, submits that a "good marriage could embody friendship, with two people intimately entwined and supported by the sanctity of law."[71]

A marriage contract, however, comes with duties and responsibilities, which is not so for all aspects of friendship. No wonder some ancient philosophers and the classical world find it difficult to include marriage relationships in the context of friendship. They reject equality between men and women, so seeing husbands and wives in the category of friendship becomes difficult. They cannot conceive of a relationship between husband and wife as a friendly one. The reality in our contemporary world is that friendship plays a key role in the building of relationships before marriage and it can continue throughout marriage. Friendship in marriage makes the couple work toward a common goal. The unvoiced commitment in friendship provides the basis of the laws governing the relationship. If dating and courtship become a time to see how each other is a good friend, then the real discoveries and virtues that grow in a relationship should not die off when the two become married.

Perhaps, Augustine is right when he intimates that a sexual relationship does not define true friendship.[72] Erotic love is not enough to make a couple live as friends or develop a love for themselves. Austin also says friendship is open to an intimacy "that is deep, like that experienced by lovers but not expressed or prepared for by an intimate physical cleaving."[73] Although Genesis 2:24 makes cleaving the final point in a marriage alliance, there is more to it than simply having sex. Friendship fuels the flames of romance in a marriage. Austin believes that being human is not predicated on sexual intimacy but on the deepening of

---

70. Pius XI, "Casti Cannubii."
71. Robert, *Faithful Friendship*, 96.
72. See Brown, *Body and Society*, 403.
73. Austin, *Friendship*, 115.

friendships, and that friendship "is the good thing that extends beyond any possible marriage."[74]

Friendship offers the best protection against feeling adversarial toward spouses. Happily married couples do not live stress-free lives, neither is there no conflict or negative feeling. Spousal friendship is driven by self-giving and sacrificial attitudes. Bernard Cooke and Gary Macy intimate that in Christianity, marriage is the symbol of selfless love and that it takes a heart of friendship to express such love.[75] A husband and wife must be friends who love at all times.[76] Couples who are friends simply learn to let their positive feelings about each other override their negative ones. As such, marriage without friendship cannot work unless it is a contract marriage aimed at securing some benefit designed for spouses, or a business-like marriage where career development is at the heart of the relationship. Couples that ignore the obligation to develop their friendship often come apart.

When a couple become friends with each other, they may feel disappointed by their partner's personality and flaws, but still feel that the partner is worthy of honor and respect. Hence, happy marriages are founded on goodwill, mutual respect, and enjoyment of each other's company.[77] Lower results of marital quality between spouses contribute to marital strain and depressive symptoms. When the couple are friends, marital strain becomes moderate.[78] In marriage, each person comes with a load or baggage of imperfections. The woman being called "a helper" does not mean the woman is perfect, but the man needs help. Both stand in need of the other's support. Marriage alliance, like friendship, is a commitment to accept each other just as the other is and build up each other based on goodwill. There will be misunderstandings, but as long as the couple know each other and are committed to being intimate and loyal, they can walk together, help each other, and promote the good of each other. Such is what friendship stands for; they are friends for a reason.

Finally, when the Lord restores and blesses the latter days of Job—he has seven sons and three beautiful daughters, and Job gives them an inheritance (42:12–14)—nothing is said about Job's wife. Her contribution to rebuilding the family is not noticed. The real issue is, if the daughters

74. Austin, *Friendship*, 12.
75. Cook and Macy, *Christian Symbol and Ritual*, 55–68.
76. Popta, "Marriage, a Covenant of Friendship."
77. Gottman and Silver, *Seven Principles for Making Marriage Work*.
78. Han et al., "Friendship and Depression among Couples in Later Life," 226.

could earn an inheritance, why is his wife left out? An instance in the Hebrew Bible where daughters inherited the property of their father is in Numbers 26:33, thus leading to special legislation in Numbers 27:1–8 and 36:1–12, but in that case, there was no son. Hence, Job giving property to his daughters can be seen as a token of the elevated status of women in a patriarchal society.[79] Job does not give any inheritance to Mrs. Job. Friends do not only share their innermost thoughts, feelings, vulnerabilities, and struggles. They also share what each one has. A good person ensures that the children and generations to come gain some inheritance (Prov 13:22), but it is important to add that depriving a wife of enjoying one's property is not a good sign. Investing in children and not one's wife is a sure way to disrupt the lifespan of an inheritance, because it is the wife who is expected to nurture children.

IMPLICATIONS

The foregoing reveals that Job and his wife are not good friends. Truly surprising is the viewpoint that the virtues of knowing each other well, intimacy, loyalty, collaboration, empowerment, goodwill, and commonality that characterize friendship cannot be found in the relationship between Job and his wife. The way they speak to each other shows that they do not know themselves well, if indeed they had nurtured ten children together. There is no cordiality between them. Job accuses Mrs. Job of disloyalty and lack of collaboration, but his words to her are not empowering. The relationship between Job and his wife reflects how wisdom is understood. Mrs. Job's counsel and question, in the view of Job, draw her into the company of foolish women whose unethical behavior and speech bring about human wrath and not divine wrath. After all, God did not pronounce Mrs. Job guilty in the epilogue. Job's accusation is very strong and bitter. Gordis,[80] S. R. Driver,[81] Janzen,[82] and Alan Cooper[83] rightly look at the word *nābāl* not in the context of intellectual ability but of religious and moral discernment, as in the case of "A fool (*nābāl*) says in his heart, 'There is no God'" (Ps 14:1). Unfortunately, some fail to recognize

---

79. Pope, *Job*, 353.
80. Gordis, "Wisdom and Job," 31–52.
81. Driver, *Commentary on Deuteronomy*, 256.
82. Janzen, *Job*, 256.
83. Cooper, "Sense of the Book of Job," 234.

how wisdom operates and claim Job's wife's intervention in the narrative is for her own self-interest.[84] Clines takes a middle position when he says that Job's wife's confrontation is ambiguous since the central issue of the narrative was not about the psychology or morality of Job's wife but Job's behavior.[85] As his wife, her care and concern are of utmost importance to this story that revolves around relationships and friendships. Nonetheless, some feminists have championed Mrs. Job's wisdom and heroic exploits.[86] Her silence after her husband "insults" her is not only a form of protestation but also a way to find space to show her wisdom.

Mrs. Job expects Job to curse God without recourse to Job's spirituality. She does not know her husband well. She cannot support Job to build his faith in the Lord. It is expected that spouses stand by each other. The sages point out that when a man finds a wife, he finds a good thing and obtains favor from the Lord (Prov 18:22). In Job's case, there was suspicion that his wife was acting like other foolish women. Incidentally, there is no evidence from the text to prove that Mrs. Job is a nagging wife and hence not a good wife. Job's description of Mrs. Job as speaking like a foolish woman echoes how Africans look down on women.

Where there is intimacy, the friendly bond between the couple will grow stronger. According to Dana Robert, "as friends come to know each other, through persistence and mutual struggle, their identities are formed anew. Through shared struggle, they bless each other."[87] When spouses engage in a friendship that only involves a growing emotional intimacy without the requisite deepening commitment to suffering together, it will result in disappointment and pain. When friendship with the spouse goes cold, it is a reflection of a cold heart toward the Lord. The Apostle Peter also looks at women as weak in some respects. He says,

> Likewise, husbands, live with your wives in an understanding way, showing honor to the woman as the weaker vessel, since they are heirs with you of the grace of life, so that your prayers may not be hindered. (1 Pet 3:7 ESV)

---

84. Clines, *Job 1–20*, 50–53; Sasson, "Literary and Theological Function of Job's Wife," 90.

85. Clines, *Job 1–20*, 52.

86. Magdalene, "Job's Wife as a Hero," 232; Gravett, "Biblical Responses," 123; Bechtel, "Feminist Approach to the Book of Job," 222–51.

87. Robert, *Faithful Friendship*, 138.

Disagreement between the husband and wife does not help them pursue a common goal and hinders prayer life. As Augustine asserts,

> Friends who disagree about things divine cannot have a full and true agreement about things human. Those who make light of things divine will necessarily value things human differently from the One who created us won't be able to love any human being in the right way.[88]

Job's words may cause his wife to be silent. His actions may lead her to abandon him because they do not agree with each other. It has been established that loyal friends stand by each other no matter what happens and not only for a season.

God's presence is in the midst of a husband and wife when they live intimately or cordially with one another. Spousal friendship requires that each person is willing to be at the side of the spouse in good times and bad. The elders say in Igbo, *Isi kotara ebu ka ebu na-agba* ("It is the head that disturbs the wasp that the wasp stings"). That is to say, troublemakers will suffer serious consequences. Mrs. Job is put right because Job feels she is trying to bring trouble. However, Job's actions and words do not show intimacy. Sharing a home with a quarrelsome wife is not easy (Prov 21:9; 25:24). The value of friendship is seen better when there is intimacy; when quarrels and feuds do not break a couple apart. If a marriage relationship is as well established as friendship, it will overcome every hurdle in reaching the moments of happiness. Mrs. Job feels that what had happened to Job has also affected her.

Job becomes blessed with lots of property and has seven sons and three daughters in his old age after God restores him. Although the writer does not mention it, Job's wife contributes to the raising of the children. She gives birth to ten children in her old age. An Akan proverb says *ɔbaa te sɛ borɔdeɛ, n'ase mpa mma* ("A woman is like a plantain tree, which sprouts all the time"). It shows how Mrs. Job is fruitful. The qualities of a good wife are enumerated in Proverbs 31:10–31, and the woman is described as having acquired and owned property.

Collaboration plays a key role in marriage and friendship. The Akan say, *nsa baako nkura adesoa* ("A single hand is never enough to lift a heavy load"). Demanding spousal responsibilities like paying bills, doing household chores, and caring for children from one of the couples alone while the other is unable to support does not show true friendship.

---

88. Augustine, *Letters* 31, 223.

A spouse who is a friend will not wait for the other's specific request to meet the need. The spouse's presence is to be shown in how they assist each other. Couples who are friends see themselves as helpmates (Gen 2:18). It is not only the wife who is a helpmate to the husband. That is to say, couples who live as friends may quarrel, but because of the friendship between them, they easily learn to put aside their differences and move on together. The writer of Ecclesiastes says,

> Two are better than one because they have a good reward for their toil. For if they fall, one will lift up the other, but woe to one who is alone and falls and does not have another to help. Again, if two lie together, they keep warm, but how can one keep warm alone? And though one might prevail against another, two will withstand one. A threefold cord is not quickly broken (4:9–12).

Such is what should be seen among spousal friends. They should stay by each other's side not only to have fun but also to support and empower each other.

Spousal friendship can be that kind of true friendship capable of accepting each other as the person is, because of the unconditional love and romantic passion between them. Job's active role in the *pater familias*, or the "*chef de clan*," clearly gives him a right to express his masculinity over his wife and other members of the family. It illustrates why his wife is passive, submissive, and feminine. He can say anything to his wife without considering how she would feel.

Friends seek to empower each other with their counsel. A friend will support and cheer the other to succeed. The words used in communication can either kill or heal. An Akan proverb goes: *Sɛ wo kokromoti poli a, wo pira wo ankasa wo ho; nanso sɛ wo kɛtrɛma poli a, ɛsɛɛ oman no nyinaa* ("If your toe slips, you hurt yourself only; but when your tongue slips, you destroy the whole society"). The sages emphasize the destructive power of the tongue (Prov 18:21; James 3:6). Good friends always aim at building each other up. For a man to jump to the conclusion that his wife is speaking like a foolish woman is not an empowering experience. Job might have known what Mrs. Job was made of. He might have had an experience of how Mrs. Job acts "foolishly" but then did not help her out. Either Job knows his wife very well or he is caught in the web of stereotyping women as "foolish." He seems to have a fixed mind, influenced by the culture. True friendship is not manufactured on biases but based on recognition of the other through love. The Akan say, *bea ɔdɔ wɔ no sum nnyi hɔ* ("where there is love there is no darkness"). Again, the Akan say, *nsuo a ɔdɔ wo na ɔkɔ wahina mu* ("water that loves you enters your pot"). That is to say, what you love most is taken to heart. Friendship is intentional and creates room for two souls to recognize something positive in each other.

Both Mrs. Job and Job speak frankly to each other. Although the text does not mention their intentions, they express their inner feelings. Africans believe that honest advice does not destroy true friendship. Job, however, does not take the advice of his wife kindly. To Job, his wife does not support him in holding on to his integrity. She does not lament to God but rather confronted her husband. The Igbo elders say, *Otu onye tuo izu, o gbue ochu* ("If one man takes a decision, he commits murder"). Murder, in this sense, is not literal but connotes any action that brings disaster to the community. This proverb means that consultation or seeking the other's opinion is the right path to take. Knowledge is never complete: two heads are better than one. Job sees his wife differently and feels that his wife is speaking like one of the foolish women. Such a statement from a man exposes the wife to public ridicule, for the Akan say, *Obea ye turom mu nhwiren, ne kunu nso ye ne ho ban* ("A woman is a flower in a garden, her husband is the fence that protects it"). By implication, the husband is to serve as a wall of protection around the wife.

Earlier, Job does not show concern for his wife as a husband should. He does not take his wife into his sacrifices and does not show any concern when she losses her ten children. To care about something is generally to find it worthwhile or valuable in some way. Caring about one's spouse is no exception. The central difference between Job and his wife is the lack of mutual care and support. Job's assertion that his wife speaks like a foolish woman does not portray a man who is caring enough. If Mrs. Job wants her husband to die, and if she finds her husband's breath repulsive and will not get close to him, then that would mean she is not caring enough. She does not show true friendship.

Job does not see his wife as a good friend based on what she says. He cannot accept his wife's point of view. He sees his wife as rebellious or treasonable. Dennis Annis stresses the reciprocal nature of friendship. He intimates that friendship requires mutual liking, attraction, and enjoyment. "It is hard to imagine two people could be friends and yet not typically like each other. Friendship allows for periods of irritation, anger, and even dislike, as long as there is overall attachment or fondness."[89] Friends may not want to see one another hurt, but one who withholds the truth from another cannot be a true friend, nor does that permit one to stand by a friend when they are doing wrong. Friends continue to tell the truth even when it hurts (cf. Prov 27:5–6). Perhaps, Mrs. Job's silence after being rebuked earns her some recognition from God. After all, no fault is found with her after God comes to judge the friends of Job.[90]

Job is somehow unfair to his wife by judging her without giving her an opportunity to explain herself. He quickly shuts her out by shaming her because she talks like a fool, affording her no room for further dialogue. He seems to have understood exactly what his wife implies. L. R. Klein observes that Mrs. Job is "the only character in the entire book who speaks without verbalizing a process of reasoning."[91] Admittedly, communication between friends oils relationships: her return to silence also does not help the situation. One wonders why the narrator did not also give her some space.

CONCLUDING REMARKS

The descriptions of the family without the specific mentioning of Mrs. Job in both the prologue and epilogue show that she is not the main character of the story, and indicate the patriarchal nature of the storyteller and the community. Job brought his seven sons and three daughters close to where he was, sanctified them, and offered burnt sacrifices on their behalf with the assumption that they might have sinned and cursed God in their hearts, but he did not do so for his wife. In the sight of God, Job is blameless and upright and fears God, but he does not show any loving relationship with his wife. Mrs. Job is not part of all that Job has, thus questioning *pater familias* ideology. It is believed that when the Adversary attacks Job's flesh and bone, it could point to Mrs. Job rhetorically, perhaps an echo of Adam calling Eve "the bone of my bones and flesh of my flesh." However, the bones and flesh were literally Job's. No matter what, spouses feel the pain when their partners are suffering. Faithful partners in marriage do not allow the other to suffer alone. Job's selfishness becomes a problem for Mrs. Job. Her pain and distress not seen by

---

89. Annis, "Meaning, Value, and Duties of Friendship," 349.
90. Magdalene, "Job's Wife as Hero," 257.
91. Klein, "Job and the Womb," 188–89.

Job make her retreat into silence; she now suffers alone in the cold. Mrs. Job also feels her husband should be blamed for not standing by her. He does not care about her. After all, she has lost her sons and daughters and is an indirect object of further attack. Job's unloving attitude toward his wife is deceptive, and as such, his integrity is questionable. Job does not mean his wife well. Giving one's wife out to another to pay for a sin committed is intimate partner violence. God hates sexual violence against women. A man who loves his wife very well will not give up his wife to be abused.

The silence between Job and his wife also widens the gap in their relationship. Job affirms that his repugnant "breath" and "anger" have caused his wife to desert him. His bad breath is interfering with their love life; she could not come close to him. There should be practical steps for couples to stand by each other if they are good friends. Where there is spousal friendship, parting ways is a difficult thing. A true friend will not wish the other to die because the loss will take away half of the friend's self. Mrs. Job is the epitome of wisdom and shows how friends are supposed to be. She advises the husband to challenge God and when he did, he was vindicated. Her silence also functions as a communicative strategy not only to indict God but also to join her husband in seeking a resolution. To be silent at certain points in life can be a mark of wisdom.

In all, the marriage between Job and Mrs. Job can be said to be full of suspicion and disappointment because they do not nurture friendship in their relationship. Job and his wife do not know each other very well. Mrs. Job does not understand why Job is holding on to his integrity. Job does not understand why his wife asks him to curse God and die. There is a lack of intimacy in the marriage, or at least a silence about marital intimacy that speaks loudly. Instead of addressing the disaster together as a couple, Job is thinking about himself. Job complains that Mrs. Job is not loyal to him and has deserted him. Job's words to his wife are not encouraging, empathic, and empowering. She is there to produce children and not as a companion. She can be sacrificed to pay for the sins of her husband, while she cannot inherit any property. All these prove that the two are not friends. Good friends may certainly disagree and fight and hurt each other's ego, but will move on to make amends because of the commitment to the ideals of friendship.

8

Extended Family Members and Acquaintances

AFRICAN SOCIETIES CONSIDER KIN as the foundation for a community. Friendship influences to a greater extent how brothers and sisters, whether in the nuclear family or extended family, treat each other. Persons of lower status, such as servants, can make friends with masters. Also, neighbors and strangers can make friends with their host. It is not the number of friends one makes that informs the quality of friendship relationships. Friends are expected to make exchanges in reciprocity and help one another in distress. The one who fails to turn up in times of distress but surfaces only in times of joy is not a good friend.

Friendship among siblings is a chance that they take and develop throughout their lifetime.[1] Martine Guichard, drawing on Gulliver, mentions how the Ndendeuli people make "better" friends with distant relatives, brothers-in-law, and second cousins. The reason for this arrangement is that whereas a relative could be trusted in times of need and accede to requests, an unrelated person was unlikely to be contacted because they have no obligations to friends or one cannot make demands from them as a right.[2] Hence, matters of obligation influence the making of friendship. For the ancient Greeks, *Philia* (translated as "friend") creates space for family members and acquaintances, placing them under

---

1. Geest, "Kinship as Friendship," 69,70.
2. Guichard, "Where Are Other's People's Friends Hiding?" 28.

different categories to relate well.³ Acquaintances and kin were all described by words like *philia* or *xenia*. Similarly, the *oikeia* or immediate family and the *genos* or kinship group were all kinds of *philia*.⁴

Africans also believe that anyone can be nice to your face, but it takes a true friend to be nice behind your back. Among the Akan it is said, *abowa bɛka wo a, ofir wo tam mu* ("if an insect can bite you, it has to be from your own clothes"). That is to say the one who is closest can hurt the most. Likewise, the one who is closest can be the greatest friend. It is people who are closer to each other that know the deep secrets of one another. Hence, siblings and kin are most unreliable because of their closeness. Guichard says there is an impression that "the way in which people deal with disappointing friends is also influenced by the local (non-)availability of relatives."⁵

Generally, acquaintance friends may include family relatives, guests, sojourners, neighbors, servants, children, and those whom one loves. An acquaintance friend is seen as a colleague bound by a social contract such as a kinsman/kinswoman, neighbor, and countryman/countrywoman. It also refers to people engaged in the same business or going along the same path who can see themselves as acquaintance friends. They are friends by virtue of the association to a common goal, not on a personal level. Acquaintance friends meet less often than regular friends. An acquaintance could be someone you know and are in contact with, but don't know very well or they are not a close friend. Other synonyms for acquaintances are companions, associates, and ordinary friends. Acquaintances share or exchange general ideas as they go about the day. They are people we cross paths with regularly: people we go to school with, work with, or live next to. The more we see someone, the more likely the chance of a friendship developing.

In what ways can we describe the relationship between the family members and acquaintances of Job? What kind of friends are they?

IDENTITY OF THE FAMILIAL FRIENDS

In the book of Job, the acquaintances and members of his extended family do not engage in any dialogue with Job. They do not say anything,

3. Baltzly and Eliopolous, "Classical Ideals of Friendship," 12.
4. See Conner, *New Politicians of Fifth-Century Athens*, 9–13.
5. Guichard, "Where Are Other's People's Friends Hiding?" 24.

but Job's perspective on them can be seen. How Job sees the nature of their relationship helps to establish what kind of friends they are and the expectations of friends. The assumption is that the concept of friendship encompasses not only non-kinship relationships but also kinship ones. Job has brothers and sisters and other acquaintances such as servants and neighbors who are mentioned in the story as a foil; these contribute to the exploration of what friendship is all about.

In *Job* 19:13–19, Job mentions his family (*'aḥay*), acquaintances (*yod'ay*), relatives (*qerôbāy*), close friends (*meyuddā 'ay*), guests (*gārê*), serving girls (*'amhotay*), servant (*'abddî*), wife (*'ištî*), family (*libene'biṭnî*), young children (*'ăwîlîm*), intimate friends (*sôdî*), and those whom he loved (*'āhabttî*). In chapter 31 he also mentions *rē'î* "his neighbors" (v. 9), *'abddî wa'ămātî* "his manservant and maidservants" (v. 13), *gēr* sojourners" and *'oraḥ* "travellers" (v. 32). Besides in Job 42:11, Job mentions *kol-'eḥāyw wekol-'aḥyotāyw* "all of his brothers and sisters."

The Hebrew noun, *'āḥ* (brother) has a wide range of meanings. A "brother" connotes:

1. one common parent (Gen 14:16; 29:12);
2. a man in the same profession or activity;
3. a fellow/companion (Gen 9:5);
4. a man who is a close friend (2 Sam 1:26; 1 Kgs 13:30);
5. a man who is of the same clan or country described as kinsman, neighbor, companion, countryman (Deut 23:7; Judg 21:6; Neh 5:7; Jer 34:9).

The Hebrew noun *'āḥōt* ("sister") also has a wide range of meanings and is used repeatedly in the Hebrew Bible for a female:

1. having the same parents as another; a niece (Gen 12:13; 20:12);
2. having one parent in common, with another, half-sister (Gen 20:12; Lev 18:9);
3. belonging to the same family or clan as another, a kinswoman (Gen 24:60);
4. of the same country (Num 25:18; Ezek 23:7);
5. figuratively for one's wife or lover (Song 4:9; 5:1; 8:8).

A similar broad idea can be observed among Africans. The Akan noun *onua*, translated as "brother" or "sister," goes beyond blood or familial relations. The Akan say, *onua ne nea wɔayɛ wo yie* ("a sibling is someone who has done good to you"). In other words, a brother or sister is one who seeks the well-being of the other. The one whose hand is seen in times of need is truly a friend. It extends to *reementaaga* (Moosi), comrades and neighbor one grows up with, or *al-chore* (Maasai), a trusted exchange partner.

JOB'S RHETORICAL CLAIMS AND SUPPORT

During his time of crisis, Job finds all his relatives and acquaintances distanced themselves from him (19:13–14). The people who used to find shelter in his home do not have any need for him because he is poor. More so, the maidservants and menservants treat him like a stranger (19:6). Job becomes disappointed that his children, neighbors, former friends, and those who depended on him have all abandoned him, and withdrawn into darkness.

Job longs for intimacy from other members of his household, a virtue that these people lacked. He complains that his family cannot show love. At that time Job has lost all his children. Hence, the reference to family (19:13a) may connote his extended family members, which include tribe, parents, siblings, nephews, and nieces. These family members are also described as "relatives" (19:14). In all, Job's family—made up of his wife who is living, extended family, and acquaintances—have all deserted him or shunned him. He also includes his wife. They are deserting him in times of trouble. Being able to fall on a family member in good times and in times of crisis is what the sages advocated for (Prov 17:17). Yet Job complains about the kind of relationship the family, relatives, children, and servants have given to him:

> ¹³ 'He has put my brothers (*'aḥay*) far from me,
> and my acquaintances (*yod'ay*) are wholly estranged (*zāru*) from me.
> ¹⁴ My relatives (*qerôbāy*) and my close friends (*meyuddā 'ay*) have failed me;
> ¹⁵ the guests (*gārē*) in my house have forgotten me;
> my serving-girls (*'amhotay*) count me as a stranger (*lezār*);
> I have become an alien in their eyes.
> ¹⁶ I call to my servant (*'abddî*), but he gives me no answer;
> I must myself plead with him.

> ¹⁷ My breath is repulsive to my wife (*'išttî*);
>   I am loathsome to my own family (*libenê bitnî*).
> ¹⁸ Even young children (*ăwîlîm*) despise me;
>   when I rise, they talk against me.
> ¹⁹ All my intimate friends (*sôdî*) abhor me,
>   and those whom I loved (*'āhabttî*) have turned against me.
> ²⁰ My bones cling to my skin and to my flesh,
>   and I have escaped by the skin of my teeth.
> ²¹ Have mercy on me, have mercy on me, you who are my friends (*rē'a*),
>   for the hand of God has touched me! (19:13–21)

Job knows that anyone who falls under the category of friend should not estrange themselves from the other. Such a person should not forget the other, or treat the other as an alien. Friends respond to each other when there is a call. They do not despise each other and talk or turn against each other.

Job expected his "friends" (*rē'ay*)—made up of his family (*'ahay*), acquaintances (*yod'ay*), relatives (*qerôbā y*), close friends (*meyuddā'ay*), guests (*gārê*), serving-girls (*'amhotay*), servant (*'abddî*), wife (*'ištî*), family (*libenê bitnî*), young children (*ăwîlîm*), intimate friends (*sôdî*), and those whom he loved (*'āhabttî*)—to show themselves to be loyal, benevolent, collaborative, other-centered and faithful. There is assonance in verse 17 to verse 21; each verse ends with the Hebrew alphabet, yod. The use of *'āhabttî* in verses 19b serves as a closure marker and reinforces "have mercy on me" repeated in verse 21, indicating a closure of the pericope.

The Hebrew *'āhab* ("to love"), which occurs 540 times in the Hebrew Bible and once in Job 19:19, holds some connotation of friendship. Traditionally, it bears the nuance of emotive love. The ideal relationship between husband and wife, parents and children, and oneself and neighbor are all properly described in terms of loving friendship. The participle forms point to "being friendly." Such a kind of friendship moves beyond mere acquaintance.[6] Wallis notes that love and behavior motivated by love cannot be separated from emotions but are also not dependent on emotion, which due to its subjectivity is ambivalent and vacillating. Nevertheless, friends have a socio-ethical responsibility for one's actions in a community. It has to be real and full of substance.[7]

---

6. Richards, *Encyclopedia of Bible Words*, 297.
7. *TDOT*, 1:110.

The noun *'aḥay* ("my brothers") may refer to Job's siblings and shares the same thinking as *benê bitnî*, literally meaning "children of my mother." The noun *yod'ay* ("my acquaintances") also connotes those who know him, and shares the same thinking as *měyuddā'ay* ("those I know well"). The Hebrew *měyuddā'ay*, translated as "my close friends" or "my acquaintances," also means "those I know." The root occurs in Job 19:13, 14; 24:1; 38:3; 40:7; 42:4. The root also connotes sexual advances. In Judges 19:22, the men of the city rush to the old man's house and request that he releases the Levite so that they have sex with him (Heb: *wěnēdā'enû*). The word *qěrôbāy*, translated as "my relative," also means those who are intimate to him or close friends, and shares the same thinking as *sôdî* intimate friends. The noun *qěrôb* translated as "family" also denotes "close relatives."

Close friend (*qěrôb*) occurs four times in *the* book of Job (19:14; 20:14; 31:37; 33:22). Basically, it denotes "come closer / draw near / make sexual advances." Physical proximity is implicit in these ideas. However, within divine–human relationship, there are some restrictions when humans come closer to God. The adjective *qěrôb* can also connote a close kinship, or intimate relations that can extend beyond family ties.[8] In Job 19:14, it is used to refer to "close friends" (NRSV; NIV), "intimate friends" (NASV), and "friend" (JSP TANAK). Job has female servants and male servants who treat him in those trying times of pain and suffering as stranger and alien.

Those whom "he loved" is likely to have included people in his household, community, and other persons. In 19:14–19, relatives, friends, guests, maidservants, servants, wife, blood brothers, little boys, and intimate friends are mentioned as constituting those whom Job loved.[9] Friendship with servants, children, and siblings is possible since it rests on how each one will be there for the other in times of need. Alexander Nehamas contends that friendships with brothers and sisters are possible as long as they, too, share mutual affection and, more importantly, wish good things for each other because it is the right thing to do.[10]

Job describes all of his brothers, sisters, and acquaintances in 19:21 as "my friends" (*rē'a'*), based on intimacy, affection, and benefaction. The LXX puts it as *hō philio* ("my friends"), expressing the familiarity and cordiality between them, but rhetorically stated to show the lack of affection Job received from them. Nehamas asserts that,

8. *TDOT*, 13:144, 145; *NIDOTTE*, 3:977.
9. Alden, *Job*, 204.
10. Nehamas, *Aristotelian Philia, Modern Friendship*, 219.

"Affection" (philēsis), which is necessary to philia, ranges from the lovers' most intense passion through the measured feelings of the virtuous to the anaemic attitude of people towards those they happen to run across in their travels or the contemptuous regard of a master for a slave. Philia may extend to all human beings, in so far as they are human beings, but if it does, it reaches most of them in a very attenuated form.[11]

In Job 29, Job affirms his virtuous life toward the people in his society. He is a great support, intimate, affectionate, and an advocate to all, especially the poor and needy. Susannah Tacciati describes Job's monologue in chapters 29–31 as "self-examination."[12] The conceptualization of his past brings to him an awareness of his social life, and his relationship with others is likened to a friend of the society. Job recounts his relationship with the community and how cordial it used to be, like a friend committed to their welfare. He says,

> 7 When I went out to the gate of the city,
>   when I took my seat in the square,
> 8 the young men saw me and withdrew,
>   and the aged rose up and stood;
> 9 the nobles refrained from talking,
>   and laid their hands on their mouths;
> 10 the voices of princes were hushed,
>   and their tongues stuck to the roof of their mouths.
> 11 When the ear heard, it commended me,
>   and when the eye saw, it approved;
> 12 because I delivered the poor who cried,
>   and the orphan who had no helper.
> 13 The blessing of the wretched came upon me,
>   and I caused the widow's heart to sing for joy.
> 14 I put on righteousness, and it clothed me;
>   my justice was like a robe and a turban. (29:7–14)

At the city gate, seats are reserved for chiefs yet Job is given one of them. Here we find a community that was ready to accept, listen, and learn from Job, counting him as one of the elite in society. The mention of "young," "old," "nobles," and "princes" (29:7–10) shows a varied group of prominent people. All these classes of people rise up to welcome Job while he comes to take his seat. Again, Job mentions the "poor,"

---

11. Nehamas, *Aristotelian Philia, Modern Friendship*, 235.
12. Tacciati, *Job and the Disruption of Identity*, 96.

wretched," "orphan," and widows" as beneficiaries of his magnanimity. Job goes on to say,

> ¹⁵ I was eyes to the blind,
>   and feet to the lame.
> ¹⁶ I was a father to the needy,
>   and I championed the cause of the stranger.
> ¹⁷ I broke the fangs of the unrighteous,
>   and made them drop their prey from their teeth.
> ¹⁸ Then I thought, "I shall die in my nest,
>   and I shall multiply my days like the phoenix;
> ¹⁹ my roots spread out to the waters,
>   with the dew all night on my branches;
> ²⁰ my glory was fresh with me,
>   and my bow ever new in my hand."
> ²¹ They listened to me, and waited,
>   and kept silence for my counsel.
> ²² After I spoke they did not speak again,
>   and my word dropped upon them like dew.
> ²³ They waited for me as for the rain;
>   they opened their mouths as for the spring rain.
> ²⁴ I smiled on them when they had no confidence;
>   and the light of my countenance they did not extinguish.
> ²⁵ I chose their way, and sat as chief,
>   and I lived like a king among his troops,
>   like one who comforts mourners. (29:15–25)

Job recounts his past relationship with the blind and lame (v. 15), and the needy and stranger (v. 16). He was their deliverer in times of trouble. When it came to advocacy, he championed their cause. He was not only there for them at the right time but also sacrificed all for their sake. If Job's word was refreshing like dew, then it was because he used his influence to empower the vulnerable, poor, and marginalized, a fact that earned him respect across the classes. His words overwhelmed the people completely with some force, although dropping as dew, lifting up spirits, and helping the broken surge to hope.[13] Being the eyes to the blind, feet to the lame, a father to the needy, and championing the cause of the stranger speaks of how such people found hope in him. Our eyes are the entrance to our hearts and minds and, as such, they provide a doorway to our very souls. Friends touch the hearts, mind, and souls of each other by their good gestures.

13. See Aidoo, "'My Words Dropped Upon Them Like Dew,'" 100–102.

Job was satisfied with what he had done for his acquaintances. He had done more than required and as such had been sure that he would die as a happy person:

> Then I thought, "I shall die in my nest (*'im-qinnî*),
> and I shall multiply my days like the phoenix (*wekaḥol*) (29:18)

Job imagined that he would die "in my nest," an idiom that means resting peacefully in his dwelling place. A nest is a place of rest (39:27; Num 24:21; Deut 32:11; Jer 49:16; Obadiah 1:4; Prov 27:8). If the particle *'im* is taken as "with," (i.e., *'im* of coordination), then the meaning of the line will be "dying with his family." Certainly, such a translation will be farfetched since all of his children had died. A paradox is, however, heightened in the second line. While the first line states that he will die peacefully, the second line gives the impression that his days will be multiplied. The waw (translated "and") adds to the difficulty. Will Job die peacefully "and" his days multiply? The noun *ḥol* can be translated as "phoenix" (NRSV; CBJ) or "sand" (NIV; ASV; ESV; NKJV). The Septuagint, the Vulgate, and Jewish interpreters favor the translation, "the phoenix bird" because it forms a parallel with "nest."

Job also describes his status in society as a noble and wise man. His counsel was well received and was always apt due to how he carried himself: "I chose their way, and sat as chief, and I lived like a king among his troops" (29:25). Job was not honored just because he was wealthy or the light of God shone over his head; his contributions to society's welfare were commendable: "When the ear heard, it commended me, and when the eye saw, it approved because I delivered the poor who cried, and the orphan who had no helper" (29:11–12).[14] So when he would take to take a seat at the city gate, all ears were ready to hear his voice. Such courtesies raised his status. As Hartley says, "he reached out to meet the deepest needs of those who were forlorn and thereby restores their sense of worth."[15] Job says he smiled at them when they had no confidence (29:24), as a sign for empowering others. The reference to "smile" (29:24) also carries the connotation of acting clumsy to amuse others and make them happy.

Fighting for the afflicted in the hands of the unrighteous can be a difficult task, yet he stood up for them like a friend: "I broke the fangs of the unrighteous, and made them drop their prey from their teeth"

---

14. The theme of commendation and social status is continued in vv. 21–25.
15. Hartley, *Job*, 391.

(29:17). This echoes the life of David, how as a shepherd boy he recounts rescuing lambs from the mouth of lions to prove he could stand against Goliath (1 Sam 17:34–37). Job was thus an advocate of social justice. Justice involves generously sharing one's resources with the poor. However, there is no one who remembers all that he has done, and Job seems stirred to remind them. Weeks says,

> It is their attempted condolences which seem to provoke his growing sense of grievance, and much of his bitterness is reserved for the way in which he is treated by humans: once a respected pillar of the community, he is now accused, shunned and ridiculed, and he looks for vindication in the eyes of humans as much as God who is doing this, but also God alone who can ultimately offer that vindication.[16]

In other words, Job's family and acquaintances are contributing to his fall from grace to grass. He remembers when his children were always around him (29:5b) but now they are wholly estranged from him. They have failed him, forgotten him, and treated him like a stranger. Habel is right when he says that "to be a friend is to be cohuman in a dehumanized situation where despairing man has lost his religion as a source of human support."[17] Such is the nature of a good friend: standing by the friend in times of need.

Job calls his acquaintances "a senseless, disreputable brood" (30:8). He says: "And now they mock me in song; I am a byword to them" (30.9). These people do not remember what Job did for them in the past. He who was once "the greatest of all the people of the east" (1.3b) has now become a laughing stock. It is fake and fair-weather friends who stand by their friend in good times but when the friend falls, they attack, mock, and judge the friend. Equally troubling are those of a lower status gathering around the fallen, pointing and laughing at a person who once enjoyed high status in society. The laughter of the children is derisive, not kind.

Job's honor before the community completely changed when he encountered suffering. The one who used to smile (śāḥăqu̇ "mock, make sport"; 30:1) at the people has become a laughing stock and they mock (śāḥăqu̇) him. The Hebrew śāḥăqu̇ echoes the relationship between a superior and an inferior.[18] If this is so, then Job's honor has been defaced; he

---

16. Weeks, *Study of Wisdom Literature*, 69.
17. Habel, "Only the Jackal Is My Friend," 230.
18. Schifferdecker, *Out of the Whirlwind*, 50.

has become inferior to the people. Since his dignity and honor is at stake, Job attacks the dignity and honor of his peers—the fathers of the children who mock him. No wonder Newsom calls Job a "master of the insult."[19] In the words of Abigail Pelham,

> Perceiving that he is laughed at, Job hurls every insult he can think of at those who find his predicament funny. "They're younger than I am! Treating them like dogs is better than they deserve! They're weaklings! They're lazy! They're uncivilized! They're outcasts! They live like animals! They're homeless! They don't have enough food to eat! They're morons! They don't deserve any respect! They don't deserve to live among civilized human beings."[20]

Significantly, Job does not go so far as to insult his family members and acquaintances. Job rather complains that persons with no significant background have attacked him (30:1–2). From the heights of honor, he has fallen so deep that those at the fringes of society laugh at him. The young people who are part of the mockers are so insignificant that their fathers are even not worthy to eat from the dog's plates or stay where their dog sleeps. All those he had been trying to protect, redeem, and help are repaying him with wickedness. They are people who are of no use to Job and he does not need their feeble strength in his workplace (30:2). They are like thieves in the community (30:5). It is these people who are supposed to be banished who are rather coming against him.

To prove that he has lived up to expectations with his relatives and acquaintances, Job decides to pronounce curses upon himself. He makes these wishes, perhaps, knowing that he will not fall foul of any of them. He says,

> ⁵ If I have walked with falsehood,
>   and my foot has hurried to deceit—
> ⁶ let me be weighed in a just balance,
>   and let God know my integrity!—
> ⁷ if my step has turned aside from the way,
>   and my heart has followed my eyes,
>   and if any spot has clung to my hands;
> ⁸ then let me sow, and another eat;
>   and let what grows for me be rooted out.

---

19. Newsom, "Book of Job," 544.
20. Abigail Pelham, "*Job* as Comedy, Revisited," 96.

> ⁹ If my heart has been enticed by a woman,
>   and I have lain in wait at my neighbor's door;
> ¹⁰ then let my wife grind for another,
>   and let other men kneel over her.
> ¹¹ For that would be a heinous crime;
>   that would be a criminal offence;
> ¹² for that would be a fire consuming down to Abaddon,
>   and it would burn to the root all my harvest.
> ¹³ If I have rejected the cause of my male or female slaves,
>   when they brought a complaint against me;
> ¹⁴ what then shall I do when God rises up?
>   When he makes inquiry, what shall I answer him?
> ¹⁵ Did not he who made me in the womb make them?
>   And did not one fashion us in the womb?
> ¹⁶ If I have withheld anything that the poor desired,
>   or have caused the eyes of the widow to fail,
> ¹⁷ or have eaten my morsel alone,
>   and the orphan has not eaten from it—
> ¹⁸ for from my youth I reared the orphan like a father,
>   and from my mother's womb I guided the widow—
> ¹⁹ if I have seen anyone perish for lack of clothing,
>   or a poor person without covering,
> ²⁰ whose loins have not blessed me,
>   and who was not warmed with the fleece of my sheep;
> ²¹ if I have raised my hand against the orphan,
>   because I saw I had supporters at the gate;
> ²² then let my shoulder blade fall from my shoulder,
>   and let my arm be broken from its socket. (31:5–22)

Job expects that familial relationships should be devoid of falsehood and deceit (v. 5) and lust (v. 7, 9). A friend should not be wicked to another who is poor, a widow, or perishing for lack of clothing (vv. 16–19). Using violence or beating up an orphan is highly unacceptable (v. 21). Any person who does this to a friend has committed a heinous crime or criminal offense (v. 11) that would destroy whatever relationship that has been developed (v. 12). A friend should be a person of integrity (v. 6), and champion the cause of others, including slaves (v. 13), because both master and servants are all created in the image of God, i.e., formed and fashioned in one womb (v. 15).

Friends should not sexually abuse others' spouses. Seow notices a wordplay in 31:9–10, with the words *we'al-petaḥ rē'î* "and at my friend's door" and *tiṭḥan* "grind," saying that they echo sexual relations.²¹ Similarly, to lay in *ʾārābttî* "wait" (v. 9b) maps with other men *ʿāleha yikreʿûn* "kneeling over her"; v. 10b), and these words reinforce the notions of rape and sexual violence. Since he has not "entered" any opening of his neighbor, no one will also "kneel over" his wife and "grind" her.

Job goes further to show some other categories of acquaintances with whom one should maintain a good relationship:

> ²⁹ If I have rejoiced at the ruin of those who hated me,
>   or exulted when evil overtook them—
> ³⁰ I have not let my mouth sin
>   asking for their lives with a curse—
> ³¹ if those of my tent ever said,
>   "O that we might be sated with his flesh!"—
> ³² the stranger has not lodged in the street;
>   I have opened my doors to the traveler—
> ³³ if I have concealed my transgressions as others do,
>   by hiding my iniquity in my bosom,
> ³⁴ because I stood in great fear of the multitude,
>   and the contempt of families terrified me,
>   so that I kept silence, and did not go out of doors—
> ³⁵ O that I had one to hear me!
>   (Here is my signature! Let the Almighty answer me!)
>   O that I had the indictment written by my adversary!
> ³⁶ Surely I would carry it on my shoulder;
>   I would bind it on me like a crown;
> ³⁷ I would give him an account of all my steps;
>   like a prince I would approach him.
> ³⁸ If my land has cried out against me,
>   and its furrows have wept together;
> ³⁹ if I have eaten its yield without payment,
>   and caused the death of its owners;
> ⁴⁰ let thorns grow instead of wheat,
>   and foul weeds instead of barley." (31:29–40)

Job knows that some people can conceal their transgression from a friend (31:33), but not a true friend. For Job, a good friend should not show contempt for the family (31:34), i.e., rejoice at their ruin or curse them (cf. 31:30). One should do good to the stranger and traveler (31:32). Job displays a high sense of social justice. Herein we find Job showing how he was a model and how human relationships ought to be. Hartley

---

21. Seow, *Job 1–21*, 80.

claims Job was testing his attitudes and motives by these curses, but his primary motive was to demonstrate that he had maintained the right relationships on all levels.[22]

Despite all that Job has done for his acquaintances and friends, he sees them as pursuing him and afflicting him all along. They are repaying evil for the good he has done to them. Reciprocity lies at the heart of friendship and is a mutual exchange of actions, goods, energy, time, emotion, etc., between friends. Reciprocating a good gesture to friends leaves a feeling of validation and a sense of worth. It proves that what one invested is valued and appreciated. It proves that one has a friend. Reciprocity energizes friends to keep going in the relationship.

In the epilogue, the narrator shows how God blesses Job and how the community and relations resurface. Job's extended family members visit him when he is restored:

> And the Lord restored the fortunes of Job when he had prayed for his friends; and the Lord gave Job twice as much as he had before. Then there came to him all his brothers and sisters and all who had known him before, and they ate bread with him in his house; they showed him sympathy and comforted him for all the evil that the Lord had brought upon him; and each of them gave him a piece of money and a gold ring. (42:10–11)

Reconciliation with his three friends contributes to Job's restoration of wealth. His fortunes are restored "when" he prays for the three. That is to say, reconciling with the three paves the way for God to restore his wealth. Human beings can enjoy the full blessings of God when they reconcile with their friends.

When all becomes well, Job's brothers and sisters come and dine with him. It seems all they are concerned with is sitting at the table with Job. As James Walton observes, Job's actions are not governed by what others do to him or do not do. He has a self-sworn ethic not to deal with others according to their folly.[23] They did not visit when Job had lost all of his property and was struggling to fend for himself because they could not sit at the table with him. Their sympathy and comfort come at the wrong time, not when it was needed most. Their money and gold rings come at a time God has already blessed Job with lots of wealth.

---

22. Hartley, *Job*, 407.
23. Wharton, *Job*, 187.

IMPLICATIONS

Job is directly blaming his extended family members and other friends for abandoning him just like how God has abandoned him. They were only available for a season; during his good days. His family, relatives, guests, servants, and young children in his home and community have also contributed to causing the suffering in his flesh, the ellipsis indicates that Job holds God accountable for the sufferings in his flesh. Job bewails his loneliness and alienation; he finds himself abandoned by relatives, close friends, and even his servants, just like what God has done to him (19:22). Job expects his family to have shown some commitment to him, although he feels the root cause is from God. If God had not caused him to suffer, the relatives and acquaintances might not have acted the way they did. In such an extreme situation, Job in his wildest imagination searches for someone somewhere of the kind of a kin redeemer.[24] He is repulsive to both wife and children; those he loves have turned against him. According to Janzen,

> Job's self-imprecations are not to be interpreted, therefore, merely as the level of abstract moral logic, and as re-statements of a rigid reward–punishment dynamic which he has earlier both denied and presupposed. These self-imprecations, rather, serve to affirm Job's loyalty to the human community and to God, and to lay the basis for his appeal to an answering loyalty from God.[25]

Turning against a friend destroys the very nature of closeness that exists among friends. In the book of Proverbs, intimacy plays a key role in friendship. The one who shows intimacy and love is worth more than a blood relation: "Do not forsake your friend or the friend of your parent; do not go to the house of your kindred in the day of your calamity. Better is a neighbor who is nearby that kindred who are far away" (Prov 27:10). The one who despises the friend is also not wise (Prov 14:2) but rather a sinner (Prov 14:21).

As Hartley observes, "in patriarchal society the bond among family members was strong, with each one being concerned for his brother's welfare."[26] Job's brothers, however, are not like that. If even someone caused them to be far away, they do not care to come back. Job's "house

---

24. Janzen, *Job*, 131.
25. Janzen, *Job*, 213.
26. Hartley, *Job*, 288.

guests" refers to those whom he had given shelter and provided food for them. They have forgotten him. His business associates, to avoid visiting Job, have traveled away.

For true friendship to exist among unequals, there must be cessation of authority, and each must see the other as equal.[27] It is ordinary friends who maintain status and class when they meet. Job does not have to treat them as if he is the head of the family, an elder, or their employer. Job had created a congenial atmosphere for a good relationship with his community, and he expects them to reciprocate with kindness and loyalty.

Interestingly, Robert Alter explains that the breaking of bread was restorative and marked the welcoming back of Job into the human community.[28] According to Alter, the ring was not that which was worn on the finger but in the ear or nose.[29] Welcoming a rich man with riches may not yield the needed impact. One wonders why he was not welcome as a poor man. Is it normal to reject the poor and welcome the rich? The writer of Proverbs says, "Giving to the rich, will lead only to loss" (Prov 22:16). That is to say, one is sure to suffer loss and come to poverty if it is all about giving to the rich.

Giving a gift in accordance with a rich person's idiosyncratic desires is vital because some things like money do not matter as much to the rich. Therefore, one needs to think about giving something that makes an emotional impact on the rich, rather than money or expensive gifts that they can afford. The writer of Proverbs says "A gift opens doors; it gives access to the great" (Prov 18:16). Perhaps, the brothers and sisters were seeking a way to have access to Job, so they had to use money and gold rings as the bait.

Earlier in chapter 31, Job explained that he did not trust in gold or put his confidence in it. He did not rejoice over his wealth and it did not go to his head (31:24–25). Such an attitude toward wealth and riches makes one godly (cf. 1 Tim 6:17). Those who trust in his riches will fall (Prov 11:28). To Jesus, it is hard for a rich man to enter the kingdom of heaven when they trust in their wealth (Matt 19:23). The prophet Jeremiah calls those who trust in their riches and not in God as boastful (Jer 49:4; cf. 48:7). Similarly, the psalmist says,

27. Lewis, *Four Loves*, 80.
28. Alter, *Job*, 293.
29. Alter, *Job*, 293.

> those who trust in their wealth
> > and boast of the abundance of their riches?
> Truly, no ransom avails for one's life,
> > there is no price one can give to God for it. (Ps 49:6–7)

Though the relatives and acquaintances of Job do not speak in the story, their actions and inaction help to understand what kinds of friends they are. All we hear about them is how Job describes them or how the narrator describes them. Acquaintance friendship and regular friendship are normally understood as being deficient in various ways relative to ideal friendship. A regular or ordinary friend, after a long time, can be a best friend. A few lessons can be drawn from the foregoing.

First, for two people to become good friends, they have to know and understand each other well. More specifically, they have to stand by each other, especially in times of need. That was what Job had done for his brothers, sisters, and acquaintances but they failed to reciprocate. Africans are expected to maintain communal relationships and have a moral obligation to engage in mutually friendly relationships—gender, status, or class does not matter. It takes self-disclosure to turn acquaintances into close friends. Opening up to the other person to share values, goals, and interests is based on trust after getting to know an acquaintance more deeply. Simply sharing a secret with someone does not make the person a close friend. For example, one can share a secret with an attorney or a pastor and that does not make them close friends.

Family members, servants, and strangers need to be sure that those in need have the basic staples of life. Showing compassion and care is essential, especially when one has received such support from others. If Job opened his arms and supported the members of his household, the poor, orphan, widow, and fatherless, and strangers, they should also reciprocate when he is going through difficulty. They should pour themselves into the life of Job to help him in a healthy way. They should mourn with him when he loses his sons and daughters. They should share what they have with Job when he loses his property, to meet his needs and show hospitality. When Job is sick, they should visit. When the three were forcing Job to confess his sins even and not listening to Job, they should have served as peacemakers.

Second, in a world filled with strife, misunderstanding, and injustice, true friends should not only support each other when things are going well. Friendship is enriched through tangible acts of good works that symbolize the extent to which each one respects the other. Generally, friendship is motivated by personal advantages that accrue to both parties when they enter into a reciprocal relationship. Friendship is a reciprocal relationship, as the Akan says: *nyimfa guar benkum na benkum so guar nyimfa* ("the right arm washes the left arm and the left arm washes the right arm"). When one shares and the other fails to reciprocate or disclose things about themselves, the friendship will break down. It is not true friendship when sought solely for the sake of the assistance it offers, and not at all from motives of feeling and affection. One gets to know people well by sharing "safe" thoughts with them first, not the issues that can land a person in trouble.

Demonstrating true friendship in times of difficulty is a wonderful testimony to validate unity in diversity in relationships. It will reveal the true nature of ubuntu and impact ways of thinking and living. Job also shows how one should be socially friendly. Vittorino Grossi quotes Augustine, who saw friendship as essential to our identity as human beings:

> Man, unable to live human life as a friend, deprived of reciprocal communication with his fellow creatures, would not live in a communion worthy of human beings but in the slavery of those who pursue illusions . . . Every human being must therefore be taught how to form friendships and be enabled to enjoy them. A human creature that is deprived of this good could not live his life at the human level, which presupposes reciprocal communication.[30]

One cannot live without being a friend since that is essential to human nature. Africans believe that to be without a friend is to be a poor person. The Akan says, *hianyi na onnyi nyenko* ("the poor person has no friend"). Hence, to live a selfish life where the emphasis is on what one would accrue from others is unacceptable. Friendship can only exist between people who are good to each other, not only the "wise." The good people are those whose actions and lives leave no question as to their honor, empathy, and liberality. Such people are not greedy, and they can be there in good times and in bad times.

In the encounter between Job and his acquaintances, Job offers them all that they need, as friends of virtue might without the expectation of receiving something of equal or greater value in return. However, these acquaintances dissolve the friendship as soon as they find out that they cannot get what they want from Job. These acquaintances see that Job has

---

30. Grossi, "Sexuality and Friendship in Early Christianity," 10.

fallen from the height of honor and reputation into shame and disgrace. Their silence is more humiliating than speech. Their actions show that they are vilifying and belittling Job. He is no longer a great person in their eyes. Therefore, they were never friends in the first place, or they were fair-weather friends; they only took advantage of Job's friendly character. The Igbo elders say, *Aka nrikwu̧o̧ aka ekpe, aka ekpe a kwu̧o̧ aka nri* ("If the right hand washes the left, the left should in turn wash the right hand"). In other words, one has to reciprocate a good gesture. If Job has been good to his acquaintances at some point in time when all was well with him, the acquaintances also have a responsibility to do good to Job in times of difficulty. The Akan elders say, *sɛ wo nyɛnko soa wo kɔhwɛ ewia, ɛnnsoa no nkɔhwɛ sum* ("if you friend carries you to see the sun, you do not carry him to see darkness"). That is to say, a good gesture should be reciprocated with goodness and not evil.

All the relatives and acquaintances are nowhere to be found when Job is suffering. However, when God restores all that Job had and becomes wealthy again, we find the brothers and sisters visiting him to share gifts and have a party with Job. Africans believe that where food is free, many will come, and a sweet-scented flower attracts many bees. Such an attitude does not fit close friends or even ordinary friends but rather fair-weather friends.

Third, intimacy plays a key role in maintaining friendship relationships. Friends incorporate the full spectrum of relational experiences, being there for each other emotionally as well as physically. As such it is expected of friends to facilitate the expression of relatedness, otherwise they can lose the support that comes from others. In good times friends know you and in bad times you get to know your friends. As such, those who stay by their friends in bad times show their true worth. As Manitza Kotse and Carike Noeth opine, "friendship can form the environment for us to be 'trained' in the characteristics of theological friendship where we are friends in freedom and without hierarchy, and, in so doing, learn to treat all human beings as equal. Where we are reminded of the relational aspects of our createdness in God's image to learn to live in intimate relation to others."[31] To Moltmann, friendship is a "free human relationship," one that "arises out of freedom and preserves freedom . . . Friendship is lived freedom."[32]

---

31. Kotse and Noeth, "Friendship as a Theological Model," 7.
32. Moltmann, *Living God and the Fullness of Life*, 119.

Friendship in this world dues to various expectations people have can easily move into realities of disappointment, thus making it lack permanence. People can disappoint one another, but true friends are willing to stay by each other. Where one eliminates affection from a relationship, a friendly culture cannot thrive. Friendship by its nature admits no pretense. If friendship springs from a natural impulse rather than a wish for receiving help, it thrives. If it is about what one can get or a deliberate calculation of the material advantage, it is likely to fail. The Swahili people say, *mtegemea cha nduguye hufaa maskini* ("the person who consistently depends on a sibling will die poor"). However, Job shows what true friendship is all about by allowing his brothers and sister to dine with him when God restores his fortunes.

Fourth, true friends strive to empower each other at all times, and not abandon the other in times of need. A friend is like the eye and the feet of the other. Someone with eyes finds life illuminated, like a lighted room, and sees things clearly. The blind depends on those with eyes to get over some obstacles and locate whatever are looking for. Similarly, the feet help in moving from place to place with some ease. Unfortunately, when Job became poor and needy, he had no one to be his eyes and feet. No one championed his cause, so he thought that without a friend, he was sure to die. Such an idea mirrors what the Shona people say: *Gara mumuzinda nwane shamwari ichakuruma nzeve kana yanza paunorechwa* ("Life without a friend, death without a witness").[33]

In the epilogue (42:11), at a time God had restored Job and blessed him with prosperity, Job's family and friends call upon him and offer gifts. This clearly shows that they are fair-weather friends. The donation of a coin and an earring would be inconsequential after God had given Job a fortune. Their appearance teaches the reader the different types of family and friends, and consequently is a key element within the core story that cannot be ignored.

Finally, friendship grows when each one is prepared to understand the other. A key virtue of friendship is being other-centered. An Akan proverb goes, *Sɛ anntse amma wo nyɛnko no mfom a, ɛtɔn wo ho* ("unless you bear with the faults of a friend, you betray your own"). That is to say, people expose their own weaknesses when they do not want to accept the weaknesses in others. Pointing one finger at another will mean pointing four fingers at oneself. If someone is not a good friend, the valid

---

33. Mhebe, *Shona Proverbs*, 165.

questions are: has one related to that person and how has one influenced that person to be good?

The Ewe elders say, *Amedzro bada dze afeto bada gbo* ("If the stranger does not behave well, he does not fit into the host society and so he is not accommodated"). One's actions will determine whether to take that person as a good friend or a bad friend. It means there are certain expectations about actions that will open doors for good hospitality and friendship. Generally, Africans believe that face to face is better than thousands of words sent through communication channels. So, priority is given to friends who stay close by and make their presence felt in the real world than online friends, especially the silent ones.

CONCLUDING REMARKS

The above discussions have revealed how Job saw his extended family members and distant friends. He gives the impression that they were friends for a season and disloyal. They were not there when they were needed most. Failing to show love, care, or friendship at a time when it is needed most is not commendable. Sometimes people can disappoint us when their presence and support is needed. We may think we know them or figure they are good friends, only to discover, through their actions, that they are not who we gave them credit for. Sometimes circumstances disappoint us. People may expect their achievements to open doors for them, but it does not happen that way. People expect affection and promotion and somebody less qualified gets it. People anticipate closing a deal and it falls through at the last moment. Other times, people also disappoint themselves. They want to do something but they cannot. They become disappointed because they suddenly realize they had not come as far as they thought. That is why friends are there to empower the disappointed.

Technology has expanded the definition of friendship in recent times, making it possible for friends to interact all over the world. It has facilitated the building of new friends—virtual and non-virtual—and also a reconnection with old friends. With the click of a button, one can make a friend without knowing the person physically. People pride themselves on having many online friends and online friends are made for several reasons. Technology also gives the opportunity to block friends who do not reciprocate a good gesture, as well as those who remain silent and stay far off. Having hundreds of online friends is not the same as having a physical friend you can turn to or be with in person. Online friends cannot be there for a friend emotionally when the other is in crisis or sick, or celebrating a happy or sad occasion. Their words of affirmation, comfort, and support make limited impact. Job calls such friends "a senseless, disreputable brood" (30:8).

9

Locating a Space for Elihu as a Friend

FRIENDSHIP IS NOT A closed world or a bounded space where only those with permission can enter. It is a free world where many can freely join or leave. Some join by default. It also does not require an official recognition. That is to say, there is no certification required to identify one as a friend. In the words of Manitza Kotse and Carike Noeth,

> Friendship should then not remain in a fenced in, enclosed area where we remain friends with those who are similar to us. Rather, we wish to put forward that friendship, as a theological model, is the space where we can practice the attributes that are developed in this contribution to enable us to live this out within the broader society with those with whom we are not necessarily friends, but with all people.[1]

What is striking in the above quote is the space provided for "all people" in the bracket of friendship. As established earlier, an acquaintance friend is someone you know or may not know very well, who crosses our path in life's journeys. It could be a companion, associate, or ordinary friend. Intimate and close friendships go deeper and broader than acquaintance friendship. Friendship networks and bonds extend beyond age peers to associates and acquaintances in the same trade or occupation. Friendship bridges the barriers of age, as expressed in the notion of equality in *bulikani* (friendship) from the perspective of the Barotse, Zambia. Among the Maasai of Kenya, friendship among age peers is

---

1. Kotse and Noeth, "Friendship as a Theological Model," 7.

more institutionalized. However, the expectation to help others, even total strangers, is very strong regardless of age.²

The Akan say, *sɛ abofra hu ne nsa ho hohor a, ɔnye mpanyimfo dzidzi* ("when a child knows how to wash the hands, they can eat with elders"). That is to say, a child can only enter into dialogue with elders when they have built the capacity to relate well. It is a child who has to be guided and directed towards gaining the right to dialogue with elders because as the Akan say, *abofra bɔ nwa na ɔmmbɔ akyekyedeɛ* ("a child breaks a snail not a tortoise"). The back of the snail is soft and with little strength one can break it, but the back of the tortoise is very thick and hard and requires a high degree of strength. However, if the child imbibes the culture and shows proficiency in the ethics of speaking, permission will be granted for that child to sit among elders and engage in a dialogue. That is why it is said that *akyekyedeɛ butu hɔ a, nnyɛ afafrantaa na opegya no* ("when a tortoise is overturned, it is not the butterfly that helps it to stand on its feet"). Great problems require great and deep thinkers.

Friends are expected to be completely honest and frank with one another. As shown in the concept of friendship among the Moosi, "to keep a reproach or a criticism to oneself or withhold gossip overheard about a friend could compromise the friendship."³

AUTHORITY OF ELIHU

Elihu, the son of Barachel the Buzite, is the one person who jumps into the dialogue after Job had argued with his three friends. Elihu is clearly not one of the friends of Job and when he joins the conversation, he turns it into a monologue. Elihu has not been spared by modern interpreters for jumping too easily into the dialogue between Job and his three friends, disrespectfully looking down on the three. He also does not show respect to Job since he was not invited to join the conversation. The Akan says *animguase to wo a, obiara tu wo fo* ("when disgrace comes upon you, everyone advises you"). Elihu knows that the three friends are elders, so as a young man, he can only stand and observe what is going on. Also, they are friends in dialogue, so if he is not a "friend" he has to be invited into the conversation.

---

2. Spencer, "Comradeship and the Transformation of Alliance Theory," 43.
3. Breusers, "Friendship and Spiritual Parenting," 77.

The narrator makes a distinction between Elihu and the three. He is not addressed as a "friend." He is like a stranger observing what is going on. A Bogon proverb goes: *Mɔɔrɛ ba jiŋ danɛ didulitiŋ ŋ* ("A stranger does not know where the room leaks"). Zuckerman rather sees Elihu as a foil to the three friends' role, whose speech is interpolation to neutralize the arguments of the three.[4] However, I consider Elihu as a friend. His language and demeanor suggest a strong emotional attachment, a deep concern, and loving care for Job and the three. By virtue of showing concern for Job and sharing his thoughts with him, Elihu acts as an ordinary friend.

It has been established earlier that friendship (*rēaʿ*) carries a wide range of meanings, including an intimate counselor, a neighbor, or a fellow. Elihu is a caring neighbor, hence a friend. By falling into the category of a friend, he becomes no longer a young man who is restricted by social norms to listen to elders; he has become a colleague who can dialogue face to face with Job. Rawlins explains that friendship is pervaded by what he calls "the spirit of equality," in the sense that hierarchical boundaries are blurred when there is friendship.[5] That is to say, the atmosphere between friends makes them appear more or less equal to each other. Although Elihu was young, he spoke as if he was a friend.

Elihu addresses Job by his name (32:12; 33:1), giving the impression that there is some cordiality between them. Again, Elihu identifies with the three, elaborating on their ideas—and arguing out their case for them puts him on another level in the story. In fact, he has been present all along when the three friends started speaking to Job. The impact of his silence and observations are implied in his speech. Elihu finds reason to be a defender, an ally, and a neighbor, hence distancing himself from the three friends. He is more like a friend's friend.

EVALUATING THE APPEALS

Focusing on what has transpired between Job and the three, Elihu does not understand why the three would give in to Job. Elihu enters the dialogue with anger because he saw that Job's friends, whom he called "wise men" (34:2, 34) could not use their wisdom to win over Job. He is a bystander listening to Job and his three friends argue out issues and concludes that none of them are "wise." They are only assuming to be

---

4. Zuckerman, *Silent Job*, 147.
5. Rawlins, *Friendship Matters*, 9.

wise in their own heart (37:24b). Seow is sympathetic to Elihu when he describes him this way: "The character flaws of Elihu should not, therefore, be grounds for disregarding his theological contribution. In fact, like Joseph and Daniel, he is seen as a divinely-gifted young man who proffers an inspired word when 'the wise' who precede him have failed."[6] As such, Elihu is angry at both Job and the three friends. His anger makes him assume a person of authority whom all must listen to. He is no longer a young man eavesdropping on what the four elders are saying.

Elihu takes over the conversation by necessity and not by invitation. For Moltmann, people can choose whom to be friends with, and furthermore one of the elements of friendship is a free human relationship, and people "do not constantly need to assure ourselves of our friendship, as is generally the case, is in love. It is enough to know that the friend is there."[7] Friendship is spontaneous and can grow anytime there is the right environment.

Tremper Longman III explains that in the ancient Near East, an elder was thought to be wise and exert more authority than a young person. The older the person, the more knowledge and wisdom the person possesses. Yet Elihu identifies with the "wise" and claims that wisdom can be associated with the young.[8] The failure of the three to contend with Job provides a rationale for Elihu to act as a counselor and wise man. He had not previously joined the conversation between Job and the three because he was a young man.

Elihu seeks to present an entirely new argument. He knows that Job is an old man and he is a young man, yet he bends the laws of propriety prevalent in the ancient Near East and confronts Job:

> So these three men ceased to answer Job, because he was righteous in his own eyes. Then Elihu son of Barachel the Buzite, of the family of Ram, became angry. He was angry at Job because he justified himself rather than God; he was angry also at Job's three friends because they had found no answer, though they had declared Job to be in the wrong. Now Elihu had waited to speak to Job, because they were older than he. But when Elihu saw that there was no answer in the mouths of these three men, he became angry. (32:1–5)

---

6. Seow, *Job 1–21*, 98.
7. Moltmann, *Living God and the Fullness of Life*, 119.
8. Longman, "Job," 381.

As John Goldingay explains, anger in the Bible may not have a moral or theological twist. It may arise when one identifies with another's cause, just as Jacob's sons identify with their sister when raped, Potiphar identifies with his wife against Joseph's alleged seduction, and Jonathan identifies with David against his father's hostility.[9]

Elihu's identifies with the three by building on their arguments. It may be a kind of remote affection, or he was a secret admirer. He admits that age was a critical factor that prevented him from identifying himself:

> 6 Elihu son of Barachel the Buzite answered:
> "I am young in years
>   And you are aged
> Therefore I was timid and afraid
>   To declare my opinion to you.
> 7 I said, 'Let days speak,
>   and many years teach wisdom.'
> 8 But truly it is the spirit (*rûaḥ*) in a mortal,
>   the breath (*nišmat*) of the Almighty, that makes for understanding.
> 9 It is not the old that are wise,
>   nor the aged that understand what is right.
> 10 Therefore I say, 'Listen to me;
>   let me also declare my opinion.'
> 11 See, I waited for your words,
>   I listened for your wise sayings,
>   while you searched out what to say.
> 12 I gave you my attention,
>   but there was in fact no one that confuted Job,
>   no one among you that answered his words." (32:6–12)

Elihu spoke to Job because the "spirit in mortals" (Heb: *rûaḥ-hî' be'ĕnōš*) urged him to do so (32:8). He uses spirit (*rûaḥ*) in a semantically parallel way to breath (*nišmat*). The spirit in mortals is the inanimate energy God breathed that brought life to the lifeless body at creation (Gen 2:7; cf. Zech 12:1). According to Proverbs, "the human spirit is the lamp of the Lord that sheds light on one's inmost being" (Prov 20:27 NIV). Hence, the nature of God is birthed in the human being through the spirit in the person. The human spirit, thus, makes it possible for one to create positive aspirations and interventions, and also deliberately will good for the other. The human spirit helps one to develop emotions, creative output, and personal passions that lie at the heart of the virtue of love and friendship.

---

9. Goldingay, "Anger," 156–58.

African ontology seriously pays attention to the spirit as well as the spiritual world in humanity as the principle that controls whatever happens in the physical realm. In the African worldview, the spirit in a person makes that individual a good or bad person. The source of spirit within each person is divine and transcends both the physical universe and time. Thus, it connects one individual to the other person, place, or thing.[10] In Akan ontology, the spirit is translated as the *okra*. The spirit is the "essence of the being or object; its intrinsic animating principle."[11] To Gyekye, spirit can be used generically to refer to all unperceivable, mystical beings and forces, and is thought to be the life-spark of the human being, an essential part of the human being that functions to explain the difference between living and non-living beings.[12] The spirit encompasses both the character and the mind of the individual.

Elihu attributes his move to dialogue with Job as the work of the spirit in him. In a sense, the same spirit that determines one's ability to flourish in relationships or to act morally—required of all persons—animates the possibility of friendship. Hence, God created humanity with a spirit to be friends and that was what was influencing Elihu's character and mind. The breath from God causes a person to gain understanding. Gordis notes that understanding "generally refers to the faculty of comprehension (Exod 31:3; Job 12:13) or the act (Pss 78:12; 136:8; Job 26:12). It also indicates the object or the content of wisdom (cf. Pr. 5:1; 19:8)."[13]

Elihu waited for an opportunity to speak to Job. Yet, when he started speaking, the tone was as if he was talking to someone who is younger than him. Zuckerman makes a profound statement about Elihu's intervention:

> If Job has a grievance, so also does the author of Elihu; moreover, if the poet of Job was driven by his anger to attack the tenets of ancient tradition, the Elihu-author is equally furious because this attack has been made. For this reason he is more than willing to match the poet of Job, outrage for outrage.[14]

Likewise, Elihu confronts the three and chastises them for their inability to stand toe to toe with Job. Elihu thinks that Eliphaz, Bildad, and

---

10. Kelland, "African Worldview and Spirituality."
11. Minkus, "Spirit in Akwapim Akan Philosophy," 182.
12. Gyekye, "Relation of *Ōkra* (Soul) and *Honam* (Body)," 59,60.
13. Gordis, *Book of Job*, 369.
14. Zuckman, *Silent Job*, 149.

Zophar do not speak well to Job (32:7, 9-11, 15-16). They do not play their role expected of them. Their mission to comfort Job has clouded their line of reasoning. Friends are also supposed to confront each other.

By using the style of positive confrontation, Elihu paves the way to express his thoughts to Job. He does not abuse Job verbally but rather develops healthy boundaries, and adopts innovative approaches to challenge Job to rethink so that he can have a better appreciation of life. Confrontation is not always an aggressive or angry attack, but boldly facing something or someone in a way that needs to be addressed proactively.

> Elihu continues to identify with the three by saying:
> ¹⁵ "They are dismayed, they answer no more;
>   they have not a word to say.
> ¹⁶ And am I to wait, because they do not speak,
>   because they stand there, and answer no more?
> ¹⁷ I also will give my answer;
>   I also will declare my opinion.
> ¹⁸ For I am full of words;
>   the spirit within me constrains me.
> ¹⁹ My heart is indeed like wine that has no vent;
>   like new wineskins, it is ready to burst.
> ²⁰ I must speak, so that I may find relief;
>   I must open my lips and answer.
> ²¹ I will not show partiality to any person
>   or use flattery toward anyone.
> ²² For I do not know how to flatter—
>   or my Maker would soon put an end to me!" (32:15-22)

The right to speak, which Elihu claims for himself, is to find relief (32:20). If he does not speak, his Maker, that is God, will take his life. He is worried because Job's three friends have nothing else to say, so he must speak on their behalf. He is not jumping to their aid for what he would get. It is not to satisfy his personal ego. However, the fact that he feels constrained, has an answer to contribute, and is so puffed inside like fermented wine ready to burst open its container makes him very emotional.

Elihu calls for Job's attention: "But now, hear my speech, O Job, and listen to all my words" (33:1). Like the three, somehow, Elihu gives Job some assurances. He claims an angel will advocate for Job for physical healing (33:25). Drawing on Eliphaz's teaching about pain and suffering, he says God has a preventive purpose to help keep a person from sinning (33:17-30) as well as a disciplinary and educational objective. God uses affliction to get human beings' attention when it comes to pride (33:17;

36:8–9). As such, Job should not lose hope. According to Larry J. Waters, Elihu purposed in his mind to encourage Job to hold on to a life of faith and trust.[15] Suffering, to Elihu, is not to punish a person but to make "lives loathe bread, and their appetites dainty food" (33:20).

Elihu presents a comparatively balanced view of God and God's relationship with humankind. He corrects Job's view of God's hiddenness by arguing that mysterious ways including dreams, pain and illness, and angels can reveal who God is (33:13–30). Job is wrong to assume that God does not speak or answer when people call. God rather speaks in dreams and visions, especially in the dark hours of the night (33:15). God speaks so that it would keep people from being proud (33:17). Elihu spoke about his view of a mediator for Job, saying,

> ²³ Then, if there should be for one of them an angel (*mal'āk*),
>   a mediator (*mēlîs*), one of a thousand,
>   one who declares a person upright,
> ²⁴ and he is gracious to that person, and says,
>   "Deliver him from going down into the Pit;
>   I have found a ransom;
> ²⁵ let his flesh become fresh with youth;
>   let him return to the days of his youthful vigour";
> ²⁶ then he prays to God, and is accepted by him,
>   he comes into his presence (way*yarě' pānāyw*) with joy,
>   and God repays him for his righteousness.
> ²⁷   That person sings to others and says,
>   "I sinned, and perverted what was right,
>   and it was not paid back to me.
> ²⁸ He has redeemed my soul from going down to the Pit,
>   and my life shall see the light." (33:23–28)

Elihu's use of an angel (*mal'āk*) is semantically parallel to the use of a mediator (*mēlîs*) and such comparison is striking (33:23). There is hardly such an angel and that is why Job is still suffering. Earlier, Job had hoped for his redeemer to intervene when he squares up with God in the courtroom (19:25). For Job, the vindicator will cause him to see God (19:25). A similar idea can be seen in Job 33:26, where the angel or mediator will make him come into God presence and see (*yarě'*) him with a shout of joy. The Hebrew way*yarě' pānāyw* rightly denotes "and he shall see his face" (cf. NASV; JPS TANAK; NKJV). For Elihu, there is no angel or mediator that can declare Job righteous.

---

15. Waters, "Elihu's Theology and His View of Suffering," 144.

The noun *mal'ak* ("angel") usually denotes a divine or human agent. In the book of Malachi, for instance, the priest (Mal 2:7) and the prophet (Mal 3:1) were also considered the angel of the Lord, and both perform mediatory roles. The priest alone has the authority to declare a person upright (cf. Lev 13:3, 6, 8, 13, 17, 20; 14:10–11). It may be valid to say that Elihu did not intend such an angelic mediation possible, from the conditional way he asked the question. In fact, an angelic intervention can be possible for one in a thousand (33:23).

God allows suffering in the life of a person, and God gives the sufferer a messenger to mediate on behalf of the sufferer. When God listens to the mediator, the sufferer will come into God's presence with joy and God repays the person for their righteousness (33:26–27). Such imputed righteousness is not because the person has not sinned, but because the person acknowledges their sins, and leaned toward what is right. Hence, God looks not upon the sin and will not pay back (33:27). "God indeed does all these things, twice, three times, with mortals to bring back their soul from the Pit, so that they may see the light of life" (33:29–30). According to John Hartley, "unlike the passionate speeches of the comforters, the Elihu speeches are a reasoned challenge to a position Job quoted in the opening speech. Thus, the Elihu speeches differ markedly in structure from the other speeches."[16]

Elihu finds it appropriate to address Job, who he describes as elderly by name: "But now, hear my speech, O Job, and listen to all my words." (33:1). Also, Elihu says,

> [31] Pay heed, Job, listen to me;
> be silent, and I will speak.
> [32] If you have anything to say, answer me;
> speak, for I desire to justify you.
> [33] If not, listen to me;
> be silent, and I will teach you wisdom. (33:31–33)

In the African worldview, only a person of status can address another person by name. Calling someone by their personal name is not only disrespectful but also a sign that the person does not have the honor to merit the respect that goes with not calling the name.[17] Such a posture taken by Elihu makes him fit the category of a friend to Job.

---

16. Hartley, *Book of Job*, 28.
17. Anchimbe, "On Not Calling People By Their Names," 1472–83.

Elihu continues to identify himself as someone with authority. He calls Job to order: "Job, listen to me" (v. 31a, 33a). He expects Job to be silent so that he teaches him wisdom (v. 33b). Certainly, Elihu is an overconfident young man. The tone here is not that of somber but harsh. He is commanding Job to pay attention to him so that he vindicates him. Earlier, Job had been looking for a redeemer to vindicate him (19:26), and Elihu also explains that if there is an angel for someone—to speak on behalf of the one the angel serves, to plead with God to redeem and ransom the sufferer—it would have been the right thing (33:23–28). Since there is no angel like that, he can act on behalf of Job to vindicate him. All that Job has to do is to keep quiet and listen to him. Even if he cannot vindicate Job, the best he will do is to teach Job wisdom (33:33). Furthermore, Elihu calls Job to listen to him if he has understanding (34:18). For Elihu, wise people listen to him (34:34b).

As Cornelis Vanderwaal observes, "Elihu is not one of the faultfinders; he does not join the others in concluding that Job must have committed some dreadful sin. Instead, he allows for the possibility that Job's suffering has a message to convey. Perhaps it is intended to deepen his life, to teach Job in his frailty to live by *grace*."[18] Elihu states that the Almighty does not pervert justice but is a sovereign, immanent, just, and impartial Ruler who does not reward people according to human terms. In that light, Job has taken the wrong position (34:12–20, 33). He recalls what Job said as follows:

> 5 For Job has said, "I am innocent,
>   and God has taken away my right;
> 6 in spite of being right I am counted a liar;
>   my wound is incurable, though I am without transgression."
> 7 Who is there like Job,
>   who drinks up scoffing like water,
> 8 who goes in company with evildoers
>   and walks with the wicked?
> 9 For he has said, "It profits one nothing
>   to take delight in God." (34:5–9)

Elihu believes that Job is overconfident in life and over-righteous. He likes jeering at people (v. 7b). The way Elihu points out Job's view seems to fit the description in Psalm 1:1 of a person who is not blessed for walking with the wicked, standing with the scoffers, and sitting with

---

18. Vanderwaal, *Job—Song of Songs*, 24.

mockers. According to Seow, "Elihu represents the response from an Elistic tradition that emphasizes divine transcendence—God as Wholly Other, who does not respond directly to human beings but through an intermediary, whether human or divine."[19]

Elihu argues that Job is deceiving himself by assuming that he is right when he is wrong. Job thinks people are taking him to be a liar but the tone of Elihu's words reveals that Job is wrong (34:6). Job is always disrespectful and mocks others (34:7b), indicating that whenever he is thirsty, what goes into him is derision. Job had earlier described his three friends as forming a company against him, but Elihu sees Job as rather joining the company of evildoers and the wicked (34:8). He sees Job as someone who mocks not only others but also God, and does not cherish his relationship with God. It is like saying Job thinks one worships God for nothing (34:9). Friends are able to tell the truth to one another even if it hurts.

Elihu supports the view that suffering is the fate of the wicked (34:11, 13, 17, 21–22; 36:6, 7). He claims that the law of divine retribution makes only the wicked suffer. He buttresses his point by affirming that God's ways are just (34:29–37). As such Job is wrong for standing on the grounds that he is righteous. He accuses Job of not knowing and speaking without knowledge (34:35; 35:16). It is strange how a "young man" would accuse Job of opening his mouth in vain and multiplying words without knowledge. However, Elihu is right after all for God made Job understand that through the whirlwind speeches of which Job conceded (42:3).

In the view of Elihu, since Job lacks the knowledge to know the just ways of God, he must repent so that he can be restored (36:11). According to Elihu, one reason God seems cruel and ignores the cries of the afflicted is that God does not hear the insincere cries of the proud (35:9–13; 36:5–6). Elihu states that a person, no matter how righteous, cannot put God under obligation (35:7).

Elihu also claims to be the spokesperson for God and as such he speaks the truth:

> ² Bear with me a little, and I will show you,
>   for I have yet something to say on God's behalf.
> ³ I will bring my knowledge from far away,
>   and ascribe righteousness to my Maker.
> ⁴ For truly my words are not false;
>   one who is perfect in knowledge is with you. (36:2–4)

19. Seow, *Job 1–21*, 70.

It is only the people God has chosen who are in the position to speak for God. Elihu's claim that he brings his knowledge from far away echoes revelatory knowledge or perhaps a prophetic status (36:3). Earlier in 33:4, one finds Elihu attributing his calling to the spirit of God, although the literal meaning of his words—"the spirit of God has made me, the breath of Shaddai gives me life"—points to how God created him and gave him the breath of life (cf. Gen 2:7). Nevertheless, the double meaning of the verse lends more toward his calling than his birth since it is not normal for one to attribute one's birth to the spirit rather than God.

IMPLICATIONS

How then does Elihu's intervention match contemporary times, and what lessons can we derive from it? McCabe, for instance, reveals how scholars do not see Elihu as a fourth friend but as a response to Job's request for an arbiter or umpire, and adds that "we should understand that a purpose of Elihu's initial apology is to present himself as the answer to Job's request for an arbiter."[20] However, he notes that "[t]he emphasis of the prose introduction on Elihu's anger is consistent with the emotional outburst of Elihu, as pictured by his *ad hominem* attack on Job in both of these speeches. Since Job's three friends have also had emotional outbursts, perhaps the Joban author is intentionally highlighting this to portray Elihu as a younger version of the friends."[21] Clines may have a similar perspective when he writes, "Job's fifth friend." Besides the three, Elihu qualifies as the fourth friend. As in African thought, the friends of a friend or companions of friends are taken as friends, or better still they are seen as casual friends.

First, one must know oneself well in dealing with friends. Paul cautions believers that when a person claims to be somebody when they are nothing, it is self-deception (Gal 6:3). Elihu is a young man but decides to intervene in the dialogue between older people due to his wisdom. Strangely, Job does not reply to his lengthy talk, perhaps judging it to be on the same level as the three. The Igbo elders say, *Ogologo abughi na nwa me tola* ("Tallness is not a yardstick to define maturity"). That is to say, maturity is not determined by the physical appearance. Whether

---

20. McCabe, "Elihu's Contribution to the Thought of the Book of Job," 50, 51.
21. McCabe, "Elihu's Contribution to the Thought of the Book of Job," 66.

one is tall or short does not matter. It is the contribution that the person makes that matters.

Similarly, the Igbo elders say, *Ogbughi ka akilu na adanọnu ka o si atọ* ("The sound of the bite of bitter kola does not correspond with its taste"). That is to say one cannot judge a thing by its outward appearance. Similarly, all that glitters is not gold.

If Elihu was not listened to and given a hearing like a friend, perhaps his voice would not have featured in the story. Such an intervention may not appeal to some cultures that draw strict lines between the young and old. To McCabe "Elihu demonstrates that youthful wisdom is an adaptation of older wisdom."[22] Christians need a similar balanced understanding of friendship with those who are of unequal status, especially young people in our contemporary world. The young have something to offer, even if they may not approach it in the right way. Elihu sets a precedent that affirms that the young should sit at the table with the old, for his theology in God's judgment was not wrong. In the view of Abigail Pelham,

> From his own perspective, Elihu is as serious as Job and the friends have been, but this is what undoes their seriousness. It is not the members of the "senseless, disreputable brood" who show us that Job is comic. Rather, it is Elihu who, by resembling Job and his friends while being so obviously a buffoon, subverts their status as tragic characters.[23]

Elihu takes a different approach from the three. But for his anger, Elihu speaks well, making Job not respond to him. Elihu has a slightly different understanding of God than the three. Elihu's spirituality affirms the omnipresent God. The meaning of the name Elihu is "He is my God," and Elihu clearly identifies with what his name means. Elihu's character and intervention do not receive much commendation, with some seeing him as pompous, a buffoon, an eavesdropper, and a raging, angry young man. God rebukes Job's friends but totally ignores Elihu and so we cannot say Elihu was incorrect in his arguments. The narrator mentions that Elihu directs his anger against Job because of Job's self-righteous attitude and against the three friends because of their philosophical incompetence; they condemn Job without finding fault and run out of arguments without having succeeded.

---

22. McCabe, "Elihu's Contribution to the Thought of the Book of Job," 75.
23. Pelham, "*Job* as Comedy, Revisited," 98.

Second, Elihu depicts himself as a friend for a reason and thus establishes strong goodwill. He disproves that reciprocity is not always a feature of friendship. He forcefully explains why he chooses to act as a "friend" and says it was due to anger, an inner urge, and his spirit. He uses a style of confrontation to draw Job's attention, yet speaks well to him. He shows concern about Job's obstinate posture, not trying to find reason in what the three friends are saying. He exhibits an open heart that would sacrifice to make things right for another, a virtue locked into the category of friendship. As Patricia Tull intimates, friendship often begins with a willing heart to show kindness toward another.[24] Friendship requires the performance of some special duties to those whom we think need some help. It takes a friendly heart to will good for the other. Being a friend calls for showing caring for the other person and meeting the person's expectations. Friends fill the gap in the other's life and provide both the human companion and the security needed by people.

Elihu also depicts himself as a friend for a season. He comes into the picture and fades out. The Luganda of Uganda also say, "Friendship is spontaneous: Friendship is like mushrooms; you cannot force them." Hence, friendships can be developed naturally and unconsciously. They are not coercive. Mushrooms spring up in conducive environments and die off when the environment changes. Elihu saw that both Job and the three needed help to understand some principles of life. Among the Swahilis, it is said *akupaye kisogo si mwenzio* ("whoever turns his back on you is not your friend").[25] Where there is no one to offer support and friendship in times of need, it can be challenging. The writer of Ecclesiastes says when one falls down, there should be another to help the other up. "But pity anyone who falls and has no one to help them up" (Eccl 4:10). In a postmodern world where each tends to concentrate on one's own affairs, lending a helping hand and being friendly can lead one into problems. However, Christians have to be persons who will show concern when another is heading the wrong way. A compassionate and friendly person will step in when there is a problem but a person who does not like to be a friend will mind their own business.

Elihu does not want the friendship between Job and the three to be disrupted by their arguments. Their hardline positions are affecting their relationships, and he feels the need to come in to manage the challenges

---

24. Tull, "Jonathan's Friendship," 142.
25. Scheven, *Swahili Proverbs*, 228.

so that all of them can hold on to one another. Hence, he takes the opportunity to penetrate the closed dialogue and to expose the strengths and weaknesses of each. He is not happy that the three have succumbed to Job and cannot convince him. In much the same way, he was not happy that Job was not speaking with wisdom and blaming God. Rather, he sees himself as wise and urged Job to listen to him.

Friends are there to correct each other and build each other up. When friends intervene in the other's life, it enhances their own self-image, but when their intervention does not end well, it can be demotivating. Friendship is indeed a reflection of the self. Being a friend, thus, does not only mean considering the benefit one would accrue from the encounter. Elihu does not show that he was in for some personal benefit. He is simply virtuous and authentic, wishing the good of Job and the three, showing unmotivated kindness and uncalculated intervention simply from the joy of companionship.

Third, friendship has to do with collaboration. Elihu wants to collaborate with the three friends. A Shona proverb says "A friend is someone you share the path with." Hence it is not only those who relate intimately or give back what is shared that can be classified as friends. One should not only expect to see a friendly relationship through the formal introduction of a person as a friend. Friendship is not by name but by actions. Elihu's type of friendship with Job can be said to be situational friendship or acquaintance friendship, which is typically structured around a specific environment. The interaction takes place within specific environments or in relation to a particular interest. Such acquaintances may not build a close connection. It could be a neighbor, a colleague you do not feel close to, or a family member's friend, who offers support when the need arises. When the "situation" changes, the friendship dissolves. It provides real solidarity and support as long as both of you are united by a similar passion. While situational friendship is positive, it lacks the commitment of reciprocal friendships.

Friendship requires that we perform some special duties to those we think need some help. It takes a friendly heart to will good for others. Being a friend calls for showing caring for the other person and meeting the person's expectations. Friends fill the gap in the other's life and provide both the human companionship and the security needed by people. An African proverb goes: "Honest advice does not destroy true friendship." Also, "to give advice as well as take it, is a feature of true friendship." Elihu thus acts as a friend by virtue of the advice he gives. He shows that friendship is driven by compassion and solidarity. What the three friends could not say well, Elihu tries to correct, thus showing that wisdom does not reside in one person's head.

Elihu forcefully explains why he chooses to act as a "friend," saying it is due to anger, an inner urge, and from his spirit. He uses a style of confrontation to draw Job's attention, yet speaks well to him. He shows concern about Job's obstinate posture, not trying to find reason in what the three friends were saying. His youthful exuberance gives him up, and his idea to project himself makes him think he is right and the elderly men are wrong. In the New Testament, Paul encourages Timothy to set an example in speech, in conduct, in love, in faith, in purity (1 Tim 4:12; cf. 1 Thess 1:6; 2 Thess 3:7, 9; 1 Cor 4:6; 11:1; Phil 3:17; 2 Tim 1:13). A young person should not feel inadequate to dialogue with elderly people with the excuse of being too young or inexperienced.

Fourth, intervening to correct a wrong impression is a good thing friends should emulate for it brings about empowerment. Friends have to draw others who are not on the right path to the right way. Elihu sees it as a matter of responsibility and mutual concern to correct a misunderstanding even if he was not directly involved in the dialogue. Perhaps he feels that is what friendship is about. A true friend will speak the truth to the other no matter what. A true friend will listen to other friends no matter what and learn from the wisdom of the conversation. Paul admonishes the Thessalonian church that they should encourage one another and build each other up (1 Thess 5:11). Good friends empower each other.

Finally, Elihu, being an unequal partner, rather shows a behavior that is not proportionate to his status before Job. This shows the privilege in friendships. No wonder Dana Roberts asserts that "sometimes friendship is a matter of being a 'holy fool,' and rushing in where angels fear to tread."[26] Elihu can be described as a hot-tempered person. He tries to suppress Job, hence does not use an acceptable way to counsel a suffering person. As such, Elihu can be described as an unfriendly person. Certainly, arrogant boasting, gushing with ambition, self-aggrandizement, and self-adulation should be out of the picture for young people. No matter how knowledgeable one is, it is unacceptable to project oneself as better than the other. Some young people tend to assume that they know more than the elderly. An Akan proverb goes: *adze a panyin tsena*

---

26. Robert, *Faithful Friendship*, 176.

famu hu no, abofra gyina tsentsen ansaana woehu ("what an adult will sit to see, a child will stand on the feet before seeing"). That is to say, it does not take one's height or eyesight to see through what is going on in life. Perhaps, that is why Job does not reply to him after his speech. Job may have been guided by what the writer of Proverbs says: Do not make friends with a hot-tempered person, do not associate with one easily angered, or you may learn their ways and get yourself ensnared" (Prov 22:24–25). Doing the right thing in the wrong way destroys the rightness of what has been done.

CONCLUDING REMARKS

The attempt to draw Elihu into the bracket of friendship has revealed some lessons. One need not to be officially recognized as a friend before acting friendly. Elihu intervenes in the life of Job and the three to show an aspect of friendship. It is believed a friend is someone who comes up to motivate the other when the person is down or build the other up. He acted as a friend for a reason. When friends intervene in the other's life, they enhance their own self-image, but when their intervention does not end well, it can be demotivating. No matter what, friends empower each other. Yet, it is not necessary to respond to some kinds of friends. Nevertheless, Elihu has set an example for young people with his rich theology. In essence, young people need guidance and support to understand the word of God as they navigate through the most challenging part of their development and as they seek to grow in their walk with Christ. Helping youth to grow spiritually in their formative years will equip them to make a commitment for friendship. Helping young people to grow in knowledge in their formative years will also equip them to make an impact in society both now and in the future.

10

God as a Friend of Job

FRIENDSHIP WITH GOD IS much obligation as well as an offering of grace. Human beings enjoy the friendship of God that rests on God's promises toward a continuing relationship. In Job's avowal of innocence in chapter 29, his perceived former relationship with God was highlighted. The most significant text that points to the friendship between Job and God is in 29:4, although this verse has its inherent difficulties, as shown in some of the translations:

MT: *ka'ăšer hāyîtî bîmēy ḥārppî běsôd 'ĕlôaḥ 'ălēy 'āhălî*

JPS TANAK:
When I was in my prime,
    when God's company graced my tent.

NJB:
Shall I ever see my days of harvest again
    when God protected my tent.

CJB:
As I was when I was young,
    and God's counsel graced my tent.

NKJV:
Just as I was in the days of my prime,
    When the friendly counsel of God was over my tent.

NRSV:
When I was in my prime,
    when the friendship of God was upon my tent.

ASV:
As I was in the ripeness of my days,
    When the friendship of God was upon my tent.

ESV:
As I was in my prime,
    when the friendship of God was upon my tent.

NIV:
Oh, for the days when I was in my prime,
    when God's intimate friendship blessed my house.

There is no agreement among translators on the meaning of *sôd* in this context. For instance, NIV uses "intimate friendship," NRSV has "friendship," while KJV uses "secret," NJB "protected," and JSP TANAK "company." Dahood[1] and Pope[2] claim it should be translated as "found" (root *sd*) while Alter sees it as "council," that is, his exclusive intimate company.[3] The Hebrew *sôd*, translated in the NRSV, ASV, ESV, and NIV as "friendship" (29:4), aptly expresses the intimacy that underlies Job's relationship with God. The noun form of the Hebrew expression denotes companion, confidant, council, and intimate company (see Psalm 55:14; Amos 3:7; Prov 3:32). The Hebrew, *sôd* meaning "friendship" occurs thrice in the book of Job (15:8; 19:19; 29:4). Etymologically, the root basically denotes "to come together," "council/counsel." In 15:8, it is used to refer to God's council. However, in 29:4, it is viewed in the context of confidential discussion, a secret plan among intimate friends.[4] Following the NIV translation, however, it can be found that Job and God were bosom friends, close friends, or intimate friends; they were close to the heart of each other with the underlying acts of intimacy and availability.

God is a relational God, always desiring to show care and spend time with human beings in the context of friendship. The quest to have a clear understanding of what it means to be a friend of God continues to be challenging. Nevertheless, divine–human friendship exists in the

---

1. Dahood, "Hebrew-Ugaritic Lexicography VII," 342.
2. Pope, *Job*, 207.
3. Alter, *Job*, 204.
4. See *TDOT*, 10:174,175; *BDB*, 619.

loving grace of God. God makes such unequal unconditional friendship, love, *agape, philia, amitica*, or *caritas*, etc., possible. Liz Carmichael avers that the mutual expression of agape, which is not different from nor opposed to friendship, makes true friendship possible. She adds, "friendship finds itself transformed by grace. God in Christ extended friendship to all human beings, and to be a 'friend of sinners', hitherto a genuine insult or impossible paradox now becomes thinkable and possible."[5] In fact, there was no period in time when divine–human friendship was an insult or impossible. Rather, it was difficult for thinkers to understand why God makes friends.

Whether assumed or explicitly stated, Job's friendship relationship with God cannot be easily dismissed. Job has challenges trying to understand his friendship with God. However, can he come to a fuller grasp of what it means to be a friend of God? In what way, then, does Job relate to God as a friend, and what kind of friendship exists between the two? How then is such friendship construed?

WHO IS GOD TO JOB?

In the book of Job, various names are used for God. Yahweh is used 32 times; occurring 27 times in the prose section, and 5 times in the poetic section (12:9; 38:1; 40:1, 3, 6). El is used 55 times and Eloah is used 41 times. *Šadday* (Shaddai) is used 31 times and Adonai occurs only twice (3:19; 28:28). The name and various titles used not only reveal God's identity but also help characterization—who God is and how God relates with the people. According to Richards, the names, titles, similes, and metaphors through which God is known "unveil the essence of who God is, they describe His qualities and character, and they depict His work both in this universe and in our lives."[6] As the Creator, all things are under God's sovereign control.

The prose prologue and epilogue of the book of Job reveal that Job is a servant of God (1:8; 2:3; 42:7). God gives good things and also bad things to people (2:10; 22:18; cf. Pss 84:11; 104:28; Luke 11:13; Jas 1:17). Job attributes all his wealth to God's provision. In the prologue, Job has 7,000 sheep, 3,000 camels, 500 oxen, and 500 donkeys. Yet, there comes

---

5. Carmichael, *Friendship*, 39.
6. Richards, *Every Name of God in the Bible*, 2.

a time God permits the Adversary to destroy all that Job has, and later to inflict him with loathsome boils.

Job sees God as the "guardian of humanity" (7:20). Job explains that God is the creator of heaven and earth, manages the mountains, the sun, and the seas, and his wisdom, and power are profound and vast (9:4–8). God's miracles are beyond understanding and uncountable (9:10). Walton shares the idea that in Job 9:5–10, the mountains, earth, sun, heavens, and constellations are all weapons God uses against those who oppose him—they do not simply teach about God's creative power. In Akkadian literature, these elements are subject to omens for either good or evil consequences. However, in the context of the book of Job, God created these elements to use "them to portend ominous events that are understood as acts of judgment."[7] Whereas Eliphaz argues that Shaddai is benevolent, Job sees him as a malevolent God (6:4; 19:21; 21:15, 17, 20). Moore states the disagreement between Job and Eliphaz succinctly with strong words: "For Job, then, Šadday appears not only as a sadistic archer who delights in shooting arrows into the chests of innocent mortals he is also a divine fowler who endlessly delights in laying snares for them as well."[8]

The presence of a divine council motif in the Bible and ancient Near East has been recognized. In biblical cosmology, not only God is in heaven but there is plurality of divine beings and a heavenly host that works in the celestial court with God. They are described as the "host of heaven," "gods," "sons of God/god," "messengers," or "angels." The group of divine beings with God is known as the divine council or divine assembly and such an idea was consistent with an Israelite understanding of God. The divine council performs two basic activities: a revelation of God's decrees and judgment, rooted in a covenant ideology; and a forum where actions and inactions are judged.[9]

There is the "sons of the God" (*běnê hā ʾĕlōhîm/běnê ʾēlîm*), and "the council of the holy ones" (*sôd qĕdōšîm*) present in both Israelite and Canaanite vocabulary to describe a heavenly assembly or some people on earth.[10] The references to God's divine assembly (Ps 82:6; 1 Kgs 22:19–23; Isa 6:1–13) and his divine army (Deut 33:2–3; 2 Sam 5:22–29; 2 Kgs 6:15–19; 7:6; Ps 68:18; Isa 13:1–22) amplifies the view that God has a group of beings surrounding him. The writer of Revelation mentions

---

7. Walton, *Job*, 170.
8. Moore, "Job's Texts of Terror," 672.
9. Cross, *Canaanite Myth and Hebrew epic*, 187.
10. Miller, "Cosmology and World Order," 55.

seven spirits who are before God (Rev 1:4). The heavenly council in the Hebrew Bible normally depicts God enthroned among the *bĕnê' hā 'ĕlohîm* ("sons of God"), the *qāhāl* ("congregation"), *'ĕdat* ("assembly"), and most importantly *sôd* ("council"). The *sôd* was a group of *'ĕlohîm* that worked closely with God. In *the* book of Job, the divine assembly includes the Adversary or Satan (Heb: *haśśāṭān*) as part (Job 1:6–7; 2:1). The noun, *haśśāṭān*, from the verb *śāṭān* meaning "to persecute, be hostile to" and also more specifically, "to accuse" with its secondary form *śāṭam*—meaning "to persecute, be hostile to" and also more specifically "to accuse" or "persecute" (Gen 27:41; 49:23)—also denotes "to entrap," in the sense of setting a snare or a trap, or putting fetters on the feet.[11] The noun "Satan" occurs in the Hebrew Bible 14 times as *haśśāṭān* (e.g., Job 1–2; Zech 3:1, 2), and 19 times as *śāṭān*. Seven of these refer to human adversaries and 19 point to a divine being.[12] Due to the use of the definite article, *haśśāṭān* (the Satan) is less a proper name or an appellative—"the adversary." The text does not indicate that *haśśāṭān* is an intruder in the council, but part of the "sons of God," the *bĕnê hā'ĕlohîm* conceived as "being belonging to the category of *'ĕlohîm*, or a single being in the divine sphere."[13]

Johnny Awwad explains that the Adversary encountered in *the* book of Job or elsewhere in the Hebrew Bible is not necessarily evil or opposed to God. The Satan does not act independently or at his own initiative. Rather, he is one of God's obedient angels serving God's purposes.[14] In the New Testament, however, Satan is presented as an opponent of God and human being, the accuser of the brethren.[15] According to Patrick Miller,

1. The system for the divine governance of the socio-political structures of society centers in Yahweh's rule over and through the divine council.

2. The divine council was present at the creation (Job 38:6) and involved indirectly in that process . . . the focus is more cosmological than cosmogonic, with order as much or more than origin.

3. The maintenance of justice and righteousness is the foundation of the universe, the responsibility of the divine council, and the issue

---

11. Kluger, *Satan in the Old Testament*, 57.
12. Hamilton, "Satan," 985.
13. Kluger, *Satan in the Old Testament*, 99.
14. Awwad, "Satan in Biblical Imagination," 112.
15. Conrad, "Satan," 112.

upon which hang both stability of the universe and the stability and effective reality of the divine world.

4. The maintenance of the world order as the manifestation of righteousness is a responsibility of the divine assembly, it is not surprising that at the key point where the issue of the justice of God and the problem of undeserved suffering comes to the fore, the divine council is the setting or the occasion for the raising of the issue.

5. The council of the Lord is the place where the goal of all creation, that is praise, begins.[16]

For Fabry, the beings in God's council (*sôd*) are charged with three functions:[17] first as a demonstration of Yahweh's omnipotence in the form of accompaniment, praise, fear or counsel in the form of obedient response; second as mediation of Yahweh's salvific will to the world of human beings; and third for the implementation of social justice. God ensures that all the members of the divine council do their work well. Hence, one cannot separate the acts of the Adversary on Job from God.

Job knew that God controls the breath of all living things (12:10). God has enormous power over the human's body and can shatter it without pity (6:9; 16:12–17). Job explains that God determines the days, nights, and months of all human beings and all creation, including the times of misery and futility (7:3; 14:5). However, Job accuses God of blatant abuse of power in the way he has been treated, assuming that he is special. God is using violence against him (19:7). How Job sees God is different from what he knows. Duck-woo Nam points out God's abusive power in strong words:

> With Job, however, the actions of God are questioned, rebuked, and ridiculed in very personal terms and manner. The very just and merciful nature of God is strongly parodied by Job to demonstrate the exact opposite: from favorable supervision to hostile surveillance, from positive expressions of anger to negative expressions of anger, and from constructive manifestation of power to destructive demonstration of abusive power. In the light of divine surveillance, anger and abusive power, the acts of

---

16. Miller, "Cosmology and World Order," 57–71. Italics are original.

17. Fabry, *TDOT*, 10:174–75. The *Targum of Job* found in Cave 11 in the Dead Sea area mentions the angels as the instruments of creation and administrators for God.

God in the world are therefore considered to be unknowable, irrational and unpredictable by human standards.[18]

In Job 13, Job describes the nature of God that he feels disturbing. God places his great hand on people and also frightens them. He wants God to do two things for him based on what he was experiencing. First, he wants God to withdraw his hand from him. Second, he wants God to stop frightening him with terror (13:21). If God can refrain from such acts, then it will be possible for Job to call on God and he will have an answer or speak for God to listen (13:22). This shows that God put people under strict surveillance which makes it impossible to do something without God seeing it. God can put his hand on an individual and nothing can break the hand loose except that God removes it. More so, God can terrify people. To Job, what God is doing is killing him, yet he will continually hope in him (13:15). Perhaps, Job sees the possibility of renewing the friendship that existed between him and God. Continued hope could mean he is envisaging a day when the strained relationship can be restored.

Although God is often seen as "merciful and gracious, slow to anger, and abounding in steadfast love and faithfulness" (Exod 34:6), God is also described as a "God of terror"—perhaps a terror that arises from horror, causing the body to shake or faint, and the bowels to move (Ps 9:20; Jer 32:21; cf. Gen 35:5–8)—and an all-powerful Judge (Heb 12:23). Creation also trembles at the terror of God (Ps 77:16; Isa 2:10, 19, 21). This is because there is an encounter with an awesome power of great magnitude causing a feeling of dread, distress, dismay, and trouble, all of which are associated with "fear" and reverential awe. Such an image echoes the message of Jonathan Edwards' preach on the theme, "Sinners in the Hands of an Angry God," on July 8, 1741, in Enfield, Connecticut, emphasizing that God's judgment will be more fearful and painful than can be imagined.

After leading the Israelites across the Red Sea, Moses sings a song acknowledging the greatness of God. Moses's song talks about the greatness of God that threw down those who opposed them, and God's unleashing of his burning anger consumed the enemies. At the blast of God's breath, the waters stood like a wall and sank like lead in the mighty waters (Exod 15:7–10). The song continues to say,

---

18. Nam, *Talking about God*, 88.

> ¹⁵ Then the chiefs of Edom were dismayed;
>   trembling seized the leaders of Moab;
>   all the inhabitants of Canaan melted away.
> ¹⁶ Terror and dread fell upon them;
>   by the might of your arm, they became still as a stone
> until your people, O Lord, passed by,
>   until the people whom you acquired passed by. (Exod 15:15–16)

Hence, nature and people became terrified at the acts of God (cf. Ps 77:16). Israel has to plead with Moses to tell God not to speak with them directly at the foot of Mount Sinai, when God speaks to the people amid thunder, lighting, fire and smoke, causing the people to tremble (Exod 19:16–18; 20:18–19). Jeremiah prays that God will not be a terror to him, but rather that his persecutors will be terrified and destroyed (Jer 17:17–18). To Isaiah, the presence of the Lord is fearful (Isa 2:10, 19, 21). The prophet Amos describes the day of the Lord as if a person runs away from a lion right into a bear (Amos 5:18–20).

Job is worried about how the splendor of God is terrifying him (9:34; 13:11). God is terrorizing him with dreams and visions (7:14). However, Eliphaz holds that it is rather the wicked whose ears can be filled with terror, distress, anguish, and trouble (15:20–24). Similarly, Bildad says that it is the wicked who are frightened with terror (18:11).

Among the Ahanta and Nzema of southwestern Ghana, the gods *Pataangye* and *Bazomgbɔkɛ*—who hate injustice, impurity, and sexual misconduct and will not delay in punishing offenders—spark fear in the minds of people.¹⁹ The name *Pataangye* is a compound word, *pata* meaning "appease" and *angyes* meaning "will not accept," which connotes how the god cannot be stopped or appeased when angry. Similarly in Greek mythology, Demois, meaning "dread," is known to be the god of terror. Demois, with his twin brother Phobos, is the personification of terror and fear, always joining hands with Eris the goddess of strife, and Enyo, the god of bloodshed, to wage war and spill blood. Demois is portrayed with wide eyes and a great mouth seeking to devour all, thus sparking fear in the hearts of human beings. His name alone brings fear to soldiers during war, as he was synonymous with loss, defeat, and dishonor.

Elsewhere in the Hebrew Bible, God is a warrior who shoots arrows at his enemies (Job 6:4; cf. Deut 32:23; 2 Sam 22:15; 2 Kgs 13:17; Pss 38:2; 45:5; 64:8; 144:3–6; Hab 3:9, 11). There are various reasons why God shoots arrows. For the psalmist, the presence of sin is one reason

---

19. Arthur, "Values and Behaviour," 147, 149.

why God shoots the arrows (Ps 38:4–5). As Seow observes, "occasionally, however, the divine warrior's arrows are directed not at the enemies of God but at God's own people when they deserve his hostility (Pss 7:13–14 [12–13]; 38:3[2]). The Divine intention in such shootings may be, as Eliphaz might argue (5:17–18), to 'reprove' and 'discipline.'"[20] The name Yahweh comes up in God's initial response to Moses, "I am who I am" (Exod 3:13–14). Like ancient Near Eastern myths from the same period, Yahweh, as a divine warrior, is believed to represent a storm god (Pss 68:4; 104:3),[21] who marches into battle in thunder (Ps 29) to defend Israel from enemies. The thunder is called God's voice, and it comes like lightning (2 Sam 22:14–16; Zech 9:14; cf. Sir 43:4–21). God as the Almighty, eternal, unchanging Creator is also a personal being who cares for all people as a father does for his child (Pss 68:5; 103:8–13).

Job argues that God cannot hide his face and think of him as an enemy (13:24). To Job, there is friendship with God as well as enmity with God. He thought he was a friend of God but God is acting like an enemy. In the book of James, either an individual is a friend of God or a friend of the world. James equates not being friends with God with marital unfaithfulness: "Adulterers! Do you not know that friendship with the world is enmity with God? Therefore, whoever wishes to be a friend of the world becomes an enemy of God" (Jas 4:4). James amplifies the marital picture of one staying faithful to the spouse with political imagery of disrupted fellowship. In other words, God's standards for friendship run at variance with the standards of the world. In the view of Robert Wall, the world's friend denies both the values and ultimate triumph of God's reign.[22] For Luke Johnson, "[t]his 'friendship' language, therefore, makes a statement about human freedom, values, and way of acting. One can choose the system of values by which one will live. One can live one's life as though God had no claim on it—be a friend to the world—or one can acknowledge that claim in faith and action as did Abraham and be a friend toward God."[23]

To Job, his suffering is caused by God and he is worried that God is not ready to see to his vindication. Job's desire is to see loyalty and justice. He does not understand why one cannot initiate a lawsuit against

20. Seow, *Job 1–21*, 445.

21. Green, *Storm-God in the Ancient Near East*, 258–80; Fleming, "Yahweh Among the Baals," 160–74.

22. Wall, *Community of the Wise*, 202.

23. Johnson, *Brother of Jesus, Friend of God*, 216.

God (9:3–4, 13–20, 32–35; 13:3, 15; 23:1–7). Job is not satisfied with God being elusive (9:11–12). Again, Job wonders why both wicked and righteous suffer the same fate (9:22–24; 10:2–3; 12:6; 21:7–26; 24:1–5). In such desperation, Job ends up accusing God of being his enemy (13:24–28; 16:9–14; 19:5–12, 22) who has betrayed the trust he had in him. Job assumes that God is using his sovereign power against him (9:22, 30–31; 13:3; 16:7–12; 19:21; 23:2; 31:35). And God has not been speaking to him as before. As Hartley observes, "God's silence terrifies Job (23:8, 9, 15)."[24]

In his disputation with his friends, Job indicates that he wants to see the Lord standing in the trial box to answer charges of arbitrary and unjust punishment against Job. God cannot be the kind of redeemer Job wants. It seems Job is skeptical for he knows that God cannot be put to trial, and if even God stands in a trial box, it would be God who will be the judge. Hence, Job wants someone else to act as a redeemer for him. He knows he could get one when he says: "For I know that my Redeemer (*goʾălî*) lives" (Job 19:25). Job identifies the *gāʾal* ("redeemer") as a different figure who after completing the task of presenting his case in court against God will enable him to be vindicated and eventually given the opportunity to see God.

In Job 19:25, the identity of the *gāʾal* seems highly debatable. The traditional interpretation is that this figure is God.[25] Some commentators also assert that the redeemer is another heavenly figure and not God.[26] Others say since the disputation is between Job and God, it is likely that Job was looking forward to another redeemer, a hypothetical figure other than God.[27] For Ringgren, the proposal that the redeemer is God is illogical.[28] Job sees the vindicator as a lawyer who will intervene to protect his legal rights.[29] Surano also suggests that the kinsman redeemer concept in Job should be understood within funerary rites. He unconvincingly disputes the courtroom setting in favor of the death threat.[30] Hartley argues cogently to reject the another-redeemer position and supports the

---

24. Hartley, *Book of Job*, 48.
25. Hartley, *Job*, 293; Alden, *Job*, 207.
26. Newsom, "Book of Job," 477–79.
27. *TDOT*, 2:355; Lindsay, "Realistic Hope or Imaginative Exploration?" 251.
28. *TDOT*, 2:355.
29. *NIDOTTE*, 1:793.
30. Suriano, "Death, Disinheritance, and Job's Kinsman-Redeemer," 49–66.

traditional view that God is the Redeemer since the author's choice of the term stands within the confessional theology of Israel.[31]

For Habel, Job will see God from his flesh. Job expresses his conviction that there is someone who will eventually rescue him from the suffering God has put him through. Job is doing the unthinkable by looking up to an unknown redeemer. Job's stance is hope in the "other" although he emphasizes that he the redeemer will make him see God.[32]

In a non-theological context, a "redeemer" indicates one speaking on behalf of the other, or buying back a field that has been sold or a person sold into slavery. Theologically, God's identity as the Redeemer is understood more in a salvific sense. Newsom contends that the function the redeemer plays in Job's thought is more important than their identity.[33] When used with God as subject, the Redeemer refers to God delivering God's people from slavery or from exile (Exod 6:6; Isa 43:1, 14; 44:6, 24; 47:4; 48:17). The word is also used to refer to God's delivering an individual from death (Ps 103:4) or taking up the cause of an orphan whose field has been stolen (Prov 23:11) or rescuing one who is praying for help (Ps 119:154).

The verb *goʾel* denoting "to redeem," "to deliver," and "to ransom" also has some correspondence with friendship. It primarily bears the legal and commercial nuances of someone who helps a friend out in times of need. In the book of Job, the word occurs in 3:5 and 19:25. The *qal* imperative in 3:5 represents "claim/redeem" while in 19:25 (participle masc const) it points to a "redeemer" who defends another person.

Job's complaint in general against God is damning, for he considers God as engaging in an unending onslaught. For instance, he says: "Will you harass a driven leaf; Will you pursue dried-up straw?" (13:25). Job's argument is founded upon his conviction that God is actively involved in human affairs and is the architect of his predicament (6:4; 10:8–14; 13:23; 16:7–14; 19:7–12). For him, it is unfair that God is too much involved in human affairs and will not spare the "dried-up straw" even when the wind is trying to blow it away (9:24). In the words of Athalya Brenner,

> Job never doubts God's omnipresence or omnipotence—his ability to exercise both good and evil is not questioned. Job's complaint is directed against his choosing to treat man in an

---

31. Hartley, *Job*, 293.
32. Habel, *Book of Job*, 293.
33. Newsom, "Book of Job," 478.

arbitrary, inexplicable, and often destructive manner. Job accuses him of being aloof and remote and of demonstrating his dark side too much in his relationship with man, so far as this relationship exists at all.[34]

On the part of Job, he does not know why God has allowed the affliction to fall on him. He does not have the answers; he has so many questions. Job sees God as an antagonist rather than a friend; one who opposes his well-being. God has become his enemy (13:24; 19:11). In the words of Zuck, "Job felt intensely the antagonism of God against him. This action of God continued to confuse and frustrate Job in his agony."[35]

Job earnestly desired to put some questions to God for answers. He takes a position to *ryb* ("contend, plead, dispute, strive") with God. The verbal root *ryb* and its cognates that occur twelve times in the book of Job (9:3; 10:2; 13:6, 8, 19; 23:6; 29:16; 31:13, 35; 33:13, 19; 40:2) seem to go deeper than a legal fight or argument. It seems Job is ready to do all it takes to confront God even if God kills him (13:15). He is poised to do this but recognizes his inability to do so, because God is Almighty and will not give him an opportunity to do so given the awesome and overwhelming nature of the Creator (9:2–3).

After Elihu's speech, God also bursts out and confronts Job with a series of rhetorical questions on how awesome creation is and how he controls everything. No wonder the whirlwind speech by God in which Job is accused of speaking without knowledge has become difficult to appreciate. Often, the debate is about whether God spoke and answered Job appropriately. Newsom does not favor the attempt by some interpreters to soften the dissonance in God confronting Job yet praising him for speaking well. She sees such discrepancy as part of the style of the entire book to highlight its polyphonic voices.[36]

God's speeches are in three parts: the first speech (38:1–39:30) corrects Job's misunderstanding of God's governance,[37] while the second speech (40:1–41:34) focuses upon God's justice or judgment.[38] The third (42:7–8) is also a judgment speech. Rowold labels God's speeches as belonging to the "challenge-to-rival" genre where in "confrontation

---

34. Brenner, "God's Answer to Job," 131.
35. Zuck, "Theology of Wisdom Books and Song of Songs," 224.
36. Newsom, "Book of Job," 634.
37. Rowold, "Yahweh's Challenge to Rival," 200.
38. Timmer, "God's Speeches, Job's Responses, and the Problem of Coherence," 294.

between rivals . . . one challenges the antagonist to duplicate the deeds that constitute his claim to authority."[39]

Scholars have long complained about God's approach of speaking in a whirlwind as demonstrating an imbalance of power between God and Job. One wonders whether God should not come to humanity and show God's awesome majesty and power. Job, knowing who God was, had prepared himself to face God, but commentators in unison think God acts with brute force and an agenda that seems to be bullying Job into submission. If Job could enumerate all that he can do, why not God?

God's first speech brings Job to understand the beautiful balance within God's creation. There is order and design in nature (38:4–6), and there also exists disorder and chaos (38:8–11; cf. Isa 40:12), all to show how God manages creation. God waters the land where no one lives so that grass might grow and torrents of rain may have a channel (38:25–27). God manages the clouds, lightning, and dust by the power of his voice (38:34–38), and God provides food for God's people, and also the wild animals (38:39–40).

Needless to say, God does not address Job as a rival, but as Yahweh (38:1). God is all-knowing but Job is ignorant, multiplying words without knowledge (cf. Job 34:35; Prov 5:23; 10:21; Hos 4:6). Reducing God to be a rival of Job is farfetched. The whirlwind is enough to show the differences in authority and power. God was not trying to argue out his case against Job, as has been requested in Job's dialogue with his three friends. God's speeches are to correct Job, but more so to restore Job's view of a distorted relationship with God. Daniel Timmer makes this point succinctly: "God's desire [was] not only to correct Job by the theophany but also to restore Job's relationship with God."[40]

God's speeches are meant to re-orient Job's understanding of God's relationship to humanity, and even more generally, of God's relationship to creation. Job had been trying to darken God's counsel, design, and power, but that should not be so. God would not be overwhelmed by Job's words and would not remain silent like the chiefs of Job's day (Job 29:21–22). After all, God had not been pouring out his anger unjustly as Job had assumed (cf. 9:5, 13–15, 17, 22, 10:17, 16:9).

Indeed, God answered Job just as Job desired, even though Job had taken it that God bruises (Heb: *yĕšûpēnî*) people with a whirlwind

---

39. Rowold, "Yahweh's Challenge to Rival," 209.
40. Timmer, "God's Speeches, Job's Responses, and the Problem of Coherence," 303.

(9:17).⁴¹ Ironically, when God answers Job in a whirlwind, Job is not bruised or crushed but broken—not in the sense of suffering emotional pain that is so strong to destroy him, but that he is mentally defeated that it ends his confrontational approach and changes the way he thinks. So, after all, God is not a silent onlooker forever. At the right time, God speaks. Job's demand for justice makes him challenge God to come up with what makes God a friend. He concludes with an invitation: "Let the Almighty answer me! . . . Like a prince I would approach him!" (31:35, 37). If God is Job's creator and king,⁴² then Job is a prince—a position he arrogates to himself—and not a servant as God testified (1:8; 2:3). In the end, Job's willpower and audacity is broken, and he repents in dust and ashes, and affirms his humanness and limitations.

In chapter 38, God begins his submission with the entreaty particle *ězār-nā'* that can literally be translated as "please," as if God is pleading for a hearing. T.C. Ham contends that the content of God's answer to Job does not callously humiliate Job nor does it constitute a condemnation or rejection of Job.⁴³ Ham reads the text against the popular view that God appearing in a whirlwind was a ploy to frighten Job. For him, God speaks from the storm, but without thundering, and gently challenges Job. Ham adds that,

> What we learn through the artfully crafted poem of ch. 38 is that God's answer is not to Job's claims of innocence but to the very heart of his suffering and cries of pain. To make this reply God appears to Job but without all of the fearful elements that caused the Israelites to tremble at Sinai. Rather the rhetorical style of the divine speech allows Job and the reader to enter the thoughts of the speaking character. We find YHWH focusing on one man, wanting to enlighten this man's darkening words without knowledge. Wondrously God does not display immeasurable power. Rather, YHWH utters "please."⁴⁴

In other words, God was not in any way trying to oppress, suppress, or overwhelm Job. It was more of a friendly encounter with the Almighty who appears distinct and spectacular, but plain and ordinary. John Gray approaches the encounter between God and Job through the whirlwind as that between equals. God was addressing Job as a *gibbôr*, that is a

---

41. NASB uses "bruises"; JPS TANAK uses "break" NRSV, NIV, NKJV uses "crush."
42. Bildad describes God as the "king of terror." See Job 18:14,21.
43. Ham, "Gentle Voice of God in Job 38," 536.
44. Ham, "Gentle Voice of God in Job 38," 541.

mature and active man, a warrior, a responsible head of a family, a man confident in his power, and an overconfident materialist.[45] Unlike how God commands and controls other creation, the relationship with Job is more reflective yet confrontational. Friends help each other to gain more knowledge through the hard way.

God demands of Job: "Shall a faultfinder contend with the Almighty? Anyone who argues with God must respond" (40:2). Job had assumed that God does not listen when people speak or does not answer when prayers are offered. However, as Elihu admitted, God answers (33:14-30). The writer opens up God's speeches this way: "Then the Lord answered Job out of a whirlwind" (38:1). Interestingly, when God questions Job (38:3; 40:7), there is no answer from Job. In fact, Job declined to answer, explaining that he has spoken once, and twice, and would not speak again (40:4-5).

When God finally speaks, Job repents in dust and ashes (42:6). The metaphor of "dust and ashes" echoes Abraham's plea with God (Gen 18:20-23), signifying how unworthy he is. In the epilogue, after putting Job right God looks positively at him and says Job has spoken concerning him what is right (42:7). The clause *kî lo' dibbarttem 'ēlay nĕkōnāh kĕ'abdî 'iyyĕōb* ("because you have not spoken to me what is like my servant Job"; 42:7) is notoriously difficult. The three who are defending God against Job's accusations do not speak well. God does not find any fault with Job's accusations and raving, however harsh they were. So, Job speaks well by accusing God and the three do not speak well by defending God. Significantly, it is plausible to claim that it is not the intention of the three that was wrong but the arguments they put up and how they said it. In the view of Samuel Terrien, the judgment—that Job spoke about what is right about God—does not take into account Job's confession that makes him repent in dust and ashes.[46] God may have held on to the privileges of friendship, that Job is his friend and thus has some privileges to confront God. Pope interprets the word *nĕkōnāh*, which denotes "to be firm, established, permanent, fix solidly," as "correct."[47] The word in the niphal also means "be treated differently, be distinguished."[48] Usually, it is used in the Hebrew Bible to refer to "a distinctive dealing revelatory of

---

45. Gray, *Book of Job*, 458.
46. Terrien, "Job," 1194.
47. Pope, *Job*, AB 15, 350.
48. Holladay, *Hebrew Lexicon*, 292.

God's presence and power."[49] Hence, what Job says conforms to what is just and true. Weeks claims it means "confirmed,"[50] but how the speeches of Job confirm who he is is not clear. Most translations understand the word as "right" (NRSV; ASV; AMP; NKJV), while others use "truth" (JB; JSP TANAK; NIV; ERV). It seems God interprets Jobs accusations and confrontations as having spoken appropriately to God (42:7, 8). I agree with Stanley Potter that the ambiguity of God's judgment in trying to understand which part of Job's sayings are "truth" or "correct" is necessary but unresolvable since human beings cannot understand how God judges all things.[51] The more people seem to know about God, the more they are overwhelmed by the ways of God. Harold Kushner's *When Bad Things Happen to Good People* captures how difficult it is to understand the ways of God.[52] Moreover, God cannot be grasped. God absconds easily from humanity's reach and no one can stop God from hiding (9:11–12). Job sees God as someone who is like an ungrateful enemy (6:4–7; 13:34; 16:7–17; 19:6–20). He feels that God knew he was innocent but had been treating him as a sinner (9:22–24; 10:4–7). God destabilizes society (12:16–25). To Job, even close friends can become enemies. A friendly relationship can end.

With all these views about God, did Job still desire to continue being a friend of God? Did Job value his friendship with God? There is a need to find out if Job can feel a sense of friendship once again.

GOD'S FRIENDSHIP WITH JOB

It is significant that God describes Job as "my servant" six times (1:8; 2:3; 42:7, 8 [3x]). The number six points to an incomplete whole. Perhaps there was more to it than being a servant. As a servant, God describes Job to the Adversary in chapter 1 in a characteristic way: (1) "None like him in the earth," (2) "Upright," (3) "Perfect," (4) "Just," (5) "Man of Integrity," (6) "Fears God," (7) "Eschews evil." Nevertheless, the master–servant model means that God still speaks as the one with authority to Job. Even where God sees Job as a friend, it does not mean they are equal as in human–human friendship. Balentine suggests that Job's lamentation seeks

---

49. Martens, *NIDOTTE*, 3:620.
50. Weeks, *Introduction to Wisdom Literature*, 67
51. Potter, "Message of the Book of Job," 302.
52. Kushner, *When Bad Things Happen to Good People*.

GOD AS A FRIEND OF JOB 261

to question not only the three friends but also God's friendship. At the end of it all it is God who emerges as the friend Job desires.[53] At the end of the story, Job does not lose his status before God as "my servant" even after the contestation and blame game (42:7).

During the dialogues, Job feels that the friendship between him and God had been short-lived. Job cannot still see the former relationship he once enjoyed with God. God has turned into an enemy instead of a close friend, echoing the view that one's best friend could be the worst enemy. His rhetoric highlights a life of a shamed and cursed one:

> 7 Surely now God has worn me out;
> he has made desolate all my company.
> 8 And he has shriveled me up,
> which is a witness against me;
> my leanness has risen up against me,
> and it testifies to my face.
> 9 He has torn me in his wrath, and hated me;
> he has gnashed his teeth at me;
> my adversary sharpens his eyes against me.
> 10 They have gaped at me with their mouths;
> they have struck me insolently on the cheek;
> they mass themselves together against me.
> 11 God gives me up to the ungodly,
> and casts me into the hands of the wicked.
> 12 I was at ease, and he broke me in two;
> he seized me by the neck and dashed me to pieces;
> he set me up as his target;
> 13 his archers surround me.
> He slashes open my kidneys, and shows no mercy;
> he pours out my gall on the ground.
> 14 He bursts upon me again and again;
> he rushes at me like a warrior.
> 15 I have sewed sackcloth upon my skin,
> and have laid my strength in the dust.
> 16 My face is red with weeping,
> and deep darkness is on my eyelids,
> 17 though there is no violence in my hands,
> and my prayer is pure. (16:7–17)

Job was growing disappointed in the actions of God, and accused God of not being a good friend. This stanza is made up of four movements (16:7–9b; 9c–10; 11–14; 15–16), and an *inclusion* (16:17). In the

53. Balentine, "Let Love Clasp Grief Lest both be Drowned," 397.

first, Job complains that God has worn him out (7a), shriveled him up (v. 8a), made him lean (16:8c), torn him in his wrath and hated him (v. 9a), and gnashed his teeth at him (16:9b). The second movement captures how the action of God has predisposed him to an attack from his friends, whom he calls "company" or "adversaries." They have sharpened their eyes against him (16:9c), gaped at him with their mouths (16:10a), struck him insolently on the cheek (16:10b), and mass themselves together against him, thus suggesting mob violence (16:10c).

In the third movement (16:11–14), God has given him up to the ungodly and wicked, broke him in two, seized him by the neck and dashed him to pieces, set him up as God's target, slashed open his kidneys, shown no mercy, poured out his gall on the ground, and rushed at him like a warrior.

The last movement (16:15–16) explains how Job has been affected by the onslaught of God: Job has sewed sackcloth upon his skin and laid his strength in the dust. His face has become red with weeping and deep darkness is on his eyelids.

> 18 O earth, do not cover my blood;
> let my outcry find no resting-place.
> ¹⁹ Even now, in fact, my witness is in heaven,
> and he that vouches for me is on high.
> ²⁰ My friends (*rēaʿ*) scorn me;
> my eye pours out tears to God,
> ²¹ that he would maintain the right of a mortal with God,
> as one does for a neighbor (*lĕrēʿhu*)
> 22 For when a few years have come,
> I shall go the way from which I shall not return. (16:18–22)

Job looks at his present state and concludes that God has worn him out and caused all of his human friends to abandon him (16:7). God has destroyed Job's body and torn him apart in such a way that his immune system is no longer protecting him, rather it's breaking him down (16:9). Like a well-built, strong, heavyweight wrestler and warrior, God holds Job by the neck and dashes him to pieces, breaking him into two (16:12, 14). Besides, God has handed him over to the wicked to struck him insolently on the cheek (16:10) and attack him with arrows (16:12). In all these attacks, Job does not respond with violence (16:17). In 17:5, Job further states: "He has made me a byword of the peoples, and I am one before whom people spit."

In all, Job looked forward to a renewed relationship. He wanted to know the right thing to do to reconcile with God:

> O that a man might plead with God
> as a man with his neighbor! (16:21 my translation)

> O that I knew where I might find him,
> that I might come to his seat!
> I would present my case before him
> and fill my mouth with arguments
> I would learn the words which he would answer
> and perceive what he would say to me.
> Would he contend with me by the greatness of his power?
> no, surely he would pay attention to me.
> There the upright would reason with him;
> and I would be delivered forever from my Judge. (23:3-7 NASB)

Job uses some key words in 16:21 and 23:3-7 to show how one can reconcile with an unfaithful friend. It takes pleading, or finding the friend, presentation of one's case, using arguments, seeking an answer, contention from the other, paying attention, and reasoning to come to terms once again. Pleading with God means having a friend back; a friend who would answer him and not contend with him using all of his power. Job wants to find God, giving the impression that God was hidden from his sight. He does not know where to find God (23:3). The concept *Deus absconditus*—the hidden God—is replete in the Hebrew Bible (Isa 8:17; 45:15; Ps 102:2; cf. Ps 10:11). God may appear but only covered with clouds and thick darkness (Ps 97:2). Jacob sees the face of God (Gen 32:30). God tells Moses that he cannot see his face (Gen 32:20). Elijah hears the voice of God and sees the back of God (1 Kgs 19:11-13). God can hide in two ways. One way for God to hide is for God to be inaccessible. God is nowhere to be found. A second way for God to hide is for God to appear right before my eyes, to speak to me, yet be so inscrutable, so indecipherable, that God remains achingly hidden.[54] The hiddenness of God shatters hope. Even after having shown his face, God remains so incomprehensible, shrouded in obscurity, that it is impossible to have a full view of God. Luther asserts, "God does many things that he does not disclose to us in his word; he also wills many things which he does not disclose himself as willing in his word."[55]

54. Gellman, "Hidden God of the Jews," 183.
55. Luther, *Luther's Works*, 33:140.

The issue of Job condemning God for frustrating divine justice comes to the fore. In the view of Daniel Timmer, Job was increasingly losing faith in God's sovereignty and good character, hence God asks Job: "Will you condemn me that you may be justified?" (40:8b). Timmer adds, "only by inverting the creature–creator relationship can Job follow to the end his intended course of prosecuting and convicting God. Ironically, only God can extricate Job from this problem, and the rest of the second divine speech shows that YHWH's gracious intention is to bring Job back into a healthy relationship with the deity."[56] Hence, God's intervention is aimed at restoring a friendly relationship with Job and not condemning him.

Job's position as the one pleading with God echoes Isaiah's prophecy to Judah. The prophet Isaiah depicts that God is ready to reason with Judah and argue out whether the people have lived right with God, although it is the people who have sinned:

> Come let us reason together;
> Though your sins are like scarlet,
>   they shall be as white as snow;
> Though they are red like crimson,
>   they shall be like wool. (Isa 1:18 my trans.)

Although presenting himself as someone pleading with a cause, Job uses a confrontational style to present his case. Deryck Sheriffs argues cogently that confrontation is a necessary part of intimacy.[57] Sometimes friends may confront each other vigorously to the displeasure of onlookers but may not necessarily be in a fight. Job confronts God aggressively for God has been "the Friend who has not turned up to commiserate with him."[58] Yet, Job maintains an unshakable conviction and trust in God's justice and continually talks to God. The first emotional outburst—the curse laments in chapter 3—makes the three astonished and perplexed. Rick Moore, juxtaposing chapter 3 with 1:21, observes that Job's assault on God in Job 3 raises suspicion about Job's integrity.[59] Anger characterizes Job's attack on God for all the suffering and alienation he had gone through. Could such anger justify how God sees Job as blameless and righteous? These attacks were, in fact, also answers to the three and Elihu for their defense of God. Zophar, for instance, claims Job's words

---

56. Timmer, "God's Speeches, Job's Responses, and the Problem of Coherence," 295.
57. Sheriffs, *Friendship of the Lord*, 210.
58. Sheriffs, *Friendship of the Lord*, 221.
59. Moore, "Integrity of Job," 30.

are agitating and insulting to him (20:2–3). In an emotional mood, Job questions God:

> If I sin, what do I do to you,
> > you watcher of humanity
> Why have me made me your target?
> > Why have I become a burden to you? (7:20)

If God has focused on an innocent man to bring this great suffering, God has been targeting the wrong man (16:12, 17; 19:6–7). God has struck him heavily (19:11, 21–22). God is treating him like an enemy (13:24; 16:9; 19:11; 33:10). Job prays that his adversary will be like the wicked and unjust (27:7).

Job questions why God binds sins in a bundle (14:16) so that the burden becomes great on the sinner. It seems Job thinks that his youthful sins have not been forgiven: God has stored them for the coming time of judgment.[60] Whereas before, Job had expected that in this moment of crisis, he would have received an equal kind of love. Throughout the book, Job acknowledges and believes in the power and sovereignty of God. What he does not understand is why God treats him unjustly (9:16–24; 11:70; 12:13–25; cf. 27:2). Job blames God for his predicament but is not quick to condemn God. He will hold on till he hears God. As Suzanne Boorer observes, Job's hope relating to vindication arises in part from his reflection on death but more so from his view that he will see God while he is alive.[61]

Job is very confident that he has played his part in his relationship with God and made this love the basis of his relationships with his family and society.[62] Job recounts his past with nostalgia. He says,

> 24 Yet God does not stretch out his hand in destruction
> > if one cries to him for help in his disaster
> 25 Did I not weep for him whose days was hard?
> > Was not my soul grieved for the poor
> 26 But when I looked for good, evil came;
> > and when I waited for light, darkness came.
> 27 My inward parts are in turmoil, and are never still;
> > days of affliction come to meet me. (30:24–27 my trans.)

60. Holt, "Why Are the Sins of Ephraim (Hosea 13,12) and Job (14:17) Bundled?" 92.
61. Boorer, "Job's Hope," 103, 104.
62. The first movement of this poem (vv. 2–10) deals with divine–human relationship. The second movement (vv. 11–20) which deals with human–human relationships flow out of the first.

Job speaks of his past when the friendship between God and himself was so intimate:

> ² O that I were as in the months of the past,
>   as in the days when God watched over me;
> ³ when he caused his lamp to shine over my head,
>   and by his light I walked through darkness;
> ⁴ when I was in my prime,
>   when the friendship (*sod*) of God was upon my tent.
> (29:2–4 my trans.)

Job is recounting a past relationship. He used to have all the blessings of wealth and favor—milk echoing wealth and prosperity, and oil representing anointing and favor. His life was established on the premise that God watched over him (29:2).

Close or intimate friendship can be understood as an enhanced version of good friendship, as seen among best friends. The link between intimacy and friendship makes it possible to identify and elucidate what might be called "intimate friendships" and "acquaintance friendships." For intimate friends, the bond between them is stronger, always bringing them near to one another. The intimate friend is able to provide warmth and love even more than close friends. Lapsley explains that the

> collocation of *mysterium tremendums* and everyday chat is the paradox at the heart of divine-human friendship. Another aspect of this same paradox can be named as well: although this is clearly a relationship between unequal partners, God enters into a friendship of such intense intimacy and care that only the language of equality can approximate the depth of its mutuality.[63]

The statement, "God was upon my tent" echoes a covenantal love and marks God's presence over Job. The joy of God's presence made him see light even when he walked through darkness.[64] Such "ruling over the tent" can be said to be a blessed fellowship of familiarity, with a loyal and unreserved relationship (cf. Ps. 4:15; 25:14; Prov 3:32). Covenantal loyalty surrounds the concept of friendship in the book of Job and this is modeled on the relation between God and humanity. The psalmist says: "The friendship of the Lord is for those who fear him, and he makes his covenant known to them" (Ps 25:14). Indeed, Job affirms that God is

---

63. Lapsley, "Friends with God?" 124.
64. Terrien, "Book of Job," 1108.

great and is the Creator (9:5–13; 12:13–25; 26:5–14). As Creator, God can rebuke all and has set limits to what he has created (26:10–15).

The kind of security God had given Job was not in the form of a servant watching over the property of a master. God had come to the level of Job and was with him along the way. Again, Alden observes that God's "'lamp' and 'light' refer figuratively to the Lord's gentle guidance and the resultant security of knowing where we are."[65] Moreover, God's glory reflected upon him and protected him as well: "his lamp shone over my head" (v. 3). As intimate friends, God was his close confidant, sharing all secrets (29:4a). It was such friendship that made his home blessed (29:4b). Hence, at that point in time when Job was in his heyday, God shared a unique relationship with him, blessing him with love and protection. He says, "When I was in my prime, when the friendship of God was upon my tent" (29:4). The Hebrew *bîmê* ("my prime") also signifies a point in harvest time, that is, a season of maturity when one bears fruit.[66]

Like Moses who encounters God on the mountain on a "face-to-face" basis, such that his face shone, Job once had a covering of God's light hovering over his head to signify friendship. The relationship between Job and God was like close confidants who share secret thoughts as "a friend to a friend." Job says,

> ⁵ when the Almighty was still with me,
>   when my children were around me;
> ⁶ when my steps were washed with milk,
>   and the rock poured out for me streams of oil! (29:5–6)

At the prime of his life, representing the early half of his years, Job was also given the red-carpet treatment. In a characteristic fashion, Job recalls when he was a celebrity. Now, gone are the days "when my steps were washed with milk, and the rock poured for me streams of oil" (29:6).

If one's friend is failing to do what is expected, then another person can be called in to act in that capacity. Job's complaint against God is that God is not fair because he has been crying out in prayer but God is not answering. God has also made it impossible for Job to access help from other friends and caused all to oppose and attack him. Job's hope has been uprooted like a tree on a path of a storm and like a city being surrounded with troops (Job 19:7–12). Now his life is miserable, finding

---

65. Alden, *Job*, 280.
66. See Keil and Delitzsch, *Commentary on the Old Testament–Job*, 119.

no support from family, friends, little children, nor his wife (19:13–21). Job knows that God is behind all of this.

Being friends with God does not diminish God's sovereignty and will. Since such friendship is between unequal, Job cannot set the standards and obligations. Divine–human friendship runs on God's principles. God expects humanity to be faithful to the relationship no matter what.

The whirlwind speeches reveal the nature of God vis-à-vis the identity of Job. God speaks like a master asking a student some questions. Job becomes aware that he knows very little about God's world and plays little role in it. He was not there when the world was created and everything will outlive him.[67] God wants Job to understand that there is enough space in the heart of God for all creation, including Job. There are lots of obligations on the part of God to take care of all creation. God cares for the animals including the wild untamed ones, the trees and plants, the sea and waterbodies and all that is in them, whatever goes on in the skies, and the heavenly places. God directs their paths and makes provision for them. Each of creation looks up to God. Job cannot be selfish by enjoying only that which is good from God. He cannot be ungrateful when he loses what he has enjoyed graciously from the hands of God—provisions that were given to him freely. When Job had lost everything, he acknowledged that it was God who had given all to him and that God had taken all (1:21). After all, it is the blessings of God that made him wealthy. His friendship with God does not mean Job should necessarily enjoy the blessings of God at all times. Moreover, there are other creatures like the Behemoth that "ranks first in the things of God" (40:19), and should be catered for. Selfishness should not creep into the favors received from friends. As Balentine observes, Job had centered his convictions on the fact that his authentic friendship depends on indissoluble commitments from God.[68] That was how Job misunderstood divine–human friendship. Longman rightly explains that "Yahweh's speeches are intended not to give Job an answer to the question of why he suffers but to reestablish the proper relationship between God and his human creature."[69]

---

67. Jones, *Study Commentary on Job*, 276.
68. Balentine, *Job*, 440.
69. Longman, *Job*, 115.

IMPLICATIONS

The book of Job begins by showing that the relationship between God and Job was a master–servant one. In time, Job sees that God is not acting his friend. When the disaster falls, Job understands clearly that his old friend, God, had allowed all that suffering to come upon him. Also, God was acting in a way that caused all the human friends, family, and acquaintances to desert Job. To Job, what kind of friend would permit the close friend would suffer physically, emotionally, and spiritually? Is God to be trusted as a friend?

In his prime, Job had God close to him. He also had his children close to him. As Gordis notes, the presence of the children around him was a sign of God's friendship and blessing par excellence (cf. Ps 127:3; Gen 15:2).[70] The writer of Wisdom highlights how the wisdom of God plays a key role in building friendship by saying,

> [24] For wisdom is more mobile than any motion;
> because of her pureness she pervades and penetrates all things.
> [25] For she is a breath of the power of God
> and a pure emanation of the glory of the Almighty;
> therefore nothing defiled gains entrance into her.
> [26] For she is a reflection of eternal light,
> a spotless mirror of the working of God,
> and an image of his goodness.
> [27] Although she is but one, she can do all things,
> and while remaining in herself, she renews all things;
> in every generation she passes into holy souls
> and makes them friends of God and prophets,
> [28] for God loves nothing so much as the person
> who lives with wisdom. (Wis 7:24–28)

Wisdom in this pericope, described as the power of God, motivates and influences the friendship between God and humanity. Friendship with God is thus construed under God's own terms and made perfect through love, forgiveness, and reconciliation. Friendship with God informs how human being makes friends with one another. The psalmist says that "the friendship of the Lord is for those who fear him, and he makes known to them his covenant" (Ps 25:14). Hence, friendship with God entails responsibilities. It also requires faithfulness and loyalty.

---

70. Gordis, *Book of Job*, 319.

At the end of the book of Job, the emphasis is on the restored relationship. God encounters Job and makes him understand that he has no clue about how God relates to all creation. If Job does not understand how God works, how can he understand the friendship between them? To God, Job was still his "servant" (42:9). Job repents for having a wrong view of God, and as such their relationship is restored, making Job regain twice as much as all that he previously possessed. God asks Job to pray for the three so that the accusation of not speaking rightly about God can be dropped. By praying for the three, Job restores the relationship between the three friends and God, and also restores the strained relationship between himself and the three. It shows clearly the heart of Job: he is there to restore and maintain former relationships no matter what.

First, friendship calls for a better understanding of the other and what friendship means. Unfortunately, Job does not know God very well. No matter how the finite mind tries to capture the infinite, there will be gaps. Human limitations in understanding the inscrutable ways of God lie at the heart of the book of Job. The three friends of Job try their best to share their views about God but in the end, they cannot speak the truth about God (42:8). Even Job has to repent in dust and ashes after confidently portraying who God is to him, because after all he spoke without knowledge and uttered things he did not understand (42:1–6). Surely, the prophet Isaiah says,

> [8] For my thoughts are not your thoughts,
>   nor are your ways my ways, says the Lord.
> [9] For as the heavens are higher than the earth,
>   so are my ways higher than your ways
>   and my thoughts than your thoughts. (Isa 55:8–9)

Job had wondered why God was acting in a strange way. He saw God as a friend who had abandoned him, hence he was not a good friend. He thought God should have been kind to him and showed loyalty to him. He thought God was more like an enemy pursuing a righteous man unjustly. He thought God was unjust and acted capriciously. However, when God points out who he really is in the whirlwind speeches, Job comes back to his senses and gains fresh knowledge. Job had not seen God as just, merciful, forgiving, and right, but that is who God really is. The suffering Job attacked God as arbitrary, malicious, and tyrannical. However, from the whirlwind, God speaks about how all creation relies on his care, providence, and benefaction. God orders the ways of all creation, including thunder, lightning, and rain. Such self-realization and new knowledge restore the friendship relationship. Friendship, thus, is best maintained when there is continuous knowledge gained about each other, for one cannot know everything about the other in one go. The more we know God, the more we can understand what our friendship with God means.

Job comes to a realization that he did not know God very well. He rediscovers God in a fresh encounter that makes him humble. He comes to understand how God works in the life of all creation in ways quite different from what he had imagined. This new understanding is what can reignite the bonds of friendship.
In the view of Emmanuel Takyi,

> The African understanding of friendship with God teaches that though God condescends to accommodate humanity, his immanence should not be taken for granted. Approaching God in any form or at any time, especially in the temple precincts, should be done in reverence and humility. It is important to remember that he is omnipresent. This understanding should inform the Christian witness on how to communicate with God, whether privately or corporately. It should also inform the way Christians relate to those who have specialized in communicating with God. Like the African our friendship with God must be covenantal. It must be a relationship "so great" because it is sealed with an *Omukago* (blood pact) of Jesus' blood.[71]

The justification to pour out lamentations to God does not mean one should not recognize who God is. The prophet Malachi points a similar idea out by saying, "If I am father, where is the honor due me?" (Mal 1:6). Jacqueline Lapsley intimates that "Like human friendship, divine friendship is not about a once-in-a-lifetime encounter, or even about casual, occasional meetings. Rather, it entails a commitment to regular encounters that form habitual practice."[72]

Second, reciprocity is one of the key foundations of friendship. It is sad, though, when one party stretches the hand and the other withdraws. Job was looking forward to God stretching out his hand to hold him and help in his time of need. Dana Robert, drawing from Frank Laubach, explains that it takes a friend of God to love God. Simply believing in God does not mean loving God for the devil believes in God, and becoming

---

71. Takyi, "Friendship with God in the African Context," 79.
72. Lapsley, "Friends with God?" 121.

acquainted with God does not help one to love God either.[73] For someone to be a friend of God, that person should cultivate the virtue of love. One way to cultivate such virtue is to love one's neighbor as oneself (Lev 19:18; Matt 7:12; 19:19; 22:37–39; Jas 2:8). Job had shown love to others, helped the poor and grieved for them, looking for their good (30:25). Hence, God should reciprocate that gesture to him, but God had not even done that. Such a lesson should inform how to understand divine–human "love."

Third, Job proves that at some point in his life God was his intimate friend and they shared counsel and secrets together (29:4). Developing an intimate friendship with God may give one the opportunity to share secrets with God, but that is not always the case. One cannot be intimate with God and keep a secret life, or hide something going on from God. Interestingly, God does not share with Job the agreement made in the heavenly council with the Adversary. Job has no clue of the permission to test him to see if he would curse God, but he is sure later along the line that God is attacking him. The view that God does not do anything unless the plan has been revealed to God's friends or servants does not work here (Ps 25:14; Amos 3:7). God confiding in his servants is but one side of the nature of God. Although God does not confide in Job, it does not mean God is a bad friend. The whirlwind speeches point out how God relies on his sovereignty in relating with all creation. Orthodox theology will insist on God confiding in his servants before embarking on any action while the story of Job, intending to show the weakness of orthodox theology, reveals another side of God.

Finally, it is said that "kind words from a friend are doubly enjoyable in dark days." Friends should desire to empower one another. Certainly, the one suffering needs comfort and compassion, not a barrage of words. The word "compassion," from the Latin root *compati*, means "to suffer with." Goetz, Keltner, and Simon-Thomas define compassion as, "the feeling that arises in witnessing another's suffering and that motivates a subsequent desire to help."[74] That is to say, it involves feeling for a person who is suffering and being motivated to act to help them. Compassion usually has to do with undeserved suffering. It is motivated by moral judgment and action. The idea is that compassion means approaching those who are suffering with non-judgment and tolerance. A compassionate heart gives the ability to remain accepting of and tolerant toward

---

73. Robert, *Faithful Friendship*, 144.
74. Goetz et al., "Compassion," 351.

another person in a difficult situation. In the view of Sung-Jin Yang, compassion is a spiritual way to restore someone who is broken and make the person connected with the sacred. It helps the person become free from suffering and brings about well-being.[75]

CONCLUDING REMARKS

The chapter has shown that divine–human friendship is not the same as human–human friendship. The privilege of making friends, however, with God, the King of Kings and the Lord of Lords, cannot be overemphasized. Friendship in divine—human perspective demands intimate worship with an eye on blessings. Worship creates a congenial atmosphere to experience God's presence. In worship, God comes to be with us and to tabernacle with his people. Befriending God calls for reverence. It calls for unlearning our old ideas about God and learning to know God better. It is about allowing God's word to abide in us so that God will confide in us what is on his heart.

Spiritual intimacy energizes physical and emotional intimacy. When spiritual intimacy is strongly nurtured, emotional and physical will follow. Disappointment can be the first major obstacle to faith in God. It can be an intruder that challenges faith. It may come in a harmless way but can be very destructive to spiritual growth and friendship. Nevertheless, it is in our moments of disappointment that God proves faithful and loyal.

---

75. Yang, "Cultivating Compassionate Living," 8.

11

Conclusion

WISDOM GLEANED IN THESE discussions is not necessarily knowledge of facts but a reflection of life. Africans uphold a social ideal where all members of society are to be treated with equity and respect regardless of age, gender, and social status. The popular wisdom sayings common to the people in any given community help to explain their world. Although there is no agreement as to what should entail wisdom or what should fall under that designation, it is true that people love the proverbs and aphorisms handed down from generation to generation. Each idea, however, is an opinion in context—once the context is removed from the saying, the meaning of the saying changes. More so, each saying has varied interpretations—or, better still, has another way of putting it. All these show the dynamic nature of African wisdom.

Friendship makes an individual a part of an ethical community. It makes sense of a social world that demonstrates the moral obligations on parties, showing how one is included or excluded in the community. The discussions on friendship, so far, have been an interplay of the "give and take" of opposing viewpoints from the characters in the story, showing a dynamic fusion of thought on the understanding of human nature. Each of the characters depicts a certain category of a friend, whether fitting or not fitting in the African worldview. The stories are intended to teach how to live rightly in a world God has created, and they help readers to confront their world of experiences and come to self-awareness of who they are. Admittedly, the author did not intend to present characters who were morally, psychologically, or theologically bankrupt, yet neither was it to show that the human characters are perfect. The human characters are set in their true nature to show what humanity really is.

There are many types of friends. A true friend is a friend indeed. Africans are to prioritize true friends over all others because true friendship offers the highest good. True friends focus on what they can give rather than on what they might receive. True friends do not flatter. In true friendship, there is reciprocity. Friends should also be a model for true forgiveness. It should not be difficult for true friends to forgive each other, even though one might not go to the same length as the other. As long as friends are more than brothers and sisters in the Lord, sharing should be a key part of their lives. Friends do not use each other to meet their parochial needs but sacrificially serve for the benefit of others. Friends should not be selfish. Toxic friends do not respect boundaries and are unsupportive, unreliable, and destructive. Their presence always makes people unhappy. And casual or ordinary friends find excuses when they have to demonstrate their friendship and are often self-justifying when they have not done so. How one develops from a fake and toxic friend to a good friend and ultimately to a best friend, intimate friend, and true friend matters a lot. Changes in identity and levels of relationship are normal occurrences. Radcliffe-Browne mentions that every social structure undergoes constant renewal of social life. The identities and actual relationship structures change from time to time, yet the social structure is expected to remain for some time. New members come into the picture and others leave from time to time—some through birth and others through death. The crucial aspect is that friends can become enemies and enemies can become friends.[1]

In the book of Job, the term "friend" can be understood in the moral sense.[2] The sages in Israel and the ancient Near East also pointed out certain conditions that could enrich the concept of friendship with the Lord and among human beings. That is to say, the concept of "friend" is inexhaustible and continues to challenge our postmodern world. Friendship embraces a wide range of people, whether related or not. It creates avenues for all and has benefits for all. McGinnis says, "people with deep and lasting friendships may be introverts, extroverts, young, old, dull, intelligent, homely, good-looking; but the one characteristic they always have in common is openness. They have a certain transparency, allowing

---

1. Radcliffe-Brown, "On Social Structure," 4
2. Hess, *NIDOTTE*, 1146.

people to see what is in their hearts."³ In other words, friendship does not promote the building of walls around oneself, living in a closed world, and minding one's own business. It allows others to get into one's world and for one to share or talk with others. Friends share part of the other's world. They do not wear masks and parade themselves behind curtains. They value self-disclosure and appreciate constructive critiques of their actions and inactions. As they make themselves fully known, they reveal who others are. Newsom also avers that the author of the book of Job was familiar with didactic tales and wisdom dialogue—two different genres— yet engaged "the sharply contrasting ways in which the two genres . . . managed to conceptualize the same situation."⁴ To consider the concept of friendship in the book of Job by considering each of the characters is helpful, situating friendship within the various contexts in which it is described.

The book of Job teaches the importance of true friendship. Friends share and shape the life and thought of each other. In all, God shows Job what it means to be his friend, not in the sense of always providing what is "good" but also withholding whatever is "good" from the friend. Job renews his friendship with his friends, brothers, sisters, family members, and acquaintances even though they were not loyal to him when he needed them most. God accepts Job who complained and accused him of injustice and unfairness. Job had argued that God had become his accuser and vindicator, but in the end, God blesses Job. He was not innocent after all but there is room for friendship. By finding the truth of God and gaining an understanding of how God works in the world, Job appreciates living within that harmony of God's order. Hence, the story helps us to learn the secrets of God—and since Africans hold firmly to God in their cosmology, and God relates as a friend, the values of friendship should always be explored.

To betray a friend is unacceptable. Betrayal can make a friend lose their personhood and feel vulnerable. It can affect self-esteem and lead to distrust. Nevertheless, friends should accept betrayal gratefully, bearing in mind that whatever happens between friends provides lessons for life. It may be hard to manage the emotions associated with betrayal but when friendship is much more valued than anything else, there will be room for forgiveness and reconciliation. The stress levels may be high but once

3. McGinnis, *Friendship Factor*, 27.
4. Newsom, "Job as a Polyphonic Text," 94.

a person can gather the strength to accept how one feels, reflect on the relationship instead of the betrayal, and take time to grieve, a heart of compassion can be developed to make moves to restore the broken relationship. One should also make time to unwind and open up to express pent-up feelings with the aim of achieving healing. If the other party cannot accept the outstretched arm of reconciliation, then that party is not a true friend. It would also be strange for true friends to find excuses not to spend their available time with their friends. There will never be enough time in life, but truly loving a friend will make one find time and space out of busy schedule to be with the friend in times of need.

True friendship does not mean one should forgo self-interests. Africans uphold communalism but respect individualism. A good balance between communalism and individualism is what Gyekye calls "moderate communitarianism."[5] Making friends is not an individual choice as if one has a right to make friends or not. One cannot choose to live without friends in African thought. Thus, there is a fundamental obligation for all to have friends, no matter the type of friends. Besides, good and true friends are surely needed. These notions of friendship are critical to social life and enhance the growth of life. Hence, the call to build a network of friends seems to teach and transmit a positive virtue to the present and future generations.

Friendship opens people up to captivating, timeless principles that examine humanity's relationship to one another and the universe. From the biblical perspective, friendship takes its source from belief in God as the foundational principle upon which all relationships must be built. Friendship reflects on practical moral principles for behavior, not only for the "people of God" but for all humanity. A person who builds friendship networks prepares for the future. Such a person is deemed to be wise. Wisdom focuses on issues facing humanity in general, especially the aspects of life that face human beings on a daily basis. Leo Perdue admits that, "Job understands that wisdom is not simply bowing the knee to the teachings by the sages, but rather it involves the testing of the tradition by experience. Wisdom as an epistemology allows for the authentic critical engagement of the past in the light of new understanding. Job also understands wisdom to be a discipline, the embodiment of virtue, especially justice and piety."[6] Knowledge is linked with wisdom and the

5. Gyekye, *Tradition and Modernity*, 41.
6. Perdue, "Wisdom in the Book of Job," 97.

fear of the Lord. The more a person gains knowledge, the more they gain wisdom. Similarly, it takes the fear of the Lord to gain wisdom (Prov 1:7; 9:10). The fear of the Lord enables one to live in a way that pleases the Lord (Deut 10:12), and is wisdom (Job 28:28). The Hebrew verb *yare* can mean "to fear, to respect, to reverence." The noun form, *yirah*, usually refers to a positive quality of giving reverence to God. When people accept the word of God and turn their ears to wisdom, it causes them to understand the fear of the Lord and find the knowledge of God (Prov 2:1–5). Such affectionate reverence, a response to God's wonder, makes a child of God humble and develops a proper attitude and relationship to God.

Wisdom is universal and exists in all places. Israel was very aware that among other nations there were people who were designated the "Wise." Wisdom offers ways to discern, reflect, and take decisions concerning life issues. It is wisdom that is passed on. The cultural settings within which Israel's reflections occur are significant, for "wisdom ideas were not tied to one particular time frame. They deal with life's basic issues (What is wise and foolish, suffering, raising children, the vanity of life without God, the need to fear God), which are forced in every age."[7] It should be noted that one's actions and thinking cannot be separated. As such one should not only become wise in thinking and speech, but also action. It is not enough to excel only in philosophical speculation but also how to relate with others. This practical aspect of life also comes with a theological perspective on wisdom, because "the fear of the Lord is the beginning of wisdom" (Job 28:28; Prov 1:7, 9:10, 15:33). A person needs to have a deep reverence and respect for God to live with the neighbor in an acceptable way.

The task of showing varied meanings of friendship from the various voices in the book of Job reveals that there is more to the concept of friendship than can be imagined. More so, every context or culture has its peculiar way of expressing reality. Readers learn the hard way that friendship is not about arguing out well or relying on self-interests. Even Job does not get it right and has to repent in dust and ashes. He presents his case poorly before God and his colleagues, making it difficult for them to easily understand his point of view. An analysis of proverbs about friendships and relationships has opened up common values and expectations that are necessary for life. The proverbs teach how people should live their lives as friends and reveal what can be extreme.

---

7. Schultz and Smith, *Exploring the Old Testament*, 127.

The ethic of self-disclosure to friends should not be taken for granted. Job is not afraid to make himself known to his three friends, brothers, sisters, household members, and acquaintances. What he had done for them was not appreciated, and his three friends saw ill motives in his good works. Job might not be perfect, but he knows himself. Expecting others to learn from him, he sets an example of creating spaces in his relationships, which they, unfortunately, failed to emulate. His concept of friendship makes him correct factual errors in his friends' minds. He vents his views and allows space for others to speak out. In the end, Job becomes convinced that he was wrong and had spoken about things he did not understand. His conviction opens his eyes to his bloated ego and miserable situation. It gives him the chance to repent, that is to turn away and begin anew on the right path. It is there that he could declare that "my eyes have seen you" (42:5), connoting he has come to new knowledge. True knowledge begins with an acknowledgment of one's powerlessness and affirmation that God created all things and sustains all things.

God desires that all people experience true friendships that inspire and encourage each other to persevere and grow. Friendship is a two-way street. They should give each other the opportunity to support and enrich their lives mutually. A godly friendship is a supportive relationship, filled with mutual service and affection. It is a mature relationship built on mutual love that is empowering. The whole design of friendship is to be there for the other (Prov 17:17; 27:10). It is not about killing loneliness or avoiding being left alone in times of hardship. It is a necessary obligation for all to be friends and to make friends. In the parables of the lost sheep and the lost coin, Jesus emphasizes how friends share in the joys of what has been found or reintroduced into the fold (Luke 15:3–7; Matt 18:10–14). Friends share successes and failures, joys and sorrows, together. David Jackson avers,

> The point stands—no man, nor any other created being, is going to call God to account. To the end of the Book of Job, even though God vindicates Job and the things he had said, the LORD does not explain to Job or his friends why he has done this, nor does he let them in on the opening scenes. Only the reader has that information.[8]

The lengthy dialogue between Job and his three friends, and God's judgement on it, shows that the three did not know what they were saying.

---

8. Jackson, "'Who Is This Who Darkens Counsel,'" 166.

They believe that good things happen to good people and bad things happen to bad people, and that Job is reaping what he has sowed. Also, in the whirlwind speeches, God confronts Job with reality and the truth, and Job sees that he had spoken out of ignorance. Hence, the story exposes the inadequate theological framework of Job as well as his three friends.

God desires that Job becomes an ethical model or paradigm and "a light to the nations" to show us what friendship means. The African church today must apply these same friendship principles as an accurate reflection of the consistency and continuity of God's purposes throughout history. The three are relying on their experience and knowledge, which falls short of who God really is. They do not say what is true about God. They have a distorted view of God because it is not the whole picture. A balanced theology serves to build relations, while an imbalanced theology can make one a dangerous counselor. Friends share ideas and give counsel where necessary. A person who is not friendly will easily find their weaknesses exposed. The good counsel of a friend is like iron sharpening iron (Prov 27:17). Such counsel is intended to make the other better, even if it turns out to be a hurting truth (Prov 27:6). True friends go a step further and offer sincere, loving corrections when necessary.

Friendship in African thought is about developing an ethical identity. Having wrong assumptions about people can block pathways of friendship. Accusing people wrongly should not be entertained in the economy of God. Relating with friends, in African thought, requires being partial, that is, offering preferential moral attention because of the obligations that exist between friends. Every human being can be seen as a neighbor yet it takes something special for one to be identified as a friend. Generally, it is unethical to withhold loyalty to one's family and community, but when it comes to friends, the demands are higher. If one is expected to offer basic support to family and neighbors, when it comes to friends the demands are beyond the basic or ordinary. The higher the level of commitment in the friendship, the higher the obligation. In other words, the obligations to an ordinary or casual friend may not be the same as a bosom or intimate friend. Again, showing a silent presence is a precious gift to people in terrible pain.

Jesus explained to his disciples that making hurtful connections between a person's situation and experience is not the right way to go. A man born blind does not mean the person is a sinner or the parents ever sinned. The disciples felt there were only two reasons for the man's situation; to Jesus, some experiences happen so that the works and glory of God might be displayed (John 9:2–3). Friends should have realistic expectations of one another. They should not be surprised when the other does not meet one's expectations. To assume that it is always the other person who falls short of being a good friend is unfortunate. The concerns of Job's friends are not about Job's identity, but are rather about Job's views and utterances. God's final judgment exposes the three friends as not acting as friends. Deryck Sheriffs says, "the debate between Job, Eliphaz, Bildad, Zophar and Elihu has ranged over many theological truths, but in one sense it can be co-ordinated with reference to the three emotions of anger, fear and guilt. Everyone has become angry, but Job has refused to feel guilty."[9] The three friends were inappropriately insisting on half-truth. Atkinson describes Eliphaz as the logician who rationalizes faith over experience, Bildad as a traditionalist whose sharp tongue professes narrow theology, and Zophar as an arrogant counselor whose approach is more confrontational.[10]

It is observed that theology that reflects on life should not be only abstract but rather address particular human needs. The three friends, like the Adversary, inflict Job with more pain, thus abusing their privileges as friends. The community and blood brothers and sisters are more like fair-weather friends. Job's hope in God as a friend is also dashed. It is the wife of Job whose concern and care, at least, can be legitimate—yet initially Job did not understand her and was not satisfied with her. God knows Job very well, but Job does not know God well. Mrs. Job does not know her husband well and also feels that one could curse God and die. Similarly, the three friends of Job do not know Job very well, nor do they know God well. Moreover, Job's three friends do not know and understand Job and his relationship with God. To become great friends, get to know your friends. This act may involve developing a listening ear and heart and avoiding criticism. What the three friends first do when they visit Job is to sit with him in silence, and that is an extravagant and costly offering. They came from a long way and were not in a rush to speak. Their presence is more soothing and comforting for seven days. It is when they are overtaken by events that they fall into the wrong path. They weep and tear their robes while Job is trying to comfort himself. They enter into Job's experience and feel sorry for him. An empowering presence requires that friends show up physically. Sometimes, social

---

9. Sheriffs, *Friendship of the Lord*, 221.
10. Atkinson, *Message of Job*, 61.

media posts, text messages, and telephone calls may play a role, but these cannot replace real presence. To be a true friend to someone in a crisis should necessarily involve our presence, intimacy, companionship, collaboration, and sacrifice.

Strong friendships can still play a role in the growth of families. Such is the teaching of the sages: "There is a friend who sticks closer than a brother" (Prov 18:24). Blood is thicker than water, so friends should be an image of blood and not water. Parents and siblings are known to have abandoned their own at certain times. Our consumeristic world has made some parents treat their own children in a business-like fashion. Others have family members who would rather not be bothered when one of them gets into problems. Yet some friends stick around much better than family members. True friends stick around when the need is really great. They are willing to jump into the fray, not counting the cost, just for the sake of love and friendship. In some sense, a true friend is seen as more dependable than a real brother (Prov 17:17). Having good friends, best friends, intimate friends, and true friends can certainly be the best thing in the world. In the words of Wesley Hill, "if your deepest fulfillment is found in personal autonomy, then friendship—or at least the close kind I want to recommend in these pages—is more of a liability than an asset."[11]

African traditional society cherishes friendship that is empowering, fruitful, and good. The egalitarian understanding of life makes a friendship work perfectly well in areas of solidarity and mutual support for each other. Refusing to have friends is not acceptable and having too many friends is unacceptable. McGinnis suggests that to salvage a faltering friendship, one should (1) locate the trouble spot, (2) apologize when you are wrong, (3) check to see if your neuroses are spoiling your friendships, (4) check to see if you employ old methods of relating that no longer work, and (5) check to see if you have an excessive need for approval.[12] Indeed, one of the lessons from the discussion is that African people are supposed to learn about building friendships with people who are suffering. Show friendship to and talking to a hurting person needs great care. Job attacks his friends with a barrage of words and laments about how they are not seeing what true friendship means. Job also accuses God of cruelty or indifference. It is possible for one to be overwhelmed by pain

---

11. Hill, *Spiritual Friendship*, 14.
12. McGinnis, *Friendship Factor*, 153.

in such a way that there is transference. It may happen that those in pain can make it difficult for others to stay close to them. They can cause a lot of pain to those who are around them because of the way they feel the pain. How they rationalize the pain may give wrong signals and prevent others from giving a candid interpretation of the pain.

The world has also accepted that friendship can be based on liking someone or following another on social networking platforms. There is less interaction physically. Such friendships do not demand the basic obligations required of casual friends. They stay connected on some level, but the actions and inactions of each other cannot be judged. One may not know the reason the other has not shown up online. Such friendship is not what we find in *the* book of Job. And it is not the friendship Africans need. And the book of Job warns against inappropriate preaching of the truth. It offers a perspective of friendship that can be ideal for African Christians. The story teaches that godly people suffer and friends can be a pain in the neck. Bad things happen to good people. It teaches us that supporting those in suffering must be holistic—body, mind, spirit, relationships, emotions, and more. It is easy for preachers to link sin with suffering just as the three friends of Job did. Preachers cannot continue to accuse people who are suffering of being in sin or confess sins that are unrelated to God's plan for that person. Preachers thus risk falling into the situation the three friends found themselves in. Job who was the victim had to pray for them before they were forgiven. May the people who may be accused by preachers develop a heart that would plead with God to forgive their "friends" for the sake of restoration and friendship.

Bibliography

Achebe, Nwando. "Love, Courtship, and Marriage in Africa." In *A Companion to African History*, edited by William H. Worger et al., 119–42. London: Wiley-Blackwell, 2018.

Ackah, C. A. *Akan Ethics*. Accra: Ghana University Press, 1988.

Ackerman, Susan. *Where Heroes Love: The Ambiguity of Eros in the Stories of Gilgamesh and David*. New York: Columbia University Press, 2015.

Adamo, David T. "Africa and Africans in the Old Testament." *Theologia Viatorum* 35 (2011) 137–66.

———. *Africa and the Africans in the Old Testament*. 1998, Reprint, Eugene, OR: Wipf & Stock, 2001.

Adams, Glenn, and Victoria C. Plaut. "The Cultural Grounding of Personal Relationship: Friendship in North American and West African Worlds." *Personal Relationships* 10 (2003) 333–47.

Agyekum, Kofi. "An Akan Oral Artist: The Use of Proverbs in the Lyrics of the Kwabena Konadu." *Research Review NS* 21 (2005) 1–17.

———. The Pragmatics of *Duabɔ* 'Grievance Imprecation' Taboo among the Akan." *Pragmatics* 9 (1999) 357–82.

Aidoo, Mark S. "'If This is of God': Choosing to Curse in Ghanaian Charismatic Christianity." *Journal for the Study of Religion* 34 (2021) 1–22.

———. *Leadership in the Book of Esther: An African Contextual Hermeneutic*. Accra: JEM, 2020.

———. "'My Words Dropped upon Them Like Dew': Towards Reimaging the Identity of African Biblical Interpreters." In *The Bible, Centres, and Margins: Dialogue between Postcolonial African and UK Biblical Scholars*, edited by Johanna Steibert and Musa W. Dube, 97–113. London: T. & T. Clark, 2018.

———. *Shame in the Individual Lament Psalms and African Spirituality*. New York: Lang, 2017.

———. "Standing on the Side of Mrs. Job." In *The Bible and Gender Troubles in Africa*, edited by Joachim Kugler et al., 129–46. Bamberg: University of Bamberg Press, 2019.

Aihiokhai, SimonMary Asese. "'Love One Another as I Have Loved You': The Place of Friendship in Interfaith Dialogue." *Journal of Ecumenical Studies* 48 (2013) 491–508.

Alden, Robert. *Job*. New American Commentary. Nashville: Broadman & Holman, 1993.

Alter, Robert. *The Wisdom Books: Job, Proverbs, and Ecclesiastes: A Translation with Commentary*. New York: Norton, 2010.

Anchimbe, Eric A. "On Not Calling people by Their Names: Pragmatic Undertones of Sociocultural Relationships in a Postcolony." *Journal of Pragmatics* 43 (2011) 1472–83.
Andersen, Francis I. *Job: An Introduction and Commentary*. Tyndale Old Testament Commentaries 14. Downers Grove, IL: InterVarsity, 1976.
Anderson, Gary A. *A Time to Mourn, A Time to Dance: The Expression of Grief and Joy in Israelite Religion*. University Park, PA: Penn State University Press, 1991.
Anderson, Jeff S. *The Blessing and the Curse: Trajectories in the Theology of the Old Testament*. Eugene, OR: Cascade Books, 2014.
Annis, David B. "Meaning, Value and Duties of Friendship." *American Philosophical Quarterly* 24 (1987) 349–56.
Appiah, Kwame Anthony. *Cosmopolitanism: Ethics in a World of Strangers*. London: Lane, 2006.
Aquinas, Thomas. *The Summa Theologica of St. Thomas Aquinas*. Translated by fathers of the English Domincan Pronvince. London: Burns, Oats & Washbourne, 1922.
Aristotle. *Nicomachean Ethics*. Translated by Sarah Brodie and C. J. Rowe. Oxford: Oxford University Press, 2002.
Arnold, Bill T. "The Love-Fear Antinomy in Deuteronomy 5–11." *Vetus Testamentum* 61 (2011) 551–69.
Arthur, Peter. "Values and Behaviour: The Literary Concept of 'Bosom' in the Akan Culture." *E-Journal of Religious and Theological Studies* 7 (2021) 143–52.
Atkinson, David. *The Message of Job*. The Bible Speaks Today. Downers Grove, IL: InterVarsity, 1991.
Audi, R., ed. *The Cambridge Dictionary of Philosophy*. 2nd ed. Cambridge: Cambridge University Press, 1999.
Augustine. *The City of God*. Translated by John Healey. London: Dent, 1931.
———. *Confessions*. Translated by R. S. Pine-Coffin. London: Penguin, 1961.
———. *De Bono Coniugali, De Sancta Virginitate*. Translated by P. G. Walsh. Oxford: Clarendon, 2001.
———. *Letters*. Vol. 2 Translation, introduction, and notes by Roland J. Teske SJ. Edited by Boniface Ramsey. Hyde Park, NY: New City, 2002.
———. *Letters: The Works of Saint Augustine: A Translation for the 21st Century*. Loschberg: Jazzybee Verlag Jurgen Beck, 2015.
———. *On Faith in Things Unseen*. Revised and edited by Kevin Knight. http://www.newadvent.org/fathers/1305.htm.
Austin, Victor Lee. *Friendship: The Heart of Being Human*. Grand Rapids: Baker, 2020.
Avrahami, Yael. "בוש in the Psalms: Shame or Disappointment?" *Journal for the Study of the Old Teatament* 34 (2010) 295–313.
Awwad, Johnny. "Satan in Biblical Imagination." *Journal of Theological Review* 26 (2005) 111–26.
Badhwar, Neera K. "Friends as Ends in Themselves." *Philosophy and Phenomenological Research*, 48 (1987) 1–23.
Baker, David W. "Aspects of Grace in the Pentateuch." *Ashland Theological Journal* 29 (1997) 7–22.
Bal, Mieke. "A Body of Writing: Judges 19." In *A Feminist Companion to Judges*, edited by Athalya Brenner-Idan, 208–30. Sheffield: JSOT Press, 1993.
Balentine, Samuel E. *Job*. Smyth & Helyws Bible Commentary. Macon, GA: Smyth & Helyws, 2006.

———. "Let Love Clasp Grief lest Both be Drowned." *Perspectives in Religious Studies* 30 (2003) 381–97.
Baltzly, Dirk, and Nick Eliopolous. "The Classical Ideals of Friendship." In *Friendship: A History*, edited by Elizabeth Caine, 1–64. New York: Routledge, 2014.
Barth, Karl. *Church Dogmatics III/1: The Doctrine of Creation*. Edited by G. W. Bromiley and T. F. Torrance. Translated by J. W. Edwards et al. Edinburgh: T. & T. Clark, 1958.
Bauckham, Richard. *God and the Crisis of Freedom: Biblical and Contemporary Perspectives*. Louisville: Westminster John Knox, 2002.
Baumeister, R. F., and M. R. Leary. "The Need to Belong: Desire for Interpersonal Attachments as a Fundamental Human Motivation." *Psychological Bulletin* 117 (1995) 497–529.
BBC. "Ethics Guide. Euthanasia." 2014. http://www.bbc.co.uk/ethics/euthanasia/overview/introduction.shtml.
Bechtel, Lyn M. "A Feminist Approach to the Book of Job." In *A Feminist Companion to Wisdom Literature*, 222–51. Feminist Companion to the Bible 9. Sheffield: Sheffield Academic, 1995.
Bergsma, Ad, et al. "Happiness in the Garden of Epicurus." *Journal of Happiness Studies* 9 (2008) 397–423.
Berry, Donald K. *An Introduction to Wisdom and Poetry of the Old Testament*. Nashville: Broadman & Holman, 1999.
Bethea, Sharon, and Tennille Allen. "Past and Present Societal influences on African American Couples That Impact Love and Intimacy." In *Love, Intimacy and the African American Couple*, edited by Katherine M. Helm and Jon Carlson, 20–59. New York: Routledge, 2013.
Bethge, Eberhard. *Friendship and Resistance: Essays on Dietrich Bonhoeffer*. Grand Rapids: Eerdmans, 1995.
Bhebe, N. M., and Advice Viriri. *Shona Proverbs: Palm Oil with which African Words Are Eaten*. Gwere, Zimbabwe: Booklove, 2012.
Biro, David. "Is There Such a Thing as Psychological Pain? And Why It Matters." *Culture Medicine and Psychiatry* 34 (2010) 658–67.
Bitzer, Lloyd F. "The Rhetorical Situation." In *Rhetoric: A Tradition in Transition. In Honor of Donald C. Bryant*, edited by Walter R. Fisher, 47–260. East Lansing: Michigan State University Press, 1974.
Bonhoeffer, Dietrich. *Ethics*. Translated by Neville Horton Smith. London: SCM, 1955.
———. *Letters and Papers from Prison*. New Greatly Enlarged Edition. Edited by Eberhard Bethge. New York: Touchstone, 1971.
———. *Life Together: The Classic Exploration of Christian Community*. New York: HarperOne, 1978.
———. *Life Together: Prayerbook of the Bible*. Minneapolis: Fortress, 1996.
Boorer, Suzanne. "Job's Hope: A Reading of the Book of Job from the Perspective of Hope." *Colloquium* 30 (1998) 101–22.
Brain, Robert. *Friends and Lovers*. London: Paladin, 1977.
Brenner, Athalya. "God's Answer to Job." *Vetus Testamentum* 31 (1981) 129–37.
Breusers, Mark. "Friendship and Spiritual Parenting among the Moose and Fulbe in Burkina Faso." In *Friendship, Descent and Alliance in Africa: Anthropological Perspectives*, edited by Martine Guichard et al., 74–96. New York: Berghahn, 2014.

Brown, F., et al. *The Brown-Driver-Briggs Hebrew and English Lexicon with an Appendix Containing the Biblical Aramaic*. Peabody, MA: Hendrickson, 2008.

Brown, G. Gordon, and James H. Barnett. "Social Organization and Social Structure." *American Anthropologist* 44 (1942) 31–6.

Brown, Peter. *The Body and Society*. New York: Columbia University Press, 2008.

Brueggemann, Walter. "Lament as a Wake Up Call." In *Lamentations in Ancient and Contemporary Cultural Contexts*, edited by Nancy E. Lee and Carleen Mandolfo, 221–36. Symposium Series 43. Atlanta: SBL, 2008.

———. *Old Testament Theology*. Minneapolis: Fortress, 1992.

———. *The Message of the Psalms*. Minneapolis: Augsburg, 1984.

———. *Theology of the Old Testament: Testimony, Dispute, Advocacy*. Minneapolis: Fortress, 1997.

Burke, Kenneth. *Language as Symbolic Action*. Berkeley: University of California Press, 1966.

Buttrick, George A. *The Interpreter's Dictionary of the Bible*. 4 vols. Nashville: Abingdon, 1962.

Campbell, W. Keith, et al. "Among Friends? An Examination of Friendship and the Self-serving Bias." *British Journal of Social Psychology* 39 (2000) 229–39.

Carmichael, Liz. *Friendship: Interpreting Christian Love*. London: T. & T. Clark, 2004.

Chitando, Ezra, and Musa W. Dube. *African Indigenous Religious in the HIV and AIDS Contexts*. Geneva: WCC Publications, 2007.

Chrysostom, John. "Homily II on I Thessalonians." In *From Nicene and Post-Nicene Fathers*, First Series, edited by Philip Schaff and translated by John A. Broadu. Buffalo, NY: Christian Literature, 1889. http://www.newadvent.org/fathers/230402.htm.

Cicero. *On Life and Death: A New Translation by John Davie*. Edited by John Davie and Miriam T. Grigin. Oxford: Oxford University Press, 2017.

Clark, Elizabeth A. "John Chrysostom and the 'Subintroductae.'" *Church History* 46 (1977) 171–85.

Clark, Gordon. *Word Hesed in the Hebrew Bible*. JSOTSup 157. Sheffield: JSOT Press, 1993.

Clines, David J. A. *Job 1–20*. Word Biblical Commentary 17. Dallas: Nelson, 1989.

———. *Job 21–37*. Word Biblical Commentary 18A. Grand Rapids: Zondervan, 2006.

———. "Job's Fifth Friend: An Ethical Critique of the Book of Job." *Biblical Interpretation* 12 (2004) 233–50.

Clines, David J. A., ed. *The Dictionary of Classical Hebrew, II*. Sheffield: Sheffield Academic, 1995.

Cocking, D., and J. Kennett. "Friendship and the Self." *Ethics* 108 (1998) 502–27.

Collins, Kenneth J., and Jason E. Vickers. *The Sermons of John Wesley: A Collection for the Christian Journey*. Nashville: Abingdon, 2013.

Cooper, Alan. "The Sense of the Book of Job." *Prooftexts* 17 (1997) 227–44.

Conejero, Ismaek, et al. "Psychological Pain, Depression, and Suicide: Recent Evidences and Future Directions." *Current Psychiatry Reports* 23 (2018).

Conrad, Edgar W. "Satan." In *The New Interpreters Dictionary of the Bible*. Edited by William O. Walker Jr., vol. 5. Nashville: Abingdon, 2009.

Cooke, Bernard, and Gary Macy. *Christian Symbol and Ritual: An Introduction*. Online ed. New York: Oxford Academic, 2005.

Conner, W. Robert. *The New Politicians of Fifth-Century Athens*. Princeton: Princeton University Press, 1971.

Crenshaw, James L. "The Concept of God in the Old Testament Wisdom." In *In Search of Wisdom: Essays in Memory of John G. Gammie*, edited by Leo G. Perdue et al., 1–18. Louisville: Westminster John Knox, 1993.

———. *Old Testament Wisdom—An Introduction*. 3rd ed. Louisville: Westminster John Knox, 2010.

———. *A Whirlwind of Torment: Israelite Traditions of God as an Oppressive Presence*. Philadelphia: Fortress, 1984.

———. "Wisdom." In *Old Testament Form Criticism*, edited by John H. Hayes, 225–64. San Antonio: Trinity University Press, 1974.

Cross, Frank M. *Canaanite Myth and Hebrew Epic*. Cambridge: Harvard University Press, 1973.

Culy, Martin M. *Echoes of Friendship in the Gospel of John*. New Testament Monographs 30. Sheffield: Sheffield Phoenix, 2010.

Dahood, Mitchell J. "Hebrew-Ugaritic Lexicography VII." *Biblica* 50 (1969) 337–56.

Davies, Eryl W. *The Immoral Bible: Approaches to Biblical Ethics*. London: T. & T. Clark, 2010.

Davis, Ellen F. "Surprised by Wisdom: Preaching Proverbs." *Interpretation* 63 (2009) 264–77.

Dei, G. "Sustainable Development in the African Context: Revisiting Some Theoretical and Methodological Issues." *African Development* 18 (1993) 97–110.

Delitzsch, Franz. *Biblical Commentary on the Book of Job*. Vol. 2. Grand Rapids: Eerdmans, 1970.

Derrida, Jacques. *The Politics of Friendship*. Translated by George Collins. London: Verso, 2020.

deSilva, David A. *Honor, Patronage, Kinship and Parity*. Downers Grove, IL: InterVarsity, 2000.

Donlan, Walter. *The Aristocratic Ideal and Selected Papers*. Wauconda, IL: Bolchazy-Carducci, 1999.

Driver, Samuel R., and George B. Gray. *A Critical and Exegetical Commentary on the Book of Job*. Vol. 2. International Critical Commentary. New York: Scribner, 2010.

Dzobo, N. K. "African Symbols and Proverbs as Source of Knowledge and Truth." In *Persons and Community*, Ghanaian Philosophical Studies, edited by Kwasi Wiredu and Kwame Gyekye, 85–98. Washington, DC: Council for Research in Values and Philosophy, 1992.

Ehrlich, Bernard. "The Book of Job as a Book of Morality." *Jewish Bible Quarterly* 34 (2006) 30–8.

Eng, Daniel K. "'I Call You Friends': Jesus as Patron in John 15." *Themelios* 46 (2021) 55–69.

Eng, Milton. *Day of Our Years: A Lexical Semantic Study of the Life Cycle in Biblical Israel*. New York: T. & T. Clark, 2011.

Etieyibo, Edwin. "Post-Modern Thinking and African Philosophy." *Filosofia Theoretica: Journal of African Philosophy, Culture and Religions*, 3 (2014) 67–82.

Exum, Cheryl. *Fragmented Women: Feminist (Sub)versions of Biblical Narratives*. JSOTSup 163. Sheffield: JSOT Press, 1993.

Fabry, H.-J. "סוד, sod." In *TDOT* 10 (2000) 171–78.

Farrell, Walter, OP. *The Fulness of Life*. Vol. 3 of *A Companion to the Summa*. New York: Sheed & Ward, 1940.

Feinberg, Charles L. "The Poetic Structure of the Book of Job and the Ugaritic Literature." *Bibliotheca Sacra* 103 (1946) 283–92.

Fleming, Daniel E. "Yahweh among the Baals: Israel and the Storm Gods." In *Mighty Baal: Essays in Honor of Mark S. Smith*, 160–74. Harvard Semitic Studies 66. Leiden: Brill, 2020.

Fokkelman, Jan P. *The Book of Job in Form: A Literary Translation with Commentary*. Studia Semitica Neerlandica 58. Leiden: Brill, 2012.

Forell, George W. *Luther's Works*. Vol. 33: *Career of the Reformer II*. Philadelphia: Muhlenberg, 1958.

Fox, Michael V. *Proverbs 1–9: A New Translation with Introduction and Commentary*. Anchor Bible 18. Garden City, NY: Doubleday, 2000.

Friedman, Marilyn. "Friendship and Moral Growth." *Journal of Value Inquiry* 23 (1989) 3–13.

Gane, Milgrom. "קָרַב qārab; קָרֵב qārēb; קָרוֹב qārôb; קִרְבָה qirbâ; קְרָב qerāb; קָרְבָּן qorebān." In *TDOT* 12 (2004) 135–45.

Garver, Eugene. "Aristotle and Kinds of Rhetoric." *Rhetorica: A Journal of the History of Rhetoric* 27 (2009) 1–18.

Geest, Sjaak van der. "Kinship as Friendship: Brothers and Sisters in Kwahu, Ghana." In *The Anthropology of Sibling Relations*, edited by E. Albert C. Coe and T. Thelen, 51–70. New York: Palgrave Macmillan, 2013.

Gellman, Jerome. "The Hidden God of the Jews: Hegel, Reb Nachman and the Aqedah." In *Hidden Divinity and Religious Belief: New Perspectives*, edited by Adam Green and Eleonore Stump, 175–91. Cambridge: Cambridge University Press, 2016.

Glazebrook, Allison, and Kelly Olson. "Greek and Roman Marriage." In *A Companion to Greek and Roman Sexualities*, edited by Thomas K. Hubbard, 69–82. Blackwell Companions to the Ancient World 100. Oxford: Wiley, 2013.

Glueck, Nelson. *Hesed in the Bible*. Translated by Alfred Gottschalk. 1967. Reprint, Eugene, OR: Wipf & Stock, 2011.

Goetz, J. L., et al. "Compassion: An Evolutionary Analysis and Empirical Review." *Psychological Bulletin*, 136 (2010) 351–74.

Goldingay, John. "Anger." In *The New Interpreter's Dictionary of the Bible*, edited by Kathrarine Doob Sakenfeld, 1:156–58. Nashville: Abingdon, 2006.

———. *The Book of Lamentation*. New International Commentary of the Old Testament. Grand Rapids: Eerdmans, 2022.

———. *Psalms 1–41*. Baker Commentary on the Old Testament Wisdom and Psalms. Grand Rapids: Baker Academic, 2006.

———. "The 'Salvation History': Perspective and the 'Wisdom' Perspective Within the Context of Biblical Theology." *Evangelical Quarterly* 51 (1979) 194–207.

Good, Edwin M. A Review of *Ḥesed in the Bible*, by Nelson Glueck. *Journal of the American Oriental Society* 89 (1969) 178.

Gordis, Robert. *The Book of Job: Commentary, New Translation and Special Studies*. New York: Jewish Theological Seminary of America, 1978.

———. "Wisdom and Job." In *The Book of God and Man: A Study of Job*, 31–52. Chicago: University of Chicago Press, 1965.

Gottman, J. M. *Why Marriages Succeed or Fail*. New York: Fireside, 1994.

Gottman, John M., and N. Silver. *The Seven Principles for Making Marriage Work*. New York: Crown, 1999.
Gravett, Emily O. "Biblical Responses: Past and Present Retelling of the Enigmatic Mrs. Job." *Biblical Interpretation* 20 (2012) 97–125.
Gray, John. *The Book of Job*. Sheffield: Sheffield Phoenix, 2010.
Green, Alberto R. W. *The Storm-God in the Ancient Near East*. Biblical and Judaic Studies 8. Winona Lake: Eisenbrauns, 2003.
Grillo, Jennie. "The Wisdom Literature." In *The Hebrew Bible: A Critical Companion*, edited by John Barton, 181–205. Princeton, NJ: Princeton University Press, 2016.
Grossi, Vittorino. "Sexuality and Friendship in Early Christianity." *L'Osservatore Romano*, English edition (1997). https://www.ewtn.com/catholicism/library/homosexuality—5–4128.
Guichard, Martine. "Introduction." In *Friendship, Descent and Alliances in Africa: Anthropological Perspectives*, edited by Martine Guichard et al., 1–18. New York: Berghahn, 2014.
———. "Where Are Other's People's Friends Hiding? Reflections on Anthropological Studies of Friendship." In *Friendship, Descent and Alliance in Africa: Anthropological Perspectives*, edited by Martine Guichard et al., 19–41. New York: Berghahn, 2014.
Gutiérrez, Gustavo. *On Job: God-Talk and the Suffering of the Innocent*. Translated by Matthew J. O'Connell. Maryknoll, NY: Orbis, 1987.
Gyekye, Kwame. *African Cultural Values*. Accra: Sankofa, 1996.
———. "African Ethics." In *Stanford Encyclopedia of Philosophy* (2010). https://plato.stanford.edu/entries/african-ethics/.
———. "The Relation of Ōkra (Soul) and Honam (Body) An Akan Conception." In *African Philosophy: An Anthology*, edited by Emmanuel Chuckwudi Eze, 59–66. Malden, MA: Blackwell, 1998.
———. *Tradition and Modernity*. New York: Oxford University Press, 2007.
Habel, Norman C. *The Book of Job*. Cambridge Bible Commentary. Cambridge: Cambridge University Press, 1975.
———. *The Book of Job: A Commentary*. Old Testament Library. London: SCM, 1985.
———. "Only the Jackal Is My Friend: On Friends and Redeemers in Job." *Interpretation* 31 (1977) 227–37.
Ham, T. C. "The Gentle Voice of God in Job 38." *Journal of Biblical Literature* 132 (2013) 527–41.
Hamilton, Victor P. "Satan." In *The Anchor Bible Dictionary*, edited by David Noel Freedman et al., 5:985–89. 6 vols. Garden City, NY: Doubleday, 1992.
Han, Sae Hwang, et al. "Friendship and Depression Among Couples in Later Life: The Moderating Effects of Marital Quality." *Journals of Gerontology: Psychological Sciences* 74 (2019) 222–31.
Harding, James E. "A Spirit of Deception in Job 4:15? Interpretive Indeterminacy and Eliphaz's Vision." *Biblical Interpretation* 13 (2005) 137–66.
Hartley, John E. *The Book of Job*. New International Commentary on the Old Testament. Grand Rapids: Eerdmans, 1988.
Hawley, Amos H. *Human Ecology: A Theoretical Essay*. Chicago: University of Chicago Press, 1986.
Heath, E. A. "Grace." In *Dictionary of the Old Testament: Pentateuch*, edited by T. Desmond Alexander and David W. Baker, 372–75. Downers Grove, IL: InterVarsity, 2003.

Heller, Agnes. "The Beauty of Friendship." *The South Atlantic Quarterly* 97 (1998) 5–22.
Helmm, Bennett. "Friendship." *Stanford Encyclopedia of Philosophy* (2021). https://plato.stanford.edu/entries/friendship/.
Hess, Richard S. רעה. In *New International Dictionary of Old Testament Theology and Exegesis*, edited by Willem VanGemeren, 3:1143–48. Grand Rapids: Zondervan, 1997.
Hill, Wesley. *Spiritual Friendship: Finding Love in the Church as a Celibate, Gay Christian*. Grand Rapids: Brazos, 2015.
Hilton, J. H. "Epicurus and Friendship." *The Classical Journal* 42 (1947) 351–55.
Hoffman, Yair. *A Blemished Perfection: The Book of Job in Context*. JSOTSup 213. Sheffield: Sheffield Academic Press, 1996.
Holladay, William L. *A Concise Hebrew and Aramaic Lexicon of the Old Testament: Based Upon the Lexical Work of Ludwig Koehler and Walter Baumgartner*. Grand Rapids: Eerdmans, 1993.
Holt, Shalom E. "Why Are the Sins of Ephraim (Hosea 13,12) and Job (14:17) Bundled?" *Biblica* 93 (2012) 107–15.
Horrell, David G. *The Bible and the Environment: Towards a Critical Ecological Biblical Theology*. London: Routledge, 2010.
Horsfjord, Vebjørn L. "Dialogue as Speech Act and Discourse: Methods to Understand what Interreligious Dialogue Does with Reference to *A Common Word Between Us and You*." *Journal of Ecumenical Studies* 48 (2013) 289–98.
Howard, Evan B. *The Brazos Introduction to Christian Spirituality*. Cambridge: Cambridge University Press, 1992.
Hruschka, Daniel J. *Friendship: Development. Ecology, and Evolution of a Relationship*. Berkeley: University of California Press, 2010.
Imasogie, Osadolor. *Guidelines for Christian Theology in Africa*. Achimota, Ghana: African Christian Theology in Africa, 1983.
Iwanski, Dariusz. *The Dynamics of Job's Intercession*. Analecta Biblica 161. Rome: Editrice Pontifico Istituto Biblico, 2006
Jackson, David R. "'Who Is This Who Darkens Counsel': The Use of Rhetoric Irony in God's Charges Against Job." *Westminster Theological Journal* 72 (2010) 153–67.
Janos, Fr. S., trans. "An Eclectic Commentary on the Book of Job: Praying for Our Children with the Jesus Prayer." https://orthodox.net/redeemingthetime/2009/05/19/commentary-book-of-job/.
Janzen, J. Gerald. *Job*. Interpretation. Louisville: Westminster John Knox, 1985.
Jayawardane, M. Neelika. "'Friend of the Family': Maids, Madams, and Domestic Cartographies of Power in South African Art." In *Ties that Bind: Race and the Politics of Friendship in South Africa*, edited by Jon Soske and Shanon Walsh, 216–42. Johannesburg: Wits University Press, 2016.
Johnson, Luke Timothy. *Brother of Jesus, Friend of God: Studies in the Letter of James*. Grand Rapids: Eerdmans, 2004.
Jones, Hywel R. *A Study Commentary on Job*. Webster, NY: Evangelical, 2007.
Josselson, Ruthellen. "Identity and Relatedness in the Life Cycle." In *Identity and Development: An Interdisciplinary Approach*, edited by Harke A Bosma et al., 81–102. Thousand Oaks, CA: Sage, 1994.
Keefe, Alice. "Rapes of Women/Wars of Men." *Semeia* 61 (1993) 79–97.
Keil, Carl Friedrich, and Franz Delitzsch. *Commentary on the Old Testament-Job*. Vol. 4. Grand Rapids: Eerdmans, 1982.

Kelland, Mark D. "African Worldview and Spirituality." https://socialsci.libretexts. org/Bookshelves/Psychology/Book%3A_Personality_Theory_in_a_Cultural_ Context_(Kelland)/16%3A_African_Perspective_on_Personality/16.02%3A_ The_African_Worldview_and_Spirituality.
Kellermann, D. רֵעַ rēaʿ. In *TDOT* 13 (2004) 522–32.
Kennedy, George A. *New Testament Interpretation through Rhetorical Criticism*. Studies in Religion. Chapel Hill: University of North Carolina Press, 1984.
Kimmel, Lawrence. "The Dialectical Convergence of Rhetoric and Ethics: The Imperative of Public Remark." In *Rhetoric and Ethics: Historical and Theoretical Perspectives*, edited by Victoria Aarons and Willis A. Salomon, 1–31. Lewiston, NY: Mellen, 1991.
Kinouani, Guilaine. "Silencing, Power and Racial Trauma in Groups." *Group Analysis* 53 (2020) 145–61.
Kitz, Anne Marie. "Curse and Cursing in the Ancient Near East." *Religion Compass* 1 (2007) 615–27.
Klassen, William. "Friend, Friendship." In *The New Interpreter's Dictionary of the Bible*, edited by Katharine Doob Sakenfeld, 2:490–91. Nashville: Abingdon, 2007.
Klein, Lalian R. "Honor and Shame in Esther." In *A Feminist Companion to Esther, Judith and Susanna*, edited by Athalya Brenner, 149–75. Sheffield: Sheffield Academic, 1995. .
———. "Job and the Womb: Texts about Men; Subtexts about Women." In *A Feminist Companion to Wisdom Literature*, edited by Athalya Brenner, 186–200. Sheffield: Sheffield Academic, 1995.
Knight, Bruce W. "Voices: Silence, Befriending Silence in Therapy." https:// charlottetherapy.com/news-notes/2018/10/15/befriending-silence-in-therapy- voices-silence.
Koehler, Ludwig, and Walter Baumgartner. *The Hebrew and Aramaic Lexicon of the Old Testament*, I/III. Leiden: Brill, 1996/2001.
Konstan, David. *Friendship in the Classical World*. Key Themes in Ancient History. Cambridge: Cambridge University Press, 1997.
———. "Friendship, Frankness, and Flattery." In *Friendship Flattery, and Frankness*, edited by J. T. Fritzgerald, 5–19. Novum Testamentum Supplements 82. Leiden: Brill, 1996.
———. "Greek Friendship." *American Journal of Philology* 117 (1980) 71–94.
———. "Patron and Friend." *Classical Philology* 90 (1995) 328–42.
Kotse, Manitza, and Carike Noeth. "Friendship as a Theological Model: Bonhoeffer, Moltmann and the Trinity." *In die Skriflig/ In Luce Verbi* 53 (2019) 1–7.
Kluger, Rivkah Scharf. *Satan in the Old Testament*. Translated by Hildegard Nagel. Evanston, IL: Northwestern University Press, 1967.
Kushner, Harold. *When Bad Things Happen to Good People*. New York: Hearst, 1981.
Landman, Christina. "Who/What Causes Suffering?': Discourses on Religious Healing in African Communities." *In die Skriflig* 54 (2020) 3.
Lapsley, Jacqueline. "Friends with God? Moses and the Possibility of Covenantal Friendship." *Interpretation* 58 (2004) 117–29.
Lewis, C. S. *The Four Loves*. New York: Harcourt, Brace, 1960.
———. *The Inspirational Writings of C.S. Lewis*. New York: Inspirational, 1991.
Lindsay, Wilson. "Realistic Hope or Imaginative Exploration? The Identity of Job's Arbiter." *Pacifica* 9 (1996) 243–52.

Lapsley, Jacqueline E. "Friends with God?: Moses and the Possibility of Covenantal Friendship." *Interpretation* (2004) 117–29.
LaSor, William Sanford, et al. *Old Testament Survey.* Grand Rapids: Eerdmans, 1996.
Lawrence, Richards. *Encyclopedia of Bible Words.* Grand Rapids: Zondervan, 1991.
Leeuwen, Raymond C. van. "Wisdom Literature." In *Dictionary for Theological Interpretation of the Bible,* edited by Kevin J. Vanhoozer, 847–50. Grand Rapids: Baker Academic, 2005.
Lidell, Henry G., and George Scott. *A Lexicon Abridged from Lidell and Scott's Lexicon.* Oxford: Clarendon, 1976.
Longman, Tremper, III. *Job.* Edited by Tremper Longman III. Baker Commentary on Old Testament Wisdom Literature and the Psalms. Grand Rapids: Baker Academic, 2016.
Lu, Peiqi, et al. "Friendship Importance Around the World: Links to Cultural Factors, Health, and Well-Being." *Frontiers in Psychology* 11 (2021). https://www.frontiersin.org/journals/psychology/articles/10.3389/fpsyg.2020.570839/full.
Lugt, Pieter van der. "Speech Cycles in the Book of Job: A Response to James E. Patrick." *Vetus Testamentum* 56 (2006) 554–57.
Magdalene, F. Rachel. "Job's Wife as a Hero: A Feminist-forensic reading of the Book of Job." *Biblical Interpretation* 14 (2006) 209–58.
Magesa, Laurenti. *African Religion: The Moral Traditions of Abundant Life.* New York: Orbis, 1997.
Malina, Bruce J. *The New Testament World: Insights from Cultural Anthropology.* Louisville: Westminster John Knox, 2001.
———. *The Social World of Jesus and the Gospels.* London: Routledge, 1996.
Martens, Elmer A. "Old Testament Theology Since Walter C. Kaiser, Jr." *Journal of the Evangelical Theological Society* 50 (2007) 673–91.
———. "פָּלָה." In *New International Dictionary of Old Testament Theology and Exegesis,* edited by Willem A. VanGemeren, 3:620. Grand Rapids: Zondervan, 1997.
Matthews, Victor H. "Hospitality and Hostility in Genesis 19 and Judges 19." *Biblical Theology Bulletin* 22 (1992) 3–11.
Mbiti, John. *African Philosophy.* London: Heinemann, 1970.
Mbuvi, Andrew. "Ancient Mediterranean Values of Honor and Shame." *Old Testament Essays* 23 (2010) 752–68.
McCabe, Robert V. "Elihu's Contribution to the Thought of The Book of Job." *Detroit Baptist Seminary Journal* 2 (1997) 47–80.
McGinnins, Alan Loy. *The Friendship Factor: How to Get Closer to the People You Care For.* Minneapolis: Augsburg, 1979.
McKane, William. *Proverbs.* Old Testament Library. Philadelphia: Westminster, 1970.
Merwe, Christo H. J. Van Der. "Lexical Meaning in Biblical Hebrew and Cognitive Semantics: A Case Study." *Biblica* 87 (2006) 85–95.
Miller, Carolyn. "Review of *Rethinking the Rhetorical Tradition: From Plato to Postmodernism.*" *Philosophy and Rhetoric* 34 (2001) 179–81.
Miller, Patrick D., Jr. "Cosmology and World Order in the Old Testament: The Divine Council as Cosmic-Political Symbol." *Horizons in Biblical Theology* 9 (1978) 53–78.
Minkus, Helaine K. "The Concept of Spirit in Akwapim Akan Philosophy." *Africa* 50 (1980) 182–92.

Mireku-Gyimah, Patricia Beatrice. "The Theme of Betrayal of Friendship in Akan Folktales." *International Journal of English language and Literature Studies* 3 (2014) 29–56.
Mogtari, Haruna Yussif. "Fulani Herdsmen Traditions and Care for the Land." In *Essays on The Land, Ecotheology and Traditions in Africa*, edited by Benjamin Abotchie Ntreh et al., 178–91. Eugene, OR: Resource Publications, 2019.
Moltmann, Jürgen. *The Living God and the Fullness of life*. Louisville: Westminster John Knox, 2015.
Moore, Rick. "Integrity of Job." *The Catholic Biblical Quarterly* 45 (1983) 17–31.
———. "Job's Texts of Terror." *The Catholic Biblical Quarterly* 55 (1993) 662–75.
Moster, Julius B. "The Punishment of Job's Friends." *Jewish Bible Quarterly* 25 (1997) 211–19.
Mufune, P. "African Culture and Managerial Behaviour: Clarifying the Connections." *South African Journal of Business Management* 34 (2003) 17–28.
Murphy, Francesca Aran. *1 Samuel*. Theological Commentary on the Bible. Grand Rapids: Brazos, 2010.
Nam, Duck-woo. *Talking About God: Job 42:7–9 and the Nature of God in the Book of Job*. Studies in Biblical Literature 49. New York: Peter Lang, 2003.
Nehamas, Alexander. "Aristotelian *Philia*, Modern Friendship." In *Oxford Studies in Ancient Philosophy*, edited by Brad Inwood, 38:213–47. Oxford: Oxford University Press, 2010.
Newsom, Carol. *The Book of Job: Context of Moral Imaginations*. Oxford: Oxford University Press, 2003.
———. "The Book of Job: Introduction Commentary, and Reflections." In *The New Interpreter's Bible*, Volume 4: *1 & 2 Maccabees; Introduction to Hebrew Poetry; Job; Psalms*, edited by Leander Keck et al., 319–637. Nashville: Abingdon, 1996
———. "The Book of Job as a Polyphonic Text." *Journal for the Study of the Old Testament* 97 (2002) 87–108.
———. "Job and His Friends: A Conflict of Moral Imaginations." *Interpretation* 53 (1999) 239–53.
Neyrey, Jerome H. "God, Benefactor and Patron: The Major Cultural Model for Interpreting the Deity in Greco-Roman Antiquity." *Journal for the Study of the New Testament* 27 (2005) 465–92.
O'Daly, Gerald. *Augustine's Philosophy of Mind*. Berkeley: University of California Press, 1987.
Ogba, Uloma. "The 5 Types of Friends Every Woman Needs in Her Late 20s and Early 30s." https://sheleadsafrica.org/5-friends-every-woman-needs/.
Okorocha, Cyril. "Religious Conversion in Africa: Its Missiological Implications." *Mission Studies* 9 (1992) 168–81.
Olyan, Saul M. *Friendship in the Hebrew Bible*. Anchor Yale Bible Reference Library. New Haven: Yale University Press, 2017.
———. "'Surpassing the Love of Women': Another Look at 2 Sam 1:26 and the Relationship of David and Jonathan." In *Authorizing Marriage? Canon, Tradition and Critique in the Blessing of Same-Sex Unions*, edited by Mark D. Jordan et al., 7–16, 165–70. Princeton: Princeton University Press, 2009.
Orr, Robert D., et al. *Life and Death Decisions: Help in Making Tough Choices about Bioethical Issues*. Colorado Springs: Nav, 1990.

Pangle, Lorraine Smith. *Aristotle and the Philosophy of Friendship*. Cambridge: Cambridge University Press, 2003.

Papini, Mauricio R., et al. "Behavioral Neuroscience of Psychological Pain." *Neuroscience and Biobehavioral Reviews* 48 (2015) 53–69.

Pardes, Ilana. "Wife of Job: Bible." In *The Shalvi/Hyman Encyclopedia of Jewish Women*. https://jwa.org/encyclopedia/article/wife-of-job-bible.

Parsons, Gregory W. "Literary Features of the Book of Job." *Bibliotheca Sacra* 138 (1981) 213–29.

———. "The Structure and Purpose of the Book of Job." *Bibliotheca Sacra* 138 (1981) 139–42.

Patrick, James E. "The Fourfold Structure of Job: Variations on a Theme." *Vetus Testamentum* 55 (2005) 185–206.

Payne, Philip B. "The Bible Teaches the Equal Standing of Man and Woman." *Priscilla Papers* 29 (2015) 1–10.

Pelham, Abigail "*Job* as Comedy, Revisited." *Journal for the Study of the Old Testament* 35 (2010) 81–112.

Pelican, Michaela. "Friendship among Pastoral Fulbe in Northwest Cameroon." *African Study Monographs* 33 (2012) 165–88.

Penchansky, David. *The Betrayal of God: Ideological Conflict in Job*. Louisville: Westminster John Knox, 1990.

Perdue, Leo G. "Wisdom in the Book of Job." In *In Search of Wisdom: Essays in Memory of John G. Gammie*, edited by Leo G. Perdue et al., 73–98. Louisville: Westminster John Knox, 1993.

Petcu, Liviu. "Saint John Chrysostom, on True Friendship Between People." *International Journal of Scientific Research* 5 (2016) 449–51.

Pfeiffer, R. H. "Edomite Wisdom." *Zeitschrift für die alttestamentliche Wissenschaft* 44 (1926) 13–25.

Pham, Xuan Huong Thi. *Mourning in the Ancient Near East and the Hebrew Bible*. Journal for the Study of the Old Testament Supplements 302. Sheffield: Sheffield Academic, 1999.

Phillips, Elaine A. "Speaking Truthfully: Job's Friends and Job." *Bulletin for Biblical Research* 18 (2008) 31–43.

Pitt-Rivers, Julian. "The Kith and the Kin." In *The Character of Kinship*, edited by J. Goody, 89–105. Cambridge: Cambridge University Press, 1973.

———. *The People of Sierra*. Chicago: Chicago University Press, 1961.

Pius XI. "Casti Cannubii: On Christian Marriage." http://www.vatican.va/holy_father/pius_xi/encyclicals/documents/hf_p-xi_enc_31121930_casti-canubii_en.html.

Polak, Frank H. "On Prose and Poetry in the Book of Job." *Janus* 24 (1996) 61–96.

Pope, Marvin. *Job*. Anchor Bible 15. Garden City, NY: Doubleday, 1979.

Popta, John L. van. "Marriage, a Covenant of Friendship." https://www.christianstudylibrary.org/article/marriage-covenant-friendship.

Potter, Stanley E. "The Message of the Book of Job: Job 42:7 as Key to Interpretation." *Evangelical Quarterly* 63 (1991) 291–304.

Rad, Gerhard von. *Genesis: A Commentary*. Translated by John H. Marks. Old Testament Library. Philadelphia: Westminster, 1961.

———. *Wisdom in Israel*. Translated by J. D. Martin. London: SCM, 1972.

Rawlins, William K. "Cross-sex Friendship and the Communicative Management of Sex-role Expectations." *Communication Quarterly* 30 (1982) 343–52.

———. *Friendship Matters: Communication, Dialectics, and the Life Course.* Hawthorne, NY: Aldine de Gruyter, 1992.
Reisman, John M. *Anatomy of Friendship.* North Stratford: Irvington, 1979.
Reyna, Stephen P. "Afterword: Friendship in a World of Force and Power." In *Friendship, Descent and Alliance in Africa: Anthropological Perspectives,* edited by Martine Guichard et al., 161–79. New York: Berghahn, 2014.
Reynierse, James H. "Behaviour Therapy and Job's Recovery." *Journal of Psychology and Theology* 3 (1975) 187–30.
Richards, Larry. *Every Name of God in the Bible.* Nashville: Nelson, 2001.
Richards, Lawrence O. *New International Encyclopedia of Bible Words.* Grand Rapids: Zondervan, 1991.
Richardson, Henry S., and Mildred K. Cho. "Secondary Researchers' Duties to Return Incidental Findings and Individual Research Results: A Partial-entrustment Account." *Genetics in Medicine: Official Journal of the American College of Medical Genetics* 14 (2012) 467–72.
Ritter, Maria. "Silence as the Voice of Trauma." *American Journal of Psychoanalysis* 74 (2014) 176–94.
Robert, Dana L. *Faithful Friendship: Embracing Diversity in Christian Community.* Grand Rapids: Eerdmans, 2019.
Roberts-Griffin, Christopher. "What Is a Good Friend: A Qualitative Analysis of Desired Friendship Qualities." *Penn McNair Research Journal* 3 (2011) 1–14. https://repository.upenn.edu/cgi/viewcontent.cgi?article=1019&context=mcnair_scholars/.
Rogerson, John. *Theory and Practice in Old Testament Ethics.* Journal for the Study of the Old Testament Supplements 405. London: T. & T. Clark, 2004.
Rorty, Amelie Oksenberg. "The Historicity of Psychological Attitudes: Love Is Not Love Which Alters Not When It Alternation Finds." *Midwest Studies in Philosophy* 10 (1986) 399–412.
Ross, W. D. "Nicomachean Ethics." In *The Complete Works of Aristotle: Revised Oxford Translation,* edited by Jonathan Barnes, 2:1729–867. Princeton: Princeton University Press, 1984.
Rowold, Henry. "Yahweh's Challenge to Rival: The Form and Function of the Yahweh-Speech in Job 38–39." *Catholic Biblical Quarterly* 47 (1985) 199–211.
Russel, Walter B. "Rhetorical Analysis of the Book of Galatians: Part 1." *Bibliotheca Sacra* 150 (1993) 341–58.
Sakenfeld, Katharine Doob. *Faithfulness in Action: Loyalty in Biblical Perspective.* Overtures to Biblical Theology. Philadelphia: Fortress, 1985.
———. "Khesed." In *The New Interpreter's Dictionary of the Bible,* edited by Katharine Doob Sakenfeld et al., 3:495–96. Nashville: Abingdon, 2008.
———. *The Meaning of* Hesed *in the Hebrew Bible: A New Inquiry.* Harvard Semitic Monographs 17. Missoula, MT: Scholars, 1978.
Sanders, James A. *Torah and Canon.* Philadelphia: Fortress, 1972.
———. *Torah and Canon.* 2nd ed. Eugene, OR: Cascade Books, 2005.
Sasson, Victor. "An Edomite Joban Text: With a Joban Parallel." *Zeitschrift für die alttestamentliche Wissenschaft* 117 (2006) 601–15.
———. "The Literary and Theological Function of Job's Wife in the Book of Job." *Biblica* 79 (1998) 86–90.
Scharbert, Josef. "ארר *'rr* , מְאֵרָה *meʾērāh*." In *TDOT* 1 (1978) 405–18.

Scheven, Albert. *Swahili Proverbs: Nia zikiwa moja, kilicho mbali huja.* Washington, DC: University Press of America, 1981.

Schifferdecker, Kathryn. *Out of the Whirlwind: Creation Theology in the Book of Job.* Harvard Theological Studies 61. Cambridge: Harvard University Press, 2008.

Scholtz, Roger. "'I Had Heard of You . . . But Now My Eye Sees You': Re-Visioning Job's Wife." *Old Testament Essays* 26 (2013) 819–39.

Schultz, Samuel J., and Gary V. Smith. *Exploring the Old Testament.* Wheaton, IL: Crossway, 2001.

Schwartz, Daniel. *Aquinas on Friendship.* Oxford Philosophical Monographs. Oxford: Oxford University Press, 2012.

Schweitzer, D. "'Curse God and Die': Was Job's Wife Completely Wrong?" *Touchstone* 14 (1996) 32–38.

Seow, C. L. *Job 1–21: Interpretation and Commentary.* Illuminations. Grand Rapids: Eerdmans, 2013.

———. "Job's Wife—With Due Respect." In *Das Buch Hiob und seine Interpretationen*, edited by Thomas Kruger, 1–39. Abhandlungen zur Theologie des Alten und Neuen Testaments 88. Zurich: TVZ, 2007.

Shapin, S. "Proverbial Economies: How an Understanding of Some Linguistic and Social Features of Common Sense Can Throw Light on More Prestigious Bodies of Knowledge, Science for Example." *Social Studies of Science* 31 (2001) 731–69.

Shepherd, David. "'Strike His Bone and His Flesh': Reading Job from the Beginning." *Journal for the Study of the Old Testament* 33 (2008) 81–97.

Sheriffs, Deryck. *Friendship of the Lord: An Old Testament Spirituality.* Carlisle, UK: Paternoster, 1996.

Sherwin, Michael S. "Friendship with God: The Christian Call to Divine Intimacy." *Nova et Vetera,* English Edition 19 (2021) 1323–43.

Shuckburgh, Evelyn S., trans. *Letters of Marcus Tullius Cicero, with his treatises on friendship and old age; And Letters of Gaius Plinius Caecilius Secundus,* translated by William Melmoth. New York, P. F. Collier. The Harvard Classics 9. New ed. rev. and enl. New York: Macmillan, 1913. https://sourcebooks.fordham.edu/ancient/cicero-friendship.asp.

Sifiano, Maria. "Do We Need to Be Silent to Be Extremely Polite? Silence and FTAs." *International Journal of Applied Linguistics* 5 (1995) 95–110.

Silverman, Sydel. "Patronage and Community: Nation Relationships in Central Italy." *Ethnology* 4 (1965) 172–89.

Snaith, Norman. *The Distinctive Ideas of the Old Testament.* New York: Schocken, 1964.

Sneed, Mark R. *The Social World of the Sages: An Introduction to Israelite and Jewish Wisdom Literature.* Minneapolis: Fortress, 2015.

Southwood, Katherine E. *Job and the Dramatised Comedy of Moralising.* Routledge Studies in the Biblical World. Abingdon, UK: Routledge, 2021.

Spencer, Paul. "Comradeship and the Transformation of Alliance Theory among the Maasai: Shifting the Focus from Descent to Peer-Group Loyalty." In *Friendship, Descent and Alliance in Africa: Anthropological Perspectives,* edited by Martine Guichard et al., 42–55 New York: Berghahn, 2014.

Spicq, Ceslas. *Theological Lexicon of the New Testament.* 3 vols. Translated by James D. Ernest. Peabody, MA: Hendrickson, 1994.

Ssettuuma, Benedict. "Friendship: An Effective Tool for Mission." *African Ecclesial Review* 52 (2010) 56–81.

Stansell, Gary. "David and His Friends: Social-Scientific Perspectives in the David-Jonathan Friendship." *Biblical Theology Bulletin* 41 (2011) 115–31.
Stauffer, Ethelbert. "ἀγαπαω, ἀγαπαω." In *TDNT* 1 (1964) 35–55.
Stein, Howard F. "A Note on Patron-Client Theory." *Ethos* 12 (1984) 30–36.
Steinmann, Andrew E. "The Structure and Message of the Book of Job." *Vetus Testamentum* 46 (1996) 85–100.
Stewart, Anne. "Job's Wife and Her Interpreters." In *Women's Bible Commentary*, edited by Carol A. Newsom et al., 216–20. Louisville: Westminster John Knox, 2012.
Strong, J. *The New Strong's Expanded Dictionary of Bible Words*. Nashville: Nelson, 2001.
Suriano, Matthew J. "Death, Disinheritance, and Job's Kinsman-Redeemer." *Journal of Biblical Literature* 129 (2010) 49–66.
Swartz, Michael D. "The Aesthetics of Blessing and Cursing: Literary and Iconographic Dimensions of Hebrew and Aramaic Blessing and Curse Texts." *Journal of Ancient Near Eastern Religions* 5 (2005) 187–211.
Tacciati, Susannah. *Job and the Disruption of Identity: Reading beyond Barth*. London: T. & T. Clark, 2005.
Tadesse, Wolde Gossa, and Martine Guichard. "Friendship Networks in Southwestern Ethiopia." In *Friendship, Descent and Alliance in Africa: Anthropological Perspectives*, edited by Martine Guichard et al., 57–73. New York: Berghahn, 2014.
Takyi, Emmanuel. "Friendship with God in the African Context." *Journal of Adventist Mission Studies* 9 (2013) 70–81.
Terrien, Samuel. "The Book of Job." *The Interpreters Bible*, edited by George A. Buttrick et al., 3:877–1198. Nashville: Abingdon, 1980.
———. *Job: Poet of Existence*. Indianapolis: Bobbs-Merrill, 1957.
"Three Types of Friends." August 16, 2022. https://online.arbor.edu/news/three-types-friendships.
Timmer, Daniel. "God's Speeches, Job's Responses, and the Problem of Coherence in the Book of Job: Sapiential Pedagogy Revisited." *The Catholic Biblical Quarterly* 71 (2009) 286–305.
Torrance, Iain. "Friendship as a Mode for Theological Engagement: David Ford's Exploration of Christian Wisdom." *Modern Theology* 25 (2005) 121–31.
Tull, Patricia. "Jonathan's Gift of Friendship." *Interpretation* 58 (2004) 130–44.
Turner, J. Hilton. "Epicurus and Friendship." *The Classical Journal* 42 (1947) 351–55.
Underwood, Marlene. "'Battered Love': Exposing Abuse in the Book of Job." In *Womanist Interpretations of the Bible: Expanding the Discourse*, edited by Gay L. Byron and Vanessa Lovelace, 165–84. Semeia Studies 85. Atlanta: SBL, 2016.
Utzschneider, Helmut. "The Book of Job and an Aesthetic Theology of the Old Testament." *Criswell Theological Review* 8 (2010) 91–100.
Uusimäki, Elisa. "Blessings and Curses in the Biblical World." In *Magic in the Ancient Eastern Mediterranean: Cognitive, Historical, and Material Perspectives on the Bible and its Contexts*, edited by Nina Nikki and Kirsi Valkama, 159–74. Mundus Orientis 3. Göttingen: Vandenhoeck & Ruprecht, 2021.
Valk, Frank. "Friendship, Politics, and Augustine's Consolidation of the Self." *Religious Studies* 45 (2009) 125–46.
Vanderwaal, Cornelis. *Job—Song of Songs*. Search the Scriptures 4. St Catharines, ON: Paideia, 1979.
VanGemeren, Willem, ed. *New International Dictionary of Old Testament Theology and Exegesis*. Vol. 2. Grand Rapids: Zondervan, 1997.

Versenyi, Laszlo. "Plato's Lysis." *Phronesis* 20 (1975) 185–98.
Vesely, Patricia. *Friendship and Virtue Ethics in the Book of Job.* Cambridge: Cambridge University Press, 2019.
Wall, Robert W. *Community of the Wise: The Letter of James, The New Testament in Context.* Valley Forge, PA: Trinity, 1997.
Wallis, Gerhard. "אָהַב *'āhabh;* אַהֲבָה *'ahabhāh;* אָהֵב *'ahabh;* אֹהַב *'ohabh.*" In *TDOT* 1 (1978) 99–118.
Walton, John. *Job.* The NIV Application Commentary. Grand Rapids: Zondervan, 2012.
Walton, John H., and Tremper Longman III. *How to Read Job.* Downers Grove, IL: IVP Academic, 2015.
Waters, Larry J. "Elihu's Theology and His View of Suffering." *Bibliotheca Sacra* 156 (1999) 143–59.
———. "Reflections on Suffering from the Book of Job." *Bibliotheca Sacra* 154 (1997) 436–51.
Weeks, Stuart. *An Introduction to the Study of Wisdom Literature.* London: T. & T. Clark, 2010.
Weiss, Meir. *The Story of Job's Beginning: Job 1–2: A Literary Analysis.* Jerusalem: Magnes, 1983.
Wesley, John. *The Works of John Wesley.* 14 vols. 3rd ed. Grand Rapids: Baker, 1978.
Westermann, Claus. *Praise and Lament in the Psalms.* Translated by Keith R. Crim and Richard N. Soulen. Louisville: Westminster John Knox, 1981.
———. *The Structure of the Book of Job: A Form-Critical Analysis.* Translated by Charles Muenchow. Philadelphia: Fortress, 1981.
Wharton, James A. *Job.* Westminster Bible Companion. Louisville: Westminster John Knox, 1999.
White, C. *Friendship in the Fourth Century.* Cambridge: Cambridge University Press, 1992.
Whitekettle, Richard. "When More leads to Less: Overstatement, *Incrementum,* and the Question in Job 4:17a." *Journal of Biblical Literature* 129 (2010) 445–48.
Wilson, Gerald H. *Job.* Understanding the Bible Commentary Series. Grand Rapids: Baker 2007.
———. "Preknowledge, Anticipation and the Poetics of Job." *Journal for the Study of the Old Testament* 30 (2005) 243–56.
Witherington, Ben, III. *Friendship and Finances in Philippi: The Letter of Paul to the Philippians.* New Testament in Context. Valley Forge, PA: Trinity, 1994.
Wolde, Ellen Van. "The Development of Job: Mrs. Job as Catalyst." In *A Feminist Companion to Wisdom Literature,* edited by Athalya Brenner, 201–21. Feminist Companion to the Bible 9. Sheffield: Sheffield Academic Press, 1995.
Wright, Chris. "The Authority of Scripture in an Age of Relativism: Old Testament Perspectives." In *The Gospel in the Modern World: A Tribute to John Stott,* edited by Martyn Eden and David F. Wells, 31–48. Downers Grove, IL: InterVarsity, 1991.
Wright, Christopher J. H. *Old Testament Ethics for the People of God.* Downers Grove, IL: IVP Academic, 2004.
Wright, P. H. "Self-referent Motivation and the Intrinsic Quality of Friendship." *Journal of Social and Personal Relationships* 1 (1984) 115–30.
Wright, Benjamin G., III. "Joining the Club: A Suggestion about Genre in Early Jewish Texts." *Dead Sea Discoveries* 17 (2010) 289–314.

Wuellner, Wilhelm. "Where Is Rhetorical Criticism Taking Us?" *Catholic Biblical Quarterly* 49 (1987) 448–63.
Yang, Sung-Jin. "Cultivating Compassionate Living Grounded in a Christian Approach for a Korean Congregation." PhD diss., Claremont School of Theology, 2014.
Young, William W., III. "The Patience of Job: Between Providence and Disaster." *Heythrop Journal* 48 (2007) 593–613.
Zobel, Hans-Jürgen. "חֶסֶד." In *TDOT* 5 (1986) 44–64.
Zuck, Roy. "A Theology of Wisdom Books and Song of Songs." In *A Biblical Theology of the Old Testament*, edited by Roy Zuck et al., 207–55. Chicago: Moody, 1991.
Zuckerman, Bruce. *Job the Silent: A Study in Historical Counterpoint.* Oxford: Oxford University Press, 1991.

www.ingramcontent.com/pod-product-compliance
Lightning Source LLC
Chambersburg PA
CBHW050623300426
44112CB00012B/1631